John Augustine Zahm

Sound and Music

John Augustine Zahm

Sound and Music

ISBN/EAN: 9783337088156

Printed in Europe, USA, Canada, Australia, Japan

Cover: Foto ©Thomas Meinert / pixelio.de

More available books at **www.hansebooks.com**

BY

The Rev. J. A. ZAHM, C.S.C.

PROFESSOR OF PHYSICS IN THE UNIVERSITY
OF NOTRE DAME

"*THOU HAST ORDAINED ALL THINGS IN MEASURE AND NUMBER
AND WEIGHT.*" — *Book of Wisdom, xi. 21*

CHICAGO
A. C. McCLURG AND COMPANY
1892

Copyright,
By A. C. McClurg & Co.
A. D. 1892.

TO

THE VERY REVEREND E. SORIN, C.S.C.,

Founder of the University of Notre Dame,

WHO HAS BEEN
FOR MORE THAN FIFTY YEARS THE FRIEND AND PROMOTER
OF HIGHER EDUCATION,

AND WHO IN AN EMINENT DEGREE

Deserves well of Science and Art.

PREFACE.

THE present volume has grown out of a course of lectures given last year in the Catholic University of America at Washington, D. C. Yielding to numerous requests to have the lectures published, my first intention was to give them to the press substantially as they were first delivered. When, however, I came to revise them, I soon found myself making many alterations and additions; and by the time the task of revision was complete, I became aware that I had practically written a new work. The object in view was to give a more complete exposition of the subject treated than had been possible in the lectures actually delivered, and to make the volume now offered to the public embrace in greater detail all the latest results of acoustical research. I have been led to retain the lecture form, as being more animated and picturesque, and as being more in keeping with the character of a work which deals so largely with apparatus and experiments.

The main purpose of the book is to give musicians and general readers an exact knowledge, based on experiment, of the principles of acoustics, and to present at the same time a brief exposition of the physical basis of musical harmony. Both in Europe and in this country musical conservatories are beginning to exact of students a theoretical as well as a practical knowledge of music;

and hence a work like the present cannot be considered as altogether untimely.

To enable the reader more readily to understand the various topics treated, illustrations of many of the instruments used in the lectures have been inserted in the text. Some of these were prepared expressly for this work, while others are to be found only in some of the more recent French and German treatises on sound and music. For the majority of the illustrations, however, I am under obligations to Dr. Rudolph Koenig and M. G. Masson, of Paris.

My most grateful acknowledgments are due to my distinguished scientific friends Professor Alfred M. Mayer and Dr. Koenig for invaluable assistance in preparing the work for the press. The former made a critical revision of the manuscript of the entire work; while the latter read all that pertained to his own inventions and discoveries. I am also indebted to my brother, Professor Albert F. Zahm, for a careful reading of the manuscript, and for many useful and practical suggestions that have enhanced materially any merit the book may possess. I have likewise to thank Mr. Frederick E. Neef, one of my students, for many of the drawings which adorn the volume.

If this contribution to the Science of Music shall in any way lead to a better understanding of the art, or to a more intelligent appreciation of the beauties and wonders of musical harmony, I shall feel that I have achieved all that I had in view in its publication.

J. A. Z.

NOTRE DAME, IND.
May, 1892.

CONTENTS.

CHAPTER I.

PRODUCTION AND TRANSMISSION OF SOUND.

Relation of the Science to the Art of Music. — Investigations and Discoveries of Helmholtz and Koenig. — The Nature of Sonorous Vibrations. — Experimental Illustrations of the Character of Sonorous Vibrations. — Difference between a Musical Sound and a Noise. — Music in Nature. — Medium necessary for the Transmission of Sound. — Experiments of Otto von Guericke, Hawksbee, and others. — Sound *in vacuo* impossible. — Opinions of Aristotle and Vitruvius regarding the Nature of Sonorous Vibrations. — Air Pulses composed of Alternate Condensations and Rarefactions. — Definition of Wave-Length. — Experiments by Mariotte and Mach showing how Sound-Waves are propagated through the Air. — Pendular or Simple Harmonic Motions. — Connection between Mind and Matter 15–53

CHAPTER II.

LOUDNESS AND PITCH.

Loudness or Intensity of Sound. — Laws governing the Intensity of Sonorous Vibrations. — Mersenne's Determination of the Pitch of a given Sound. — Experiments by Sauveur, Hooke, Chladni, Savart, and Cagniard de la Tour. — The Vibroscope of Duhamel, and the Phonautograph of Koenig and Scott. — Definition of a Sinusoid or Harmonic Curve. — Description of Koenig's *Grand Tonomètre Universel.* — Variations in Standards of Pitch. — The French or International Standard. — The Gamut. — The Limits of Audibility. — The Compass of the Human Voice, and of Various Musical Instruments. — Delicacy and Accuracy of the Ear as compared with the Eye 54–93

CHAPTER III.

VELOCITY, REFLECTION, AND REFRACTION OF SOUND.

Opinions of Aristotle, Lucretius, and Mersenne concerning the Velocity of Sound. — Determinations of the Velocity of Sound by Mersenne: by the French Academy of Sciences; *Le Bureau de Longitudes;* and Numerous Subsequent Experimenters. — Newton's Theoretical Investigations. — Corrections by Laplace. — Law of Mariotte and Boyle. — Velocity of Sound in Gases, Liquids, Solids. — Chladni's, Kundt's, and Bosscha's methods of determining the Velocity of Sound. — Wheatstone's Experiments on the Transmission of Sound through Solids. — Doppler's Principle. — Koenig's Experiment with two Tuning-Forks. — Laws of the Reflection of Sound. — Echoes. — Refraction of Sound. — Researches of Tyndall and Henry. — Diffraction of Sound. — Distances to which Sound-Pulses may be transmitted by the Earth and the Atmosphere   94-130

CHAPTER IV.

MUSICAL STRINGS.

A String as understood in Acoustics. — The Origin of Stringed Instruments. — Experiments by Pythagoras. — Laws of Vibrating Strings as determined by Mersenne. — Observation of Upper Partials by Mersenne. — Experiments by Sauveur, Noble, and Pigott on Subdivisions of a Vibrating String. — Nodes and Ventral Segments. — Experiments by Young regarding the Number and Order of Partial Tones in any given Compound Tone. — Harmonic and Inharmonic Partials. — Harmonics in Acoustics not the same as Harmonics in Music. — Illustration. — Melde's Method of demonstrating the Laws of Vibrating Strings. — Longitudinal and Torsional Vibrations   .   .   .   131-167

CHAPTER V.

VIBRATIONS OF RODS, PLATES, AND BELLS.

The Use of Rods and Bars in Musical Instruments. — Chladni's Researches. — Transversal Vibrations of Rods. — Laws governing the Transverse Vibrations of Rods. — The Inharmonic Partials of Bars and Tuning Forks. — The Longitudinal Vibrations of Rods. — Experiments by Savart. — Chladni's Method of determining the Velocity of Sound in Rods of Different Materials. —

Vibrating Bars examined by Polarized Light. — Torsional Vibration of Rods. — *Son rauque*. — Vibrating Plates. — Chladni's Figures. — Wheatstone's Analysis of Chladni's Figures. — Koenig's Experiments with Rectangular Plates. — Experiments of Faraday. — The Vibrations of Bells. — The Requisites of a Good Bell. Vibrating Membranes. — Delicacy of the Tympanic Membrane of the Human Ear 168–212

CHAPTER VI.

SONOROUS TUBES.

Definition of Wind Instruments. — The First Wind Instruments used in Music. — Mouth Instruments and Reed Instruments. — Laws governing Sonorous Tubes. — Open Pipes and Stopped Pipes. — Methods of determining the Positions of Nodes and Ventres in Sonorous Tubes. — Koenig's Manometric Flames. — The Results of Theory as compared with those yielded by Experiment. — Experiments by Mersenne and Savart. — Cavaillé-Coll's Empirical Law for Organ-pipes. — Various Kinds of Reeds used in Musical Instruments. — Descriptions of some of the more Common Wind Instruments. — The Human Larynx. — Singing Flames. — Sensitive Flames. — Kundt's Method of Determining the Velocity of Sound in Gases 213–259

CHAPTER VII.

RESONANCE AND INTERFERENCE.

Mechanical Illustrations of Co-vibration and of the Cumulative Effects of Slight Periodic Impulses. — Illustrations of the Phenomena of Resonance by means of Tuning-Forks. — Savart's Bell. — The Sound-Boards of Musical Instruments. — Sympathetic Vibration of Strings. — Helmholtz's Resonators. — " The Lost Chord." — The External Auditory Passage of the Ear as a Resonator. — Resonance in Bodies whose Periods of Vibration are different. — Mayer's Sound-Mill. — Curves corresponding to two Wave-Systems of varying Periods, Phases, and Amplitudes. — Interference of Sonorous Vibrations as illustrated by a Tuning-Fork: by Vibrating Plates: by Organ-pipes; by Quincke's Apparatus: by Koenig's Manometric Flames. — Sonorous Vibrations compared with the Vibratory Motions of other Forms of Energy . 260–300

CHAPTER VIII.

BEATS AND BEAT-TONES.

The Nature and Cause of Beats. — Beats illustrated by Curves, produced by Tuning-Forks and Organ-pipes, and examined by means of Manometric Flames. — Beats studied by means of Singing Flames. — Two Japanese Gongs. — The Value of Beats in Tuning Musical Instruments. — Tonometers and their Uses. — Lissajous' Optical Illustration of Beats. — Koenig's Apparatus for Studying Beats. — Theories of Helmholtz and Koenig regarding Beats. — Lower Beats and Upper Beats. — Beat-Tones produced by the Blending of Beats. — Beat-Tones used in Music. — How to calculate their Pitch. — Primary Beats and Beat-Tones. — Secondary Beats and Beat-Tones. — Beats and Beat-Tones yielded simultaneously by the same Sonorous Body. — The Wave-Siren, and what it teaches. — Beat-Tones subjective, not objective . 301–340

CHAPTER IX.

QUALITY OF SOUND.

Meaning of the Word "Quality" as applied to Sound. — Investigations of Mersenne and Chladni. — Simple, Single, Compound, and Composite Tones. — The Number and Order of Occurrence of Partial Tones in Various Sonorous Bodies. — Analysis of Compound Tones by Means of Helmholtz's Resonators and by Means of Manometric Flames. — The Nature of Vowel-Sounds. — Koenig's Researches. — Analytical and Synthetical Methods of examining Compound Sounds. — Helmholtz's Apparatus for the Artificial Production of Compound Tones of Different Qualities. — Quality of a Compound Tone affected by the Differences of Phase of its Constituent Simple Tones. — The Results of Theory and Experiment compared. — Descriptions of Different Forms of Wave-Sirens. — Their value as Instruments for Research. — Discoveries of Corti and Hensen. — Helmholtz's Theory of Audition 341–386

CHAPTER X.

MUSICAL INTERVALS AND TEMPERAMENT.

Musical Intervals. — Temperament. — Intervals defined. — Names of the Principal Intervals employed in Music. — Consonant and Dissonant Intervals. — Addition and Subtraction of Intervals. — The Origin of the Diatonic Scale. — Oriental Scales. — Melody. — Harmony. — Major Chords. — Minor Chords. — The Harmonic or Sub-minor Seventh. — Experimental Examination of Intervals and Chords by Pendulums; by Sirens; by Tuning-Forks. — Optical Tuning. — The Graphical Method of Studying Intervals. — Difference between Consonance and Dissonance. — Researches of Koenig and Mayer. — Difference between Sharps and Flats. — Pure Intonation. — Mean Tone Temperament. — Equal Temperament. — The Advantages and Disadvantages of Equal Temperament. — Mathematics and Music, Science and Art . 387-438

APPENDIX.

I.

Frequencies of the Notes of the Musical Scale and Compasses of the Human Voice, and of some of the more Common Musical Instruments 439-440

II.

Playing in Pure Intonation 441-443

INDEX 445

God spoke, and through the soundless realms of space
    The keynote of created music rolled;
    And time felt harmony within its hold, —
The pulse-beat of eternity's embrace.
The Infinite in finite hearts we trace,
    As ages strike the chords by Love controlled;
    The earth is vibrant, and with rhythm untold,
All sounds in Nature's orchestra find place.
O Sound! thou art the echo of a word
    That broke the primal stillness by command. —
An echo, through whose strains our souls have heard
    A promise of the choral raptures grand.
    That, voicing love and praise, forever rise
    In Music's natal home beyond the skies.

SOUND AND MUSIC.

CHAPTER I.

PRODUCTION AND TRANSMISSION OF SOUND.

AS a period of remarkable intellectual activity in every department of natural and physical science, the latter half of the nineteenth century must ever remain memorable. Never in the world's history has so much been accomplished in the same space of time. The fauna and flora of every continent and of every sea have been studied and compared; the forms of life of the dim and distant past have been unearthed and assigned their places in the scheme of creation. Aided by appliances he never dreamed of a few decades ago, the astronomer has penetrated the depths of stellar space, and can now literally unfold to us the story of the heavens in the light of the radiant orbs that are the constant objects of his nightly vigils. Worlds of untold magnitude and atoms of inconceivable minuteness — the infinitely great and the infinitely small — are alike the subjects of earnest quest and patient investigation. It would be difficult indeed to say in which department of knowledge the most work has been accomplished, and in which line of research the most energy has been expended. The facts observed and the discoveries made are almost incredible to one who has not made an attempt to keep abreast with the advance of science; and they show, in a most striking manner, what can be accomplished by unity of action and persistence in properly directed effort.

We may also state of the different branches of the various sciences what can be said of the sciences themselves. Marvellous strides have been made in every direction. This is pre-eminently true of the science of physics. The forces of heat and light, of magnetism and electricity, have been studied by thousands of investigators; and many contributions, of the utmost practical as well as theoretical importance, have been made to our pre-existent store of physical knowledge. Sound, too, — a subject which one would think musicians had exhausted ages ago, — has, in the hands of modern research, proved almost equally with the other forms of energy to be prolific in results of the greatest value both to music and science.

It is, indeed, only recently that the science of music became possible. The art, it is true, had been cultivated from the earliest times; but the physical principles underlying this art were unknown. While the fundamental facts of musical science were unknown it was obviously impossible to formulate anything like a true theory of sound or of music. The two go together, — the elements of music as a science, and a correct theory of that form of energy which in physics is known as sound.

And here we have a most interesting illustration of the intimate connection that may sometimes exist between art and science. The art of music and the science of sound — Acoustics — are so correlated that it is impossible to give an explanation of the simplest cases of musical harmony without a knowledge of the nature and laws of sound. The conviction of the truth of this is becoming so strong, especially in England, that in some of the best schools of music a course in acoustics is demanded from all candidates for musical degrees.

The relation, then, of acoustics to the most popular and the most universal of the arts, — music, — its intrinsic interest and importance no less than the wonderful advance it has made as a branch of science during the last few years, will, I am sure, be a sufficient reason for selecting it as a subject upon which to address you.

It is scarcely thirty years since the appearance of the work which completely revolutionized the subject of acoustics. I refer to the masterly "Die Lehre von den Tonempfindungen" of Professor Hermann Helmholtz, one of the most illustrious of German physicists. In this noble monument of profound thought and marvellous experimental research, Professor Helmholtz laid the foundations of musical science, and gave us, for the first time, a rational explanation of many of the most complicated forms of musical composition. It has been truthfully said that this great work has done for acoustics what Newton's "Principia" did for astronomy.

In the course of the lectures I shall deliver before you, I shall endeavor to follow Helmholtz as closely as possible in what pertains to the philosophy of musical sounds, and to give you experimental illustrations of his most important discoveries. It would be impossible to follow him in detail, as that would require far more time than I have at my disposal.

But while sounding the praises of Helmholtz, I must not forget to speak of another distinguished scientist, — one who, not excepting even the eminent German philosopher just mentioned, has contributed more than any other person to the advancement of the science of acoustics. The one to whom I refer is the celebrated acoustic mechanician of Paris, Dr. Rudolph Koenig. Dr. Koenig's book, bearing the modest title of "Quelques Expériences d'Acoustique," is, indeed, a necessary appendix to Helmholtz's learned work. It explains what Helmholtz failed to make clear; it supplies his omissions, and corrects a number of errors that, in such difficult problems as the German professor grappled with, were almost, if not entirely, inevitable. To be unacquainted with Dr. Koenig's contributions to acoustics is to be ignorant of some of the most important facts and discoveries that go to make the science what it is to-day.

It is not, however, simply as an investigator of the nature and laws of sound that Dr. Koenig merits recognition. He has probably a greater claim on students of acoustics throughout the world for enabling them, by means of delicate and exquisitely finished apparatus of his own design, successfully to pursue their researches in the realms of sound, and also to verify the results of preceding investigators. Were it not for Dr. Koenig, I should not attempt to give the present course of lectures on sound before such an audience as the one that now greets me, as I should feel that I could not do so with any degree of satisfaction either to my hearers or myself. With Dr. Koenig's apparatus around me, however, I can always be assured that I have the means of entertaining you, and of illustrating, in a way that would otherwise be impossible, the most salient facts and phenomena of sound. Indeed, before accepting the invitation to lecture before you, I made sure that Dr. Koenig would supply me with all the more delicate and important instruments. It was not that I could not get similar apparatus from other makers of acoustic instruments, but because I know from experience that for some, at least, of the experiments I shall make for you, the only apparatus that can be depended upon for exactness and never-failing operation are those made by the learned and painstaking Dr. Koenig. The making a perfect instrument — especially if that instrument be a tuning-fork or a wave-siren — is for Dr. Koenig a labor of love. It is for this reason that the tuning-forks which bear his stamp are so universally sought, and, when secured, are so highly prized. In our collection here we have tuning-forks of all forms and sizes, yielding from the lowest to the highest audible notes. Their importance as instruments of research we shall see as we advance.

I have hastened to make you acquainted with Professor Helmholtz and Dr. Koenig, not only because they are our two greatest authorities on the subject of sound, but also because I shall have occasion to make frequent references to them in the course of our investigations and experiments. It is important, therefore, that at the outset you should have a just appreciation of their standing in the world of science, and particularly in that realm of science in which they have won such distinction.

We are now prepared, without any further preamble, to enter upon the elucidation of the subject of to-day's lecture, — namely, "The Production and Transmission of Sound."

What is sound? How is it produced? How is it transmitted? We shall endeavor to answer these questions experimentally, — the only way in which they can be answered with any degree of satisfaction. "The nature of sounds," writes Lord Bacon, "hath in some sort been inquired, as far as concerneth music, but the nature of sound in general hath been superficially observed. It is one of the subtilest pieces of Nature."

For the majority of people sound is still what it was for the scientific student of Bacon's time, — something that is ill understood, something that may truthfully be reckoned as "one of the subtilest pieces of Nature."

The subject of sound has engaged the attention of philosophers from the earliest times, and the ideas entertained by them regarding its nature and production are often such as to surprise us for their exactness. They show us that the views of the philosophers of Greece and Rome concerning sound were in many respects very nearly identical with those which obtain among students of science in our own day.

Thus Aristotle, who seemed at times to have almost an intuitive knowledge of science and of the nature of the phenomena that constitute the subject-matter of physics, declares that "Sound, in act, is always produced by a body towards another and in another. It is a shock that determines it."[1]

Seneca asks, "What is the sound of the voice if it be not the disturbance of the air occasioned by the movement of

---

[1] Γίνεται δ' ὁ κατ' ἐνέργειαν ψόφος ἀεί τινος πρός τι καὶ ἔν τινι πληγὴ γὰρ ἐστιν ἡ ποιοῦσα. — *The Soul*, viii. 2.

the tongue? ... And to come to details: What song could be heard were it not for the elasticity of the air? And are not the sounds of horns and trumpets and hydraulic organs also explained by the same elastic force of the air?"[1]

Locke, referring to this subject, says: "That which is conveyed into the brain by the ear is called sound, though in truth, until it come to reach and affect the perceptive part, it is nothing but motion. The motion which produces in us the perception of sound is a vibration of the air caused by an exceedingly short but quick, tremulous motion of the body from which it is propagated, and therefore we consider and denominate them as bodies sounding."

The English philosopher makes here a distinction we cannot too carefully bear in mind, — namely, the distinction between sound as a sensation, which is merely subjective, and exists only in the brain, and sound as a mode of motion, which is objective, and the physical cause of sensation. Physiologically, then, or psychologically, if you prefer it, sound is a sensation excited in the brain, through the organ of hearing, by the vibratory motion of bodies external to the ear. Sound, therefore, as a sensation has no objective existence, — does not and cannot exist independently of the brain and auditory nerve. As a sensation it is comparable with the sensations excited through our other senses, — to wit, taste, smell, sight, -- although entirely different from them. There is nothing external to any of our senses that corresponds to the sensations experienced. Neither is there anything capable of causing sensation except matter and motion. Touch, taste, and smell are generally excited by matter in direct contact with the nerves of these special senses. In

---

[1] Quid enim est vox nisi intensio aeris, ut audiatur, linguæ formata concussu? ... Ad minora veniamus. Quis enim sine intensione spiritus cantus est? Cornua et tuba et ea quæ aliqua pressura majorem sonitum reddunt, quam qui ore reddi potest, nonne aeris intensione partes suas explicant? — L. ANN.EI SENECÆ *Quæst. Nat.*, ii, 6.

the case of smell, matter must be in the gaseous state, or in a state of fine subdivision, and in the case of taste it must be in the liquid state, or a solid in solution. But matter is not, in any of these cases, the same as the sensation produced. Matter is the stimulus, sensation is the result. In the case of sight and hearing, however, it is not matter, but motions of matter, which are the stimulating agent.[1] Physically then, and externally to the ear, sound is merely a mode of motion, and nothing more. But the kind of motion that is competent to stimulate the optic nerve has no effect whatever on the auditory nerve. We cannot see a sound, and we cannot hear a color, not because the motions producing sound and color are different in kind, but simply because the auditory and optic nerves are of different degrees of sensibility. The motions giving rise to the sensation of light are too minute to originate the sensation of sound; and, conversely, motions capable of producing sound are too gross to generate light. Both light and sound, externally to the ear, are only modes of motion, but modes of motion that require specially adjusted organs, and organs of different degrees of sensitiveness, for their transmutation into the sensations of light and sound.

If then sound, considered apart from the brain and ear, be only a mode of motion, it follows that if there were no ears and brains in the world, sound, as a sensation, would be impossible. This may appear paradoxical, and yet it is literally and absolutely true. The motions of matter, the vibrations, as they are called, would be the same as they are now, but all would be silence,—a silence so complete and universal that nothing in our experience can give us any adequate idea of its character.

Sound, then, is produced by motion. The kind of motion, however, that goes to produce sound is not that of masses of matter precisely, but rather of the molecules, or ultimate particles, of which matter is composed. When

---

[1] Dr. William Ramsey, in his admirable "Essay on Smell," has advanced the hypothesis that the sense of smell is excited by vibrations of a lower period than those which give rise to the sensations of light and heat.

the state of equilibrium of an elastic body is disturbed by a shock or by friction, it tends to regain its condition of equilibrium, but does so only after a greater or less number of vibrations, or oscillatory movements, of the molecules of which the mass of the body is composed.

We are now prepared to show that in all cases where the sensation of sound is produced, motion is a necessary antecedent, and is always the efficient cause. Before going any farther, however, permit me to explain a few terms of constant recurrence. The term *vibration* has been used several times, and this term must be defined first of all. It is, too, more frequently used than any other, and when employed in connection with sound it has a very precise and definite signification.

A movement of a particle, or molecule, to *and* fro constitutes what is called a *complete* or *double vibration*, and is

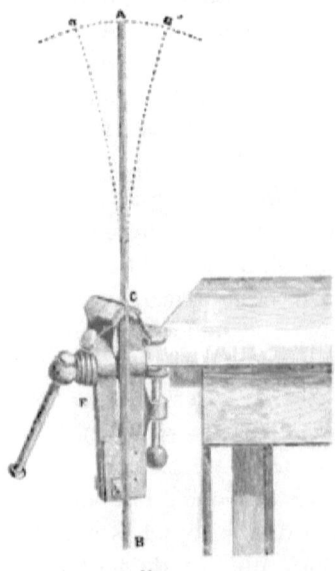

Fig. 1.

the kind of vibration I shall always speak of, unless otherwise stated. In France, however, a movement of a particle to *or* fro is called a vibration. This we should denominate a *single*, or *semi-vibration*. It is also called an *oscillation*. Newton measured by double vibrations, whereas Chladni always used single, or semi-vibrations.

Let me illustrate. In a vice, E (Fig. 1), is fastened an elastic steel strip or bar, $B\ C\ A$. Drawing the free end aside to a, and letting it go, the elasticity of the strip will carry it back to its original position A; but the energy now stored up in it will cause it to move onward to a', nearly as far from A as a is. At a and a' the motion, as is evident, will be *nil*, while at

A, intermediate between a and a', its velocity will be at a maximum. At points between aA and Aa' the velocity will be accelerated or retarded, according as the strip moves to the right or the left.

Once started, the bar will continue to move to and fro for some time, the distance through which it passes gradually decreasing, until it finally comes to rest. The motion from a to a' constitutes a single vibration; that from a to a' and return, is a complete vibration. The time required for executing a complete vibration is called its *period*,[1] and when a motion always returns to the same condition after equal intervals of time, it is said to be *periodic*. The distance through which any particle of the bar moves, as from a to a', is called the *amplitude* of vibration. The movements themselves are of the kind called *vibratory*.

The period of the successive vibrations of an oscillatory, or sounding, body, like those of the pendulum, are equal. The term used to express this equality of periodic vibration is *isochronous*.[2] Thus two or more vibrations, executed in the same time, are said to be *isochronous*, and the motions themselves are said to *synchronize*. In the case before us, the vibrations, by reason of the length of the strip, may be perceived by the eye. As the strip is shortened, however, the amplitude of the vibrations is lessened, and they also become so rapid as to be no longer visible. But if we cannot see them, we can hear them. A musical sound is the result of the vibratory motion communicated to the strip, and you will observe that as the length of the strip is shortened, the pitch of the sound it emits becomes higher and higher.

In the experiment just made, you have seen how a vibrating body may generate sound. In the place of a straight strip, or bar, let me take a bent one mounted on

---

[1] Mersenne appears to have been the first to employ this term — Latin, *periodus* — in the sense here indicated, in his *Harmonicorum Libri*.

[2] This is the word — ἰσόχρονοι — used by Mersenne, *Harm. Lib. ii.*, Prop. 29, in which the law of synchronism is discussed. It is from the Greek ἴσος, equal, χρόνος, time.

a box (Fig. 2). The bar thus fashioned is called a tuning-fork, and is the most useful instrument the student of acoustics has at his command. The box reinforces the sound produced by the fork for a reason we shall see later on.[1]

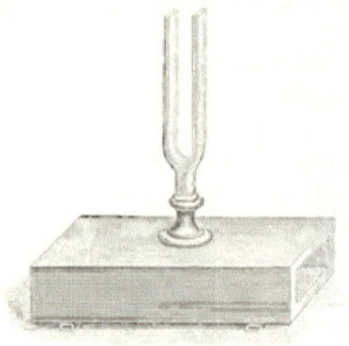

FIG. 2.

When a violin-bow is drawn across the end of one of the prongs of the fork, a loud, clear note is produced. You cannot, however, see the motion of any part of the fork, although every part of it, as well as of the box, is in a condition of violent oscillation. By touching one of the prongs, or even the box, one can feel the tremors that agitate them and give rise to the sound that fills the room. Permit me now to give you a simple proof of the existence of these unseen vibrations.

Close beside one of the prongs of the fork (Fig. 3) is suspended a small pith ball. Exciting the fork as before, you again hear the sound emitted, and you remark at the same time that the pith ball is thrown aside with considerable force. Every time it comes in contact with the fork it is violently repelled. Here, as in the case of the vibrating bar, sound is a concomitant of motion. And although the rapidity and small amplitude of the vibrations

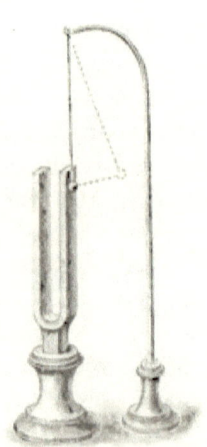

FIG. 3.

---

[1] The tuning-fork was invented by John Shore, a trumpeter in the service of George I. of England, in 1711,— nearly two hundred years ago. The resonant case was added subsequently by a French instrument-maker, Marloye.

prevent them from being directly perceived by the eye, the repulsion of the ball, when it comes in contact with the fork, leaves us in no doubt as to their existence. Holding a lead pencil against one of the prongs gives the same results. The loud clatter that follows, assures us of the reality of the motion of the sonorous body.

We may now go a step farther. Instead of a bar of steel I shall take a circular plate of brass (Fig. 4), mounted on a heavy iron support. On agitating the plate with the bow, a very marked sound is heard, and, in the case of the lowest sounds that may be produced, the motion of the plate is visible to the eye. When, however, the higher notes which the plate is competent to yield are sounded, the motions of the plate are lost to the unaided vision. But there is a way of showing their presence in a most simple yet most beautiful and striking manner. Strewing some find sand upon the plate, and drawing the bow across one of its edges, we not only evoke a musical sound, but call into existence, as if by magic, a figure of the most exquisite design and symmetry. The mirror behind the plate enables you to see the figure by reflection. Each note, as we shall see in its proper place, has its characteristic figure.

FIG. 4.

It would be easy to fashion this plate into a bell, as a tuning-fork is made, by bending, out of a straight bar. Instead of taking a metal bell, it will answer our present purpose much better to have one of glass. Almost in contact with the edge of the large bell, *A* (Fig. 5), is suspended, from a convenient support, a small ball of cork, *B*. On drawing the bow across the edge of the bell, a loud, pure sound is emitted. But observe: directly the sound is emitted, the ball is violently agitated, and keeps up a rapid oscillatory motion as long as the sound lasts. This experiment should convince any one that the molecules of the glass bell are in a state of tremor; but it is easy to vary the experiment so as to demonstrate the same fact in an equally conclusive manner.

Fig. 5

We may do this by removing the cork ball and pouring a little water into the bell. By causing it to vibrate as before, beautiful ripples play over the surface of the water, and if the bow is vigorously drawn, the water is projected as spray from the portions of the bowl where the quivering motion is greatest. If a little more force were applied to the bow, the bell would shiver into fragments.

Every one is familiar with the fact that when stringed instruments like the violin, piano, or harp emit a note, the string producing the note is in a state of greater or less vibration. Frequently the vibrations can be seen; they can always be felt.

We have in the apparatus before us (Fig. 6) a simple and effective means of showing the vibrations of strings. It consists of a black board, and a white string passing over two bridges, A and B. The tension of the string is regulated by the peg C. When stretched but slightly and plucked, one is able without difficulty to follow its to-and-fro motion on either side of its position

Fig. 6.

of equilibrium. As the tension is augmented, the vibrations become more rapid. The string now appears as an airy, transparent spindle. Increasing the tension still more, the vibrations become sufficiently rapid to generate an audible sound, while the motion of the string remains as marked as before. But when the vibratory motion of the string ceases, the sound due to this motion becomes extinct.

With the organ-pipe the case is different. One may, it is true, by the sense of touch become aware of the vibratory motion in an organ-pipe, but the invisibility of air prevents our seeing the condition of the particles constituting the aërial column. As it is the vibration of the column of air within the pipe, and not the pipe itself, which chiefly gives rise to the note of an organ-pipe, it is well that we are able to render evident to the eye that this motion actually exists. This can be done very easily indeed. Into an organ-pipe, one of whose sides is of glass, is lowered a thin membrane stretched on a frame and strewn with fine sand. As soon as the pipe is made to speak, the sand is violently agitated, as may be seen by one who is near, and the rattling noise produced by the grains of sand dancing about on the membrane is sufficiently loud to be heard some distance away.

The existence of the vibratory motion of a column of air in a sonorous tube can be shown still better by another method. Before the condensers of the lantern is placed a glass whistle, the inside of which is strewn with a very light powder such as amorphous silica. As soon as the whistle is sounded, the powder forms groups of thin vertical plates, which are now projected on the screen. As long as the sound persists, the powder retains its present position. When it ceases, the powder falls to the bottom of the tube.

But it may be urged that the agitation here produced is really due to a current of air from the mouth, and not to a vibratory motion of the particles of the aërial column. The form and the grouping of the vertical plates of powder should convince any one who reflects on the matter that this is impossible. To remove all doubt, let us modify the experiment somewhat, and excite the air column in another way. Taking the mouthpiece away from the whistle, we have left only a glass tube, stopped at one end. Let us now excite this tuning-fork, which emits the same note as the vibratory column of air within the tube. As soon as the fork is sounded, the powder springs up into groups of plates as before, and that notwithstanding the fact that the fork is several feet away from the tube. The

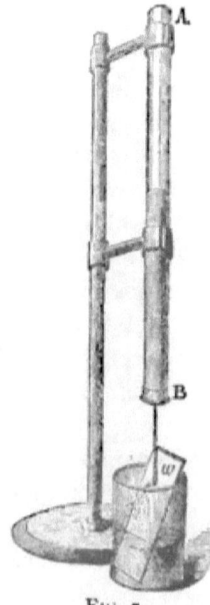

Fig. 7.

vibratory motion of the fork, it is obvious in this instance, is communicated to the air enclosed within the tube through the medium of the air separating the fork from the tube. When the sound of the fork dies out, the agitation of the air in the tube ceases, the powder becoming quiescent as before.

Supported on a suitable stand, we have a large glass tube, $A B$ (Fig. 7), about three feet in length and two inches in diameter. Its lower extremity is covered by a brass cap, in the centre of which is a circular orifice whose diameter is equal to the thickness of the cap. If we fill this tube with water and allow it to issue from the orifice below, striking at w, we shall hear a low, variable note of great purity and sweetness. It is produced by the intermittent flow of the water through the aperture, the rhythmic action of the flow communicating a vibratory motion to the entire liquid column above. This experiment is due to the distinguished French physicist, Félix Savart, to whom, as we shall learn, we are indebted for many interesting apparatus and methods of research in acoustics.

Let me now show you how sound can be generated by a motion different from any we have yet considered.

Before you, mounted on a rotator, is an instrument (Fig. 8), called, from its inventor, Savart's wheel. It is nothing more than a toothed wheel made of brass, and is very like a small circular saw. There are in reality four of these wheels attached to the stand, but we shall for the present employ but one of them, — it is immaterial which. When the wheel is turned, and the teeth are allowed to strike against a card, you hear at first a succession of taps. But by giving the wheel a more rapid motion, these taps coalesce and form a continuous sound, — a sound that can be rendered so loud and shrill as to become actually painful to the ear. A circular saw rapidly revolving in the air, or cutting wood, produces a

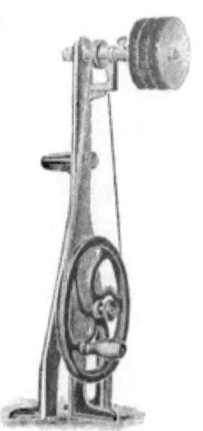

FIG. 8.

similar sound, and for the same reason. A circular saw, as we shall soon learn, gives a louder sound than the serrated wheel we have just used, because of the greater force applied, and a higher pitch, on account of its more rapid revolutions.

FIG. 9.

In this connection permit me to show you a still more remarkable way of producing sound by taps. The instrument used consists (Fig. 9) of a peculiarly shaped brass bar and a block of lead. It is named Trevelyan's rocker, from Mr. Trevelyan, who invented it and first gave an explanation of its mode of action. The brass bar is made so as to move from side to side, under the influence of slight impulses. The rocker is heated, and on placing it upon this cold lead block, you at once hear a musical note. By pressing on the rocker with the point of a pencil the pitch of the sound is made higher, and any variations in the pressure, however slight, give rise to a corresponding change in pitch.

The origin of this singular sound is not difficult to account for. As soon as one side of the heated bar touches the lead, it induces, by communication of heat, sudden expansion of the part touched, which causes a tilting of the bar itself. This process is repeated from side to side, giving the bar a sufficiently rapid rocking, or vibratory motion, to produce the sound emitted. The sound may be made to vary with the size, form, weight, and arrangement of the bar, but it is in all cases the result of a more or less rapid oscillatory motion.

I turn now to an entirely different method of producing sound. In this case the motion required for the eliciting of an audible note takes the form of a rapid succession of puffs of air. On the rotator just used there is, in addition to Savart's wheel, a disk of brass having near its circumference a number of equidistant orifices. The instrument in this form was designed by Seebeck, and with it, under various forms, he made many interesting experiments. A modified form of the siren, together with the tuning-fork, will, as you shall see in our subsequent lectures, constitute our most efficient aids in elucidating the mysteries of sound. Bringing the nozzle of a small tube, connected with an acoustic bellows, over the circle of perforations of the disk, and causing the disk to revolve, you hear, when the air escapes from the bellows through the tube, first a succession of puffs, and then, as the wheel revolves more rapidly, the sound becomes more shrill, and reminds one of the weird wailing of the wind on a dark wintry night.

I hold in my hand a little instrument called the mill-siren of Cagniard de Latour. It is essentially a cylindrical tube of brass, at the end of which is a revolving fan. When one blows into the mouthpiece the fan is made to revolve. The fan thus renders the current of air intermittent, and we have produced, therefore, the vibratory motion which, as we have seen in the preceding experiments, is the necessary precursor of sound.

By increasing the blast of air the speed of the fan is accelerated, and the pitch is heightened as in the case of the siren just used.

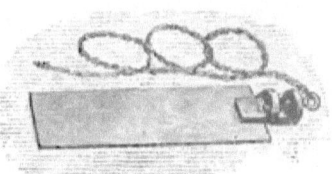

FIG. 10.

There is but one step from the mill-siren to a very simple and primitive instrument, to which I wish now to direct your attention. I show it to you to emphasize what I have thus far been insisting on, — namely, that sound externally to the ear is merely a mode of motion, and that when motion is properly timed, sound is always the result.

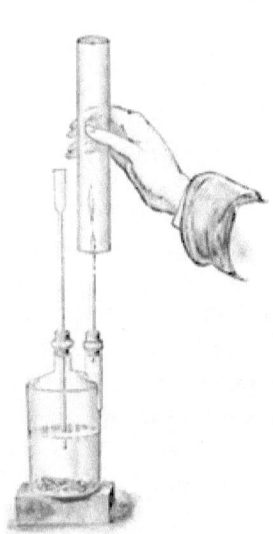

FIG. 11.

The instrument referred to is called a musical sling, and consists of simply a thin plate of metal (Fig. 10) about three by six inches in size, and attached to a string. I take hold of the string and give the plate a whirling motion, making it describe a circle in the air. The resistance of the air causes the plate rapidly to revolve around its longer axis, and to give forth, first a flutter, and then the more acute musical sound which is distinctly audible in every part of the room.

A more interesting way of throwing the air into periodic pulsations is by means of a jet of burning gas, preferably hydrogen. On introducing an ignited jet of this gas into a glass tube (Fig. 11) there is at once heard a note of singular purity and power. By causing a cubical mirror to revolve near the tube, we can see that the flame is rapidly extinguished and rekindled; and this rapid extinction and rekindling it is that causes the aerial column within the tube to vibrate so as to emit the sound you all hear. Such a flame is called a singing flame, and we shall have occasion to investigate it more in detail in a subsequent lecture.

Wertheim has taught us how we may vary our experiments by using electricity as an agent for producing the vibratory motion necessary to generate sound. We have here (Fig. 12) an iron bar firmly clamped in the middle to a solid metal stand. Around one of the ends of the rod

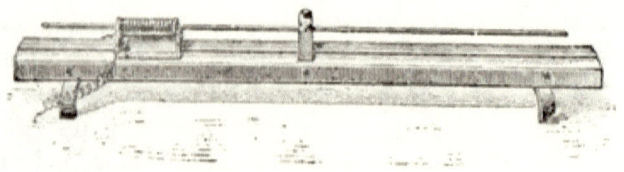

FIG. 12.

is placed a coil of insulated copper wire, through which may be sent a current of electricity. We allow a current from a battery to pass through the coil, and then intercept its flow by breaking the circuit. Every time the circuit is closed or broken, a faint sound is the result. When the current is passing through the bobbin the bar is magnetized; but as soon as the current ceases to flow, on account of the conductor being disconnected, the bar loses its magnetism. The alternate magnetization and demagnetization of the bar throw its molecules into such a state of vibratory motion that it at once becomes perceptible as sound.

A still more interesting sound-producer is the radiophone, a simple form of which is before you. In a test-tube is placed a small tube of brass covered with lampblack. Through the perforated disk on the rotator, intermittent flashes of heat, converged by a concave reflector from the gas jet, are allowed to impinge on the soot-covered brass tube. This, by producing rapid changes in temperature, causes corresponding expansions and contractions in the metal tube, and a continuous sound follows in consequence. The pitch of the sound depends on the number of flashes made to impinge on the tube. The more rapid the revolution of the disk, the greater the number of flashes of radiant energy, the higher the pitch of the resulting note.

M. Mercadier has devised a more elaborate instrument (Fig. 13), by means of which we can get the four notes of

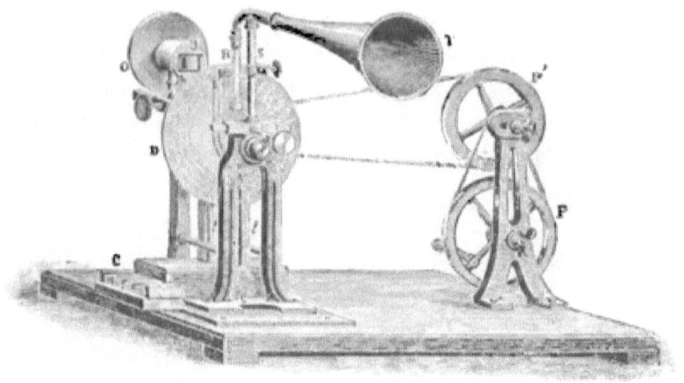

FIG. 13.

the perfect major chord [1] by pressing on suitable keys at C, connected with $t\ t$. By converging a beam of light through $O\ U$, from a powerful electric lamp on the soot-covered brass tube R, and reinforcing by a trumpet-shaped resonator, $S\ T$, the notes emitted, we can, by rotating, by means of the pulleys, $P\ P'$, the perforated wheel, D, with sufficient velocity, elicit notes that can be perceived at a considerable distance from the instrument.

In the experiments so far made we have seen a few of the many ways in which sound may be generated. In some cases it is directly caused by friction, as when a bow

[1] See chapter x., on Intervals, etc.

is used. In other instances it is produced by taps or puffs, as when Savart's wheel or the siren is used, or by a series of rapid explosions, as was observed in the singing flame. In others, still, the sounds elicited have their origin in rapid molecular motions induced by the intermittent action of heat or electricity.

In all cases motion precedes and accompanies sound. It appears sometimes as segmental mass-motion, when a part or a whole of the sound-producing body, divided into a greater or less number of segments, is seen to be in a state of rapid oscillation. More frequently, the motions which give rise to audible notes are nearly or entirely invisible. In the latter cases it is molecular rather than mass-motion — the motions of the molecules or ultimate particles of the vibrating body, rather than those of the vibrating body, considered as a whole — that is the cause of sound. We may not, however, separate the two motions, as they are always, to a greater or less extent, concomitant in all cases where sound is produced. Molecular motion gives rise to mass motion, and *vice versa*. In all cases under discussion one necessarily depends on the other. When, for instance, the tuning-fork is excited by the bow, the whole mass of the fork is set in periodic vibration, — a motion which would be impossible, were it not for the elasticity of the steel, — and at the same time there is a corresponding tremor of the smallest particles, the molecules, of which the fork is composed.

The physical cause, then, of sound is motion, — in all cases motion. If this one fact is duly appreciated, a great advance is made towards properly understanding what will follow.

We are now prepared to answer a question that must have suggested itself to all of you ere this; that is, "What is the difference between a musical and a non-musical sound, between a musical sound and noise?" As a sensation, every one can, under ordinary circumstances, distinguish one from the other. The extremes of musical and non-musical sounds are easily separated.

But there are many instances in which the separation is not so easy.

Physically, musical sounds, as Helmholtz tells us, are always produced by periodic vibrations, noises by non-periodic vibrations.

But musical sounds may be so combined as to produce a noise. If, for instance, one were to sound simultaneously all the eight notes of the gamut on a piano or harmonium, the result would be designated as a noise, although each of its components, taken separately, is recognized as a musical note. Similarly, what is usually regarded as a noise may be shown to be, in reality, a distinct musical sound. In my hand is a small piece of wood, which I let fall on the table. Certainly no one would think of calling the sound musical. And yet it does possess quite a marked musical character when one's attention is properly directed to it, and when the sound is compared with others of the same kind in a proper sequence.

When the same piece of wood is dropped again, and, in succession, seven others of gradually decreasing size, you at once recognize the notes of the gamut. Choosing three from the number, and allowing them to fall on the table as before, you distinguish a series of sounds that constitute, in music, the perfect major chord. If all three are let fall at once, the sound is still agreeable.

The sounds thus generated are not, if you will, as pure as those furnished by the harp or the flute, but they must be classified as musical, and are, indeed, used in music. The instrument known as a xylophone is made up of just such pieces of wood. Substituting metal bars for wood, we have the well-known instrument called the metallophone. Pieces of glass or compact stone, like slate, might be used, and these would give us what are known as glass or rock harmonicons. The Chinese, in an instrument called the *king*, use pieces of flint suspended from cords, and by striking the flints they manage to elicit from them quite agreeable music. The well-known "Anvil Chorus" is another illustration of how what are ordinarily reckoned as noises, may be made to do service as music.

But we may go still farther. When a cork is drawn from a bottle you hear a quick, explosive report. Surely no one would call this a musical sound. Let us compare it with a proper sequence of similar sounds. Drawing corks from these three bottles, whose sizes vary according to a fixed ratio, we have three sounds of different pitch produced. Every one near recognizes the same sequence of sounds as was produced with the three wooden bars. The sounds are unmistakably those of the major chord. With a sufficient number of properly tuned bottles a skilful performer could, by merely withdrawing the corks, easily evoke a simple melody that every one would recognize.

Koenig has devised an interesting piece of apparatus (Fig. 14), in which sounds are elicited in the manner just illustrated. Here, instead of bottles, we have four brass tubes attached to the same base, and furnished with accurately fitted pistons. When these are withdrawn in succession, you hear the notes C_5, E_5, G_5, C_4, constituting the perfect major chord.[1]

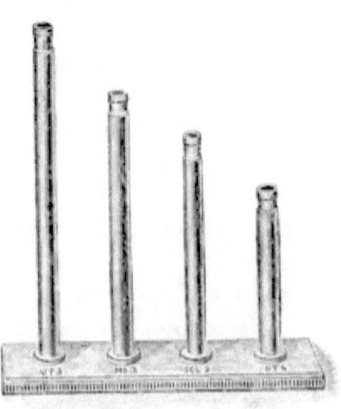

FIG. 14.

From these experiments it is obvious that the line of demarcation between musical sounds and noises is not so easily drawn as one might imagine. Dr. Haughton gives an excellent illustration of the truth of this statement. "The granite pavements of London," he says, "are four inches in width, and cabs driving over this, at the rate of

[1] See Appendix I. for value in musical notation of the notes here mentioned.

eight miles an hour, cause a succession of noises at the rate of thirty-four in the second, which corresponds to a well-known musical note that has been recognized by many competent observers; and yet nothing can be imagined more purely a noise or less musical than the jolt of the rims of a cab-wheel against a projecting stone. Yet if a regularly repeated succession of jolts takes place, the result is a soft, deep, musical sound that will bear comparison with notes derived from more sentimental sources."

So, too, we may hear musical notes in the plashing of a fountain, the roar of a cataract, the murmur of a river, the howling of the wind, the hum of machinery, the rumble of a railway train passing over a bridge or through a tunnel, and in the complex result occasioned by the manifold noises of a neighboring city. Carlyle, therefore, tells a profound truth when he says, "See deep enough, and you see musically; the heart of Nature being everywhere music, if you can only reach it." Byron expresses the same idea still more elegantly when he sings, —

> "There's music in the sighing of a reed;
> There's music in the gushing of a rill;
> There's music in all things if men had ears, —
> Their earth is but an echo of the spheres."

Equally true, and almost equally beautiful, are the following lines of another poet: —

> "We have not heard the music of the spheres,
> The song of star to star; but there are sounds
> . . . . . .
> That Nature uses in her common rounds, —
> The fall of streams, the cry of winds that strain
> The oak, the roaring of the sea's surge, might
> Of thunder breaking off afar, or rain
> That falls by minutes in the summer's night:
> These are the voices of earth's secret soul,
> Uttering the mystery from which she came."[1]

We do not hear many of the musical sounds that keep the atmosphere in a state of constant tremor, because we

[1] Archibald Lampman, in "Scribner's Magazine."

do not give ear to them, or because we are not in the habit of expecting musical sounds except from musical instruments. It is true that musical instruments afford us the most agreeable tones, but there are instruments used in music that emit sounds which are far from pure, and frequently anything but agreeable. Among these are drums, tom-toms, cymbals, castanets, timbrels, tambourines, harmonicons, triangles, and others of the same class. They are, for the most part, used for keeping time, and the tones produced, are fortunately so modified by accompanying sounds that they lose most of their harshness.

From what has been said, and from the experiments made, we must conclude that the popular distinction between sound and music is singularly vague. Helmholtz's distinction, however, is always literally true. Periodic vibrations, whatever the source of sound, whatever the instrument used, always yield musical notes. They are smooth and agreeable to the ear, while, on the other hand, noises, or non-periodic vibrations, produce on the tympanic membrane a kind of jolting sensation, — a sensation of irregularly recurring shocks. A noise thus affects the auditory nerve painfully, just as a flickering light gives rise to a painful sensation in the nerves of sight.

But the motion, periodic or non-periodic, of sonorous bodies cannot be apprehended as sound except through the intervention of some medium connecting these bodies with the organ of hearing. This medium is, ordinarily, the air. Any other substance, however, solid, liquid, or gaseous, may serve as a transmitting medium.

Let us then inquire into the mode of the propagation of sound. If we can picture this clearly to our minds we shall have made a second important step in our investigations. That air or some other medium is indispensable for the transmission of sonorous vibrations has been known from the earliest stages of physical inquiry. We have seen how Seneca considered the elasticity of air as essential to the production and transmission of sound. That some medium was necessary was evident, but it was not possible to demonstrate experimentally the necessity of a medium until the invention of the air-pump by Otto von Guericke, in 1650. It was then shown by the inventor of this most useful instrument that sound cannot travel *in vacuo*, — that air or some other medium is always necessary for its propagation from one point to another.

We may here repeat the experiment of the illustrious burgomaster of Magdeburg, which is no less instructive than interesting. Thanks to improved forms of apparatus, we can now secure much better results than were possible in Von Guericke's time.

On the plate of our air-pump (Fig. 15) is placed a piece of clockwork, H, C, which causes a small hammer, a, to strike a bell, T. The clockwork is now wound up and set going. The bell-glass is next placed on the plate, and covers the clockwork; but still you hear the bell with almost undiminished intensity. A few turns of the crank of the pump are, however, sufficient to exhaust the air in the receiver to such an extent that the sound now audible becomes comparatively feeble. A few more strokes of the piston produce almost a perfect vacuum, and the sound is now so faint as to be inaudible even to those who are nearest the instrument. The hammer is still striking the bell, as you may observe, but it is entirely noiseless. To secure this result we have isolated the clockwork from the plate of the pump by interposing a layer of non-conducting material. Had the mechanism operating the bell been in contact with the plate, the strokes of the hammer would have been communicated to the outside air by the material of the plate itself.

FIG. 15.

As soon as air is re-admitted into the receiver, the sound of the bell again breaks forth, so as to be heard by every one in the room.

Let us now admit hydrogen gas into the receiver instead of air, and note the result. Hydrogen is about fifteen times lighter than air, and sounds generated in such a medium are more feeble than they would be in a denser medium. Although the receiver is now filled with this gas, the sound of the bell is, as you remark, much weaker than when the receiver was filled with air. Exhausting the receiver as before, the sound disappears more rapidly, and becomes inaudible sooner than it did when air was used. This experiment shows that the more attenuated the medium, the less competent it is to convey sonorous vibrations to the ear. We might experiment with other gases or vapors, and we should find that the intensity of the sounds heard would in all cases depend on the density of the media employed.

Later on, in 1685, Papin repeated Von Guericke's experiment before the members of the Royal Society in London. As a source of sound, he used a whistle instead of a bell. In 1705, Hawksbee made the experiment in a somewhat modified form, using a simple bell suspended by a string instead of one operated by clockwork.

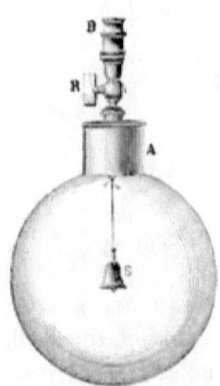

Fig. 16.

By means of a large glass globe (Fig. 16), in which is suspended a little bell, we may repeat Hawksbee's experiment in a very pleasing and effective way. Swinging the globe back and forth while full of air, the bell is made to ring so as to be clearly heard throughout the hall. Connecting it by means of the metallic part, *A B*, with our pump, we withdraw the air from it, and then close the tube by the stopcock *R*. Now, on agitating the bell anew, we find that the sound is so faint as to be barely perceptible.

These experiments, then, prove conclusively that sonorous vibrations cannot be propagated in a vacuum; some medium is necessary. Ordinarily it is air, but all elastic bodies are capable of transmitting sound, and some of them, as we shall see, with much greater readiness and velocity than others.

From the foregoing experiments we should infer that in a vacuum there is absolute silence, and that, if we could exist *in vacuo*, we should be able to hear nothing, not even the most powerful detonations. Balloonists, in the higher regions of the atmosphere, encounter conditions which afford an approximation to this utter silence. Those who have ascended very high mountains have noted a similar circumstance. The sensation is strange, indescribable, awe-inspiring, almost startling. It is so entirely different from any experience that one can have near the earth's surface, where there is always more or less sound, even when everything is apparently in perfect quiescence.

I had some years ago an opportunity of experiencing a sensation of this kind on the summit of the volcano of Popocatapetl. This peak, as you know, has an elevation of nearly eighteen thousand feet above sea-level. The feeling that then came over me is something I shall never forget. The silence there is "the silence that is in the starry sky," — a silence where no sound is uttered, where no sound may be, a silence that —

> "Pours a solitariness
> Into the very essence of the soul."

And here again it will be interesting to know what opinions the early physical investigators entertained regarding the subject we are now discussing. We are often wont to imagine, and without any warrant for so doing, that the theories of the ancient philosophers in matters of physical science were entirely futile, and that their consideration is simply a loss of time. But the truth is that their views on many subjects in physics are often nearly identical with our own. They seemed at times to have had an almost intuitive conception of the truth. The wonder is how they were able to acquire such exact notions about matters that even now are not easily understood. Nothing indeed can be more interesting or instructive than to observe their gropings after truth, and to see how closely they anticipated, in many instances, the discoveries and generalizations of modern science. It is simple justice to these old students of Nature to give them credit for what they have achieved, and to admit that many of the theories and doctrines that are usually regarded as the fruits of modern research, had, in reality, their starting-point in the observations and hypotheses of those who labored and thought long ages ago. If there is evolution in the organic world, there is evolution also in the world of science; and the grand intellectual achievements of our own time owe not a little of their lustre to the glory of the distant but brilliant past.

We have a striking illustration in the question before us, — the mode of propagation of sound. Aristotle in his treatise on "Sound and Hearing" says: "Sound takes place when bodies strike the air, not by the air having a form impressed upon it, as some think, but by its being moved in a corresponding manner; the air being contracted and expanded and overtaken, and again struck by the impulses of the breath and the strings. For when the air falls upon and strikes the air which is next to it, the air is carried forward with an impetus, and that which is contiguous to the first is carried onward; so that the same voice spreads every way as far as the motion of the air takes place."

In reading this we could almost fancy we are perusing some modern treatise on sound, so nearly does the view of the illustrious Stagyrite coincide with that now held by all men of science. Indeed, as Whewell truthfully observes: "The admirers of antiquity might easily, by pressing the language closely, and using the light of modern discovery, detect in this passage an exact account of the production and propagation of sound."

Let us take another opinion, — that of Vitruvius, the celebrated Roman architect. His views regarding the motions of the air which give rise to sound, and the illustration which he uses, seem more like those found in a modern text-book on physics than those of an author who wrote two thousand years ago. He says: "Voice is breath flowing and made sensible to the hearing by striking the air. It moves in infinite circumferences of circles, as when, by throwing a stone into still water, you produce innumerable circles of waves, increasing from the centre and spreading outwards till the boundary of the space or some other obstacle prevents their outlines from going farther. In the same manner the voice makes its motion in circles. But in water the circle moves breadthways upon a level plain, the voice proceeds in breadth, and also successively ascends in height."[1]

Let us now, in the light of modern research, investigate the condition of the air when under the influence of vibratory motion. And that we may better understand this

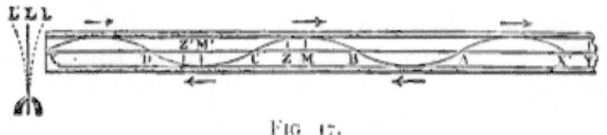

FIG. 17.

motion, let us suppose an elastic strip to vibrate at one of the extremities of a cylindrical tube (Fig. 17). A little reflection will make it apparent that each time the strip moves from L to L'' it will impress on the vertical layer of air, X, a series of condensations whose intensity increases during the first half and decreases during the last half of its excursion. Every time, however, that the strip moves in the opposite direction — that is, from L'' to L' — the layer X will be subject to a series of rarefactions whose intensity increases during the first half, and decreases during the last half of its swing. And as long as the strip continues to vibrate, this terminal layer X will be subject

[1] Quoted in Whewell's "History of the Inductive Sciences," ii. 25.

alternately and periodically to similar conditions of condensation and rarefaction.

But these condensations and rarefactions are not confined solely to the terminal layer X. They are communicated in succession to all the succeeding layers, and affect the entire mass of air enclosed in the tube. As the vibrations of the elastic strip are periodic and isochronous, so also are the pulses of condensation and rarefaction periodic and isochronous. Condensations and rarefactions of equal length alternate with one another, and persist as long as the strip continues to vibrate. A simple vibration of the strip — that is, an excursion to *or* fro — generates a single wave of condensation or rarefaction. A complete vibration of the strip — that is, an excursion to *and* fro — produces a complete wave, one, namely, that is composed of both a condensation and a rarefaction.

Fig. 17, as we see, exhibits the condition of the aërial column after the elastic strip L has executed five single vibrations. We have, accordingly, five single sonorous waves, of the same length, abutting one another. These waves, composed of alternate condensations and rarefactions, are graphically represented by a continuous curve, which cuts the axis of the tube at the points X, D, C, B, A, X'. The portions of the tube above the axis are conventionally considered to represent waves of condensation, of which we have here three, while the parts below the axis represent waves of rarefaction, of which two are exhibited.

Arrows indicate the direction of movement of the air particles constituting the condensed and rarefied pulses. The direction is always the same for pulses of the same kind, but opposite in condensed from what it is in rarefied pulses.

The perpendiculars to the points Z and M represent the degrees of condensation and the velocities of movement of the air-particles at these points. Similarly, the ordinates at the points Z' and M represent the amount of rarefaction and the relative velocities at the points intersected. At the points where the continuous curve cuts the axis of the tube the air is in a state of equilibrium, and there is neither condensation nor rarefaction, and consequently no movement. But even at the points of maximum condensation and rarefaction the amount of displacement for any determinate particle is extremely small.

The time required for the bar L to execute a complete vibration is, as we have learned, called its period. The time required for a particle of air set in motion by the vibrating bar to make a complete vibration is called its period. The periods of both the bar and the air-particles excited by the bar are obviously equal. The wave-length is the distance from one condensation to the next condensation, as from N to C, or from one rarefaction to the next rarefaction, as from D to B, or from any one given particle

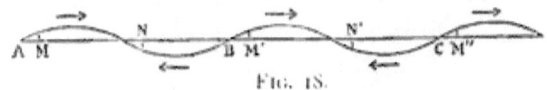

FIG. 18.

to the next particle in a like position and moving in the same direction.

The wave always moves one wave-length in the time required for a particle to make one complete vibration. Any two points separated by one or more wave-lengths are in similar conditions, and are said, therefore, to be in the same *phase*. If any two points are separated by an interval greater or less than one or more complete wave-lengths, they have phases which are different. Thus in Fig. 18 the points where M, M', M'', cut the continuous curve are in the same phase. Similarly the points cut by the ordinates N and N' are in the same phase. M and N, or M and N' are in different phases.

In Fig. 19 we have a very instructive graphic representation of sonorous waves. It must, however, always be borne in mind that it is only an arbitrary representation, a symbol, and not a picture, of a sound-wave that is indicated by such curves and lines. From what has been said, the figure needs but little explanation. The portions of the curve above the horizontal line correspond, as has been said, to pulses of condensation, while those below represent pulses of rarefaction. The letters n, c, and r, in (1), and n, c, d, in (2), indicate respectively the nodal points where there is no motion, and the points of greatest condensation and rarefaction, or elevation and depression.

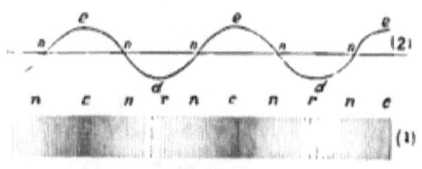

Fig. 19.

So far we have been considering sonorous waves that move in one direction only. Ordinarily, however, sound is propagated in many, or in all directions, simultaneously. When a skylark, for instance, is singing in the air, the sonorous pulses which it originates are propagated in all directions. Spherical waves or shells are thus formed, which recede from the centre of disturbance with the velocity of sound, alternate condensations and rarefactions being generated precisely in the same manner as when the sound-pulse travels only in one direction.

This is well illustrated by the accompanying diagram (Fig. 20). A is the source of sound. During the first half-vibration, motion is communicated to the entire sphere, PQ, whose centre is A and radius AR. During the time of the next half-vibration, all the space between PQ and $P'Q'$ is set in movement. Thus in the second interval of time a sphere of twice the radius of the first is made to vibrate. In the third interval of time the space between $P'Q'$ and $P''Q''$ has been set in vibratory motion. The volume of

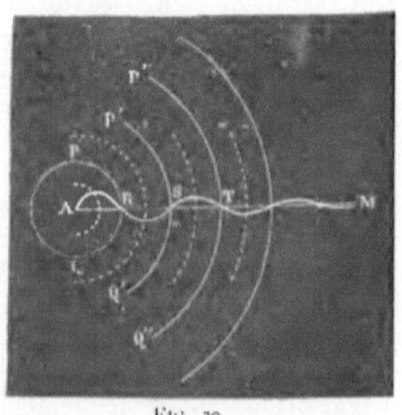

Fig. 20.

air, therefore, which is agitated augments in proportion as the spherical sound-wave recedes from the centre of disturbance. The amount of air set in vibration at any given instant varies directly as the surface of the sphere, or as the square of the radius of the sphere. And as the intensity of sound, as we shall learn, depends on the amplitude of motion of the sonorous body, its intensity, in any given case, will vary inversely as the square of the distance from the centre of agitation. This is illustrated by the curve $ARST$, which represents the condition of the air at a determinate instant in the direction AM. The amplitude of movement at any given point of the curve would, as you know, be represented by a perpendicular drawn from that point to the horizontal line AM. The wave-lengths are all equal, being independent of the amplitude of movement and of their distance from the origin of motion. The intervals of time are also equal, because the vibrations considered are of the class called isochronous.

It is now apparent, I think, that our modern notions regarding the propagation of sound are only a natural development of theories held by Aristotle, Vitruvius, and others of their time. We have simply cleared up their conceptions, but have not, I venture to say, introduced any essential modifications. We can state their theory more accurately than it was possible for them to do, and, thanks to our modern delicate instruments of research, we are able to demonstrate experimentally what they were able only to infer.

We must, then, view sound as conveyed by waves or pulses. Newton tells us in his "Principia" that "Sounds, since they arise in tremulous bodies, are no other than waves — *pulsus* — propagated in the air." It is a *motion* that is transmitted, not a *substance*. There is a transference of a *condition*, or a *system of conditions*, of matter, but no transfer of *matter itself*. The waves that strike on the drum of the ear are similar to those that are excited in the sonorous body, but they are not the same. The sonorous body communicates its vibratory motion to the air-particles nearest to it, and these in turn deliver their motion to the particles adjoining. Motion is thus conveyed from particle to particle, until it finally reaches the organ of hearing, where it is taken up by the auditory nerve and transmitted by it to the brain, which converts or translates it into the sensation which we call sound.

A simple illustration will show you how a transfer of motion, like that which obtains in the case of sound, is possible.

Before you is an apparatus devised over two hundred years ago by the distinguished French physicist, Abbé Mariotte, one of the ablest and most successful investigators of his time. On a stand (Fig. 21) are suspended

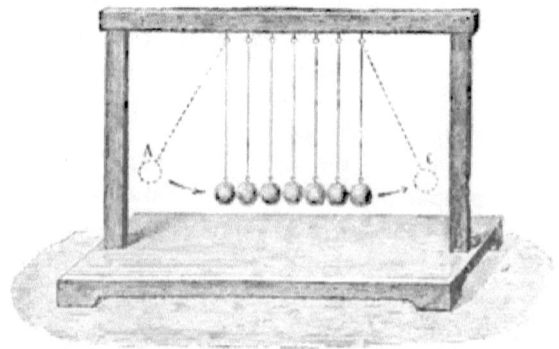

FIG. 21.

seven elastic balls of lignum vitæ, each of which almost touches its neighbor. Drawing the ball A aside from its position of rest and allowing it to impinge against the one nearest to it, you observe that directly the first ball touches the second, it is stopped in its course, and its motion imparted to the second. This, in turn, transfers its motion to the third, which gives it up to the fourth; and so on until the motion reaches the seventh ball, C, which at once flies off to the right, while the other six remain motionless. What then has taken place? The motion which was primarily imparted to the first ball was communicated to the succeeding six, but only the last of these showed the visible effects of this motion.

Were it not for the elasticity of the balls, this transfer of motion, as just shown, would be impossible. If the balls were perfectly elastic — they are far from it — the motion of the seventh ball would be equal to that given to the first. By using ivory balls, or, better still, glass balls, the loss of motion would be less, as ivory and glass are more elastic than is lignum vitæ.

Imagine, now, these wooden balls replaced by particles of air. Imagine also the particle of air nearest a sounding body taking up the motion of that body and imparting it to the adjoining particles in the direction of the ear, and imagine further this motion transferred in succession to all the particles intervening between the sonorous body and the ear, and you have a true picture of what actually takes place in nature when vibratory motion is propagated in straight lines through air or any other medium whatever, and perceived as sound.

Let us take another illustration, which shows even more strikingly the mode of propagation of sonorous vibration. I hold in my left hand one end of a brass wire-spiral, twenty feet long, made of the best spring brass. The other end of the spiral is attached to a small box. With my right hand I grasp the spiral about six inches from my left, and pulling the turns of the spiral some distance apart, I suddenly relax my hold with the right hand. In virtue of the elasticity of the wire the turns that were separated from each other tend to return to their orignal position. At the same time, however, a vibratory motion, or pulse, is sent through the whole length of the spiral, and announces its arrival at the other end by a loud rap on the box. This pulse on reaching the box is reflected immediately, and quickly returns to its starting-point at my hand. Thence it again returns to the box, repeating the tap you heard before, and is again reflected to my hand. This oscillatory motion is repeated several times, each time becoming weaker, until it entirely disappears.

When the pulses are first produced they can not only be heard, but seen as well. To and fro you see them move, each pulse making the excursion from one end to the other of the spiral in the same period of time.

If we examine closely the condition of the spiral as the pulses pass along its length we shall find that, at a given instant, some of the coils are farther apart than others. As the pulse first starts forward towards the box we observe that at the end I hold in my right hand, several coils are closely pressed together, followed by others more widely separated from each other. As the pulse is carried onward, the condition of compression and separation is seen to be propagated from one end of the spiral to the other. On reaching the box these same compressions and separations are reflected back to their starting-point, and this motion is repeated as long as the pulse continues its forward and backward motion.

This, as has been stated, is exactly what takes place when sound is transmitted through the air. When a tuning-fork, for instance, is excited, its prongs, in moving away from each other, crowd together the air particles in contact with their outside surfaces. These air-particles compress those in front of them, whilst those first compressed by the tuning-fork tend, by reason of their elasticity, to return to their normal condition. But the return of the prongs of the fork to their original position pulls the particles that were at first crowded together farther apart from each other, and farther apart even than they were before the fork was set in vibration.

As in the wire spiral some of the coils were closer together than others, so when sound is transmitted through the air we have the air-particles alternately compressed and separated. This condition of compression and dilation, as in the spiral, is carried forward from the source of sound until the motion gradually dies away, or until it encounters some obstacle, when it is reflected back in its path, as in the spiral, or off in some other direction.

Mariotte's apparatus illustrates how one particle of matter can communicate its motion to a contiguous particle. The wire spiral exhibits the transfer of motion by the formation of pulses of compression and dilation. Mach, however, has provided us with an apparatus which beautifully exhibits both of these phenomena simultaneously. Such an instrument is before you (Fig. 22). It is about ten feet long and four feet high, and, taken altogether, is by far the best means yet contrived for showing the nature of all kinds of vibratory motion, both transversal and longitudinal. As you observe, twenty-one white metal balls are suspended from the cross piece *c d* of a frame *p a g b*. On a long bar, *s t*, are fixed a number of pegs, at different

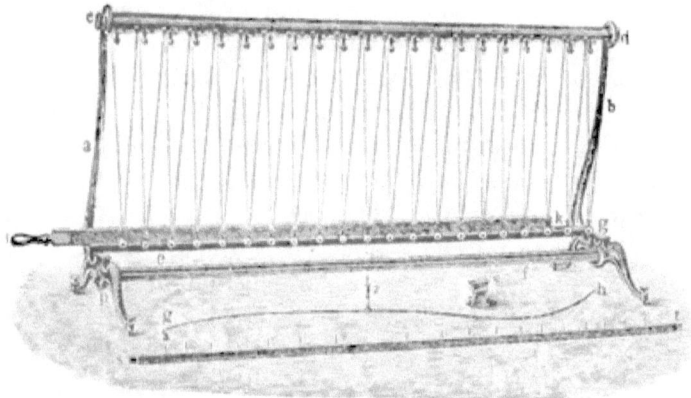

FIG. 22.

distances from each other. These pegs are so placed as to represent one complete sonorous wave, composed of one condensed and one rarefied pulse. When the balls are held in position by these pegs, the former as well as the latter exhibit a complete sound-wave. If, now, when the balls are in this position, the bar is suddenly withdrawn, they will commence to swing in the same plane, and while swinging they will retain the same relative positions with reference to each other which they had before they were put in motion. They are now oscillating all in the same plane and in the same period. But in addition to the excursions made by each individual ball, you see, in a most striking manner, a transfer of pulses of condensation and rarefaction from one end of the series of balls to the other. This is exactly what takes place in every sonorous wave, and we could have no better illustration of the character of sonorous vibrations than that here given. It gives us in a moment a more exact idea of the nature of condensed and rarefied pulses than could be obtained by hours of the best-directed efforts of the unaided imagination. Indeed, we could scarcely desire a better instance than this of the capability which a well-devised and well-executed experiment possesses of furnishing us with a clear mental picture of certain physical processes that otherwise would remain quite obscure, if not unintelligible.

The motion of each ball in the experiment just made is like that of the bob of a pendulum. The motion of each particle of air agitated by the ball is the same. Such motions are accordingly called *pendular motions*. They are also known as *simple harmonic motions*. We shall use either term indifferently. The motions of each particle of a medium, transmitting a sonorous wave, are always in a direction parallel to the line of propagation of sound. In this respect they differ from the motions of the individual particles of a water wave, which are always at right angles to the direction of the wave itself. Sound-vibrations are likewise different from light-vibrations, for the latter, like vibratory motions of particles of water, are always transverse to the line of propagation of luminous rays.

What has been said of the mode of the propagation of sound in air applies with equal truth to all other media, whether gaseous, liquid, or solid. Sound is transmitted in pulses. Whatever the media, then, by which sonorous vibrations are carried from one point to another, we must regard the molecules of this media as being the active agents in the transfer of the motion impressed on it. While conveying sound the molecules are in a state of invisible, but most energetic tremor, and when this tremor ceases, the sensation of sound ceases also.

How wonderfully the mechanical action of these infinitesimal molecules, the physiological action of the organ of hearing, and the psychological action of the brain are related to each other! Who can tell us how they are connected, or how one gives rise to, or influences, the other? No one. Such questions are "above the reach and ken of mortal apprehension." They bring home to us with telling force the fact that there are mysteries in the natural as well as in the supernatural order, — mysteries that only an angelic, possibly only the Divine, mind can fathom.

CHAPTER II.

LOUDNESS AND PITCH.

MUSICAL sounds differ from each other in three ways, — in loudness, in pitch, and in quality. To-day we shall discuss the subjects of loudness and pitch, and reserve that of quality for a subsequent lecture.

In speaking of the loudness of sound we must carefully distinguish between the sensation of loudness and the mechanical action that gives rise to it. Generally speaking, there is no measure for the loudness of sounds, so far as sensation is concerned. Acute sounds, even when of the same mechanical intensity as grave sounds, seem louder than the grave ones. A bass note, therefore, to sound as loud as a treble note, must be executed with proportionally much more force. The reason of this is that the ear is not equally sensitive to all sounds.

Mechanically considered, the loudness of sound depends upon the energy of vibration of the sonorous body. I draw a bow across the prong of a tuning-fork, and you hear a loud, clear note. At the same time those of you who are sufficiently near can see that the prongs are actually in motion. Gradually, however, the sound dies away, and simultaneously, and at the same rate, the vibratory motion of the fork disappears. From this experiment we learn that the loudness of sound for any given note depends upon the amplitude of vibration of the sonorous body. The greater the amplitude, the louder the sound. As the result of many careful experiments, it has been found that the intensity or loudness of sound varies as the square of the amplitude of the oscillations of the vibrating body.

Here are two tuning-forks, *A* and *B*, that are made to give exactly the same note. If *A* could be caused to vibrate with an amplitude of exactly one fifth of an inch, and *B* with an amplitude of one tenth of an inch, *A* would have twice the width of swing of *B*, and would give rise to a sound just four times as loud as *B*.

The loudness of sound varies also with the distance of the sonorous body from the ear. A little consideration will enable us to determine the law that governs the rate of variation. Exciting the tuning-fork before me, it gives off sonorous waves in all directions. But the amount of matter put in motion at a distance of one foot from the centre of disturbance is, as geometry tells us, only one fourth of that which is agitated at a distance of two feet, and only one ninth of the amount caused to vibrate at a distance of three feet. In other words, as we learned in our last lecture, the amount of matter set in vibration increases directly as the square of the radius of the shell affected. But as the volume of air put in motion increases, the loudness of the sound decreases, and in the same proportion. The rate of diminution is put in the form of a law by stating that *the loudness of sound varies inversely as the square of the distance of the sonorous body from the ear.*[1] At this rate, to one standing twenty feet away from the fork just used, the sound would be only one fourth as loud as to one but ten feet away. It would, however, be difficult to compare accurately the relative degree of loudness in this way. The experiment could be made more satisfactorily in another way. If one tuning-fork were to be placed ten feet away, and four others, giving exactly the same pitch and intensity as the first, were to be placed twenty feet off, we should find that the sound emitted by the fork ten feet distant equalled in loudness the aggregate sound of the four other forks twice the distance away. We thus see that doubling the distance reduces the loudness of the sound to one fourth. Trebling the distance would

---

[1] Mersenne gives this law in Prop. 14, lib. i., Harm.

reduce it to one ninth, and quadrupling it would, for the same reason, bring down the intensity to one sixteenth.

Loudness of sound is also modified by the density of the air in which it is excited. We saw in our last lecture the effect of rarefied air in diminishing the intensity of vibrations set up by a sonorous body. Using hydrogen gas, which is about fifteen times lighter than air, we obtained a similar result. In a heavier gas, like carbonic acid, the loudness of sound is augumented. The effect of air of slight density in diminishing the loudness of sonorous vibrations is illustrated in a very marked manner on the summits of very high mountains. Here the report of a pistol, as has frequently been remarked, sounds much like the discharge of a small fire-cracker

Again, the loudness of sound produced by a sonorous body is strengthened by the proximity of other bodies capable of vibrating with it. I hold in my hand a small tuning-fork. It is unlike those hitherto used in that it is not mounted on a resounding box. When it is struck against the table and set in vibration, the sound is so feeble that it is scarcely audible; but when its base is placed upon the table, it immediately breaks forth into a clear, powerful note. The board on which the fork rests is also thrown into a state of vibration, and hence the increased loudness of sound as a result. Later on, we shall study more in detail this phenomenon of co-vibration, — resonance, as it is called, — and we shall see what an important part it plays in reinforcing sound in many of the more important instruments of music. It is sufficient here to allude to it as one of the important factors that materially augment the intensity of sonorous vibrations.

We have said that there is no measure for the loudness of sound as far as its sensation is concerned. Prof. A. M. Mayer has, however, attempted to determine the mechanical equivalent of a given sonorous aërial vibration, though much yet remains to be done in this direction. He found that the sonorous air vibrations produced by a C_3 fork, placed before a suitable resonator during ten seconds, was equivalent to the mechanical energy necessary to lift 54 grains one foot high. Joule's mechanical equivalent of heat, or thermal unit, being 772 foot-pounds, the intensity of the sonorous vibrations of the fork used was, therefore, only about the $\frac{1}{10000}$ part of a Joule unit. Professor Mayer's investigations are interesting, because, among other reasons, they indicate a universal method for the exact determination of the relative intensities of sounds of different pitch. Some method, like the one referred to, is quite a desideratum, and, when discovered, will enable the acoustician to solve many problems that constantly present themselves to him in the course of his researches.[1]

We come now to consider the second characteristic of sound, — its pitch. In some of the experiments made in the last lecture with Savart's wheel and Seebeck's siren, we were given a hint as to what constitutes pitch.

Galileo seems to have been the first to suspect the true cause of pitch. He noticed that in passing a knife over the milled edge of a coin, a musical sound was produced, and that the pitch of the sound was higher as the number of serrations passed over in a given time was greater.

But the first one to investigate thoroughly the cause of pitch, and the first to determine the pitch of a known musical note, was the illustrious French ecclesiastic, Father Mersenne, of the order of Minims. Père Mersenne, as he is usually known, is justly called the Father of Acoustics. He did for the science of musical sounds what Galileo did for mechanics, and what Copernicus and Kepler achieved for astronomy. He put it on a solid scientific basis, and by the number and variety of his experiments, in almost every department of acoustics, he made the way easy for subsequent investigators. Besides being an excellent musician, he was one of the most eminent mathematicians of an age of great mathematicians. He was the intimate friend and correspondent of Descartes, and was the real founder of the French

[1] See the American Journal of Science and Arts, No. 47, vol. viii. p. 365.

Academy of Sciences. He translated and made known in France the works of Galileo, and made many discoveries in mathematics and physics. But the greatest monument of his genius is his work on sound and music, the first edition of which appeared in French in 1636, and is called "Harmonie Universelle." A later edition, in Latin, revised and corrected, is entitled "Harmonicorum Libri XII."[1] It is to this edition that I shall always refer. In this admirable but little known work, the learned author gives evidence, on nearly every page, of his skill as a clever and industrious experimenter and profound thinker. Indeed, many of the laws governing sonorous vibrations are to-day given in almost the same language in which he first formulated them. Mersenne, Chladni, — of whom more anon, — Helmholtz, and Koenig may be considered as the four great pillars of the science of acoustics, as they, by the number and originality of their experiments, have contributed more to its advancement than any other four that could be mentioned.

To establish the fundamental law regarding the pitch of sound, Mersenne stretched a hempen rope over ninety feet in length, so that the eye could easily follow its displacements. It did not then emit any sound, but one could easily count the vibrations it made in any given time. He then shortened the cord by one half, and found it then made twice the number of vibrations in the same length of time. In reducing it to a third or a fourth of the original length, he observed that the oscillations became three and four times as rapid. He also made similar experiments, with like results, with a brass wire. He thus established the law that, all other things being equal, the number of vibrations of a cord is inversely as its length. When the cord was sufficiently shortened it gave forth

---

[1] The full title of the "Editio Aucta," published in 1648, of this extraordinary, but almost forgotten, work is, "Harmonicorum Libri XII, in quibus agitur de Sonorum Natura, Causis, et Effectibus: de Consonantiis, Dissonantiis, Rationibus, Generibus, Modis, Cantibus, Compositione, Orbisque totius Harmonicis Instrumentis."

a sound, and this sound became higher in pitch in proportion as the cord was further shortened. In this manner he proved that the pitch of sound depends upon the number of vibrations made, and is heightened exactly in proportion as the number of vibrations is augmented.[1]

This law being once established, it is obvious that knowing the length of a string and the note emitted by it when in vibration, it is an easy matter to calculate the note that would be given by another string of the same size and material, and under the same tension, but of different length. Thus Mersenne " took a musical string of brass three quarters of a foot long, stretched it with a weight of six and five eighth pounds, which he found gave him by its vibrations a certain standard note in his organ; he found that a string of the same material and tension, fifteen feet, that is, twenty times as long, made ten recurrences in a second; and he inferred that the number of vibrations of the shorter string must also be twenty times as great; and thus such a string must make in one second of time two hundred vibrations."[2]

The next one, after Mersenne, to attempt to determine the pitch corresponding to a given sound was Sauveur, about the year 1700. He endeavored to solve the problem in two ways: first, by the method known as that of beats, and secondly, by the application of mechanical principles to the vibrations of strings. Both of these methods, although indirect, gave quite accurate results; but they are rather too recondite for discussion here. It will therefore be sufficient simply to refer to them, without entering into details.

In 1681, Robert Hooke improved on the experiment of Galileo by using a serrated wheel of brass instead of a coin. He found that on striking the teeth of such a wheel a distinct musical sound was emitted. Stancari repeated a similar experiment before the Academy of Bologna in 1706, and showed that the pitch of the sound produced increased with the velocity of rotation of the wheel; and

[1] Harm., lib. ii. Prop. 18.   [2] Op. cit., lib. ii. Prop. 21.

the number of teeth being known, it was easy to compute the number of vibrations per second corresponding to a determinate note.

About the beginning of the present century, Chladni endeavored to determine the pitch of sounds by means of vibrating bars similar to the one shown in Fig. 1 of our last lecture. The vibrating portion of the bar was at first sufficiently long to enable him to count the number of vibrations in a given time. By a series of carefully conducted experiments, Chladni found that the number of vibrations per second varied inversely as the square of the length of the bar. When the bar was made sufficiently short, it emitted a musical note, the pitch of which became higher as the bar was made shorter.

It is obvious that Chladni proceeded in essentially the same way with vibrating bars as did Father Mersenne with vibrating strings. In practice, however, it has been found that the results yielded by bars were not so exact as those afforded by strings; and for this reason the determinations made by Chladni have not the same accuracy as those made by his distinguished predecessor.

Let us take Savart's wheel again, which was used in our last lecture, and push our experiments a little farther. By pressing a card against the wheel, sound is at once produced, as before. Turning the wheel more rapidly, a more acute sound is the result; and the more rapidly the wheel is rotated, the shriller, as you observe, the sound becomes. Evidently, then, pitch depends upon the number of vibrations produced in a given time. The time spoken of in experiments of this kind is always one second. When we wish to determine the pitch of any sound, we find out how many vibrations it makes per second. With the wheel before us this is an easy matter. It is only necessary to count the number of teeth, and the number of revolutions the wheel makes per second, to know the number of vibrations produced. As one vibration is made by each tooth, the entire number of vibrations will obviously be equal to the product obtained by multiplying the number of teeth in the wheel by the number of revolutions it makes in one second.

We have here the means of showing in another beautiful way that pitch depends on the number of vibrations. On the rotator before you are four of Savart's wheels, with 48, 60, 72, and 96 teeth respectively. Placing a card against the wheel having 48 teeth, and then against the one with 60, you observe that the latter gives the higher note, although the rate of revolution of the wheel has remained unchanged. The musicians present will notice something more. They will remark that the two notes emitted, whether sounded in succession or simultaneously, constitute what is called a major third. The third wheel has 72 teeth, and the fourth 96. By turning the rotator at the same speed as before, and touching the wheels with the card, you hear notes that are more acute than either of the two sounded previously. The fourth wheel, with 96 teeth, gives just twice the number of vibrations that the first with 48 teeth makes. Sounding the two notes together, we have the interval called in music the octave. Sounding all four wheels together, we have the perfect major chord.

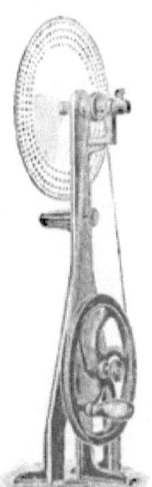

Fig. 23

But let us compare the results given by Savart's wheels with those obtained from Seebeck's siren. In the siren we shall now use (Fig. 23) there are four concentric series of holes. The first circle has 48 holes, and the next three 60, 72, and 96, respectively. The number of holes in the four circles of the siren corresponds exactly with the number of teeth in the four toothed wheels. At the same rate of revolution, therefore, the siren should give the same number of vibrations as the wheels. Let us try. Taking a small bent tube, bringing it over a point in the circle having 48 holes, blowing through the tube, and turning the rotator, you hear a note which you recognize to be in unison with the one that is given by the wheel having 48 teeth. Sounding in succession the four notes of the siren, beginning with the lowest and going to the highest, you notice not only a rise in pitch, but also that the pitch of the notes emitted corresponds exactly with that given by the four serrated wheels.

The siren and the toothed wheels prove, therefore, conclusively that pitch depends on the rate of vibration of the sonorous body, although the sounds emitted are comparatively feeble, and are accompanied with so much noise that a great part of their musical nature is lost.

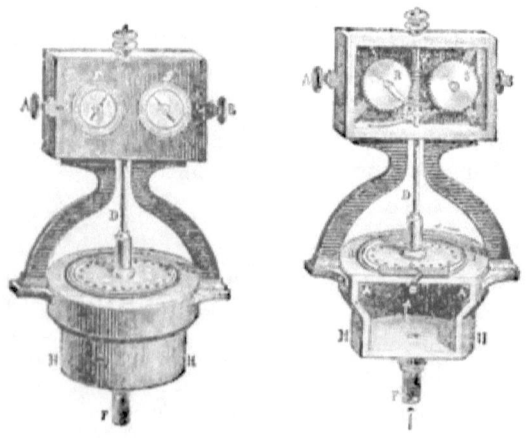

FIG. 24.

It is now time to make you acquainted with an instrument that is capable of yielding much louder and purer tones, and of giving much more satisfactory results. It is, in reality, only a modified form of Seebeck's siren, but is in every way a superior instrument. It is known, from its inventor, as the siren of Cagniard de la Tour. It was called a siren because it can be made to sing under water. The notes are not, however, such as we are wont to associate with the songs of the sirens of Homer.

As you will observe, the instrument (Fig. 24) is composed of a cylindrical wind-chest, *HH*, in the top of which are fifteen holes equidistant from each other, and equidistant from the centre of the circle which they form. Above the wind-chest is a disk, BB, attached to an axis, D, to keep it in place. Like the wind-chest, the disk is pierced with fifteen holes, those of the latter being immediately above those of the former. In both, the orifices, a and b, are inclined to the perpendicular, those of the disk being inclined opposite to those of the wind-chest. When air is urged through F from the wind-chest of a bellows, it passes through the apertures in AA, and impinges against the sides of the holes in the disk, and with sufficient force to cause it to revolve, — the rapidity of the revolution depending on the pressure of the air. When the disk makes one revolution, fifteen puffs of air are given off, and fifteen vibrations are the result. Air is now admitted from the bellows into the siren, and immediately the disk begins to revolve. At first the movement is so slow that the puffs can be counted. Gradually they succeed each other more rapidly, and soon the puffs blend into a continuous sound. Augmenting the air pressure, the sound gradually rises in pitch until the notes becomes so loud and piercing as to be positively painful. By diminishing the pressure of air or placing the finger on the disk, the pitch is instantly lowered, showing, as in the preceding experiments, that pitch depends solely on rapidity of vibration.

By means of clockwork, $R S$, in $A B$, which can be connected with an endless screw, $V K$, on the axis which carries the revolving disk, we can determine, by merely looking at the dials, $r s$, the number of vibrations corresponding to any given sound. It is, indeed, just such an instrument as this that some of the most distinguished scientists have employed in their researches on the pitch corresponding to various notes, and as given by different sonorous bodies. The eminent French physicist, M. Lissajous, had recourse to it in his very difficult and delicate task of determining the pitch of the standard tuning-fork of France, — the "Diapason Normal" of the French Conservatory of Music.

Let me now give you an idea of how the work is done. One cannot make any pretensions to great accuracy in a lecture experiment, as exact results would require greater time and more attention to many details than can be given now. In an illustration, however, exactness is not necessary. It is only the method we wish to understand, and not the great delicacy of which it is susceptible.

In one of the orifices of the wind-chest of the acoustic bellows is placed an organ-pipe, near that occupied by the siren. We now cause air to enter both pipe and siren at the same time. The tone of the organ-pipe comes out at once, loud and clear. The siren starts with a succession of puffs, and gradually reaches the same note as is emitted by the pipe. When the siren gives exactly the same note as the pipe, it is said to be in unison with it, and when it is in unison it gives the same number of vibrations. And what is true in this particular case is true universally. When two or more instruments give the same note, they are in unison, and when they are in unison, their frequency — that is, the number of vibrations they execute in a given time — is the same.

As soon as the siren is in unison with the organ-pipe, the clockwork is set in motion and kept going for some time, — say ten seconds. If the siren can be kept steady, — and this is not an easy matter, — we have only to read off from the dials of the clockwork the number of revolutions made by the rotating disk of the siren. Multiplying the number of revolutions by the number of apertures in the disk, we have the number of vibrations made by the siren in ten seconds. Dividing this product by ten, we have the number of vibrations made by the siren in one second.

But as the two sounds were kept in unison during these ten seconds, it follows that the number of vibrations we have found for the siren answers also for the number of vibrations of the pipe. In a similar manner, we could find the pitch of the human voice, or of a musical note emanating from any sonorous body whatever.

This method of determining, by means of the siren, the number of vibrations corresponding to any given sound, is, you will say, quite satisfactory. So it is. It is simple and ready, and, with proper precautions, capable of giving results that are correct to a fraction of a vibration. Surely, one might think, this ought to be sufficiently near the truth to satisfy any one. Scientific men, however, are very exacting, and demand a more certain and more delicate instrument than even the most perfect form of siren.

Such an instrument is before you. It is ordinarily called the vibroscope of Duhamel. It can be used for several most delicate and most interesting experiments. The

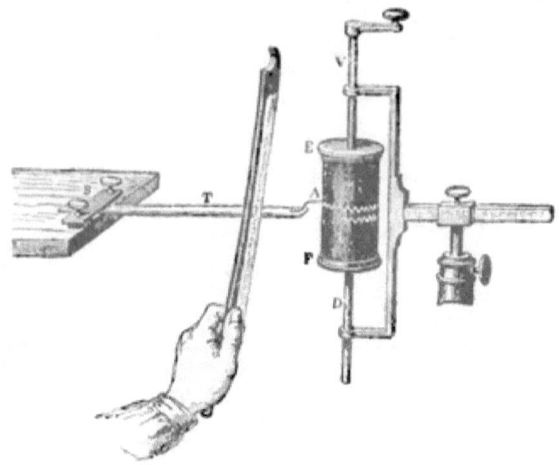

FIG. 25.

apparatus we shall now employ is, as you may observe, composed of a cylinder, EF (Fig. 25), mounted on an axis, VD, on which a screw is cut in such a manner as to permit axis and cylinder to move endwise when the crank attached to the axis is turned. Around the cylinder is gummed a sheet of smoked paper, and in front of it is fastened an elastic strip of metal, BT, to the end of which is attached a light style, A. The end of the style is made just to touch the smoked paper. By moving the style along a line parallel to the axis of the cylinder, a straight line is traced. On turning the cylinder when the style is at rest, the latter will again inscribe a simple straight line on the smoked paper, but at right angles to the axis of the cylinder. By bowing the elastic strip it is set in vibratory motion; and if at the same time the cylinder is turned, we get as a resultant of the double motion, a beautiful wavy line instead of the straight one we obtained before. By this means the elastic strip writes out its own motion, and tells, in a manner that cannot mislead, the exact number of vibrations it executes in a given time.

Instead of the thin elastic bar just used, let us make the same experiment with a tuning-fork. This can be done very simply, by attaching a light point, b, to the fork, A (Fig. 26), and passing under it a plate of smoked glass,

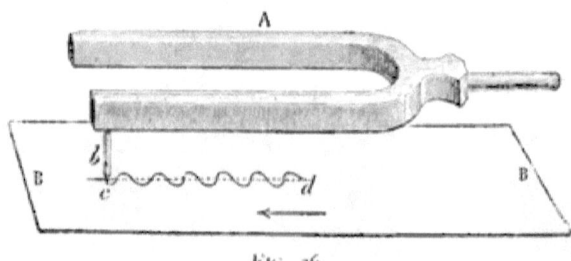

FIG. 26.

$B B$. If the fork is quiescent, and the plate is moved in the direction of the arrow, the point attached to the prong will inscribe a simple straight line, cd. But if the fork is set in vibration, and the plate is moved as before, a sinuous curve will be formed, similar to the one traced by the vibrating elastic bar. The movement of the plate being uniform, divisions of equal lengths on the straight line, cd, would correspond to equal periods of the vibrating fork. We might, in a similar manner, cause a string vibrating under the influence of molecular forces only to write out the story of its motion, and the curve obtained would be identical with those just examined. Vibrating plates and membranes will also, under proper conditions, give the same curve. The air particles in an organ-pipe, vibrating between fixed nodal surfaces, likewise yield just such curves. Mach has devised an instrument — which, however, cannot be used here — whereby they can be made to give a record of their motion.

If, again, we were to cause a plate of smoked glass, like the one used in Fig. 25, to pass, with uniform motion, under an oscillating pendulum in such a manner that the line *c d* should move in a direction at right angles to the plane in which the pendulum swings, we should obtain a sinuous curve in all respects similar to those afforded by the tuning-fork and the vibrating bar.

Let us now examine the record that has been made in the cases considered, because it is important, before going farther, that we should become acquainted with this form of writing. We shall frequently have occasion to study it hereafter, and if we understand how to decipher its meaning, it will tell us many and wonderful things. Indeed, some of the most striking conclusions in the science of sound have been deduced from a close study of similar undulating inscriptions.

The motion in all these cases is, as already stated, called *pendular* motion, because it is like that of a pendulum. It is also, as you will remember, called simple *harmonic* motion. The curve traced by the pendulum, and by the other vibrating bodies referred to, is called the *curve of sines*, a *sinusoidal curve*, a *sinusoid*, or, better still, a *harmonic curve*. In Fig. 25 there is a series of such sinusoids, or harmonic curves. As one complete vibration traces out a complete curve of the sort we are now studying, we have in Fig. 25 six harmonic curves connected with one another so as to exhibit a continuous undulating line. When considered as a symbol of wave-motion, the indentations, or portions of the curve above the straight line *c d*, are called *crests*, while those below are called *troughs*. A trough and a crest form a complete wave. A succession of waves, as in Fig. 25, constitutes an *undulation*. The distance the wave travels in one period is one wave-length.

Water-waves and sound-waves are alike in this, that there is no transference of matter by the waves in either case.

In the case of water-waves, the progressive motion of the masses of water that constitute the wave is only apparent. The individual particles of water in each wave have nothing more than an up-and-down motion at right angles to the line of progression. It is ordinarily said that these particles move in straight lines perpendicular to the direction of the wave's motion; but this is not strictly true. Each particle in reality describes a curve — a circle or an ellipse — in a plane in the line of progression. In the case of sonorous waves, however, the particles composing the waves have, as we now know, a motion parallel to the direction of propagation of the wave. The motion of the particles, then, is simply a *to-and-fro* motion, one of advance and retreat; and the results, as already explained, are conditions of compression and dilation known as waves, or pulses, of condensation and rarefaction.

Like the motions of the pendulum, the periods of sonorous vibrations are independent of their amplitude. Whether the width of swing of a sonorous body, or of the air particles excited by a sounding body, be great or small, the pitch of the sound remains the same. The amplitude of vibrations may change, as they do when this tuning-fork is excited with the bow and then left to itself, but the pitch of the sound remains unchanged. Whether the pitch of the sound be strong or weak, you recognize it as the same note. A change in amplitude of vibration, then, means simply a change in loudness or intensity, and nothing more. The period, therefore, of sound-vibrations, as well as of pendulum-vibrations,[1] is independent of amplitude.

The knowledge of these facts will enable us still better to understand the sinuous line our tuning-fork has described for us. In the particular figure we have been studying, we observe that the lengths of the waves remain the same. This depends, if you will, on the uniform motion of the glass plate during the production of the figure; but were there any change in the pitch of the note emitted, the

---

[1] The period of pendulum-vibrations is independent of their amplitude only when the arc through which the pendulum oscillates is small.

wave-length would vary, notwithstanding this uniform motion. The pitch remains the same because the wave-lengths remain the same. This, however, is only another way of stating what has already been said; namely, that the vibrations of any given continuous sound are periodic, and they are periodic because the wave-lengths remain unchanged.

By counting the number of indentations, or sinusoids, made by the fork in one second, — and this is a very simple matter, — we at once obtain the *vibration-number*, or what is more appropriately called the *frequency*,[1] of the fork. By this method we can determine with great accuracy, not only the number of the vibrations of the fork we are now using, but also that of any other sonorous body whatever.

In a small vice is fastened an elastic steel rod whose point just touches the smoked paper around the vibroscope. Near by a tuning-fork is so placed as to register its vibrations alongside those of the steel rod. Exciting the rod and the fork by means of a bow, we cause them both simultaneously to trace their sinuous curves on the revolving cylinder. The number of vibrations made by the tuning-fork has been determined by the maker, and knowing the frequency of the fork, it is an easy matter to calculate that of the rod. The fork we are now using makes one hundred vibrations per second. Counting the number of vibrations registered by the fork and the rod on the paper during the same time, we find that while the fork writes out indentations corresponding to 75 vibrations, the rod inscribes 125. Now, as the tuning-fork makes one vibration in the $\frac{1}{100}$ part of a second, it will make 75 vibrations in $\frac{75}{100}$ of a second. But during this time the rod makes 125 vibrations, or one vibration in the $\frac{75}{100 \times 125}$ of a second. In one second, therefore, it makes $\frac{100 \times 125}{75}$, or $166\frac{2}{3}$ vibrations. This method of determining pitch, known as the graphical method, is due to Dr. Thomas Young, and is competent to give very accurate results.

Let us now replace the fork we have been using by

---

[1] This is the term — in Latin *frequentia* — employed by Mersenne.

another which is kept in vibration by a current of electricity. The advantage of such a fork is that it can keep in motion indefinitely, and thus we can secure records extending over periods of time longer than would be possible with a fork actuated by a violin-bow. By allowing the fork to vibrate for one hundred seconds, for instance, and counting the sinuosities produced, we can get the average rate of vibrations per second, by dividing the total number of sinuosities by 100. This is known as the electrographic method, and is even more accurate than the graphical method just described.

Prof. A. M. Mayer has, by ingenious additions, so modified the electrographic method and improved its efficiency that it is now almost all that could be desired.

Let us now see if we can determine the number of vibrations produced by a given note of the human voice. To do this it will be necessary to make use of some appliance that will take up the vibrations of the voice in such a manner that they can be recorded.

Such an instrument (Fig. 27) is before you. It is the Phonautograph, as devised by Scott and improved by Koenig. As its name indicates, it is a self-registering sound apparatus. It is a modification of the cylinder and tuning-fork we have been using, with an attachment for collecting sound-waves of whatever character, or however delicate. As you will notice, this attachment, *A*, is in the form of a concave paraboloid. This particular form is chosen because it possesses the property of reflecting all parallel waves to a point called the focus, near the smaller end. Just at this point is stretched a delicate membrane on a frame, *D*. All the waves that enter the paraboloid impinge on this membrane and throw it into vibration. On the side of the membrane next to the cylinder is attached a very fine and light style, which faithfully inscribes on the smoked paper around the cylinder the slightest motion given to the membrane. By means of a small adjustable clamp, *G*, held in position by a screw, *V*, it is possible, with a second screw, *V'*, to regulate at will the tension of any given point of the membrane. In this way we can obtain a record of any sonorous wave that enters the paraboloid. By this instrument we find that each sound traces out its own characteristic curve, — writes out its own distinguishing autograph. Some sounds give indentations much like those of the tuning-fork, while others, like those of the human voice, give rise to sinuosities of much greater complexity.

By means of a tuning-fork, which is kept in vibration simultaneously with the style, the frequency of any sound

FIG. 27.

can be determined with the greatest ease and precision. The process is identical with that used a few moments ago in estimating the rate of vibration of an elastic rod. We have traces of both the sounds made on the smoked paper; and knowing the frequency of the fork, we have only to count the number of sinuosities of each sound corresponding to any given distance on the paper, when a simple proportion will give us the number of vibrations made per second by the sound collected by the paraboloid and recorded by the style attached to the membrane.

Let some one now sing a prolonged note into the open

end of the reflector. On turning the cylinder we have the curve peculiar to this note, and at the same time we have the sinuous line produced by the tuning-fork. Let us next count the number of vibrations made by the voice for any given length of time, and suppose we find that the voice makes one hundred and eighty sinuosities while the fork makes seventy. What is the frequency of the note sung, that of the fork being one hundred? When the fork makes seventy vibrations, the voice makes one hundred and eighty; when the fork executes one hundred vibrations, the voice executes x vibrations. Putting this in the form of a proportion, we have, $70 : 180 :: 100 : x$, from which we find the value of x to be $257\frac{1}{7}$, which corresponds almost exactly with middle C of the pianoforte.

To give you an idea of the variety and beauty of the tracings obtainable, I will project on the screen[1] a number of them as produced by the various notes and combinations of notes of organ-pipes of different frequencies.

The upper sinuous line (Fig. 28) in each pair of undulating tracings was inscribed by a tuning-fork making two hundred and fifty-six vibrations per second. The numbers at the left hand of the figures indicate the relative frequencies of the notes used. Thus the second sinuous line was produced by the joint action on the membrane of the phonautograph of two notes whose relative frequencies were as $4 : 5$. Near the middle of the figure is a curve resulting from the combination of three notes, whose relative frequencies were as $4 : 5 : 6$. The lowest curve was generated by the sonorous pulses proceeding simultaneously from four organ-pipes whose relative frequencies were $4 : 5 : 6 : 8$.

After some familiarity with these and similar curves,

---

[1] Professor Mayer uses an excellent and ingenious means of obtaining traces from a rotating cylinder on a transparent surface. He takes a band of *thin mica*, and binding it around the cylinder, fastens it down with rubber bands. It is then smoked with camphor smoke. The trace having been made on it, it is taken from the cylinder, and thin *white* negative varnish is flowed over the lampblack. It may then be mounted between plates of glass for the lantern projection.

one can see at a glance whether the sounds that produce
them are simple or complex. Not only this, one can also
tell how the constituents of complex sounds are related
to each other, and discover, with equal readiness, their
comparative intensities.

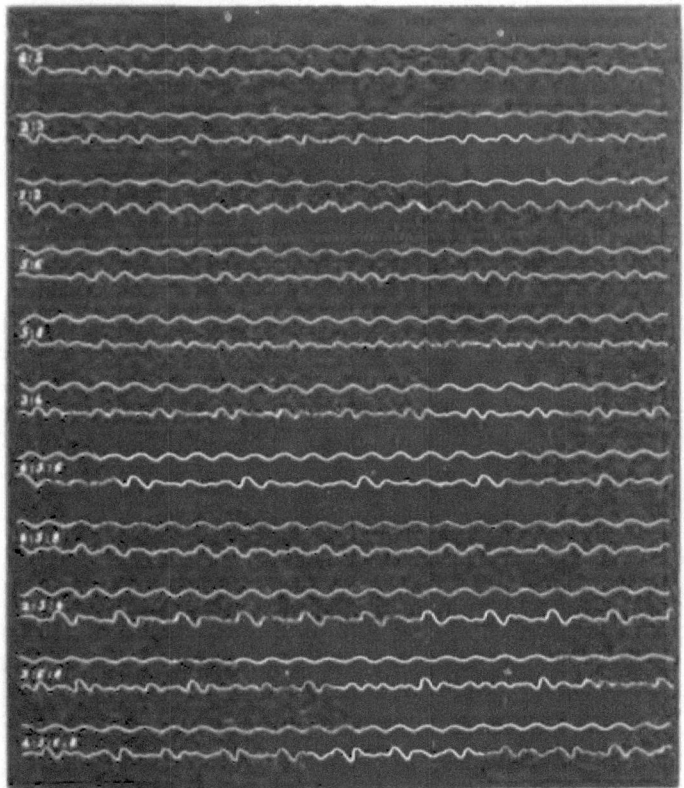

Fig. 28.

The experiments just made have familiarized you with
some of the principal methods employed by physicists
for determining the pitch of sounds. There are indeed
many others, some of which are more difficult and complicated than those just illustrated, but we have not time
to consider them now. And even if we had the time,
some of them are of such a character as to preclude

the possibility of their being introduced in lecture experiments.

In his very exact determination of the pitch of the Diapason Normal, which Lissajous intended should give 435 vibrations, at 15° C., Koenig used a large fork connected with clockwork, the whole acting as a single system. This clock-fork, as Koenig calls it — and a most elaborate apparatus it is — was kept vibrating in a practically constant temperature for many hours at a time, and the experiments extended over a period of several months. The result obtained is probably as near an approximation to the truth as it would be possible to obtain. By this means it was found that the Diapason Normal at 15° C., or 59° F., executed 435.45 instead of 435 vibrations per second. This is a very slight difference, you will say; but it is only one among many instances of the accuracy with which modern scientific apparatus is constructed, especially by such a mechanician as Koenig. Of the large number of forks made by him, which you see here, all are, I dare say, tuned with equal care, and all will give exactly the number of vibrations which his stamp, affixed to each fork, says they will give.

Indeed, nothing is better or more accurate for determining pitch than a carefully constructed set of tuning-forks. And strange though it may seem, the first one to propose and construct a tuning-fork tonometer — an instrument for determining pitch — was a silk manufacturer, J. Heinrich Scheibler, of Crefeld, Germany. In one of the tonometers constructed by him, there were as many as fifty-six tuning-forks, all tuned with the utmost care and accuracy. The tonometers made by Scheibler were long used as the standard for similar sets, and nothing comparable to them was attempted until some decades later, about 1860, when Dr. Koenig began his marvellous career as an acoustic mechanician.

Dr. Koenig has made many sets of tuning-forks similar to those designed by Scheibler, having in his larger tonometers as many as sixty-seven forks. But his most wonderful work is a tonometer commenced in 1877, and now very near completion. It consists of one hundred and fifty forks of exquisite workmanship, and tuned with infinite care and skill. It embraces the entire range of audible sounds, and extends from 16 to 21845.3 vibrations per second. For the compass of sounds employed in music, the forks are so adjusted that no fork differs from the one that precedes or succeeds it by more than four vibrations. For the lower sounds the difference is only one half of a simple vibration.[1]

By means of this extraordinary instrument, the frequency of any note can at once be determined with absolute accuracy. No such work has ever been essayed by any one before, and it is quite safe to assert that no such herculean task will ever again be undertaken by any one else. Only untiring patience, exceptional skill, and a phenomenal love for his work could ever have enabled Dr. Koenig to accomplish a task demanding such care and time and labor. It is a most remarkable achievement of industry and genius, and a monument of which any man might be proud.

If now it can only be secured by some musical organization that will take proper care of it, it could be used for a long time as a standard about whose accuracy there could be no question. And furthermore, if the musicians of the world would only agree to take this for an international standard, it would be a happy solution of many difficulties that have beset musical composers, performers, and manufacturers of musical instruments for several generations past. Nothing better could be desired, and certainly nothing more complete has ever been carried into execution. The musical world has no standard of pitch,[2] and this marvellous tonometer would answer the purpose admirably, and with due care would last for all time to come. The standards of weight and measure of France and England have been worked out with all the nicety and delicacy that

---

[1] The largest forks, which are about five feet in length, are provided with great cylindrical resonators of copper. The largest resonator is an immense affair. It is twenty inches in diameter, and nearly eight feet in length. All the resonators are adjustable in length, so as to be used for notes of different pitch.

[2] See note on following page.

human ingenuity could suggest; but I do not think they are any more exact in their sphere than is the *grand tonomètre universal* on which Dr. Rudolph Koenig has spent so many of the best years of his life.

I have spoken of the desirability of having a standard of pitch that would be universally recognized. One would imagine that such a standard would have been agreed upon long ago; but when one thinks of the various and often imperfect standards of measurement that obtain in other branches of science and art, one is not surprised that musicians also are behindhand in this respect. The French, it is true, have done something in this direction, for in the Diapason Normal, already referred to, they have a national standard. But even in France this standard is not universally employed. The Government has no power to enforce it except in the schools, theatres, and conservatories which it subsidizes. In churches, private theatres, conservatories, concerts, and orchestras, the pitch of the instruments used is far from being uniform.

So it is elsewhere. The pitch varies, not only in different countries, but in different cities of the same country, and even in the different theatres of the same city.

But more than this. The pitch varies not only in place, but also in time. It is quite different now from what it was a century ago. Then it was comparatively low. Since then it has been growing higher and higher, until the opinion begins to prevail, almost everywhere, that it is time to call a halt. And to avoid the constant fluctuations of pitch that have obtained so long and so extensively, it is felt now more than ever that an international standard of pitch is almost, if not quite, a necessity. The first step in this direction was made by an international conference of musicians held in Vienna in 1885, when the French pitch was unanimously adopted.[1] So far, however, this adop-

---

[1] The French pitch was adopted by Russia in 1860, by Spain in 1879, and by Belgium in 1885. The Royal Academy of England accepted it as the standard, June 20, 1885, and a few months subsequently, Feb. 12, 1886, it was formally adopted by the English Society of Arts. Italy, having sent representatives to the Congress of Vienna, adopted French pitch in 1885.

tion has amounted to nothing more than an acceptance, in theory, that the French pitch is desirable, and should therefore be adopted. As yet little or nothing has been done towards carrying out in practice what the conference deemed not only advisable but necessary.[1]

The French standard of pitch, the Diapason Normal, which is preserved in the Musée du Conservatoire in Paris, was designed to make 435 vibrations per second, but actually makes, as we have seen, 435.45.

The starting-point for pitch in music is the second open string of the violin, which gives the tuning note for orchestras. It corresponds to A_3 above middle C of the pianoforte, which in musical notation is written. A_3, of a vibration-number of 435, was chosen in 1859 as the result of a report made by a special commission appointed to determine a standard pitch. Previously to this date, in 1834, the German Society of Physicists, assembled as Stuttgart, had adopted as a standard of pitch a note which had a frequency of 444. Physicists employ a fork whose frequency is much lower, — their A_3 having a vibration-number as low as 426.6. This is very near the frequency of the A_3 fork used by Handel in 1751; its vibration-number was 422.5. Mozart's pitch was a little less, being A_3 421.6. The lowest church pitch, in Mersenne's time (1648), was A_3 373.7. The so-called chamber pitch, at that date, according to Mersenne, was A_3 402.9.

Since Mersenne's time, as is apparent from the foregoing numbers, the rise in pitch has been very great indeed. But without going back any farther than the days of Mozart and Handel, we find that the rise in pitch has

[1] Since the above was written, "The Piano Manufacturers' Association" of New York and vicinity have unanimously selected the French pitch as the standard for all instruments made by the members of the Association. At a meeting held by this body Nov. 6, 1891, it was "Resolved, that the standard musical pitch adopted by the piano manufacturers of the United States, giving that A which vibrates 435 double vibrations in a second of time at 68° Fahr., shall be known as the 'International Pitch.'" It was further decided that this resolution should go into effect July 1, 1892.

been so great as frequently to make it difficult to sing and play the works of these great masters with proper effect. In England, for instance, in spite of all the efforts that have been made to keep it down to A_3 444, orchestra and pianoforte pitch has risen higher and higher, until it now runs from A_3 449.7 to A_3 454.7. In some parts of the United States, especially in New York, pitch, in some instances, has gone up as high as A_3 460.8. A Chickering piano is tuned by a standard fork which gives A_3 451.7, and a piano by Steinway is tuned to A_3 458. Between Mozart's pitch and that used by Chickering and Steinway there is, therefore, a difference of between thirty and thirty-one vibrations, amounting practically to three fourths of a tone.

The disadvantages, especially to vocalists, consequent on such a rise of pitch, are apparent. Music written by Mozart, Handel, Beethoven, and Haydn must be sung more than a semitone higher than it was intended to be sung. For the higher notes this is often difficult without straining the voice. Besides, the effect produced by this elevation of pitch is often entirely different from that which was aimed at by the composer, and which would be secured if the music were sung at the pitch for which it was written.

Orchestras and military bands are, in the main, responsible for this undue elevation of pitch. Wind instruments especially have more brilliancy of tone when tuned to this high pitch, and, for this reason, popular taste has demanded from the manufacturers of such instruments that they should give them the high pitch which now prevails.

The "tuning note" for orchestras, as above stated, is A_3 of the frequencies already given. For pianos, however, the tuning note is the first C above A_3, namely, C_4. This C_4, according to the old theoretical pitch, which is that now used by physicists, has a frequency of 512. In French equal temperament, with A_3 435, C_4 has a frequency of 517.3. The pitch of C_4 of the English Society of Arts, based on the German standard pitch, A_3 440, is 528. In modern concert pitch the frequency of C_4 is still higher, being 540.

The frequency, 512, of the standard C_4 of the physicist, is the ninth power of 2, and gives, consequently, vibration-numbers to all the C's which are powers of 2. This number was proposed by the distinguished acoustician Sauveur, and subsequently, in 1830, adopted by Chladni. It has above all others the advantage of simplicity. For this reason, although considerably lower than other pitches in use, it is almost universally employed by physicists and acousticians. All the forks that we shall employ in our experiments, unless otherwise specified, are tuned to this standard of pitch. In musical notation this note C_4, of 512 vibrations, would be written .

To get C_5, an octave above this, it is only necessary to multiply 512 by 2, which gives 1024. Dividing 512 by 2 will give C_3, the octave below having 256 vibrations. In general, by doubling the number of vibrations corresponding to any given note we obtain a note an octave higher, and by halving it we get a note an octave lower. Having the notes, then, of one octave of what is called the diatonic scale, we can readily obtain all the others used in music by simply multiplying or dividing by 2 or a multiple of 2.

The notes of the gamut are variously designated in different countries. In France the first six notes still bear the names given them by the monk Guy of Arezzo in 1026. They are the beginnings of words which occur in a hymn to Saint John the Baptist,[1] and are as follows: *ut, re, mi, fa, sol, la*. The seventh syllable, *si*, was added in 1684 by Lemaire. In Italy *do* has been substituted in place of *ut*, because more easily pronounced in singing. In England the notes are named after the first letters of the

---

[1] The words are, —

"*Ut* queant laxis *re*sonare fibris
*Mi*ra gestorum *fa*muli tuorum,
*Sol*ve polluti *la*bii reatum,
    Sancte Joannes."

alphabet, and are called C, D, E, F, G, A, B. In Germany H is substituted for B.

But we must go farther. The letters and syllables just given distinguish the notes of an octave from each other, but it is necessary besides to have a means of designating the different octaves of any musical instrument. In Germany and England this is ordinarily done by using capital letters, one unaccented, and the others variously under-accented or under-lined for the lower octaves, and small letters, one likewise unaccented and the others over-accented or over-lined, for the higher octaves. The C's of the eight octaves of the organ, when accented or lined, are usually written as follows: —

$$C_{\prime\prime} \quad C_{\prime} \quad C \quad c \quad c' \quad c'' \quad c''' \quad c'''' \quad c'''''$$

$$\underline{\underline{C}} \quad \underline{C} \quad C \quad c \quad \dot{c} \quad \ddot{c} \quad \dddot{c} \quad \ddddot{c} \quad \dddddot{c}$$

The French method of designating the same notes is the following: —

$$Ut_{-2}, \quad Ut_{-1}, \quad Ut_1, \quad Ut_2, \quad Ut_3, \quad Ut_4, \quad Ut_5, \quad Ut_6, \quad Ut_7.$$

The tuning-forks that we shall use give for these notes the following frequencies, unless stated otherwise: 16, 32, 64, 128, 256, 512, 1024, 2048, 4096. As we shall have occasion to refer frequently to these notes, octaves, and vibration-numbers, and as it is important that we should be able to locate them at once, it is desirable to give them as written in musical notation, together with their names and frequencies.

In this manner we may recognize them at a glance.

German:	C''	$C,$	C	c	c'	c''	c'''	c''''	c'''''
French:	Ut_{-2}	Ut_{-1}	Ut_1	Ut_2	Ut_3	Ut_4	Ut_5	Ut_6	Ut_7
Frequency:	16	32	64	128	256	512	1024	2048	4096
	C_{-2}	C_{-1}	C_1	C_2	C_3	C_4	C_5	C_6	C_7

The last line is a partial combination of the French and the German systems, and is, in many respects, more convenient than either. For this reason we shall adopt it in preference to either of the other two. I shall frequently have occasion to speak of higher notes and higher octaves than those used in any musical instrument, and with this last system one can indicate any given note with the greatest facility and accuracy. Thus C_9, one of the forks of a series on the table, gives a note just two octaves above C_7, the highest note of the organ. F_9 designates a fork of the same series four notes higher. G_{10}, the highest note for which any tuning-fork has yet been made, is full three and a half octaves above the highest note used in music. Its relation to a corresponding note of any of the lower octaves is seen as soon as one knows the frequency of the fork.

The notes of the diatonic scale, with their corresponding vibration-numbers, for what is known as the "two-foot" or "one-stroked" octave, are in musical notation as follows:

c'	d'	e'	f'	g'	a'	b'	c''
C_3	D_3	E_3	F_3	G_3	A_3	B_3	C_4
256,	288,	320,	341.3,	384,	426.6,	480,	512.

By multiplying or dividing the vibration-numbers of the notes of this octave by 2, or some power of 2, we can, as just stated, readily determine the frequency of any note of any octave, high or low.

The subject we have been studying has prepared the way for a question of considerable experimental interest; namely, what are the limits of audible vibrations? Very few persons, I fancy, have any idea of the many and apparently conflicting answers given to this question.

According to Sauveur's experiments with organ-pipes the lowest audible sound corresponds to $12\frac{1}{2}$ vibrations per second. Biot's and Chladni's experiments with strings raised the number to 16. Savart in his investigations used a rotating rod striking through a narrow slit, and came to the conclusion that 8 vibrations were sufficient to produce a continuous sound. By means of a specially constructed sounding-box, over which a string was stretched, Helmholtz finds that the lowest limit for grave tones is about 30 vibrations. "At B_{-2}," he says, "with $29\frac{1}{3}$ vibrations in a second, there was scarcely anything audible left;" and he concludes with the statement that "although tones of 24 to 28 vibrations have been heard, notes do not begin to have a definite pitch until about 40 vibrations are performed in a second."[1] According to Mr. Ellis's observations with a large tuning-fork, the lowest audible sound was in the neighborhood of 30 vibrations. "For 30 vibrations," he observes, "I could still hear a weak drone; for 28 scarcely a trace." With the same instrument Prof. W. Preyer, of Vienna, was able to hear a continuous sound at 24 vibrations. But by using specially loaded tongues in reed pipes made by the acoustician Herr Appunn, of Hanau, he declares that he was able to hear tones as low as 15 vibrations. Preyer's conclusions are that no musical tones are produced by less than 15 vibrations, that air-pulses begin to coalesce into a tone at about 20 vibrations, and that the musical character of bass tones is perceived only when their frequencies exceed 24 vibrations per second. According to Despretz, the lowest limit of audible sounds is 16 vibrations,—the note that is given, or supposed to be given, by the thirty-two foot organ-pipe. There is grave doubt among experimenters whether the thirty-two foot organ-pipe actually gives a continuous note of 16 vibrations, or whether the sound heard is not in reality due to

---

[1] See Mr. A. J. Ellis's admirable translation of Helmholtz's "Tonempfindungen," chap. ix.

what are called "upper partials," which we shall consider in the sequel. According to Helmholtz, the vibrations of this pipe can always be heard as separate pulses, and never blend into a continuous sound. Its value, then, depends entirely on its power of reinforcing the notes of the octaves above it, and on the so-called upper partials, which are always produced simultaneously with the note having 16 vibrations, which it is supposed to produce.

Regarding the limits of audibility of acute sounds, there is the same diversity of opinion. Sixty-four hundred vibrations, according to Sauveur, constitute the highest perceptible note. Chladni made the number 8,192, and Walloston 25,000. By means of a large toothed wheel, similar to the one used here, Savart showed that it was possible to hear a sound corresponding to 24,000 vibrations. Using tuning-forks tuned for him by Marloye, Despretz was able to obtain sounds whose frequencies were over 36,000 vibrations. Employing a very large Seebeck siren, Preyer heard a sound produced by 24,000 vibrations, although this sound was quite inaudible to other persons present. The highest tuning-fork made by Koenig gives 21,845 vibrations, but he makes a set of short steel cylinders, of which the shortest is calculated to give 32,768 vibrations per second. This note corresponds to C_{10}. Herr Appunn makes a set of thirty-one tuning-forks, the highest of which is G_{10}, which makes 49,152 vibrations per second. One of these G_{10} forks I hold in my hand. As you see, it is exceedingly diminutive. It is about half an inch long, two fifths of an inch wide, and its tines are but one eighth of an inch thick. Many persons have been able to hear the note yielded by this fork; but a question may arise whether it really gives a note of the high pitch claimed for it. Without here entering into an explanation of the manner in which the pitch of such forks is determined, I may observe that Herr Appunn, in a letter to me about this and other forks of very high pitch which he furnished me, states that he can guarantee that the frequencies of the forks correspond absolutely with the numbers stamped on them. No one can doubt the skill of Herr Appunn as a mechanician, and the delicacy of his ear for very acute sounds is, according to the testimony of all who are acquainted with him, something quite astonishing. It would probably be impossible for one with a less delicate ear to tune such a fork, even if he were familiar with the method of tuning employed in such cases. We are consequently, by the very necessities of the case, compelled to accept Herr Appunn's estimate as that of an expert and that he is an expert in his specialty no one can gainsay.

Only ears that are specially sensitive to acute sounds are capable of perceiving the notes of such tiny forks. For most persons, especially those advanced in years, the limit of audition is ordinarily below C_9, giving 16,384 vibrations per second.

Such acute sounds, however, are anything but agreeable to the ear. They have a peculiar grating, rasping effect that, at times, becomes extremely painful. In other cases they produce a peculiar indefinable feeling of discomfort, which persists for some time. Dr. Koenig has often told me that he does not like to experiment with these high notes, as they frequently continue to ring in his ears for days, and even weeks afterwards. Prof. W. Preyer, who has distinguished himself by his experiments on the limits of the perception of tone, speaks also of the disagreeable character of the higher notes. In describing his experience with the notes above C_9, he says they affected him "as if a thin wire were drawn through both ears towards the middle, and thence towards the top of the head."

Permit me now to illustrate experimentally the subject we have been discussing. As you already understand how Savart's wheel and Seebeck's siren can be used to determine the limits of perceptible sounds, whether grave or acute, — having seen these instruments used in other experiments, — we shall have recourse to other and more exact instruments.

For investigating the limits of grave sounds we have here a very large fork (Fig. 29), made by Koenig, and similar to the ones used by Mr. Ellis in his researches. It is mounted on a heavy cast-iron base, and to its prongs, which are nearly thirty inches long, are attached two sliding weights about three inches in diameter, by means of which the pitch of the fork can be raised or lowered. The range of the fork is from C_{-2} to G_{-2}; that is, from 16 to 24 vibrations. There is a scale along each prong to show where the weights are to be adjusted in order to produce the different vibrations marked thereon.

Clamping the weights at the top of the prongs, at the place marked for 16 vibrations, we now cause the fork to vibrate; but although you can see that the prongs are in motion, I am quite sure that no one present is able to perceive the sound corresponding to 16 vibrations. You may, when the fork is first excited, hear a deep musical note; but this is one of the upper partial tones to which allusion has been made. It is an octave higher than C_{-2}, and is not, therefore, the note for which we are seeking. In working with the fork, the ear is brought as close as possible to one of the sliding weights, which, on ac-

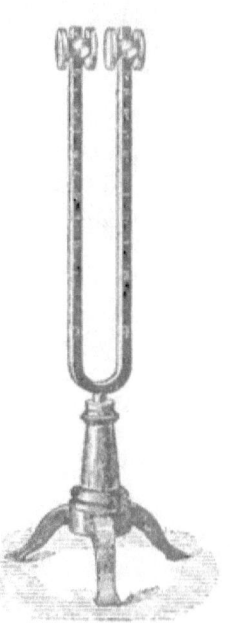

FIG. 29.

count of their great surface, act as an aid to hearing. But notwithstanding numerous experiments which I have made with many persons having an acute ear for musical sounds, I have never yet been able to find even one who could detect what would be denominated a pure musical note.

I bring the weights down to the bottom of the prongs, to the tone marked 24 vibrations, and again agitate the fork. The result is practically the same as before. You can see the vibratory motion of the fork, but you cannot hear the note G_{-1}, that answers to the 24 vibrations. If, however, the ear is placed as close as possible to one of the sliding disks, it is possible for some persons to hear a kind of low drone, probably the nearest approach to a musical note, — at least with such apparatus.

Tuning-forks are also the best means for determining the limit of acute sounds. Reeds have been used, as well as sirens of various kinds; but the results obtained by these means are not so trustworthy as those given by well-tuned forks. Before you is a superb series of forks for the notes from C_7 to F_9. They are so arranged on a support that it is easy to excite them in succession by merely drawing a violin-bow across their prongs.

C_7 corresponds to the highest note of the organ, and when excited by the bow, its tone comes out clear and

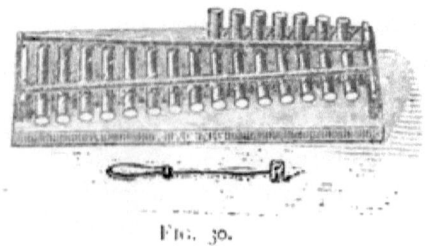

FIG. 30.

loud. Setting the others in vibration in the order of their pitch, the sound becomes correspondingly higher and more piercing. As we approach C_9 the sounds will die out for some of you, while they will remain unpleasantly painful for others. The nearer the forks are to the ear, the more these effects are intensified. Above C_9 the forks will, I think, be inaudible to most of you, no matter how vigorously I draw the bow across them, or how near you may be to them. We have reached the border-land of acute sounds, and by the most perfect means that science has thus far at its command.

Koenig employs another method for showing the limit of perceptibility for acute sounds, which may be illustrated here, as it possesses considerable interest and is capable of giving quite reliable results.

The instrument used for this purpose consists of twenty-two cylindrical steel rods (Fig. 30), giving notes as high as C_{10}, making 32,768 vibrations per second. The lowest note, C_9, is given by the longest cylinder, and the notes become higher in proportion as the cylinders are made shorter. Striking the longest cylinder with an ivory hammer, made for the purpose, you at once perceive a clear, penetrating sound that almost quenches the sound of the hammer itself. When we strike in succession the shorter bars, the musical note becomes more acute, and the shock of the hammer comparatively louder. With the shortest rods the notes due to their vibrations become almost, if not entirely, inaudible, and one hears only the sound of percussion when the hammer comes in contact with the cylinders. With such cylindrical rods, G_7 is heard with difficulty by ordinary ears, and C_9 marks the limits of audition for elderly persons generally, while even the most sensitive ear scarcely ever reaches G_9.

By means of a small whistle (Fig. 31) Captain Douglas Galton has been able to obtain sounds which are said to be as acute as any of those we have been considering, if indeed they are not more acute. Such a whistle I hold in my hand. The air is supplied by a little rubber bulb,

Fig. 31.

and the vibrating column of air, by means of a scale attached to the whistle, can be accurately shortened by such a small amount as the $\frac{1}{250}$th of an inch. When the whistle is made to sound, you hear a very high note, resembling somewhat that emitted by some of the smaller mammalia. The sharp, attenuated notes of white mice, which probably many of you have heard, are not unlike some of the notes we can evoke from this whistle when it is properly adjusted.

By means of this simple little contrivance, one may readily estimate the pitch of very acute sounds. With it I have been able to determine the pitch of a creaking door, which yielded a note full two octaves above the highest note used in music.

From the foregoing we learn that the range of audition extends somewhat over eleven octaves.

Light, like sound, is due to a mode of vibratory motion, and the various colors, like notes of different pitch, have their origin in different rates of vibration. The extreme red of the spectrum corresponds to the gravest musical notes, while the more acute sounds correspond to the extreme violet. Intervening colors correspond to the notes between the most grave and the most acute. But the range of perception for the different rates of vibration is much less for the eye than it is for the ear. For the former it is at most an octave and a half; for the latter it is nearly eight times as much. The frequency of the extreme violet is never more than three times that of the lowest red, — ordinarily it is not much more than twice as great, — whereas the frequency of G_{10} of Appunn's fork is over three thousand times that of the note of the thirty-two foot organ-pipe.[1]

Only an exceptional ear, as we have seen, has a perception extending over the entire eleven octaves of sound. But no human ear, however acute or well trained, is able to separate all audible sounds from each other. It requires a good ear to distinguish the lower notes from each other, but it is a far more difficult matter to discriminate the higher notes from each other after they rise above C_6.

Experimentally we have been dealing with sounds hav-

[1] "Assuming, then," — I quote from Ellis, — "that the yellow of the spectrum answers to the tenor C in music, and Frauenhofer's 'line A' corresponds to the G below it, Professor Hemholtz, in his 'Physiological Optics,' gives the following analogies between the notes of the piano and the colors of the spectrum: —

$F\sharp$,	End of the Red,	c,	Yellow,	$f\sharp$,	Violet,
G,	Red,	$c\sharp$,	Green,	g,	Ultra-violet,
$G\sharp$,	Red,	d,	Greenish-blue,	$g\sharp$,	Ultra-violet,
A,	Red,	$d\sharp$,	Cyanogen-blue,	a,	Ultra-violet,
$A\sharp$,	Orange-red,	e,	Indigo-blue,	$a\sharp$,	Ultra-violet,
B,	Orange,	f,	Violet,	b,	End of the Solar Spectrum."

ing a compass of something over eleven octaves. The largest organ never has more than eight octaves, the ordinary small organ never more than seven; the piano, as usually constructed, embraces from seven to seven and one half octaves. The violin has three and one half octaves, and the compass of some other instruments is still less. On the organ and the piano, neither the lowest nor the highest octave, as compared with the intervening ones, is much used; this reduces the practical range of these instruments to about five octaves.

In tempered instruments, like the organ, piano, and harmonium, for instance, the number of notes available for each octave is also limited. Counting white and black keys, there are only twelve notes to each octave. This gives for the five octaves employed in ordinary music only sixty different notes, — sixty notes out of the fifty thousand different rates of vibration which we have been considering! In the case of the violin only about forty different notes are used, — less than the $\frac{1}{1000}$th part of the number with which the acoustician deals.

In the human voice the range is much less than that of any of the musical instruments just named. For the ordinary voice the compass, or register, as it is called, is about two octaves. In extraordinary cases the register may embrace two and a half octaves, and in a few phenomenal instances an octave more.

The average human voice, therefore, in singing a solo, in which the key remains unchanged, does not ordinarily use more than twelve or fifteen different notes; and yet, with these few notes, it is able to execute those marvels of melody that so charm the ear.

The human voice has well been compared to the viol family, which embraces four different instruments, — bass, tenor, alto, and soprano. Besides these there are also two intermediate voices, baritone, between bass and tenor, and mezzo-soprano, between soprano and alto.

Male voices are known as bass, baritone, and tenor, and female voices are classed as alto, mezzo-soprano, and soprano. The ordinary compass of these various voices is indicated in the following musical notation: —

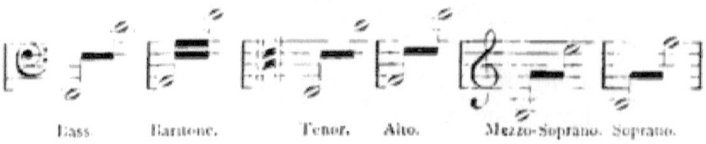

Bass. Baritone. Tenor. Alto. Mezzo-Soprano. Soprano.

Amongst phenomenal voices were those of Gassner and the brothers Fischer, who were at the court of Bavaria in the sixteenth century, all of whom were able to sing as low as F_{-1}. The voice of Forster, the Dane, had a compass of three octaves. The highest voice on record was undoubtedly that of Lucrezia Ajugari, who sang for Mozart in Parma in 1770. She could sing as high as C_6, and descend as low as G_2, and had therefore the marvellous compass of three and one half octaves. But with all this, her voice, even in its highest tones, remained, according to the testimony of Mozart's father, as pure as a flute. Nilsson and Patti have also attained marvellous heights. The voices of Catalani, Farinelli, and the younger of the sisters Sessi were extraordinary for their depth and compass, having in each case a range of three and a half octaves.

The greatest observed compass of the human voice, from the lowest bass to the highest soprano, is, then, fully five and a half octaves, extending from F_{-1}, of 43, to C_c of 2,048 vibrations per second. This range, expressed in notes, is as follows: —

The compass of the wonderful voices of Sessi and Farinelli is indicated by the following notes: —

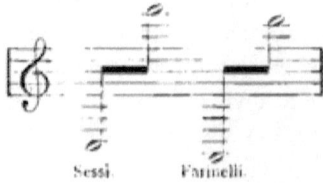

Sessi. Farinelli.

The lowest note used in the orchestra is C_{-1}, and is given by the double bass. As usually made, it gives 33 vibrations per second. The highest note employed in orchestral music is the D_7 of the piccolo-flute, giving, according to the physicist's pitch, 4,608 vibrations per second, but a much higher frequency according to the standard of pitch at present in use. The lowest note, A_{-2}, on a grand piano, is made to give about $27\frac{1}{2}$ vibrations per second. The highest note, C_7, has a frequency of about 4,200 vibrations per second.

In our experiments we have discovered that the range of hearing varies greatly with different persons. One will be astonished at the extent of this variation when he comes to examine the matter with a little attention; he will find, to his surprise, that there are many sounds in nature that are very unpleasant to some, but are entirely beyond the perception of other ears. There are many to whom the multifarious sounds of insect life are inaudible, while these same sounds are disagreeably shrill and piercing to others. There are those, even, who are capable of enjoying music, who cannot hear the upper notes of the piano or organ, or distinguish in the lowest octave one note from another.

Some savages have remarkably acute powers of hearing, but only for certain sounds. Their range of audition is frequently as limited as their perception of some sounds is acute.

Then, again, the sensitiveness of the ear varies greatly for the different notes. It is not as marked for high or low notes as it is for those which are intermediate. Strike in succession the notes of the highest or the lowest octaves of the piano, and you will find that there is not by any means such a marked difference in pitch between the consecutive notes as there is in the intervening octaves. I have known a piano-tuner, for instance, who was an expert in tuning all the octaves except the lowest. In this octave he lost completely his perception of pitch and intervals, and — what was more remarkable, in his case — he was utterly unconscious of his lack of musical appreciation in this part of the scale, and could not be brought to believe that his ear was less sensitive to low than to high notes.

But notwithstanding all this, the ear is a wonderfully comprehensive instrument. As compared with the eye, it is vastly superior in the extent of the sensations it is capable of experiencing. The eye possesses barely an octave and a half of sensations, whereas the average ear, as we have seen, has a range of six or seven, while more acute ears have a compass of fully eleven octaves.

And then the ear is a wonderfully accurate instrument, and capable of appreciating minute differences that would be wholly impossible in the case of the eye. According to Dr. W. H. Stone, "an architect or draughtsman who, between two lines neither parallel nor in one plane, made an error of estimation by eye not exceeding one thirtieth, would gain credit for unusual precision. But in the ear one thirtieth amounts to a quarter of a tone, and by ear one forty-fifth of a tone is easily determined." A skilful pianoforte-tuner can do much more. He is called upon, for instance, to distinguish between a true and an equally tempered fifth, where the difference is only the one hundredth of a tone. He should, accordingly, be able to recognize at least six hundred different sounds in an octave. More than this, according to the investigations of Professor Mayer, it is possible, under specially favorable conditions, and for sounds whose pitch is near that of C_3, to distinguish from each other notes which do not differ by more than the $\frac{1}{120}$th of a semitone.

In the rapidity of its appreciation the ear is equally remarkable. In a fraction of a second it can accurately refer any note to its place in the scale, and can just as easily and as quickly separate from each other several widely different notes. According to recent investigations, the ear is capable of hearing a sound when only two vibrations are made. It should therefore hear the middle notes of the pianoforte in the two or three hundredth part of a second. It requires more time, however, for the ear to distinguish the full characteristic of a note. To do this, according to the experiments of Exner, Auerbach, and W. Kohlrausch, from 2 to 20 vibrations are necessary.

With proper training and practice the organ of hearing can be rendered remarkably sensitive and accurate. There is rarely any physical defect in the ear itself. The defects ordinarily noticed and spoken of are such as can be easily remedied by cultivation. It may, it is true, never be able to attain the remarkable range of audition we have spoken of above, it may never become so "apprehensive and discriminant" as the ear of Mozart; but its delicacy can be increased and its general appreciation of musical sounds wonderfully improved. This is especially true if the work of instruction is begun in childhood, when the organ of hearing is naturally most sensitive and most readily susceptible of cultivation.

In making experiments with rods and tuning-forks giving very acute sounds, I have frequently been struck with the very great difference in the ability to perceive such sounds as manifested by young and old persons. Even when the latter were trained musicians they were incapable of hearing sounds that were quite audible to children who had no musical training whatever. This fact, like many others that might be adduced, is a striking commentary on the necessity of beginning early the training of the young, when eye and ear, not to speak of the other senses, are ever on the alert, and quick to detect sounds and forms and colors which at a later period would entirely escape their observation, or that of one who had never been taught the wonderful powers and capabilities of the five senses when properly educated.

CHAPTER III.

VELOCITY, REFLECTION, AND REFRACTION OF SOUND.

SOUND, as every one knows, requires an appreciable time for its transmission from one point to another. The earliest observers were cognizant of this fact. Thus Aristotle, whose observation nothing seems to have escaped, remarks that one sees a boatman strike the water with his oar a second time before the sound of the first stroke reaches the ear. In another place he observes: "The flash of lightning succeeds the noise of the thunder, but is perceived before it, because the sense of sight is quicker than that of hearing."[1]

Lucretius, who has preserved for us, in exquisite Latin verse, so much of the physical knowledge of the old Greek and Roman philosophers, refers to the same illustration as that last quoted from Aristotle; and then adds another, that has been used and paraphrased until the present time. Permit me to repeat what he says: —

> "Then earlier see we, too, the rushing blaze
> Than hear the roar, since far the fluent films
> Of sight move speedier than of laggard sound.
> As, when the woodman fells some branch remote,
> It drops conspicuous ere the bounding blow
> Strike on the ear, — so the keen lightning far
> Anticipates the thunder, though alike
> Reared from one cause, from one concussion reared."[2]

---

[1] Γίνεται δὲ μετὰ τὴν πληγὴν, καὶ ὕστερον τῆς βροντῆς· ἀλλὰ φαίνεται πρότερον διὰ τὸ τὴν ὄψιν προτερεῖν τῆς ἀκοῆς. — ARISTOTLE: *II. Meteor.*

[2] Sed tonitrum fit utei post auribus adcipiamus,
  Fulgere quam cernant oculei, quia semper ad aureis
  Tardius adveniunt, quam visum, quæ moveant, res.
  Id licet huic etiam cognoscere; cædere si quem

The rate at which sound travels in a unit of time is called its velocity. The unit of time ordinarily employed is one second. But no attempt to make anything like an accurate determination of the velocity of sound was undertaken until about two hundred and fifty years ago, when the matter was taken up by the illustrious Father Mersenne.

"Light," says Mersenne, "spreads through the sphere of its activity in an instant, or if it require time, it is so short as not to be observable. Sound, on the contrary, requires time to fill the sphere of its activity, the duration of which time is in proportion to the distance of the sonorous body from the ear. This has been proved experimentally in several ways. Thus, it has been observed that the axe of the woodman will have struck a second blow before the first is heard, when he is distant six hundred paces or thereabout."

He then describes experiments by which one may determine the velocity of sound. Among these he mentions that of counting the beats of the pulse from the moment one sees the flash of the musket, or of a piece of artillery, until the sound is heard. Although the observations which had been made by others, and to which he refers, gave quite discordant results, Mersenne held that the velocity of sound was not so great as that of a ball from an arquebus. And he bases his opinion on the fact that "birds are often seen to fall dead from the branches of trees before the sound of the arquebus is heard, although it be quite close at hand."

Mersenne's measurements of the velocity of sound were based on the phenomenon of reflection known as an echo. By means of a pendulum he had determined that seven syllables could be pronounced in a second. But he found

> Ancipiti videas ferro procul arboris auctum
> Ante fit ut cernas ictum, quam plaga per auras
> Det sonitum ; sic fulgorem cernimus ante,
> Quam tonitrum adcipimus, pariter qui mittitur igni
> E simili causa, concursu natus eodem.
> T. LUCRETII CARI: *De Rerum Natura*,
> Lib. vi. 163 *et seqq.*

that an echo at the distance of 519 feet would give back seven syllables. It requires one second to pronounce them, and they are heard coming back the second second. Sound then travels 519 feet in going, and the same distance in returning, that is, 1038 feet, in one second. "We may therefore," says Mersenne, "consider this as the velocity of reflected sounds, which I have always found to be the same, whether the sound proceed from trumpets, arquebuses, stones, or voices, acute or grave." This result, considering the means employed, is a remarkably close approximation to the value now received as correct.

About the same time that Mersenne was carrying on his researches on sound, the Academy of Florence took up the vexed question of the velocity of sonorous vibrations. In this instance the experiment was made by noting the time that elapsed from the appearance of the flash of a cannon until its detonation was heard. The result obtained was about 1,148 feet per second,—a value that is considerably higher than that assigned by Mersenne.

It was necessary, however, before any reliable results could be obtained, to employ more precise methods of measurement than any yet indicated. This was not done until nearly a century later, when in 1738 the matter was taken up by the French Academy of Sciences. A commission composed of Cassini de Fleury, La Caille, Maraldi, and a number of associates, chose as stations from which to make their observations the Observatory of Paris, the Pyramid of Montmartre, the Mill of Fontenay-aux-Rose, and the Château de Lay, at Montlhéry. Cannons at Montlhéry and Montmartre were fired alternately, and the observers at the four stations noted, by means of pendulums beating seconds, the time that elapsed between the arrival of the flash and the report of the guns. As the average of many observations they found that the velocity of sound at a temperature of 6° C. was 1,106 feet per second. As the velocity of sound increases almost two feet for every degree centigrade, this would make the velocity at 0° C., 1,094 feet per second.

The conditions under which the above observations were made were such as to show the effect that wind has on the propagation of sound. The velocity of sound is accelerated when its direction is the same as that of the wind, and retarded when wind and sound move in opposite directions. When the wind blows obliquely to the direction of propagation of sonorous waves, the velocity of sound is augmented or diminished according to the angle subtended by the lines along which wind and sound are carried. When, however, the wind is at right angles to the direction of propagation of sound, its influence is *nil*. The same observations likewise demonstrated that the velocity of sound in air is independent of atmospheric pressure, and that sonorous waves always pass over equal distances in equal times.

Subsequently, numerous other observations, with a similar object in view, were instituted in various other parts of the world. Observations were made by La Condamine at Quito and Cayenne; by Espinoza and Banza at Santiago in Chili; by Köstner and Müller at Göttingen; by Benzenberg near Düsseldorf; and by the English astronomer Goldingham at Madras. As a mean of eight hundred observations, the latter observer found the velocity of sound at a temperature of $0°$ C. to be 1,089.9 feet.

In 1822, at the instance of Laplace, the Bureau de Longitudes undertook to measure anew the velocity of sound. The commission appointed to do the work embraced some of the ablest mathematicians and physicists of the time. Among them were Arago, De Prony, Humboldt, and Gay-Lussac. The stations selected were Montlhéry and Villejuif, distant from each other nearly twelve miles. The observers were provided with the most accurate chronometers obtainable, recording from the tenth to the sixtieth of a second. As in 1738, cannons were used at both stations, and the time intervening between the arrival of the flash and the report of the guns was accurately measured. As a mean of numerous observations, after making due allowance for wind, temperature, and moisture, it was calculated that the velocity of sound at 0° C. would be 1,086.1. According to Arago, the probable error in this result, due to mistakes in measuring the distance between the stations, and in the estimation of time, cannot amount to more than four feet. It is probably less.

The year following, two Dutch physicists, Moll and Van Beck, as a result of a carefully conducted series of experiments, in which the influence of the wind, whose velocity and direction were indicated by good anemometers, was noted, calculated the velocity of sound at 0° C., in dry air, to be 1,089.4 feet per second. This result agrees closely with that which had been obtained by Goldingham.

All the preceding observations were made at stations that had practically the same elevation above sea-level. Besides, the direction of sound in all these cases was horizontal. But would the results be the same were sound to be transmitted in a direction oblique to the horizon? Theory answers this question in the affirmative.

According to Newton, who made the first theoretic investigations into this subject, the velocity of sound, as propagated in the air, depends both on the elasticity and the density of the air. The result at which he arrived is best expressed by the formula, $V = \sqrt{\frac{e}{d}}$,[1] in which V represents the velocity of sound, e the elasticity, and d the density of the air. This means that the velocity of sound in air is proportional to the square root of the ratio between the elasticity and the density of the air. But as, according to the law of Mariotte,[2] the elasticity of the atmosphere

---

[1] This formula, which is the one usually given, for the sake of simplicity, does not specify the value of e. e, according to Newton, is $= \Delta \cdot H \cdot g$, which, expressed in C. G. S. units, gives $\Delta = 13.596 =$ density of mercury. $H =$ normal barometric height $= 76$ cms. $\frac{e}{d} = \frac{981}{\text{density of air}} = .0012932$. The formula thus corrected is subject to calculation and is written $V = \sqrt{\frac{\Delta \cdot H g}{d}}$.

[2] In England usually called Boyle's law. As a matter of fact the law was discovered by Mariotte and Boyle independently and about the same date. Their discoveries were published in the early part of the latter half of the

varies as the pressure to which it was submitted, and the density varies also as the pressure, it follows that density and elasticity vary in the same proportion, and that the ratio between elasticity and density, for the same temperature, will always remain constant. Hence the velocity of sound will be the same in all directions. It will therefore be the same whether its direction of propagation be oblique or parallel to the horizon.

Two Austrian physicists, Stampfer and Myrbach, in 1822, were the first to demonstrate this experimentally. Twenty-two years later, in 1844, two French philosophers, Bravais and Martins, repeated the experiments in the Bernese Alps. They found that the velocity of sound from the base to the summit of the Faulhorn was the same as that from the summit to the base. According to their computations, this velocity at 0° C. in dry air was 1090.3 feet per second.

But the formula, $V = \sqrt{\frac{e}{d}}$, expressing the results of Newton's theoretical investigations, requires a correction to tally with the results of experiments. Newton himself was aware of the necessity for such a correction, but was not able to supply it. Basing his calculations on the known elasticity and density of the air, he found the velocity corresponding to the temperature of 0° C. to be 916 feet per second. The result thus obtained was about one sixth less than it was proved to be by observation. He offered a

---

seventeenth century. In strict justice the law should be known as the law of Mariotte and Boyle.

Mariotte, like his distinguished countryman, Mersenne, is not known as well as he should be, considering the great services he has rendered to science. A perusal of his published works, embracing two massive tomes in quarto, would show that we are indebted to him for many of the experiments and laws found in our modern works on physics. He, like Mersenne, was a monk, and like him, too, was one of the original members of the French Academy of Sciences. Condorcet in speaking of him says "Mariotte was the first one in France who introduced into physics a spirit of observation and doubt, and who inspired that scrupulousness and caution so necessary to those who interrogate Nature and interpret her responses."

conjecture as to the cause of the discrepancy, but it was reserved for the illustrious French mathematician, Laplace, to point out the true cause of the great difference between theoretic and observed results. This difference, as Laplace proved, was owing to changes of temperature produced by the sonorous wave itself. Compression, it was shown, augmented the temperature and, consequently, the elasticity of the air, while dilation caused a diminution of the temperature; but the net result of these changes in the temperature of the sound-wave was to cause an acceleration of velocity.

"Laplace," says Lord Rayleigh, who summarizes the question with characteristic lucidity, "considered that the condensations and rarefactions concerned in the propagation of sound take place with such rapidity that the heat and cold produced have not time to pass away, and that, therefore, the relation between volume and pressure is sensibly the same as if the air were confined in an absolutely non-conducting vessel. Under these conditions the change of temperature corresponding to a given condensation or rarefaction is greater than on the hypothesis of constant temperature, and the velocity of sound is accordingly increased."

"The only question," as Lord Rayleigh well observes, "which can possibly be considered open, is whether a small part of the heat and cold produced may not escape by conduction and radiation before producing its full effect. Everything must depend on the rapidity of the alternations. Below a certain limit of slowness the heat in excess or defect would have time to adjust itself, and the temperature would remain sensibly constant. In this case, the relation between pressure and density would be that which leads to Newton's value of the velocity of sound. On the other hand, above a certain limit of quickness the gas would behave as if confined in a non-conducting vessel, as supposed in Laplace's theory. Now, although the circumstances of the actual problem are better represented by the latter than by the former proposition, there may still, it may be said, be a sensible deviation from the law of pressure and density involved in Laplace's theory, entailing a somewhat slower velocity of propagation of sound."[1]

According to the hypotheses both of Newton and Laplace, there is no dissipation of energy during the propagation of sonorous undulations. Sound-waves do not generate heat. No work, therefore, is consumed. If there were such a conversion of sonorous vibrations into heat, — if work were done, — the distance to which sound could travel would be very limited indeed. Adding Laplace's correction to Newton's formula, it is found that theoretic and observed results agree exactly.

According to the experiments just referred to, the velocity of sound, in dry air, at a temperature of 0° C., would be, in round numbers, 1,090 feet per second. More recent observations by Le Roux and Regnault, in which all the refinements of modern experimental science were brought into requisition, show that this figure is probably too high, and that a nearer approximation to truth, for the velocity of sound at 0° C. is 1,083 feet per second. Le Roux estimates that this result, making allowances for all sources of error, is true to within six inches at most. As Le Roux and Regnault made independent observations and employed different methods, and give as their results the average of a large number of painstaking experiments, their figures may be accepted as substantially correct.

I have spoken thus at length of the experiments made to determine the velocity of sound to give you an idea of the immense amount of labor required to establish with certainty a single fact in science. And in what has been said, your attention has been called to a few only of the many experiments that have been made during the past two hundred years in various parts of the world. No one, who has not reflected on the matter, has any idea of the amount of energy expended on investigations of this nature, and of the ingenuity displayed in eliminating all possible sources of error. And what has been said con-

---

[1] Theory of Sound, vol. ii. pp. 19, 23, 24.

cerning observations made to determine the velocity of sound, may, with equal truth, be asserted regarding every fact that now constitutes a part of that very comprehensive branch of knowledge which we call physical science. We shall have several equally striking illustrations of the truth of this statement during the course of our investigations in the domain of sound. What are now accepted as simple facts, often, apparently, of slight importance, represent, each one of them, weeks, months, yea, years, of labor on the part of one or more of the enthusiastic students of Nature and Nature's laws.

From the foregoing we have seen that the velocity of sound is independent of the density of the air, and, consequently, of its pressure, but that it is modified by temperature, moisture, and the direction of the wind. The question may now be asked, Is the velocity the same for all sounds, grave or acute, feeble or intense?

It is within the experience of every one that all sounds travel equally fast, whatever their pitch. If this were not so, a melody played on a musical instrument, and heard at a distance, would undergo alteration in the order in which the different notes follow each other; but such is not the case. Biot demonstrated this conclusively by his experiments on the velocity of sound in iron pipes. He caused a well-known air to be played on a flute, at one end of a pipe over three thousand feet in length, and, stationing himself at the other end, he found that the notes bore the same relation to each other, and that their sequence was the same, at one end of the pipe as at the other. From this and other observations, he concluded that all sounds, whatever their pitch, travel equally fast. And what is true for one instrument is equally true for any number of instruments. Thus the music of an orchestra or brass band remains unaltered whether the hearer be hard by or farther away.

It is proper to state here that Biot's observations require a slight correction. The correction, however, applies only to what might be called exceptional cases. Regnault's experiments prove that very intense sounds, especially when passing through gases in pipes of small diameter, travel more rapidly than feeble sounds. But it is only when this difference in intensity is very marked that any variation in velocity is discernible. For ordinary sounds, under ordinary circumstances, no perceptible difference is ever observed.

When the velocity of sound in air is known, it is, obviously, an easy matter to compute the distance of any source of sound. As the velocity of light is so great, — about 190,000 miles per second, — its time of transmission, in all experiments on the velocity of sound, is so infinitesimal that it may be neglected. Counting, for instance, the number of seconds elapsing between the lightning's flash and the peal of thunder, and multiplying this number by the velocity of sound in air, according to its temperature, we have at once the distance of the point of discharge. It is only when the lightning's flash and the thunder's peal are nearly simultaneous that any danger from lightning is to be apprehended. In a similar manner the distance of any other source of sound can be computed.

The velocity of sound in gases may be determined both directly and indirectly. Regnault filled long tubes with gas, and thus measured the velocity of sounds directly. The results he arrived at agreed remarkably well with those required by theory, as expressed in Newton's formula, corrected by Laplace. Dulong, acting on a suggestion given by D. Bernouilli, measured indirectly the velocity of sound in air and various gases, by means of organ-pipes. I will not go into the details of his experiments, but simply tabulate the results at which he arrived: —

Velocity of sound in gases at the temperature of 0° C.

	Velocity.
Air	1092 feet.
Oxygen	1040 "
Hydrogen	4164 "
Carbon dioxide	858 "
Carbon monoxide	1107 "
Nitrous oxide	859 "
Olefiant Gas	1030 "

The preceding table affords a remarkable experimental confirmation of theoretical results. According to theory, as expressed in Newton's formula, $V = \sqrt{\frac{e}{d}}$, the velocities of sound in any two gases are inversely proportional to the square roots of their densities. The density of hydrogen is, to that of oxygen, as 1 is to 16. Hence, according to theory, the velocity of sound in the former should be to its velocity in the latter as 4 is to 1. The velocity in oxygen being 1,040, the velocity in hydrogen, according to the law indicated, should be 4,060.

FIG. 32.

Experiments, as made by Dulong, fix the velocity of sound in hydrogen at 4,164.

The velocity of sounds in liquids may also be determined both directly and indirectly. Beudant, at Marseilles, was the first to measure the velocity of sound in water. But the most exact determination of the velocity of sonorous waves in water was made by two French physicists, Colladon and Sturm, in 1827, in the Lake of Geneva. The method adopted was similar to that employed by Beudant. The two observers stationed themselves on boats (Fig. 32), at opposite sides of the lake. The source of sound was a submerged bell, C, attached to one of the boats. The signal, announcing when the hammer, B, moved by the lever, L, connected with a torch, M, struck the bell, was a flash of gunpowder, P. On the other boat the observer was provided with a peculiarly shaped ear-trumpet, OM, the bell of which was held in the water, and a good stop-watch, by means of which he was able to register exactly the time of the arrival of the sound-pulse through the water. As an average of many observations, it was found that the velocity of sound in water, at a temperature of 8.1° C., was 4,707 feet per second, more than four times greater than it is in air.

By means of a specially constructed apparatus, that need not be described here, Wertheim was able to measure indirectly the velocity of sound in other liquids as well as water. The following table gives the velocity in feet per second obtained for the liquids mentioned at the temperatures given:

	Temperature	Velocity
River Water (Seine)	15 C	4,714
" " "	30	5,013
Sea Water (artificial)	20	4,768
Solution of Common Salt	18	5,132
Solution of Sulphate of Sodium	20	5,194
Solution of Carbonate of Sodium	22.2	5,230
Solution of Nitrate of Sodium	20.9	5,477
Absolute Alcohol	23	3,804
Ether	0	3,801

The velocity of sound in liquids, as in gases, increases with the temperature. But the changes of temperature, which are due to the condensations of sonorous undulations in water, are so insignificant as to affect no appreciable change in the medium. For this reason we may apply Newton's formula, $V = \sqrt{\frac{e}{d}}$, without Laplace's correction, for calculating the velocity of sounds in liquids, and the results given closely approximate to those obtained by experiment. Thus by direct measurement the velocity of sound in water was found to be 4,708 feet per second; by Wertheim's indirect method it was found to be 4,714 feet; and by the application of Newton's formula a velocity of 4,671 feet is given. As the elasticity and density of any given liquid can always be determined experimentally, it is an easy matter, by using Newton's formula, to calculate the velocity of sound in any liquid whatever. And since Wertheim's method is almost equally comprehensive in its application, it is evident that the results arrived at by the two methods can serve as checks for one another, and that in no case can the calculations made vary from the truth by any considerable quantity.

In solids the elasticity, as compared with the density, is usually greater than in liquids, and hence the rate of transmission of sounds is correspondingly greater.

Biot determined the velocity of sound in cast iron by means of an iron pipe over three thousand feet in length. One end of the pipe was struck by a hammer, and an observer stationed at the other end heard two sounds, one transmitted by the air, the other by the metal. It was thus found that iron transmitted sound about ten and one half times as rapidly as air.

By calculations based on their coefficients of elasticity, which may be experimentally determined, Wertheim was able to deduce the velocity of sound in the solids named in the following table: —

Velocity of Sound in Metals at 20° C.

Lead	4,030 feet	Gold	5,717 feet
Silver	8,553	Copper	11,666
Steel Wire	15,470	Iron	16,822

Velocity of Sound in Wood along the Fibre.

Pine	10,900 feet	Oak	12,622 feet
Ash	13,314	Elm	13,516
Fir	15,218	Aspen	16,677

From the preceding tables we observe that the solids in which the velocity of sound is greatest are iron and steel for the metals, and fir and aspen for the woods. According to Chladni's measurements, however, the velocity in fir is much greater than that given in the table. His experiments gave for this wood a velocity of 19,685 feet, — fully twelve times the rapidity of transmission of sonorous pulses in air.[1]

It is to be noted that the rate of propagation of sound-vibrations is not the same in all directions in wood. The figures above given are true only when the direction of transmission is along the fibres. When sound is made to pass parallel or across the rings of the wood, its velocity is very much less.

It is to be remarked, also, that augmentation of temperature in metals has not the same effects which it has in gases and liquids of increasing the velocity of sound. The result, except in the case of iron between 20° and 100° C., is just the opposite. Increase of temperature entails a corresponding decrease in velocity. Iron is an exception to the rule which obtains with other metals, by reason, very likely, of some peculiar molecular structure; for it has been observed that iron and steel, prepared in different ways — iron and steel as wire and cast steel, for instance — do not transmit sound-waves with the same velocity.

Chladni and Kundt have devised two beautiful methods of calculating the velocity of sound in different solids, which I shall dwell on more at length when we come to study the vibrations of rods.[2] Interference of sound also affords us an interesting way of computing the rate of propagation of sound-vibrations in air and gases. But we shall see more of this in the sequel.

Many methods have been devised for measuring the velocity of sound at short distances. The best and simplest of these is, probably, that contrived by Bosscha. His method depends on the principle of coincidence of two sounds coming to the ear from points at different distances. The apparatus required consists essentially of two electric sounders, A and B (Fig. 33), which, under the influence of a vibrating spring, beat exactly ten times a

---

[1] Prof. A. M. Mayer has recently made a very accurate determination of the velocity of sound in clear white pine (American), thoroughly seasoned. This wood had a density of .395, and the velocity in it at 24° C. was 17,260 feet per second.

[2] See chapter v.

second. When the two sounders are placed side by side, as they are now on the table, they sound as one, because as the sounds of both reach the ear, O, at the same time, it is impossible to distinguish one from the other. As soon, however, as the instruments are separated the sounds they emit cease to coincide. You now hear twenty instead of ten strokes per second, — ten from each sounder. The reason of this is that the sounds emitted by the instrument farthest from the ear are behind those emitted by the nearer one. If the sounders were to be so placed that one should be about 112 feet farther from the ear than the other, then the sounds coming from the two sources would again coincide. The explanation of this is to be found in the fact that at the temperature of this hall, 112 feet is the

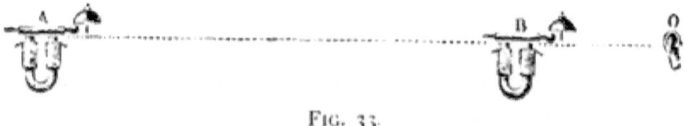

FIG. 33.

distance that sound travels in one tenth of a second. For a similar reason the sounds from the two instruments would be coincident whenever the distance separating them is any multiple of 112 feet. It is obvious that the same appliance could be used for measuring the velocity of sound both in gases and liquids.

The vibrating spring is, as you see, provided with a mirror, as is also a tuning-fork making forty vibrations per second, which forms a part of the apparatus. By means of a discovery of Lissajous, of which we shall see more in its place, the spring can be so adjusted as to close and break the circuit exactly ten times per second, and thus cause the sounders to strike with unfailing regularity the tenths of a second as long as may be desired. This is not an apparatus for giving rigorously exact measurements, and yet the results obtained are probably more reliable than those obtained by any other instrument for measuring the velocity of sound at short distances.

Sir Charles Wheatstone, to whom the sciences of acoustics and of optics are indebted for many beautiful inventions, has devised a means of exhibiting, in a most pleasing manner, the transmission of sound through solid bodies. On the table is a music-box wrapped in several layers of felt. Although the instrument is now in operation, not the slightest sound is perceptible. I hold in my hand a rod of fir three feet long, the lower end of which is now brought into contact with the lid of the music-box. Still, no sound is heard. On the top end of the rod is now placed a guitar, and all at once it appears to be animated with the spirit of music. The harmony that was buried in the manifold layers of felt has now found a means of making itself audible. Through the fir rod the sounds in the box are carried to the guitar, and this, acting as a sounding-board, — it does nothing more, — communicates to the air, in perfect rhythm and cadence, all the most delicate shades of harmony that have their origin in the complex mechanism in the box below. So faithfully is every note and every chord of the piece that is being played reproduced, so perfect is the illusion as to the real source of sound, that it is difficult at first to realize that the sweet sounds to which you are listening are issuing from a shapeless mass of felt, and not from the guitar itself.

The rod that connects the box with the guitar might be of any other wood as well as of fir, or might be made of metal, and the result would be the same. Or, instead of being only three feet long, it might be several hundred feet in length, and still the result would be unchanged. Instead of a music-box, we might use a piano, or any other musical instrument, and in lieu of a guitar we might substitute a violin, mandolin, or simply a resonant box. The only purpose served by the musical instrument, or box, placed on top of the rod, connected with the music-box, is, by exposing to the air a large surface, to distribute to it all the tremors which the revolving cylinder and steel tongues of the instrument engender. The rod alone is incompetent to render the sounds of the box audible, because of the small amount of surface it exposes to the air. But I shall not forestall what properly belongs to the subject of resonance, which will be considered in another lecture.

The toy called the string telephone, with which every one is familiar, is another pretty illustration of the facility with which solids transmit sounds. The telephones before you are composed of two brass tubes, the smaller ends of which are covered with a thin membrane. The centres of these membranes are connected with each other by a light cord, and by this simple means sounds, otherwise inaudible, can be heard at a distance of a thousand feet or more.

A simple experiment will show the capacity that liquids have for transmitting sounds. On this resonant case is placed a long, narrow jar filled with water, and into the water at the top of the jar is placed the foot of a tuning-fork. As soon as the fork touches the water a loud, clear note is heard, where before all was silence. Any other liquid would answer the purpose as well as water.

Here I must call your attention to an interesting property of sound which was first pointed out by Doppler in 1842, in a remarkable memoir on the colors of double stars. If an observer approach a source of sound it is obvious that the number of sonorous pulses which will reach his ear will be increased in proportion to his rate of motion. The pitch of the sound, therefore, will be heightened. If he recede from the sonorous body, the number of sound-waves that will reach him will be diminished in proportion, and the sound, consequently, will appear more grave. The same results will be observable if the hearer remain stationary and the sounding body be put in motion. Thus, if one could move with nearly the velocity of sound towards a brass band playing a piece of music, its pitch would be so greatly augmented that, although the performance would still be in time, its character would be entirely altered, and it would be nearly, if not quite, inaudible except to ears specially sensitive to very acute sounds. If, on the contrary, one were to move away from such a musical source with a velocity approaching to that of sound, the sounds heard, if at all audible, would be proportionally flattened. If, further, the observer were to recede from the band with a velocity greater than that of sound, a piece of music commenced after he had started would never reach him, but "sounds previously executed," as Lord Rayleigh observes, "would be gradually overtaken, and heard in the reverse of the natural order."[1] And, finally, if the observer's velocity were to be twice that of sound, he would "hear a musical piece in correct time and tune, but backwards."

An illustration of the effect of motion on the pitch of sound is afforded by the whistle of the locomotive as it approaches or recedes from the observer. In the former case the pitch is augmented, in the latter it is diminished. Thus, for a train moving at the rate of thirty-eight miles an hour, the velocity is about fifty-five feet per second. This, calculation shows, is sufficient to raise the pitch of the whistle a semitone as it approaches the observer, and to lower it by the same amount as the locomotive retreats. Thus, if, when both locomotive and observer were stationary, the whistle were to give the note A_1, it would, with the velocity above mentioned, give the note $A\sharp_1$ as it approaches, and $A\flat_1$ as it leaves him. Just at the moment of passing by the observer there would be a change of a whole note, that is, from $A\sharp_1$ to $A\flat_1$. By doubling the velocity of the train the whistle would be augmented by a whole tone when approaching, and diminished by a whole tone on leaving. If two express trains, each going at the rate of thirty-eight miles an hour, were to pass each other, the whistle of the engine of one train would appear, when approaching an observer in the other train moving in an opposite direction, to be a whole tone higher than when whistle and observer were both stationary. After the two trains had passed each other the note of the whistle would appear a whole tone lower than it would if both observer and whistle were stationary. At the instant of passing

---

[1] Theory of Sound, vol. ii. p. 240.

there would be a change of a major third, or of two whole tones. If instead of thirty-eight miles the velocity of the two trains were to be equal to that which is now frequently attained by some of our limited express trains, there would be, at the instant of passing, a transition equivalent to an interval greater than a fourth, and approximating to a fifth.[1]

Doppler's principle, as it is called, at first only a theory, has, in its application to sound, been experimentally verified by Buys-Ballot and Scott Russell, by means of musical instruments carried on locomotives, whose pitch was determined by musicians stationed along the road over which the engines passed.

By applying the same principle to luminous vibrations, astronomers have been able to determine, not only the direction of motion, but also the velocity of many of the stars as they approach or recede from the earth.

A simple laboratory instrument for showing the influence of motion on the pitch of sonorous bodies has been devised by Mach. It is composed of a tube six feet in length, mounted on a stand, and turning about an axis at its centre (Fig. 34). At one end of the tube is fixed a reed, which is sounded by forcing air into the tube through an aperture at its axis of rotation. If, while the tube is rotating, an observer stand in the prolongation of its axis of rotation, he will hear a note of constant pitch. If, on the other hand, he be stationed in the plane of rotation, he will hear a note which alternately rises and falls in pitch according as the sonorous body approaches or retreats from him.

---

[1] Designating by n the number of vibrations of the sonorous body when at rest, by V the velocity of sound, by V' the velocity of the sonorous body when approaching or receding from the observer, and by n' the number of vibrations corresponding to the sound perceived by the observer, we have the two following formulæ:—

$$n' = \frac{n(V + V'')}{V}$$ as the sonorous body approaches observer.

$$n' = \frac{n(V - V'')}{V}$$ as the sonorous body recedes from observer.

Koenig illustrates this phenomenon in another way equally striking. For this purpose he employs a pair of tuning-forks mounted on resonant cases, like those now before you. The frequency of one of them is C of 512 vibrations, and that of the other is exactly four vibrations higher. They thus, when stationary and sounding together, give four beats per second. If now I excite the two forks, and leaving the more acute one on the table, move the graver one towards it, in a line joining my ear and the stationary fork, over a distance of about two feet,—approximately the wave-length of the fork,—in a second I thereby lower the pitch of the graver fork by one vibration. This increases the difference between the forks to five vibrations, and gives rise to five beats per second. A movement in the opposite direction would, for a like reason, produce three beats a second. Thus by properly timing the movement of the graver fork between the ear and the fork on the table, we have alternately three and five beats per second,—three beats as the fork is brought towards the ear, and five beats as it moves away. By this means, also, it is evident one can determine approximately both the wave-length and the pitch of a sound.

FIG. 34

A modification of this experiment will enable you all to see at a glance the effect of motion on the frequency of sonorous vibrations. For this we shall use two forks on cases that are exactly in unison with each other. And in this experiment I shall anticipate, to some extent, what I shall have to say on the subject of resonance and sympathetic vibration. When one fork is agitated, the other, although at some distance, immediately begins to vibrate, as you see by the small pith ball that is projected away from the prong against which it was suspended. This happens, however, only when both forks are stationary. If now one of them is moved rapidly backwards and forwards in a line connecting the two forks, the perfect unison that previously existed between them is destroyed. For from what has been said, when one of the forks approaches the other, the pitch of the fork in motion is heightened, and when it recedes the pitch is lessened. And as in this experiment perfect unison is necessary in order that one fork may excite sufficient vibratory motion in another to produce the effects noted, we see at once in the absence of such motion what influence the movement of one fork towards or away from the other has on the pitch of the sonorous vibrations in question.

In a homogeneous medium sonorous waves are propagated in the form of concentric spheres. When, however,

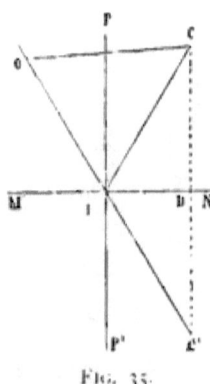

Fig. 35.

the homogeneity of the medium is disturbed, or an obstacle is encountered, sound-waves suffer partial or total reflection. In this respect they obey the same laws as those which govern rays of light and radiant heat. If, in Fig. 35, MN represent a fixed elastic surface, a sound produced at C will be heard by an observer at O both directly in a straight line, and by reflection from the point I. The sound in the latter instance appears to come from I or from C', a point in the line OI produced. Making PI perpendicular to the reflecting surface MN, and calling CI the incident, and IO the reflected, ray[1] of sound, it is found that in all cases the angle of incidence, CIP, is equal to the angle of reflection, PIO.

---

[1] A *ray* of sound, as is obvious from what has been said concerning the nature of sonorous vibrations, must be considered as a simple abstraction, and nothing more. In explaining the laws of reflection and refraction of sound it is a convenient term to use, and for this reason only is it introduced.

It is found also that the incident and reflected rays are always in the same plane, and that this plane is perpendicular to the reflecting surface.

When concentric sound-waves encounter a fixed obstacle they return upon themselves, as if emanating from a second centre on the opposite side of the obstacle. Thus, in Fig. 36, the sonorous waves whose source is O, on arriving at the fixed surface $A B$, are reflected in such a manner that they seem to proceed from the point O' on the other side. A single ray of sound from O, impinging against the point I, would be reflected to the point M, along the

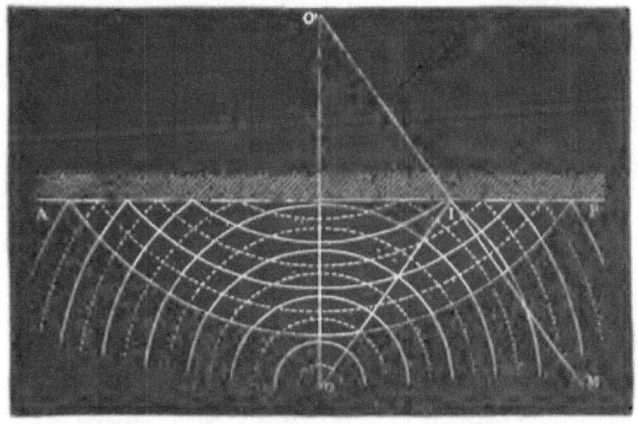

Fig. 36.

line $I M$. This line may be regarded as a continuation of that drawn from O', the virtual centre of the waves reflected from the surface $A B$.

It is an easy matter to show experimentally the reflection of sound. Before you are two curved mirrors on metallic supports, A and A', about six yards apart. These mirrors — which are shown in section in Fig. 37 — have the property of converging parallel rays of light, heat, or sound, to a point called the focus. When, however, the rays start from the focus and are reflected from either mirror, they are given off in lines that are parallel. In the focus, F of one of the mirrors, M, is suspended a watch, and at the focus, F', of the other mirror, M', is a small funnel, which is connected with my ear by means of a rubber tube. By a special effort I am able to hear the ticking of the watch with the unaided ear; but by means of these two mirrors I can hear its ticking with remarkable distinctness. The sound-rays from the watch strike against the mirror adjacent, and by it are reflected to the one more distant; and by this last the rays are concentrated at a single point, which, by means of the tube, is now in direct communication with my ear. By this means the ticking of a watch can be distinctly heard at a distance of two or three hundred feet, whereas the

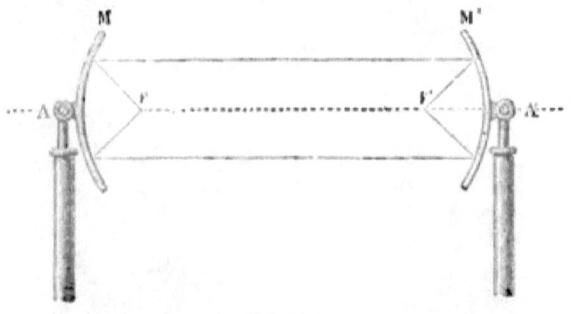

FIG. 37.

unaided ear would be unable to detect the slightest sound at a very small fraction of this distance. Good results may likewise be obtained from one mirror, as can be easily demonstrated. Leaving the watch suspended as it is, I turn the adjacent reflector so as to direct the sound-rays towards the audience. With a little attention I think that even those in the most distant part of the room can hear the ticking of the watch, when the reflector is so adjusted that the reflected sonorous waves shall strike directly the tympanic membrane of the ear.

Mr. Cottrell has devised a very ingenious instrument for exhibiting the reflection of sound and showing that the angles of incidence and reflection are equal and in the same plane. It consists (Fig. 38) of a tube, RB, by means of which the acute sound of a small reed is directed against a mirror, *M*, by which it is reflected into another tube, *AF*, carrying at its extremity a sensitive flame. The axes of the two tubes can be turned towards the mirror at any angle, and the support is so graduated that the angles of inclination of the tubes to the normal of the mirror can be read off at a glance.

When the angles are equal and the reed is sounded, the sonorous pulses are reflected from the mirror into the tube bearing the sensitive flame. The flame, as you observe, is now violently agitated, and this disturbance persists as

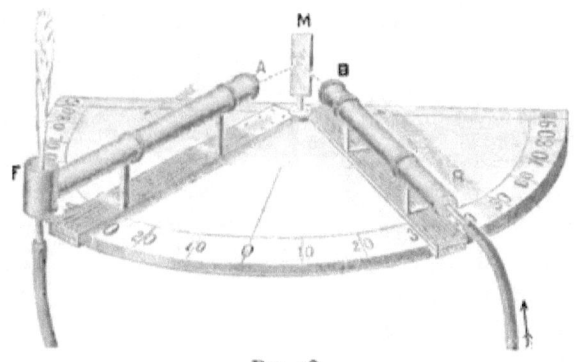

Fig. 38.

long as the sound continues. If, however, the angles are unequal, the sensitive flame will remain quiescent. I now make the angle of reflection greater than the angle of incidence, and sound the reed as before; the flame remains perfectly quiet. Nothing could be more sensitive than the flame, when properly adjusted, or illustrate more clearly the laws governing the reflection of sonorous rays.

But it is not by any means necessary to have a solid surface, such as this mirror, for a reflector. Liquids and gases have also the power of reflecting sound. Every one may recall instances of the reflecting power of liquids, especially the water at the bottom of wells or under the arches of bridges. But the power which gases have of reflecting sounds is not so well known. It can nevertheless be strikingly exhibited by the apparatus which we have just been using. Substituting a jet of burning coal-gas for the glass mirror, and proceeding as before, we find that the sonorous pulsations coming from the vibrating reed are reflected so as powerfully to agitate the sensitive flame. By lowering the flame and causing the sound-waves to impinge against the sheet of heated air which arises from the flame, the result is unchanged. Substituting a red-hot bar of iron for the gas jet, the sensitive flame is still agitated. The stream of hot air now rising from the bar is the reflecting surface, although entirely invisible.

These last experiments explain many facts concerning the behavior of sound under circumstances that, until recently, were an enigma to all investigators. Humboldt, indeed, suspected the action of non-homogeneous air on the transmission of sonorous waves, and offered an explanation of a fact that is within the experience of every one; namely, that sounds are heard with greater distinctness at night than during the day. Speaking of the sound due to the Great Falls of the Orinoco, in South America, he says: " During the five days we passed in the neighborhood of the cataract we remarked, with surprise, that the noise of the river was three times as loud during the night as during the day. The same thing, it has been observed, holds true for all the waterfalls of Europe. What can be the cause, in a wilderness, where nothing disturbs the silence of nature? It must probably be sought in the current of hot air which ascends during the day, and which arrests the propagation of sound, but which ceases during the night, when the earth is cooled." Air rising from rocks or the bare ground would be more heated than that which rises from soil covered with water or vegetation. We should thus have produced air-columns of different temperatures, and, consequently, of different densities. In passing through such an atmosphere, sound would undergo successive reflections, which would entail a corresponding diminution of intensity. During the night, when the homogeneity of the air is restored, such reflections are absent, and sound reaches the ear with proportionally augmented intensity. The admirable observations and experiments of Tyndall have cleared up all doubts regarding this matter, and what Humboldt and others only suspected, is now received as one of the established truths of science.

The familiar phenomenon of resonance, or echo, is due to the reflection of sound. If one speaks in a moderately large room with bare walls and little or no furniture, the sound-waves reflected from the walls and ceiling of the room reach the ear shortly after the direct waves, and both combine in such a manner as to augment the resultant sound. Such an augmentation is known as resonance. If the room be larger, the direct and reflected waves reach the ear in appreciably different times, and the result is that the words spoken appear to be doubled, and, for this reason, confused, and distinguished with difficulty.

But when the reflecting surface is about 110 feet distant from the speaker, he hears twice each syllable he pronounces, — one directly, and the other by reflection. The latter sound is known as a *simple* echo. If the reflecting surface is 220 or 330 feet away, the speaker will hear two or three syllables by reflection. Such a phenomenon is called a *polysyllabic* echo. The farther away the reflecting surface is, the greater the number of syllables that one may hear. Dividing the distance of the obstacle throwing back the sound by 110 will give approximately the number of syllables which an echo will furnish. I say approximately, because I proceed on the assumption that one can pronounce distinctly only five syllables per second. As sound at the ordinary temperature of the air travels about 1100 feet per second, this would allow about 220 feet for each syllable, or the half of this number for the distance of the object from the speaker. When sound is reflected from several different objects at suitable distances, or when it undergoes a series of reflections from parallel walls, for instance, we have what are called *multiple* echoes.

One of the most remarkable multiple echoes ever known was one formerly heard in the Château of Simonetta, near Milan. According to Father Kircher, a sound was here reflected no less than forty times. An echo in Woodstock Park, in England, repeats a sound seventeen times during the day, and twenty times at night. All European travellers are familiar with the celebrated echoes at the Gap of Dunloe, at Killarney, and that which is heard between Bingen and Coblentz, where the waters of the Nahe flow into the Rhine. The most remarkable echoes I know of in this country are found in the cañons of the Rocky Mountains. These deep chasms, as one might imagine, by reason of their precipitous and oftentimes parallel cliffs, are particularly well adapted to reflecting sound and to furnishing echoes of all kinds. I have also heard in the Grand Cañon of the Colorado River, in Arizona, some most extraordinary echoes, comparable, I think, with any that are to be heard elsewhere.

In whispering-galleries we have another illustration of the peculiar effects produced by reflected sounds. Sometimes the sound is greatly augmented, as in the crypt of the Panthéon in Paris, where a slight clapping of the hands gives rise to reverberations of great power and volume. In the large chambers and long passage-ways of the Great Pyramid of Gizeh the reverberations excited by the slightest noise are equally striking.

Large domes, like those of St. Peter's in Rome or of St. Paul's in London, are interesting examples of the perfect manner in which sound is reflected by curved surfaces. In both cases the slightest whisper is conveyed by reflection, or by a series of reflections, from one side of the dome to the other, without any appreciable enfeeblement of sound. Two persons stationed at opposite sides of the dome can, without any difficulty, carry on a conversation that is almost, if not quite, inaudible to bystanders only a few feet distant. The dome of the Capitol in Washington is an almost equally good place for reflecting sounds and augmenting them by resonance. But perhaps the most remarkable building for reflections and echoes to be found anywhere is the curiously designed Mormon Tabernacle in Salt Lake City, Utah. It is in the form of a semi-ellipsoid, and is capable of seating over ten thousand people. The speaker, as I can testify from personal experience, can be heard distinctly, and without the slightest effort on his part, in every part of this vast edifice. When the hall is empty, a whisper at one end of the building is easily heard at the other. Indeed, two persons may here carry on a conversation in a whisper, although over two hundred feet apart, so perfect is the reflection from the curved surfaces of the walls and ceiling. I do not think there is any other place in the world where a speaker can make himself heard by so many and with so little exertion. The acoustic properties of the building are certainly extraordinary, and as unexampled, I think, as the architectural style of the structure is unique.

Strange as it may appear, architects are still in the dark as to the laws governing the acoustic properties of buildings. For places of assembly, like public halls, theatres, churches, one would think that, by this time, architects would be able to determine, at least empirically, the best form to give to a building of determinate size; but they are not. Success is a matter of accident. There are many halls in this country that, from an acoustic point of view, are all that a speaker or singer could desire; while, as is well known, there are many others that are almost useless for the purpose for which they were designed. And what is said of the defectiveness of halls may be predicated more particularly of churches, especially those that are at all large. Gothic churches seem to suffer most in this respect, and it would appear that the Gothic style of architecture is incompatible with good acoustic effects.

Even in ordinary halls several expedients must frequently be resorted to in order that a speaker or singer may be heard to advantage. It is observed, for instance, that in certain halls there is too much resonance, — so much, indeed, as to interfere materially with a distinct perception of what is said or sung; and the only remedy is to dampen the sound by draping the walls, or to make the surface of walls and ceiling so irregular that resonance and echo are so diminished as not to be appreciable. Public speakers all know the difference in resonant effect observed in speaking in an empty hall and in one crowded with people. In the former case the resonance may be so great, and the direct and reflected sounds so interfere with each other, that what is uttered is indistinguishable. The presence of an audience in a hall in which such a difficulty is observed, is often sufficient to dampen this excess of resonance so that every word spoken or sung can be heard and understood. There is certainly much yet to be learned in the science of acoustics as applied to the construction of build-

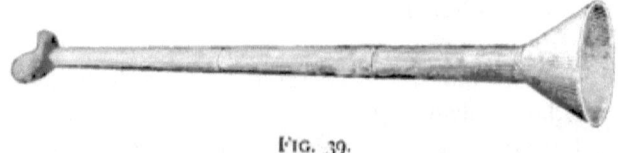

FIG. 39.

ings, and the one who shall supply even a part of the information still needed will confer a boon both on hearer and speaker.

Among the practical applications of the laws of reflected sounds may be mentioned speaking-tubes and speaking and ear trumpets. Sound, as every one knows, is conveyed to a much greater distance in tubes than in the open air. Hence their adoption in buildings and other places where it is desirable to carry on a conversation at any considerable distance. The smoother the interior, and the more elastic the material of such tubes, the less rapidly is the intensity of sound diminished, and the farther, consequently, is it carried.

A speaking-trumpet is usually of metal, conical in form (Fig. 39), with a mouthpiece at its smaller end, and a wide opening, called the bell, at the end opposite. Experience shows that the bell renders the trumpet more effective; but the office it performs is not yet understood. By means of a series of reflections in the interior of the trumpet, the sonorous rays are rendered more or less parallel, and, hence, capable of being transmitted to much greater distances than would otherwise be possible. The loudness of the sound produced is most likely due to resonance.

An ear-trumpet is just the reverse of a speaking-trumpet. The smaller end is inserted in the ear, and the sound to be heard is produced at the larger end. By a series of

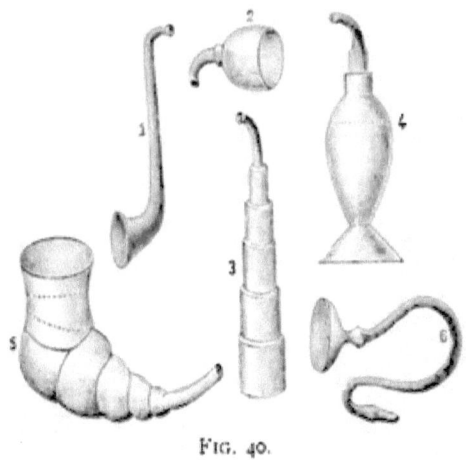

FIG. 40.

reflections the sonorous waves are condensed as they enter the tube, and, on arriving at the tympanic membrane, are of sufficient intensity to excite the sensation of a sound that the unaided ear could not perceive. Although the general principle obtaining in all ear-trumpets is identical, many forms have been devised A few of these are shown in Fig. 40, the *modus operandi* of which is apparent.

Sound, like light and radiant heat, when passing from one medium to another of different density, or from one point to another in the same medium, when it lacks homogeneity, deviates more or less from a direct course. It is then said to be refracted. From theoretical considerations, based on the different velocities of sound in media of different densities, Poisson and Green demonstrated that sonorous waves are subject to laws of refraction similar to those that prevail for light and heat.

Sondhaus was the first to demonstrate this experimentally by means of lenses of peculiar construction, and Hajech, shortly afterwards, showed that the same results are obtained by using suitable prisms filled with gases or liquids of different densities. A lens (Fig. 41) similar to the one employed by Sondhaus in his researches is before you. It is made of a broad brass ring, to the two sides of which are attached sheets of thin India-rubber, A.

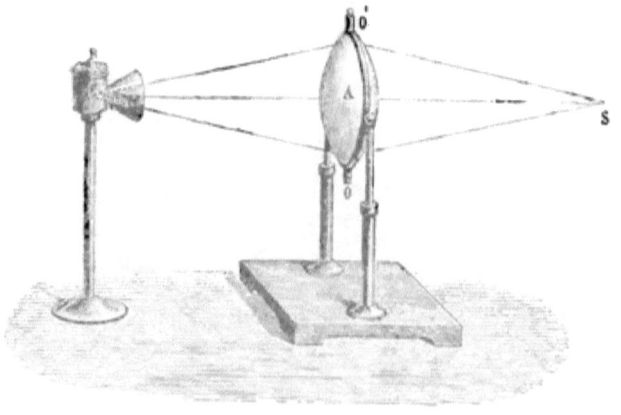

FIG. 41.

Through a stopcock, O or O', carbonic-acid gas is admitted into the apparatus until the sheets are sufficiently distended, and have the form of a double convex lens. As carbonic-acid gas is more dense than air, a sound produced in the surrounding air has its velocity retarded while passing through the heavier gas in the lens. The result is that sonorous rays, which were divergent before entering the lens, are made to approach each other when leaving the lens on the opposite side and to converge to a focus. Suspending a watch in the axis of the lens on one side, the sound-pulses are collected at a point on the axis on the other side. Bringing the ear to this point, the ticking of the watch is far more distinctly heard than would be possible with the unaided ear.

This concentration of sound-rays by means of a lens can also be exhibited in another way devised by Sondhaus. At the point occupied by the ear is placed a small cylindrical box, F, covered with a thin membrane, B, strewn with fine sand, and a funnel which collects the sound-rays and conveys them to the interior of the case. When a note of suitable pitch and of some intensity is sounded at S (Fig. 41), the sonorous pulses are concentrated at the other side of the lens, and cause the sand to dance about on the membrane as long as the sound lasts. To prove that there is really a refraction of sound in this instance, it is only necessary to remove the lens, when the movement of the sand subsides.

Refraction and reflection explain many phenomena connected with the propagation of sonorous waves that would otherwise remain unintelligible. The investigations of Prof. Joseph Henry and Professor Tyndall on the audibility of fog-signals have disclosed many facts before unknown regarding the transmission of sound-waves; but there are many apparently abnormal acoustic phenomena which are far from being understood. Henry seems to think that the very capricious action sometimes observed in fog-signals can in almost all cases be explained by refraction. Tyndall lays more stress on reflection; and the experiments made in support of his views are, in at least some instances, apparently conclusive as to the truth of his theories. We have shown experimentally that a sheet of heated air or gas is capable of reflecting sound, and according to Tyndall, a heterogeneous condition of the atmosphere is competent to produce reflections of sufficient power to produce an echo. In Tyndall's opinion the reverberations of cannon and thunder are in many, if not in all, cases due to limiting surfaces of strata and columns of heterogeneous atmosphere, and not, as has been long supposed, to clouds or other reflecting surfaces.

If sound-waves encounter an obstacle in their path, and this obstacle be large in comparison with the length of the waves of sound, it will give rise to what is aptly called a sound-shadow. The sound behind the object is much less intense than that in front of it, and if the object be sufficiently large, the sound may be quenched entirely. But if the obstacle encountered is small, as compared with the length of the sound-wave, the wave will pass around it, and there will consequently be no sound-shadow. This property which waves of sound, like waves of water and light, have of bending around obstacles in their path, is known as *diffraction*.

It is ordinarily supposed that both sound and light rays travel only in straight lines; but this statement requires modification. Both luminous and sonorous rays are capable of diffraction; that is, of being bent round opaque bodies, to a greater or less extent. With diffraction of light we are not at present concerned; but it were an easy matter to instance numerous examples of sonorous diffraction. A railway train passing through a tunnel and around hills is a familiar example of the variation in the intensity of sound due to diffraction. In a mountainous country like Colorado, where the curves are sharp and the cuttings deep, and where there are numerous castellated buttes facing the road along which the train passes, the effect is particularly striking. All visitors to Manitou, the great summer resort of the Rockies, must have observed the peculiar and remarkable effects produced by the train on the "Midland Railway" as it passes around the base of Pike's Peak, now going through tunnels and deep cuts, now behind knolls and hillocks and immense masses of rock that have been detached from the mountain high overhead. A more interesting and instructive example of the diffraction of sound could not be found.

A remarkable illustration of diffraction is afforded when a person in motion puts between himself and a brass-band, playing some distance away, objects of varying sizes. The result is that the notes played are differently diffracted according to their respective wave-lengths. In some instances the objects passed may give rise to more or less perfect sound-shadows for the notes of higher pitch, while the graver notes bend round the object with but little diminution in sonorous intensity. The result is that the acute notes seem very much feebler comparatively than the grave ones, and there is, consequently, a change in the quality of the music that no one could fail to observe. For this reason, in order to hear music to the best advantage, one should always be in full view of the performers, where there will be no danger of sound-shadows for any of the notes played.

Diffraction also explains the peculiar behavior of some of the great dynamite and powder explosions that have taken place in the country during the last few years. It has often been remarked as strange that the windows on all sides of the houses near where these explosions have occurred have been forced inwards by the terrible concussion which was occasioned. The reason is simple. The sonorous waves in coming from the centre of disturbance encircled the houses, in which the phenomena referred to were observed, with a wave of condensation of such power that the windows on all sides of the houses were forced inwards at practically the same moment. Were it not for diffraction,—the property that sound-waves have of bending around obstacles,—such results as those indicated could not have occurred. And furthermore, were it not for diffraction, sound produced on one side of an object could not be heard on the side opposite, except by transmission directly through the obstacle, which in nearly all the cases alluded to would have been impossible.

The distance to which sound travels is often very great. Of course the distance to which it will be conveyed in any given case will, as we have seen, depend on circumstances,—on the elasticity and temperature of the medium through which it is transmitted, on the intensity of the sound itself, and on a number of other factors which need not now be indicated.

Thus, in 1762 the cannonading at Mayence was heard at Timbect, a village 148 miles distant. The booming of the cannon which preceded the taking of Paris in 1814 was heard at the distance of 132 miles, and the firing at Waterloo was audible at Dover. The cannonading at Antwerp in 1832 was, we are told, heard in the mines of Saxony, about 370 miles from the scene of action. According to Humboldt, the report of the volcano of St. Vincent was heard at Demerara, 750 miles off. In respect of distance, this would be the same as if an eruption of Vesuvius were heard in the north of France. At the time of the great eruption of Cotopaxi, in 1774, subterranean detonations were heard at Honda, on the Magdalena. The distance between these two points is over five hundred miles, and their difference of level is nearly 18,000 feet. Besides this, they are separated by the colossal mountains of Quito, of Pasto and Popayan, and by valleys and ravines without number. Evidently, then, sound in this case was not transmitted by the air, but by the earth, and at a very great depth.

It would appear from the last two examples, in which there can be no doubt that the earth was the medium by which sonorous vibrations were propagated, that the range of sound, under favorable circumstances, is very great indeed. But it may be asked, Is the reach of sound ever thus great in air? We have no means of answering this directly; but certain facts recorded by competent and trustworthy observers show that sound in air is sometimes, even under unfavorable circumstances, transmitted to almost incredible distances.

Chladni, for instance, tells us of meteors whose explosion was not heard until ten minutes after the appearance of the luminous globe. This would indicate that the meteor had an altitude of at least 125 miles at the time of the explosion. A meteor observed in the south of France in 1864 exhibited the same peculiarity, and the observers noted an interval of full four minutes between the appearance of the flash and the hearing of the detonation. Speaking of this subject, M. Daubrée declares that "in order that an explosion produced in air so rarefied may give rise at the earth's surface to a report of such intensity, and over such an extended area, we must admit that its violence in these high altitudes far exceeds anything with which we are acquainted here below."

The amount of matter, solid, liquid, and gaseous, put into a state of tremor by the explosions just referred to is measured by hundreds of thousands and millions of cubic miles. But although we may make some attempt to express in numbers the magnitude of the disturbance, the mind fails to grasp their full significance. No better illustration could be asked of the elasticity of the different kinds of matter which compose the earth's crust and its circumambient atmosphere, nor could we desire stronger evidence of the extreme sensitiveness of the auditory apparatus capable of appreciating, at such distances, vibratory motion that must, for individual particles, be all but infinitesimal.

In all the cases cited, however, sonorous waves are originated by titanic forces. But even when the source of sound is quite insignificant, the amount of matter set in motion is simply amazing. Thus the lark, as it rises in the air and breaks forth into its morning carol, may put into vibration many millions of cubic feet of the medium in which it warbles its notes of gladness.

But far more remarkable for their ability to impart vibratory motion to large masses of air are certain crickets, locusts, and grasshoppers. "The stridulation produced by some of the locustidæ," says Darwin, "is so loud that it can be heard at night at the distance of a mile." Calculation shows that it thus excites, according to the condition of the atmosphere, sonorous tremors in no less than from five to ten million tons of matter. And yet the insect that accomplishes this extraordinary work does not weigh more than a quarter of a pennyweight.

Facts like these bring us face to face with phenomena that seem to elude the equations and the formulæ of the mathematician, and to defy all attempt to bring them within the range of mathematical analysis. In the instance last given the magnitude of the volume of matter set in motion by a tiny, insignificant insect is something calculated to excite our astonishment. But more wonderful still, when we come to think of it, is the fact that notwithstanding the small amplitude of movement of the air particles a mile distant from the stridulating locust, the vibratory motion excited by this insignificant little insect is still competent to excite the sensation of sound. We know, indeed, that very slight, almost infinitesimal, periodic tremors are sufficient to generate sonorous pulses. Lord Rayleigh has shown that sound-vibrations may be produced when the amplitude of movement is not more than the $\frac{1}{250000000}$th part of an inch. But such reflections and calculations, far from detracting from the marvellous in the case we are considering, tend only to enhance it and to place it in a brighter light. Nothing could give us a better idea of the transcendent delicacy of the ear, nor could we have a better example of the perfect conservation and correlation of force, than that afforded by the illustration just given. But here I must close. We have again come into contact with more of those innumerable mysteries of the natural order which hitherto have baffled all attempts at their solution, and which will, most likely, ever remain as they are at present, — fascinating, yet inscrutable.

CHAPTER IV.

MUSICAL STRINGS.

REVIEWING the ground over which we have thus far travelled, we shall find that we have been dealing with only the more general laws and phenomena of sound. We are now prepared to consider, in greater detail, the laws and phenomena that are observed in connection with special forms of sonorous bodies. Most of our attention will, naturally, be given to such vibrating bodies as are used in music. Chief among these are strings, wires, reeds, bars, plates, bells, membranes, and various forms of sonorous tubes.

To-day we shall occupy ourselves in studying the very interesting phenomena which characterize the vibration of wires and strings. By the term *string*, in acoustics, we mean "a perfectly uniform and flexible filament of solid matter stretched between two fixed points." It thus includes wires as well as strings properly so-called. An acoustic string, however, is quite ideal, as no string is perfectly elastic or perfectly uniform. The most that is ever realized in the strings employed in musical instruments is a more or less close approximation to the ideal string which the mathematician has in view in all of his calculations.

From the earliest times strings have been used in the construction of musical instruments, for we have records of them that date back to the twilight of fable. Figures of what are evidently primitive forms of the harp and the lute are to be found on Egyptian monuments all along the Nile valley. Similar instruments were used by the earliest inhabitants of western Asia, as is evidenced by inscriptions found among the ruins of the great cities that once graced the plains of Chaldea and Mesopotamia. The favorite instrument of the Hindoos — the vina, resembling somewhat the guitar — was given to mankind, we are told, by Sarasvati, the benevolent consort of Brahma. And then we must recall other stringed instruments scarcely less ancient, — the kinnor and hasur and psaltery of the Israelites, and the lyre and cithar of the Greeks, not to speak of many similar instruments employed by other nations of antiquity. According to the Greeks, the lyre was invented by Apollo, while the Hebrews tell us that a similar instrument was devised by Jubal. The Egyptians attribute the glory of a like invention to Mercury. "The Nile," says Apollodorus, "after having overflowed the whole country of Egypt, when it returned within its natural bounds left on the shore a great number of dead animals of various kinds. Among the rest was a tortoise, the flesh of which being dried and wasted by the sun, nothing was left within the shell but nerves and cartilages. These, being braced and contracted by dessication, were rendered sonorous. Mercury, in walking along the banks of the Nile, happening to strike his foot against the shell of this tortoise, was so pleased with the sound it produced that it suggested to him the first idea of the lyre. This he afterwards constructed in the form of a tortoise, and strung it with the sinews of dead animals."

No attempt was made to inquire into the scientific basis of music until the time of Pythagoras, the seventh century B. C. Of this distinguished philosopher and mathematician it is said that —

> "A stream
> Of song divine stole on his raptured ears,
> And round him burst the music of the spheres."

To illustrate his theory of musical harmony, as based on numbers, he invented the monochord, — an instrument that is still employed in many investigations regarding the nature and mysteries of the tonal art.

A modified form of the instrument devised by the Greek sage is before you. It is known as the differential sonometer of Marloye, who invented it, and it differs from the monochord in that it has two strings instead of one, and is available for a greater number of experiments. We shall have frequent occasion to use it during the course of this lecture, as with it can be illustrated all the leading laws of vibrating strings. As you will observe (Fig. 42), it is constructed of a long resonant case of fir, MN, on which are stretched two wires. One of the wires, $a\ d$, is stretched between two pins, by means of a piano key, p, the other, $b,\ R$, passes over a movable pulley, and is stretched by a weight, P, which can be varied at pleasure. Near their

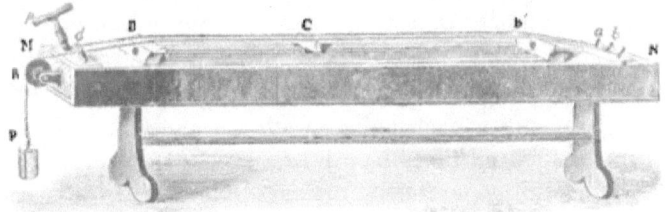

FIG. 42.

extremities these wires rest upon fixed bridges, B and B'. A movable bridge, C, rests under the wires, and permits a variation in the lengths of the vibrating parts. A scale divided into millimeters is fixed on the top of the box, and gives the length of the strings between the bridges.

I now pluck one of the strings and cause it to vibrate as a whole. It gives the lowest note it is capable of yielding with the tension to which it is at present subjected. The lowest note emitted by any sonorous body musicians call the *fundamental*, or the *prime*. By means of the movable bridge, the string is now divided into two exactly equal parts. Plucking either one of the halves, we get a note that the musicians present will recognize as the octave of the fundamental. That a string sounding an octave is only one half the length of a string emitting its fundamental, is one of the first discoveries made by Pythagoras with the monochord. By placing the movable bridge so that the string is divided into two parts whose lengths are as the numbers 2:3, he found that the sounds yielded are those that are separated by the interval known as a fifth. Thus, if the longer string gives the note C_3, the shorter one will give G_3. Continuing his experiments, he divided the string in such a way that the relative lengths of the two parts were as the numbers 3:4. Such strings he found gave the interval known as the fourth. As before, if the longer string were to sound C_3, the shorter would emit F_3.

Although the Greek philosopher made many other observations with his monochord and designed several other instruments, among which was his famous tetrachord, he does not appear to have discovered any other intervals used in modern music. If he did make such discoveries, he certainly did not employ them in his system of music. One of the most pleasing intervals in modern music was not introduced till the fifteenth or sixteenth century. It is known as the *major third*. It is obtained on the monochord by causing two strings to vibrate whose lengths are to each other as 4:5. In this instance if the longer string yields C_3, the shorter will give E_3. In lieu of this interval, Pythagoras employed one much more complicated. It is called, after its inventor, the *Pythagorean third*. The relative lengths of the vibrating strings in this interval are 64:81. True, the difference between this interval and our major third is small, — so small as scarcely to be recognized in ordinary music.

As a result of his investigations, Pythagoras discovered the law that *the simpler the ratio of the two parts into which the vibrating string is divided, the more perfect is the consonance of the two sounds*. But no explanation of this relation of simple whole numbers to musical harmony was given until the appearance of Helmholtz's great work, "Die Lehre von den Tonempfindungen," in 1859. The school of Pythagoras made the fact simply the basis of fantastic mathematical and philosophic speculations, the most famous of which was their theory regarding "the harmony of the spheres."

Full two thousand years elapsed after the time of Pythagoras before any other notable advance was made in the science of musical harmony. The subject was then taken up by one of the ablest experimenters and most profound thinkers of modern times. I allude to the illustrious Franciscan friar, Père Mersenne, who has justly been called the "Father of Acoustics."

Taking up the investigations of Pythagoras, he found that the simple harmonic intervals above mentioned demanded not only that the lengths of the strings should bear a simple ratio to each other, but also that *the ratio of vibration of these strings should be equally simple*. Thus he found that the octave vibrated with twice the rapidity of its fundamental;[1] that the fifth vibrated three times, while its fundamental vibrated twice; and that the rate of vibration of the fourth to its fundamental was as 4 to 3. In a similar manner he discovered that the same law held good for all intervals whatever. In other words, he first laid down the all-important law that *the number of vibrations in any case is inversely proportional to the length of the string*. Moreover, he was the first to demonstrate the fact that *pitch depends on the rate of vibration; that the greater the number of vibrations per second, the higher the pitch*. Going still farther, he proved that this law regarding pitch applied not only to vibrating strings, but to all sonorous bodies whatever. This was indeed a gigantic step forward, and threw new light on the mystical numbers of the Pythagoreans.

Pythagoras had made some observations on the effects of tension on vibrating strings, but does not seem to have arrived at any definite results. Mersenne took up the problem and determined the law as it now stands; namely, *the number of vibrations per second of a string is proportional to the square root of its tension*.[2] This means that if a string stretched by a weight of one pound

---

[1] *Op. cit.*, lib. i. Prop. 15; and lib. ii. Prop. 6. [2] *Op. cit.*, lib. ii. Prop. 8.

gives forth a certain note, it will yield a note an octave higher if the weight be four pounds. By making the weight nine pounds, the string will execute three times the number of vibrations, and the note produced will be the fifth of the second octave above the note emitted by the string stretched by a weight of one pound. Similarly, a weight of sixteen pounds would cause the string to vibrate four times as fast, and the resultant note would be two octaves higher than the first. Thus, if the same string be successively under a tension of one, four, nine, and sixteen pounds, and the note given by the string with one pound be C_2, the note given by the string with the other weights will be C_3, G_3, and C_4. This means that if C_2 give 128 vibrations per second, C_3, G_3, and C_4 will give 256, 384, and 512 vibrations respectively.

Continuing his experiments with strings of different thicknesses, but of the same tension, Mersenne found that any given string must be twice as thick as another in order that the thicker string may yield a note an octave lower than that emitted by the thinner one.[1]

From this and similar observations is deduced the law that *the number of vibrations varies inversely as the thickness of the string.* Thus, if two strings of the same material, length, and tension have diameters which are to each other as 2 to 1, the thicker string will execute one half the number of vibrations of the thinner one. If one string be three or four times as thick as another, it will vibrate three or four times more slowly than the one of smaller diameter.

A fourth law, which the preceding seems, in a measure, to indicate, is that, the length, thickness, and tension being the same, *the number of vibrations of a string is inversely proportional to the square root of its density.* Thus, other things being equal, if two strings, A and B, whose densities are respectively as 1 : 4, be set in vibration, A will execute twice the number of vibrations made by B. If the ratio of the densities of the two strings be 1 : 9, the

---

[1] Lib. ii Prop. 7.

lighter one will vibrate with three times the rapidity of the heavier one. The specific gravities of aluminum and copper are respectively 2.6 and 8.9, and hence their relative densities are as 1 : 3.46, nearly as 1 : 4. If, therefore, two wires, one of aluminum and one of copper, be caused to vibrate, the aluminum wire will vibrate with very nearly twice the rapidity of the copper one. Catgut and brass have specific gravities that are to each other approximately as 1 : 9. Hence, the relative frequencies of the notes yielded by two strings, one of catgut and one of brass, both being of the same length, diameter, and tension, will be as 3 : 1, — the catgut string vibrating three times as rapidly as the one of brass.

All the foregoing laws can be roughly illustrated by any stringed instrument. For their more exact verification an instrument like the sonometer is necessary. With such an apparatus, we can regulate the length and tension of the strings with the greatest ease and accuracy.

The laws of vibrating strings have been determined mathematically as well as experimentally. The first one to attempt a mathematical solution of the problem involved was the English mathematician, Brook Taylor, in 1715. His solution, however, was incomplete. Later the problem was attacked, in turn, by the ablest mathematicians in Europe. Among these were John and Daniel Bernouilli, D'Alembert, and Euler. The celebrated mathematician Lagrange eventually completed the work at which the others had so indefatigably labored.

But it was soon discovered that the results of theory and experiment did not agree. As early as 1736 Mersenne recognized the existence of this discrepancy.[1] Thus, when a string is divided into two parts, each part does not when set in motion give *exactly* the higher octave of the note emitted by it when vibrating as a whole. The higher note is *flat* by about a quarter of a tone. And the shorter the string, and the greater the diameter, the more pronounced the difference between theory and experiment.

[1] Lib. ii. Prop. 8.

When one string is twice the thickness of another, this discrepancy for the law of diameters may amount to as much as a half tone. N. and F. Savart attempted a solution of the difficulty; but although they employed every refinement in their experiments that ingenuity could suggest, and devised many special forms of apparatus in the course of their investigations, they were utterly unable to make the results of their experiments agree with the formula of the mathematician. Finally, it was pointed out that it was impossible for the experimenter to have such a string as the mathematician assumed in his calculations, — one, namely, that is *perfectly flexible*. All strings used by the experimenter are more or less *rigid*, and their rigidity, and this alone, supposing the strings to have the same diameter and homogeneity throughout, accounts for the differences observed between experiment and theory. When, however, the experiments are made with the requisite amount of care, these differences are ordinarily so small as to be scarcely recognizable.

This instance, and it is only one among many, well illustrates the difficulties, inherent in the nature of the materials at his disposal, that the man of science meets with in his investigations, and in his attempts to make the results of his experiments agree with those of calculation. Our conclusions, indeed, when based solely on experiments, are in many cases only approximately true at best, and it is impossible in the nature of things to make them other than approximate. In such cases as those under consideration our experimental results approach more nearly to truth just in proportion as they more nearly coincide with the demands of theory. If the experimenter could have at his disposal a perfectly flexible, uniform, and homogeneous string, he could without doubt make his observations conform with the formula of Lagrange, but not otherwise.

All the foregoing laws of vibrating strings are applied in the construction of the various forms of stringed instruments. Thus, in instruments like the harp and pianoforte, the strings designed to give acute sounds are short, light, and thin. Those calculated to produce graver tones are proportionately longer, heavier, and thicker. To avoid increasing the thickness of a string or making it inconveniently long, it is sometimes loaded. In the violin, for example, three of the strings are of catgut of different thicknesses, and subject ordinarily to different tensions. The fourth string is rendered heavier by a spiral of silver wire. This device obviates rigidity, and at the same time renders the notes emitted as grave as may be required. Similarly, those strings of the harp and pianoforte that are designed to sound the lower notes are weighted by being wrapped with wire.

The tensile force with which the wires of a modern pianoforte are stretched is quite surprising. It varies all the way from one to five hundred pounds. The aggregate tension of a Broadwood instrument is equal to about eighteen tons weight, while the total stress of a Steinway Grand is fully twice that amount. It is found by experiment that the greater the tension and the longer the string, within certain limits, the richer and more harmonious the tones produced. This great increase of tension necessitates a heavy framework, and hence the massiveness of our modern pianofortes.

In the pianoforte there is a separate string, or group of strings, for each note. In the harp the notes are arranged to yield the notes of the diatonic scale. These, however, can be sharpened or flattened by means of pedals. In the banjo and guitar there are only a few strings, but as the length of these may be varied by pressing them against the frets with which such instruments are provided, a comparatively large number of notes may be elicited from them. The violin and violoncello have only four strings, and yet their compass is remarkably great. In such instruments the performer must be guided by his judgment and his ear and by practice as to the amount by which a string is to be shortened for the production of any given note. He has no mechanical aids like those afforded by the guitar and the banjo, whose frets serve as a guide as to how much a string is to be shortened for any determinate case.

Besides the note which a string of any given length emits when vibrating as a whole, and which is called its fundamental note, it also gives forth certain superior tones, which are sometimes called natural harmonics. Mersenne makes special mention of them in his great work.[1] He tells us that he was able to perceive tones corresponding not only to the first and second octave above the fundamental, but also the fifth of the second octave, the major third of the third octave, and the major second of the fourth. Supposing that the string gave as its fundamental the note C, the superior tones, or natural harmonics, heard along with their fundamental by Mersenne, would in musical notation be written as follows: —

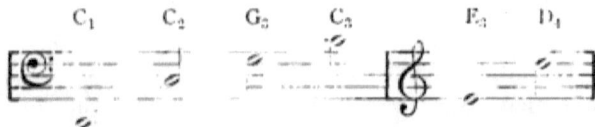

We now know — what was unknown but probably suspected in the time of Mersenne — that a string emitting a musical note rarely, if ever, vibrates as a whole without at the same time vibrating in segments which are aliquot parts of the whole. The motion of these segments is usually superposed on that of the string vibrating as a whole. For this reason *harmonics* — a term introduced by Sauveur — are more properly called *upper partial tones*, or, considering the compound nature of the note composed of the fundamental and upper partial tones, as simply *partial tones*. In this case the fundamental would be the first partial of the compound tone, the octave the second, the fifth of the second octave the third, and so on. The fundamental is, of course, ordinarily more prominent than are any of the other partial tones. Nevertheless, in certain exceptional cases some of the upper

[1] Harm., lib. ix. Prop. 33.

partials may sound louder than the prime. The pitch of the compound note heard is gauged by that of its fundamental; the quality of the tone is determined, as we shall see later on, by the number and relative intensity of the concomitant upper partials.

Mersenne's observations have been verified and explained by a number of subsequent investigators, chief among whom are D. Bernouilli, Riccati, Rameau, Sauveur, and Chladni. Rameau in 1722 attached so much importance to upper partial tones that he made them the basis of his system of musical harmony. Chladni gives a detailed explanation of them and shows that they are found in nearly all sonorous bodies, and that they are especially marked in organ-pipes, wind instruments, and bells.

Sauveur in 1701 appears to be the first to give a satisfactory explanation of the existence of upper partials. He attributes them to the string vibrating in parts, while at the same time vibrating as a whole. After showing how this can take place, he declares that "each half, each third, each fourth part of a string has its own special vibrations, while at the same time the string vibrates as a whole." And then, after enumerating the successive partials that accompany the fundamental note of a string, he observes: "It seems, therefore, that whenever Nature makes for herself, so to speak, a musical system, she employs only such sounds. Nevertheless, they have so far not been received in musical theory."

While speaking of Sauveur, I must not fail to mention what you will surely regard as a striking circumstance. He is justly regarded as one of the founders of the science of acoustics. He first applied the word *acoustics* to designate the science of sound. And yet he was mute until the age of five years, and remained almost deaf during his entire life. Hüber was blind when he carried on his wonderful investigations regarding the nature and habits of bees, which have made him one of the greatest authorities on the subject treated. Plateau, who was so distinguished for his wonderful discoveries in optics and molecular mechanics, did most of his work while deprived of sight. But even their achievements, astonishing as they are, seem to pale before those of Sauveur, who, although deprived almost entirely of the sense of hearing, was yet able to contribute more to the science of sound than any one of his age, and to detect the existence of tones that even cultivated musical ears did not recognize.

The number of upper partials that may accompany any given tone depends upon circumstances and upon the nature of the sonorous body itself. Sometimes only three or four may be detected; occasionally we may be able to demonstrate the existence of fifteen or twenty. They sometimes occur in the order of all the natural numbers, 1, 2, 3, 4, 5, etc.; at other times in the order of the odd numbers only. In the former case the first sixteen partials, beginning with C_1, as a fundamental, succeed each other as follows: —

C_1 C_2 G_2 C_3 E_3 G_3 B_3 C_4 D_4 E_4 F_4 G_4 A_4 B_4 B_4 C_5

1 2 3 4 5 6 7 8 9 10 11 12 13 14 15 16
64 128 192 256 320 384 448 512 576 640 704 768 832 896 960 1024

The seventh, eleventh, thirteenth, and fourteenth partials are, as will be observed, indicated by crotchets, while the positions of the others are shown by minims. The former do not occupy exactly the position marked, as they have not the pitch of any note used in music. Their positions, therefore, can be indicated only approximately in the ordinary musical notation.

The second row of figures below the staff shows the frequencies of the corresponding partials. Inspection will show that the frequency of each partial is some multiple of that of the fundamental.

Only the lower partials, however, are usually considered in music. Ordinarily no importance is attached to those above the fifth or sixth. As a rule they diminish in intensity as they ascend. Nevertheless, as we shall see, in some special cases, particularly in bars, bells, and tuning-forks, the higher upper partials may be so loud as to be unpleasantly sharp and piercing.

The first six partials, counting the fundamental as one, constitute in ordinary musical instruments a compound tone that is perfectly harmonious. To these may be added the eighth, tenth, twelfth, fifteenth, and sixteenth, without impairing in the least the harmony that characterizes the tone due to the combination of the six first. The seventh, eleventh, thirteenth, and fourteenth do not, as we have seen, belong to the musical scale. The eleventh and the thirteenth, together with the ninth, — D_{1}, — are discordant, and cannot be combined with the first-mentioned partials without marring the harmony which these latter yield alone. In an instrument tuned in pure intonation, — a harmonium, for instance, — the seventh and fourteenth partials, contrary to what musicians usually maintain, may be added to the six first partials, and give a compound tone of superior richness, brilliancy, and harmony.

The relative intensity of the various partials constituting a compound tone depends chiefly on the nature of the stroke, the point struck, and the rigidity, density, and elasticity of the string.

The same string will give a different sound according as it is struck or plucked or bowed. The harp and the guitar are plucked with the finger, and give a sound that is characterized by softness, richness, and the predominance of the lower partials. The zither and the mandolin are plucked with a point of wood or metal very much in the same manner as the ancient varieties of the harp were excited by the plectrum. The tones of these instruments are distinguished from those of the guitar and harp by the number and intensity of their upper partials; the sound is therefore shriller and more tinkling in character. The strings of the pianoforte are struck with soft elastic hammers of felt, and yield the pure, rich tones that contribute much to make this instrument so popular. In the best instruments, particularly when new, the first six partials predominate, to the exclusion, almost, of all higher ones. The strings of the violin family are bowed. This method of exciting vibration brings out a large number of partials, both high and low, and we have, in consequence, the sharp, full, brilliant tone of the "most perfect" of musical instruments.

The point struck or bowed always determines the presence or absence of a certain number of partials. In the pianoforte the string is struck in such a manner as to allow the formation of the first six partials, and to exclude or weaken those which are higher, — especially the seventh and the ninth, the latter of which is very discordant. To secure this result, the hammers are made to strike the string at from one seventh to one ninth — preferably one ninth — the distance from the end of the vibrating length of the string. The reason for this we shall see presently. Eliminating or weakening all partials above the sixth, there are left only such tones as enter into the formation of the major chord, because in the first six partials we have only octaves, fifths, and major thirds of the fundamental.

Again, the force and number of upper partials are greatly modified by the thickness and material of the string. Thick strings, by reason of their rigidity, do not permit the formation of very high partials, while very thin strings yield them quite readily and in great numbers. On a string of very fine iron wire Helmholtz was able to isolate the eighteenth partial tone. These high partials, however, form a series of very dissonant tones. The reason of this is because they lie so close to each other in the scale that the intervals formed are highly inharmonious. Above the eighth they are less than a whole tone apart, and above the fifteenth they are separated by an interval which is less than a semitone.

Every one has observed the difference in quality of tones emitted by metal and catgut strings. Other things being equal, a string of catgut, on account of its greater lightness, should produce higher partial tones than one of metal. But by reason of the inferior elasticity of the former, its higher partials are sooner damped than those of the latter. Hence the acute tinkling sounds that frequently characterize thin metal strings, as in the mandolin, and the comparative softness of the tones of strings of catgut, as in the harp or violin.

All the phenomena we have been discussing can be beautifully illustrated by the sonometer. But before going farther, we must examine more particularly the manner in which strings vibrate, and the way in which they subdivide so as to yield the partial tones we have been considering.

Mersenne had observed that when a string was set in vibration, a neighboring string in unison with it would also vibrate, although it might not have been touched. And he found this to be the case not only when the strings were in unison, but also when the second is an octave or a twelfth below the first. The same observation was afterwards made by Noble and Pigott at Oxford, and communicated by Wallis to the Royal Society in 1674. They showed that when the second string was two or three times the length of the first, it was divided into two or three equal vibrating segments, each segment being separated from the one adjacent by a point at rest, and each being of the same length as the vibrating portion of the first string. The existence of these points of rest was cleverly shown by placing paper riders along the string. Those on the vibrating segments were instantly thrown off, whereas those on the points of rest remained undisturbed. The tones excited by the first string in the second one are what are known as sympathetic tones, and we shall learn more of them later. What we are now more particularly interested in is the formation of the vibrating segments, and the points of rest discovered by Noble and Pigott.

In 1701 Sauveur, without any knowledge of the discoveries of the English investigators, made the same experiment in a somewhat different way. Instead of using two strings he employed but one. Bowing a string so as to cause it to emit its fundamental, and to vibrate, therefore, as a whole, he touched it with a feather at points one half, one third, and one fourth its length from one of the extremities, and he then heard the octave, the twelfth, and the second octave of the fundamental. He made evident to the eye the subdivisions of the string by means of riders, some of which were white, others black. The former were placed at the points of rest, which Sauveur called *nodes*, and the latter on the vibrating segments which he named *ventres*.

All the laws and phenomena that we have been discussing can be clearly and accurately illustrated by the sonometer.

To repeat Sauveur's experiment exhibiting the nodes and ventres, I damp the middle of one of the strings by pressing a feather gently against it, and draw the bow across one of the halves. Immediately the other half is set in vibration, as is evidenced by the paper rider being at once thrown off. In this instance we have two *ventres*, or *ventral segments*, as we shall call them, and one node which is an immovable point in the centre of the string.

Damping the string at one third of its length from one of its extremities, and exciting it as before, we have formed three ventral segments separated by two nodal points. Placing red riders on the ventral segments, and white ones on the nodes, and bowing the string as before, the red riders are cast off, while the white ones remain undisturbed.

When the string is damped at one fourth of its length from one of the fixed bridges, and the shorter segment is set in vibration, the longer one is immediately divided into three equal parts, separated by two nodes. The whole string is now made up of four ventral segments separated from each other by three nodal points. As before, the red riders on the ventral segments are all rejected, while the white ones on the quiescent nodes retain their places.

In like manner the string might be divided into five, six, or more segments, separated from each other by nodal points, and the existence of both segments and nodes could be shown in the same way as before.

If the string is sufficiently tense, and we listen to the notes emitted by these successive subdivisions, we shall find that they are the upper partials of which we have been speaking. Thus, one half of the string yields the second partial, or the octave of the fundamental, one third of the string gives the twelfth, one fourth the second octave, while the fifth and sixth subdivisions give the major third and the fifth of the second octave. More minute subdivisions would of course give higher partials.

By simply striking the string with a pencil or a small metal bar, we can evoke all these partials in such a manner as to be distinctly audible to all who are near the instrument. In this case, however, we have not only the individual partials distinct and alone, but also their fundamentals, and a number of other tones due to various subdivisions of the string. Striking the string in succession at the centres of the ventral segments corresponding to the various partials, we elicit the corresponding notes with the greatest ease. You hear others, it is true, but the partials specially excited come out with greater purity and force than any of the others, except, it may be, the fundamental, which is always present with considerable power. If the string is struck sharply at points one half, one third, one fourth, one fifth, one sixth, and one seventh of its length from one of its extremities, and then in the inverse order at the same points, the notes referred to come out from the general mass of sound in a way that is quite surprising. With a little practice, one could thus play a simple melody on a single string, without changing its tension or its length.

A series of experiments made by Young in 1800 enables us to account for the absence or the prominence of the partial tones that we have been considering. He demonstrates that if a string be excited at its middle point, the octave and all the evenly numbered partials that have nodes at this point vanish from the compound tone that is emitted. This results in a note that is hollow and nasal in character. In like manner, when the string is excited at a distance of one third its length from either of its points of attachment, the third partial is quenched, as are also the sixth, ninth, and higher multiples of the third. The tone is still hollow, but less so than when the even partials were absent. The more nearly the point of excitation approaches the end of the string, the more pronounced become the higher partials, and the poorer and more tinkling the quality of the sound produced. In general, according to Young, there are always wanting in any given compound sound, all those upper partials that have their nodes at the point of excitement. According to the researches of Ellis and Hipkins, however, this principle enunciated by Young seems to require some modification, at least for the higher partials. They found that when a pianoforte string is struck by a soft or hard hammer at a node, the corresponding partial, especially if it be one of the higher ones,—the eighth, for instance,—is not necessarily extinguished. So far, no one seems to have offered a satisfactory explanation of this singular phenomenon.[1]

In speaking of the upper partial tones as existing in any compound sound, I have spoken of them as having frequencies related to the fundamental, as the natural numbers 2, 3, 4, 5, etc., are to 1. This is the general impression both among musicians and acousticians. It was because he believed they were so related that Sauveur gave to these partials the name they still bear, *harmonics*. But it is quite rarely that the upper partials bear such relations to their fundamental. Instead of having their frequencies related to that of the fundamental as the whole numbers 2, 3, 4, 5, etc., are to 1, upper partials have, in the majority of cases, frequencies whose ratios to that of the fundamental cannot be expressed in whole numbers. This is particularly true of bars, plates, and bells, as we

---

[1] Sensations of Tone, pp. 545, 546.

shall learn in our next lecture. When the succession of partials as to their frequencies differs from the order of the natural numbers, we have what are called *inharmonic partials*, as contradistinguished from *harmonic partials*, whose frequencies are to those of the fundamental exactly as 2, 3, 4, 5, etc., are to 1.

In organ-pipes, open or stopped, and in vibrating strings, although the upper partials are not so inharmonic as those formed in bars, plates, and bells, they are far from being perfect.

Wertheim found, during his researches, that the partial tones of pipes are higher than the theoretical harmonics. Koenig, in experimenting with a certain open organ-pipe, discovered that the eighth partial tone — he calls it a *sound of subdivision* — was nearly a whole major tone higher than the true harmonic, and that, consequently, it almost coincided with the theoretical ninth harmonic partial.

In the case of strings, the upper partials would correspond to true harmonic partials, if we could have a string uniform in thickness and homogeneous in texture, and entirely devoid of rigidity. But such an ideal string cannot be obtained. In the catgut strings of a violin the irregularities in form and density are so great that one often finds a difference of a semitone, or even of a whole tone, in the notes emitted by the halves of the same string.

The difference between harmonic and inharmonic partials cannot always be detected by the ear, especially when these differences are very small; but by means of the graphical method of registering vibrations, it can always be shown to have a real existence in fact. Koenig, in Fig. 43, gives a graphic trace furnished by a steel wire in which had been simultaneously excited the fundamental and its octave. These two tones were but very slightly separated from the true interval of an octave, but though the difference was but slight, it was indicated by the continually changing form of the successive waves. The upper partial, as disclosed by the trace, was sharper, by one wave in 180, than a perfect harmonic octave. The record is divided into five parts, in order to be more easily inscribed in the text. Had the two notes constituted the interval of a theoretic harmonic octave, the waves would have remained unchanged, and the wavelet due to the upper partial would have retained the same position on the larger wave denoting the fundamental, from one end of the record to the other.

By the graphical method just illustrated, we have the means of making clear to the eye the amount by which the interval in question deviates from a true interval, while it would be difficult, if not impossible, to appreciate such difference by the ear.

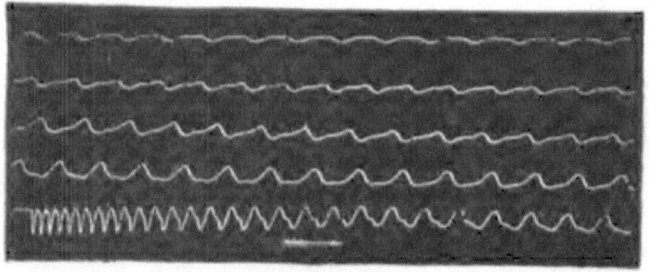

FIG. 43.

Free vibrating reeds, unlike strings and organ-pipes, may, and in most cases do, generate true harmonic partials. In the case of reeds, however, we have not such subdivisions as occur in strings and other sonorous bodies. Reeds vibrate as a whole, and their vibrations, so far as the most careful observation can determine, are perfectly simple and pendular. But strange as it may appear, these same simple pendular vibrations have the power of exciting the air in such wise as to generate compound tones. Such compound tones, as G. S. Ohm has demonstrated, the ear has the power of analyzing and resolving into a series of simple tones, each simple tone corresponding to a simple pendular vibration of the air transmitting the sound.

Some sonorous bodies — tuning-forks, for instance, which have long, thin prongs, and execute vibrations of great amplitude — may generate both harmonic and inharmonic partials. Koenig has recognized as many as five harmonic partials in tuning-forks of this kind, in addition to the usual inharmonic partials found in all forks. Long, thin strings, executing vibrations whose amplitude is very great compared with the thickness of the string, may also give rise both to harmonic and inharmonic partials. The inharmonic partials are due to subdivisions of the string, whence the name Koenig gives them of sounds of subdivision. The harmonic partials are constituents of a compound tone corresponding to a compound vibration made up of a certain number of pendular vibrations. The fact, then, that there is such a marked difference between these two kinds of tones, and the further fact that they frequently coexist in the same sonorous body and accompany the same fundamental, show clearly the necessity of carefully discriminating between them. The majority of sounds, then, employed in music have partials which, instead of being harmonic, are inharmonic. This is contrary to what is usually supposed and taught by those who are eminent both in the art and science of music, and by those, too, who are distinguished as teachers of the science of acoustics.[1]

And while speaking of this subject, it must be observed that harmonic partials, or harmonics, — as the term was understood by Sauveur, and as it is generally employed in acoustics, — are not identical with harmonics as ordinarily designated in music. In acoustics, the term *harmonics* is used to designate simple tones only, — tones, namely, that enter into the composition of a determinate compound tone. In music, on the contrary, harmonics are in nearly all cases compound tones. In the violin and harp, for example, the notes yielded when some of the aliquot parts of a string vibrate, are said to be harmonics of the notes emitted by the same string vibrating as a whole.

[1] Compare Koenig, Quelques Expériences d'Acoustique, pp. 218 *et seq.*

Let me illustrate. Suppose that under a certain tension the string on this sonometer gives the note C_1 as a fundamental. Its first sixteen partials, including its fundamental, will, as we have learned, be written in musical notation as follows: —

I.

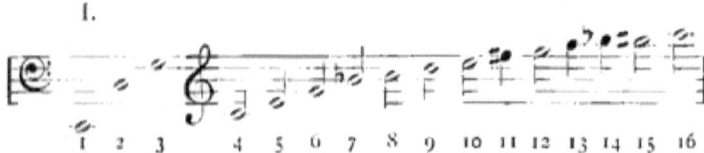

Taking one half the string, its partials, with fundamental, would be written thus: —

II.

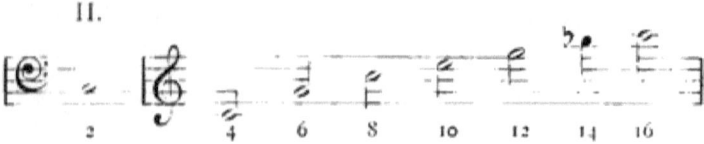

Proceeding in the same manner with one third the string, we should obtain: —

III.

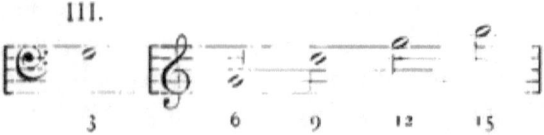

One fourth the string, for a similar reason, would give:

IV.

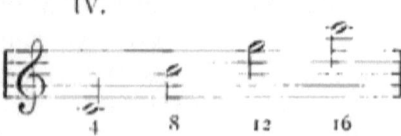

Inspection of I. and II. of the preceding diagrams will show that when only one half of a given string is set in vibration, its partials correspond only with the even partials yielded by the string vibrating as a whole. Thus, of the sixteen partials entering into the composition of the compound tone (tone emitted by the string vibrating as a whole), only those, as indicated, which in I. are numbered

2, 4, 6, 8, 10, 12, 14, 16, are found in II. When one third the string is caused to vibrate, only the odd partials of I., as shown in III., constitute the components of the resulting compound tone. When one fourth of the string vibrates, we have, as seen in IV., only half of the evenly numbered partials of I., namely, 4, 8, 12, and 16. IV., as will be observed, bears the same relation to 2, as the latter bears to I. I. has sixteen partials, II. has eight, III. has five, and IV. has four. Each note in I., II., III., IV., answers, as you remember, to what we have called a partial tone; or, to distinguish it from an inharmonic partial, each note is an harmonic partial. And all the upper partials, that is, all the partials exclusive of the fundamental, are what Sauveur called *harmonics*, and what many acousticians still denominate *harmonics*.

But the musicians' harmonics are quite different. They discard all partials, and consider only fundamentals. Thus C_2, in II., is the first harmonic of I., G_2 is the second harmonic, and C_3 the third harmonic. But as in these cases we cannot separate the partials from their fundamentals, the harmonics musicians actually refer to are compound tones, and not simple tones, as their language would seem to imply. Such being the case, the first harmonic of C_1 would not be simply C_2, but all the partials, as seen in II., which accompany this note. For a similar reason, the second harmonic would be G_2 and its four upper partials; and the fourth harmonic would be C_3 and its three upper partials. For the sake of simplicity, I have taken no account of any sounds that might be due to subdivisions of the string. These, as is obvious, would simply add other partials to the harmonics of which the musician speaks, and make them proportionally more complex.

To avoid all confusion, I shall therefore adhere to the terms *harmonic partials* and *inharmonic partials*, as already defined. This is important, as we shall avoid many errors and misconceptions that arise from confounding the two meanings so frequently given to the unqualified term *harmonic*.

It is now time to answer a question that must have already presented itself to your minds; and that is, "How can one and the same cord give rise to several sounds simultaneously?" In the case of a string, for instance, the segmental vibrations, which, alone, would yield certain partial tones, are superposed on that of the string vibrating as a whole; and those corresponding to its various segments are so combined as to yield a compound motion as a resultant. In Fig. 44 we have represented two of the simplest cases of this kind. The string $A M B$, $A C B$, when vibrating as a whole, emits only its fundamental, and while doing so does not undergo any subdivision. The string $A' M' B'$ yields simultaneously its fundamental and its first partial. In this case it assumes the form $A' C' B'$, indicated

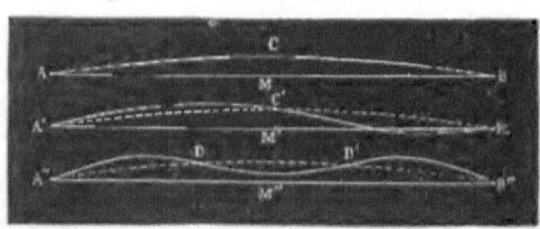

FIG. 44.

by a continuous line, — that is, while vibrating as a whole, it at the same time divides itself into two parts, $A' C'$ and $C' B'$, each of which vibrates with twice the rapidity of the whole, as would strings having one half the length of the whole. The same string, represented in $A'' M'' B''$, gives simultaneously its fundamental and its third partial. It then assumes the form $A'' D M'' D' B''$; which means that while vibrating as a whole, it is at the same time subdivided into three segments, each of which has a rapidity of motion three times as great as that of the whole string, and therefore vibrating as rapidly as would a cord one third of the length of the whole. In the latter two cases, the fundamental is represented by dotted lines, while the resultant compound tone is represented by lines which are continuous.

If a larger number of partials were superposed on the fundamental, a more complex tone would result, and the form assumed by the vibrating string in yielding such compound tone would depend on the number and relative intensity of the partials present. And if in addition to the harmonic partials, inharmonic partials were added, as is sometimes the case, the movements of the string would be still further modified.

Thus far we have been employing the sonometer in elucidating the laws of vibrating strings. We can, however, investigate them with other apparatus and from other points of view. The experiments to which your attention is now invited, beautifully corroborate those already made. They also add materially to our knowledge of the laws of vibrating strings, inasmuch as they enable us to see clearly and in a different light what we have seen only imperfectly in our experiments with the sonometer.

Chief among the phenomena to which I wish to direct your attention is that which concerns the formation of nodes and ventral segments. The illustrations so far have been on only a small scale, and none of you, except those very near the sonometer, have been able to see the nodes and ventral segments referred to, unless indirectly by the device of the riders employed.

There are various methods of rendering visible at a distance the nodes and ventral segments of vibrating strings. The first one we shall have recourse to is merely mechanical, but it is none the less instructive or beautiful.

In my hand I hold one end of the brass spiral which we used in illustrating the propagation of sound through the air or other media. The other end of the spiral is fastened to a hook in the wall at the other side of the room. By properly timing the motion of my hand, I can cause the spiral to vibrate as a whole, giving, as you see, one long vibrating segment. Doubling the rapidity of motion of my hand, the spiral also is made to vibrate with twice the rapidity it did before. This time, however, it does not vibrate as a whole, but divides itself into two ventral segments, separated from each other by a stationary node. Trebling or quadrupling the rapidity of motion of the hand causes the spiral to divide itself into three or four segments, separated by a corresponding number of nodes. By moving the hand yet more rapidly, I can still further increase the number of subdivisions. There are ten of them now, each segment presenting the appearance of a gauzy spindle, and separated from its neighbor by a dark and apparently motionless node.

I say "apparently motionless," because, as a matter of fact, the node is never a point of no motion, otherwise the formation of vibrating segments would be impossible. But the amplitude of vibration of the node, in comparison with that of the ventral segment adjoining, is ordinarily so small that the node seems to be a point of absolute rest. By moving my hand through a very small distance, an inch or so, I can give to the ventral segment of the spiral an amplitude of motion equal to a foot or more. The same result might be accomplished if the part held in the hand were to have a transverse motion of only the fraction of an inch. The motion at the point clasped by the hand soon accumulates at the ventral segments to such an extent that their amplitude of vibration far exceeds that of the point held by the hand. And what holds true of the part grasped by the hand — which is in reality a node — holds true of the various nodes separating the ventral segments from each other.

At the end of the wire attached to the hook in the wall is also a node, for it is customary to regard both ends of a vibrating string as nodes. At the fixed end of the wire, however, no motion is necessary, for the pulse sent along the spiral from the hand is, on reaching this point, reversed in position and direction, and returned to its starting-point in accordance with the laws of reflection.

But in all cases, be it observed, the period of my hand must be the same as that of the vibrating spiral. If it is not so, if the impulses given are not properly timed, if the period of the hand does not synchronize with that of the spiral, it will be impossible to produce the subdivisions alluded to, or to secure the perfectly uniform motion and beautiful results you have just witnessed. With a little practice, however, one can so time the motion of the hand as to bring out with comparative ease and readiness the various segmental motions that we have been illustrating.

Instead of imparting motion by the hand we might impart it by any mechanical contrivance whatever. But by far the most interesting and instructive method is that due to M. Melde, of Marburg. Tuning-forks were employed

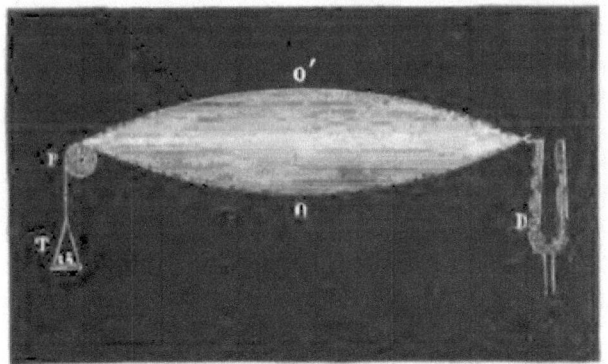

Fig. 45.

by him to generate the initial impulses necessary for the production of the vibrating motions which we have just been studying. And as his method at the same time illustrates in a most striking manner the formation of nodes and ventral segments, it affords us a new means of verifying the different laws of vibrating strings as determined by the sonometer.

Before you are four tuning-forks, C_2, C_3, G_3, C_4, whose frequencies are 128, 256, 384, and 512 vibrations per second. Their relative rates of vibration are therefore as the numbers 1, 2, 3, 4. To the prong D of C_2 (Fig. 45 is fastened, by means of a small hook, one of the extremities of a small silk cord, $O\,O'$. The other extremity passes over a pulley, P, and has attached to it a scale-pan,

T, for carrying weights, which can be increased or decreased at pleasure. Setting the fork in vibration, its motion is communicated to the string, and it is found that with a certain tension and a determinate length of string, the string vibrates as a whole.

Substituting the fork C_3, for C_2, and keeping the stretching weights the same, we find that the length of the string that will now vibrate as a whole is only one half of what it was for C_2. Employing in turn the forks G_2 and C_4, and retaining the same tension as before, we discover that the length of the strings required are respectively one third and one fourth of what was necessary for C_2. The relative frequencies of the forks, as stated, are as the numbers 1, 2, 3, 4. The relative lengths of the strings set in vibration by these forks are, as we have just seen, the reciprocals of these numbers, namely, $1, \frac{1}{2}, \frac{1}{3}, \frac{1}{4}$. Hence, by this novel method we have corroborated experimentally the truth of the law already established, which is that *the number of vibrations is inversely proportional to the length of the string.*

We may now repeat the experiment in another way. This time we shall keep the tension constant, as in our previous experiment, and instead of varying the length of string for the various forks as before, we shall retain the same length of string for the four forks. With the fork C_2, the string vibrates as a whole, and gives, as you see, but one segment (Fig. 44). With the fork C_3, however, the case is different. The vibrations of this fork being twice as rapid as those of C_2, the cord must divide into two segments, as in Fig. 46, I, in order that it may synchronize with the increased number of vibrations by which it is actuated. Substituting G_2 for C_2, the string, in order to accommodate itself to the period of the fork, breaks into three segments, separated by two nodes, as in Fig. 46, II. In like manner, and for a similar reason, the fork C_4 would cause the string to vibrate in four segments, separated by three nodes. The number of ventral segments of the string is therefore in proportion to the number of vibrations of the fork with which it is connected.

The number of ventral segments may also be varied by retaining the same fork and length of string, and changing the weights. If with any given weight the string vibrate as a whole, it will, with one fourth of this weight, divide itself into two segments, and with one ninth the weight it will form three segments. And in general, whatever the diminution of the weight, it will always be found that the number of ventral segments will be inversely proportional to the square root of the tension.

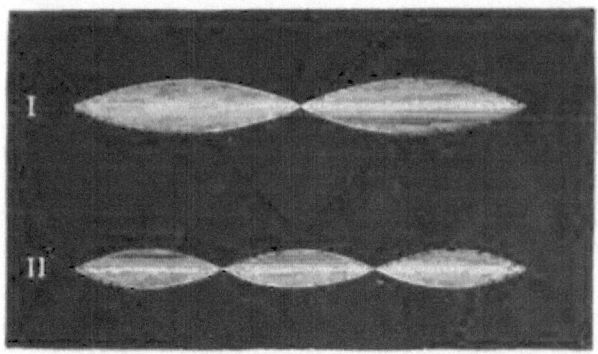

FIG. 46.

Taking again the forks C_2 and C_3, let us attach to them two strings of the same length and diameter. Stretching the string fastened to C_2 with a weight of one gram, it vibrates as a whole. Making the tension of C_3 equal to four grams, it also vibrates as a whole. The number of vibrations of C_3 is, as you know, just twice that of C_2, and yet in both cases we have but one ventral segment. But to obtain this result the tension of C_3 must be four times that of C_2. Hence the law established by the monochord: *the number of vibrations of a string is proportional to the square root of its tension.*

So far we have been considering the case of vibrations given to the cord by motions of the fork which are parallel with the length of the cord. Here we have the *longitudinal* vibrations of the fork changed into *transverse* vibrations in the cord. A brief examination of the manner in which the fork communicates its motion to the cord will reveal how this change of longitudinal into transverse vibration is effected. By referring to Fig. 45 one will see that when the prong D of the fork moves towards the pulley P, the cord will relax and reach the position O. When, however, the prong of the fork returns to its original position, the cord will do the same. A second excursion of the prong of the fork towards the pulley will cause the cord to move to O', and when the prong returns to the point from which it started, the cord will again go back to its position midway between O and O'. The fork, therefore, executes two complete vibrations while the cord

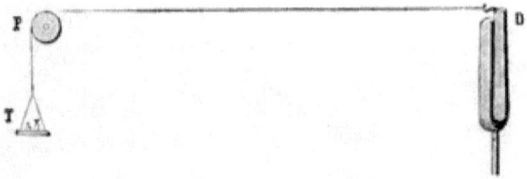

FIG. 47.

makes only one. If, then, the cord could emit a tone, such tone would be an octave below that produced by the fork.

If now we turn the fork through a right angle, as in Fig. 47, the vibrations will be executed in a direction transverse to that of the cord. Each time the fork moves backward or forward, it is followed by the cord. The number of vibrations of the latter are, in consequence, the same as those of the former. And if the frequency of the vibrations were high enough to render them audible, the notes given by the fork and the cord would be in unison.

To exhibit these phenomena we shall use a large electrically mounted fork devised by Mercadier. The advantage of using such a fork is that we can have vibrations of uniform amplitude continued for any length of time desired; and then, by regulating the strength of the current, we can obtain ventral segments of great or small width of swing, as may best suit our purpose.

Such a fork is before you. Attached to one of the prongs are two silk cords, one of which, A, is in the direction of the vibrations of the fork, and the other, B, is perpendicular to this direction. Both cords pass over pulleys, and are stretched by weights of equal mass. I now determine by trial what length the string A, with the tension to which it is subjected, must have, in order to vibrate as a whole. After some adjusting, I find the length is five feet. The vibrating portion of the string B is also made five feet in length. The forks are now set in vibration by causing the current from a good-sized Grenet cell to pass through the electro-magnet that is held in place between the two prongs of the fork. Immediately both cords take up the motion imparted by the fork. But behold! while A vibrates as a whole, and forms only one ventral segment, B undergoes instantaneous subdivision, and forms two segments, each of which is just one half the length of that furnished by A.

If we diminish the tension of A until a certain point, the string will form two segments in place of the one it had before. Lessening the tension of the string B in the same proportion, we have four segments in place of two. When we relax both strings still further, keeping the weights the same in both cases, A is thrown into three, and B into six, segments. Continuing to decrease the stretching weight of the two cords, we get in succession four, five, six, and more, ventral segments for A, and always, simultaneously, just twice the number of segments for B.

If now we attach a third cord, C, to the same prong to which the other two are fastened, and give it the same length and tension which A and B have, and place it midway between the two latter,—having it thus make an angle of forty-five degrees with its fellows,—it will, on being made to vibrate, have a compound motion made up of vibratory movements which characterize A and B. If the cords A and B vibrate in such a manner as to form one and two segments respectively, one being the octave of the other, *C* will vibrate with a motion which is the resultant of the other two components. I, II, III (Fig. 48), exhibit some of the forms which the string *C* assumes when under the joint influence of the movements which actuate *A* and *B*.

If instead of having one and two segments, as in the previous case, *A* and *B* have respectively one and three segments, the superposition of these two motions, as seen in *C*, would have a new form. Such a form would distinguish the interval of the twelfth, as the preceding forms

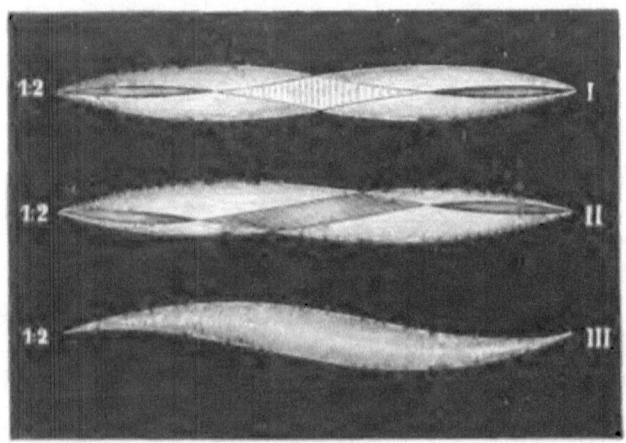

FIG. 48.

do that of the octave. In both cases the forms produced disclose the two component motions. With some experience, one could readily unravel forms of much greater complexity.

Before you is a most ingenious apparatus, contrived by M. Schwedoff, of Odessa, for illustrating the motions of cords such as we have just been investigating. It is far more convenient for the purpose than anything else with which I am acquainted, and besides it is universal in its action. As you will observe (Fig. 49), it is composed of a heavy metal stand supporting a board *P*, at one end of which is an electro-magnet, *E*. Above the board is a black graduated bar of wood one metre in length. In front of the bar is stretched a white silk cord attached to C and to the little spring armature of the electro-magnet E. By means of a milled-headed screw, T, the tension of the cord can be modified with the greatest facility.

The current from a small Grenet cell near by is now allowed to pass through the magnet, and at once the little spring is set in vibration. In its present position the motion of this spring is parallel to the length of the string, and consequently the frequency of the spring is one half that of the vibrating armature. By loosening the screw that holds the magnet to the board P, and turning the magnet through an angle of ninety degrees, which can be done without changing the length of the cord, the vibra-

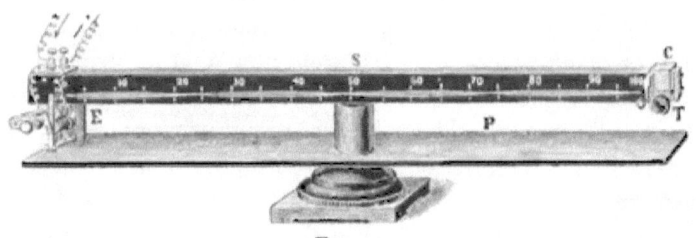

FIG. 49.

tions of the spring become perpendicular to the length of the string. This is at once revealed by the number of ventral segments, which is just twice what it was before.

Loosening or tightening the screw P, the number of segments is augmented or diminished at will. With the tension now applied to the string it vibrates as a whole. Gradually relaxing the tension, the number of segments increases, until there are now twelve or fifteen. Only with certain tensions, however, do we get perfectly defined segments. When the string has not the required tension, there is only an irregular flutter distinguishable, in place of the beautiful gossamer spindles and the stationary nodes otherwise observable.

By moving the magnet so as to give it a position intermediate between the positions which it occupied before, we get the compound motion afforded us by the large electric tuning-fork with which we were experimenting a few moments ago.

But the beauty and complexity of the forms now produced are much greater than any we have yet seen. By modifying the tension of the cord, or the position of the magnet, or both, we are able to produce an almost endless variety of gauzy forms of the most marvellous symmetry and delicacy.

Placing the magnet in such a position that it gives simple, well-defined ventral segments, and loading one section of the cord with a small white bead, we have at once a beautiful illustration of the effect of augmenting the density of the string. It vibrates in segments as before; but, as you will observe, the weighted segment is much shorter than the one that has no extraneous load to carry. Adding another bead, or replacing the one now on the string with a heavier one, would make the ventral segment which carries it still shorter. The relative lengths of the loaded and unloaded segments can be read off at a glance on the graduated metre scale before which the cord vibrates.

By means of our little white bead we are able also to make another interesting observation in connection with the manner in which strings vibrate, especially when under the influence of two or more vibratory movements.

When the string vibrates in a direction parallel to that of the cord, the latter moves almost in a vertical plane. When the spring's motion is at right angles to the length of the cord, the vibrations of the latter are in a plane that is nearly horizontal. Looking at the bead, brightly illuminated, when the cord is vibrating either in a vertical or a horizontal plane, its path is found to be a simple straight line. Turning the magnet around, however, so as to compound the cord's parallel and transverse motions, we get quite different results. Instead of moving in a straight line, the bead now describes curves of various forms and degrees of complexity. Sometimes we have circles, sometimes ellipses, sometimes the figure 8. These curves are modified by the superposition of smaller vibrations on that answering to the vibration of the string as a whole, and then their outlines are broken by loops and sinuosities which give rise to constantly changing figures of indescribable beauty.

These figures were first observed by Dr. Thomas Young, who obtained them by allowing a ray of sunlight to strike a wire on the pianoforte. The point thus illuminated described, when the wire was caused to vibrate, figures which were in many cases identical with those obtained with the apparatus before you. Some of the curves given under such circumstances are shown in Fig. 50. We shall see in the sequel that the quality of tone depends on the form of the sonorous wave. It is manifest, then, that even when

FIG. 50.

the tension, length, and material of a vibrating string remain the same, the tones elicited from it may vary in quality, just as its vibratory motions may vary. This is strikingly illustrated by the tones obtained from a violin by a beginner and by a virtuoso. Although the string emitting a given note may remain unchanged as to tension, length, and material, the sound produced is in the one case peculiarly rasping and scratching in character, while in the other case it is remarkable for great purity, steadiness, and volume. The bowing, and the motions of the string consequent on the bowing, are the sole causes of the great difference in the quality of the tones in question.

Thus far we have been considering the *transverse* vibrations of cords. We may now study their *longitu-*

dinal vibration, and learn in what respect one kind differs from the other.

The sonometer affords us a ready means of obtaining and examining these longitudinal vibrations. Taking a piece of chamois leather on which is strewn some finely powdered resin, and passing it to and fro along the wire, I cause it to yield a loud pure note. Placing the movable bridge in the centre of the wire, and rubbing one of the halves of the wire, I elicit a note that is an octave higher than that elicited when the string was excited as a whole. Rubbing in succession one third and one fourth the length of the wire, we obtain the twelfth and the fifteenth (or second octave) of the fundamental. We thus find that the law for longitudinal vibrations is the same as that for transverse vibrations; namely, that *their number is inversely as the length of the vibrating string*.

Let us change the tension of the string first by augmenting, and then by diminishing, the stretching weight. This, as you observe, has no appreciable effect on the pitch of the note emitted. The reason is that longitudinal vibrations do not depend on the tension applied to the wire, unless the tension be very great, but on the elasticity of the wire itself. The tone, moreover, within certain limits, at least, is independent of the diameter of the wire or string. These facts can be well illustrated with the three catgut strings of a violin. Passing the bow successively along the direction of these strings, we observe no appreciable difference in the pitch of the tones produced. And unless the tension is very greatly modified, it is impossible to detect any difference of pitch due to tension. Thus the E_4 string of the violin gives, when set in longitudinal vibration, a note approximating F_6. If now the tension of the string be so diminished that the note due to its transverse vibration becomes E_3,—a fall of an octave,—we shall find that the pitch of the note due to the longitudinal vibration of the string is almost the same as it was before. As a matter of fact, the fall is hardly equal to a comma,—the smallest interval used in music.

From the fact that a cord cannot execute transverse vibrations without undergoing a change in length, it is obvious that such transverse vibrations must in all cases be accompanied by longitudinal vibrations. These longitudinal vibrations may sometimes be recognized in the A string of the violoncello.

More than this. It is found that in addition to the transverse and longitudinal vibrations executed by all strings, whether bowed or plucked, they likewise have a third motion, which Chladni called *turning* or *rotary*. The vibrations peculiar to this motion are executed through a small arc of a circle around the axis of the string, and are alternately in opposite directions. They are ordinarily known as *torsional* vibrations, because they are due to a greater or less twisting of the string. But such vibrations have a mathematical rather than a musical interest.

As will be remarked, the notes due to longitudinal are much more acute than those due to transverse vibrations. Hence the importance on the part of the violinist of using the bow in such a manner as to produce only transverse vibrations; as in the event of his exciting longitudinal vibrations simultaneously with the former, the result would in most cases be in the highest degree discordant.

From what has been said regarding the vibration of strings it is manifest that there may be an infinite variety of tones evoked from the same string. But as these tones differ from each other so slightly, the majority of them appeal even to the most sensitive and highly cultivated musical ears as one and the same sound. It is as impossible for the musician to distinguish the various tones produced as it is for the geometer to analyze the amazingly complex curves to which this infinitude of tones corresponds.

CHAPTER V.

VIBRATION OF RODS, PLATES, AND BELLS.

IN our last lecture we considered the laws which govern, and the phenomena which characterize, the vibrations of strings. To-day we shall devote the time at our disposal to the discussion and illustration of the vibrations of rods, plates, and bells. And as the subject is so very comprehensive, we shall be obliged to confine ourselves chiefly to the examination of such matters as are connected directly or indirectly with the science of music, and of special interest, therefore, not only to those who are interested in the science of music, but also to those who desire information regarding certain mysterious points bearing on the art of music.

It is still a moot point as to which were the first forms of musical instruments used by our race. Stringed instruments, as we saw in our last lecture, were employed at a very early period. Playing on pipes probably antedated the use of stringed instruments. Nevertheless, if we may judge by analogy based on the customs of the barbarous nations of our own time, we should infer that instruments of percussion were first introduced; that these were followed by wind instruments; and that stringed instruments were the last in the order of time with every people, whether ancient or modern.

Pieces of bone and bars of wood and metal readily lend themselves to the production of musical notes, and for this reason the first musical instruments invented by prehistoric man were probably not unlike the various rude harmonicas which are in vogue in our own day in different parts of Asia and Africa. In some places pieces of bone or rock are employed, in others pieces of wood or metal. In Java the principal music of the natives is produced by various forms of harmonicas and gongs. When the rods of such harmonicas are made of the outer silicious layers of the bamboo, and reinforced by resonators, as is frequently the case, the notes yielded are wonderfully full and pure. And what is true of Java applies in great measure to Siam, China, and Japan. Here instruments of percussion predominate over all other kinds. Tomtoms of all forms and sizes, cymbals, wooden clappers, bars and plates of wood or metal, and gongs of every shape or design, are the chief instruments that go to make up the ordinary orchestra of these semi-barbarous nations of the Orient. The deep booming thunder of their large drums, and the sharp rattle of their smaller ones, seem to possess a charm for Chinese and Japanese ears which makes them prefer instruments of percussion to either stringed or wind instruments.

The vibrations of rods, like those of strings, have been very carefully studied both mathematically and experimentally. D. Bernouilli in 1741 was the first to attempt a mathematical solution of the problem involved in the transverse vibrations of rods. Nevertheless it was reserved for the illustrious mathematician Euler to give the first satisfactory answer to the difficulty propounded. Later on, the problem was taken up and further developed by other mathematicians scarcely less eminent. Among those whose mathematical contributions to the subject are especially notable were Riccati, Poisson, Cauchy, Strehlke, Lissajous, and A. Seebeck.

The first one to attack the problem experimentally with any success was one who has immortalized himself by his experiments and researches in the domain of acoustics. — Ernst Florens Friedrich Chladni, a German physicist, whose work, "Die Akustik," published in 1802, is still justly regarded as a classic. We shall learn more of the character of his achievements when we come to study the nature of vibrating plates, to which, for many years, Chladni gave especial attention.

In studying the laws governing the transverse vibrations of rods, we must carefully distinguish the various ways in which such rods may be held or supported. There are six cases, all told, which may present themselves. Either one end may be fixed and the other free; or one end may be supported and the other fixed; or one end supported and the other free. Or, again, both extremities of the rod may be supported or fixed in a holder of some sort, or free. Of these six cases, however, we shall consider only the first and the last; namely, that of rods having one extremity free, and the other fastened to a support, or that of a rod having both extremities free. I choose these two cases, as they are the only ones that have been utilized in practical music.

The first case, then, that shall occupy our attention is that of a rod fixed at one end and free at the other. In a vice we have strongly clamped a rod like the one used in our first lecture (Fig. 1) to illustrate the nature of vibratory motion. I draw the free end of the rod from its position of equilibrium to the point a. On being liberated it oscillates about its former position of equilibrium, and executes a series of perfectly isochronous vibrations of gradually diminishing amplitude. The vibrations in this case, unlike those of strings, are not sustained by external tension applied to the rod, but by the elasticity of the material of the rod itself. The rod is now so long that the vibrations it executes may easily be counted. As they are only three or four per second, they are of course inaudible. But if the length of the vibrating portion of the rod is diminished, the number of oscillations is augmented. They are now sufficiently numerous to yield a distinctly audible sound. By means of the graphical method of registering the number of vibrations, or by means of the siren or a tuning-fork, we could determine exactly the number of oscillations the rod is now executing. Let us suppose that the number is 32, corresponding to the note C_{-1}. If, now, we diminish the length of the rod by one half, and again excite it, you observe that a note much higher in pitch than the last is the result. If we were to determine the rate of vibration of the rod by any of the methods just mentioned, we should find that it is now making four times as many vibrations as it did before. The note yielded is consequently the second octave above C_{-1}, and corresponds to C_2, 128 vibrations per second. Making the rod one third as long as it was when it gave the note C_{-1}, the number of vibrations is rendered ninefold greater. The note now emitted is D_3, of 288 vibrations. If one fourth the rod were caused to vibrate, it would execute sixteen times as many vibrations as before; if one fifth entered into vibration, the number of oscillations would be twenty-five times greater than it was when it emitted the first note.

According to theory, the number of vibrations per second is inversely proportional to the square of the length of the vibrating part of the rod. Acting on the supposition that theory and experiment agreed in this case, Chladni constructed a tonometer made of bars, whose rates of vibration were determined as above. With this he hoped to be able to determine the rate of vibration of any sonorous body whatever. More exact investigations, however, have shown that the results given by experiment only approximate those demanded by theory. Chladni's tonometer, therefore, could not be relied upon when it was desirable to make anything like exact measurements.

In another vice near the one I have been using, there is fastened a strip of steel terminating in a disk at its free end, which beautifully illustrates the principle of Chladni's tonometer. It was made for me by Herr Appun, of Hanau, and is designed for determining the lowest audible number of vibrations. The vibration-numbers marked on the strip run from 4 to 24. But the vibrations corresponding to any given length of the strip were determined by means of some of the exact measurements above indicated, and not by the method proposed by Chladni. The results afforded by this little strip are as satisfactory as the instrument is simple. For the purpose of determining the lowest limit of audible sounds it replaces admirably the more costly and complicated apparatus which were employed in the second lecture.

Small rods, fastened at one end and free at the other, are used in the construction of the so-called nail-fiddle, or *violon de fer*. Such an instrument is on the table before you. As you observe, it is composed of a number of rods of steel arranged in the form of a semicircle on a resonant case. Their lengths are so regulated, according to the law just enunciated, that when excited by a bow they give the notes of the gamut. The tones emitted are far from being disagreeable, and with a little practice one could make this homely little instrument yield fairly good music.

Music-boxes are constructed on the same principle. In them, however, the rods of the *violon de fer* are replaced by plates or tongues of steel. These are placed side by side like the teeth of a comb on a common base, and are of various lengths, according to the notes they are designed to produce. Those which yield the lowest notes are loaded with some extraneous material, so that they may thereby vibrate more slowly. A cylinder provided with teeth suitably arranged is kept in motion by clockwork. Each tooth raises one of the steel tongues and sets it in vibration. The air played will obviously depend on the manner in which the teeth are distributed on the cylinder's surface.

The reeds used in harmonicas, concertinas, mouth-harmonicas, accordions, organs, and other instruments of music, operate in essentially the same manner as the tongues of the music-box and the rods of the nail-fiddle. In all these instruments the vibrating element is free at one end and fixed at the other. They vary simply in length, thickness, and the manner in which they are set in vibration.

The *guimbarde*, or "jews-harp," instead of a reed or tongue, has a long spring, which is set in vibration by striking its free end with the forefinger. The fundamental note it yields is modified by the various forms assumed by the cavity of the mouth; hence the peculiar variations of tone which characterize the instrument.

In none of the instruments thus far spoken of has any reference been made to any other notes than the fundamental. True, like the notes of most other sonorous bodies, the tones of the rods, tongues, and reeds spoken of are more or less compound tones; but in all cases it is the fundamental that determines the pitch of the note heard.

It is now time for us to turn our attention more directly to the consideration of the upper partial tones that rods and bars are competent to produce. Our first experience will show us that there is a very marked difference between these tones and those afforded by vibrating strings. In the case of strings, as you remember, the order of the partial tones was practically that of the natural numbers 1, 2, 3, 4, 5, 6, etc., and for this reason, as was stated, they are called harmonic partials. The upper partials of vibrating rods follow quite a different order, and have anything but a harmonious relation to their fundamental. Hence, as said before, they are termed inharmonic partials.

The frequency of a rod vibrating as a whole as compared with that of its first subdivision — that is, the frequency of its fundamental as compared with its first upper partial — is very nearly as the square of 2 is to the square of 5, or as 4 : 25. After the first subdivision of the rod, the rates of vibration, and consequently the frequencies of the notes produced, are approximately as the squares of the odd numbers 3, 5, 7, 9, 11, etc. For this reason the pitch of the upper partials in rods rises far more rapidly than does that of the partials of vibrating strings.

Supposing the rod vibrating as a whole to yield the note C_{-1}, Chladni gives for the first six partials, including the fundamental, the following series of notes, together with their relative rates of vibration and the order in which they occur: —

C_{-1}	$G\sharp_2$	D_4	D_5-	E_5	F_6+
1	$6\frac{1}{4}$	$17\frac{1}{3}$	$34\frac{1}{4}$	$56\frac{1}{4}$	84
$(1.2)^2$	3^2	5^2	7^2	9^2	11^2

According to theory, partial tones, commencing with the third, succeed each other exactly in the order of the squares of the odd numbers, the relative frequency of the fundamental being $(1.194)^2$, and that of the second being $(2.989)^2$.

The minus sign after D_5, and the plus sign after F_6, indicate that the number of vibrations in these two cases does not correspond exactly with any fixed musical notes. In the former case the number of vibrations is less than C_5, and in the latter greater than F_6. A little arithmetical computation will show that the theoretic and observed values above given are by no means identical. In some instances, indeed, they differ by quite an appreciable quantity. But this should not surprise us, as we have found in other similar instances how difficult it is to get the results of experiment to coincide with those required by theory.

Chladni viewed the tuning-fork as vibrating like an ordinary bar free at both ends. The only difference between the two, in his estimation, was that the former was bent, the latter straight. But the law of succession of the upper partial tones and the absolute number of vibrations of the fundamental of a tuning-fork show that its mode of vibration resembles rather that of a rod fixed at one end and free at the other. When the fork vibrates so as to emit its fundamental tone, it forms two nodes, one at the base of each branch, as shown in Fig. 51. Each of these nodes represents exactly the point of attachment of a rod fixed at one end and free at the other. The part of the fork intermediate between the two nodes, to which the stem is attached, vibrates in unison with the two branches, and when fixed to a resonant case sets it in vibration also. When a fork emits its first upper partial, whose frequency, as in a rod fixed at one end, is $6\frac{1}{4}$ times that of the fundamental, it has four nodes, as shown in the second diagram of the subjoined figure. But when the fork vibrates so as to yield its third partial, it possesses six nodes, and the frequency of the partial, as indicated in the figure exhibiting its mode of division, is $17\frac{1}{2}$ times that of its fundamental. The nodes and ventral segments in all the three cases illustrated in the figures are precisely the same as those of simple vibrating rods yielding the same partials. The upper partials of a tuning-fork, then, succeed each other according to the law which governs the same notes in the case of a simple fixed rod, and the frequencies of these upper partials, in both cases, have the same ratios to their primes.

It would nevertheless be a mistake to infer from what has been said that the upper partials of tuning-forks have

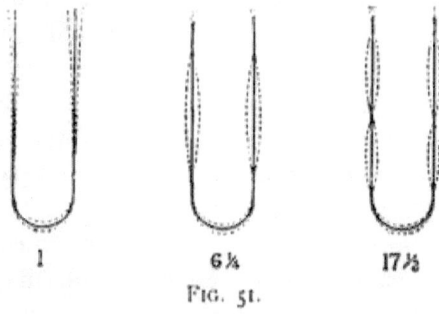

FIG. 51.

always the same pitch as compared with their fundamentals. Such is by no means the case. In a number of forks examined by Helmholtz, the first inharmonic partial executed between 5.8 and 6.6 as many vibrations in a given time as the fundamental. The number will vary slightly, according to the form of the fork and the material of which it is made.

Before you are three tuning-forks mounted on resonant cases. The largest one, which we shall here regard as the fundamental, is C_2, executing 128 vibrations per second; the second one is G_4, the sixth partial of C_2, making 768 vibrations per second; and the third one corresponds to the seventh partial, and executes 896 vibrations per second.

The larger fork is now struck so as to elicit its first upper partial. You hear it loud and clear. The second fork, G_1, is next excited, so as to yield its prime tone, and you will perceive that its pitch is very nearly that of the upper partial of the large fork. But there is a difference of several vibrations, as is disclosed by the beats that are heard. The prime tone of the third fork is compared in a similar manner with the upper partial of the first fork, and, as before, we get very distinct beats. But now they are much more numerous than with the other fork. This shows that the first upper partial of the large fork more nearly approaches the note emitted by the fork G_1 than that yielded by the fork giving the seventh harmonic partial of C_2. In other words, the frequency of the first upper partial of the large fork is more nearly six than seven times the frequency of its fundamental. By counting the number of beats made by the fork G_1 when sounding with the first upper partial of C_2, — and this could be done with little difficulty, as the beats are not rapid, — we could determine exactly the frequency of the first partial of the fork C_2 as compared with its prime.

Again, two forks which are identical in appearance, and whose fundamentals are in perfect unison, may, and generally do, give rise to beats when the same upper partials are educed. Here are two forks, each making exactly 512 vibrations per second, and therefore in perfect unison. If we excite the forks in such a way as to bring out their first upper partials, beats are at once heard, due to a want of unison on the part of these upper partials. The second set of upper partials might be excited in a similar manner, and the results would be the same.

Ordinarily when a tuning-fork is set in vibration, one hears in addition to the prime tone, one or more of its upper partials. But these are in most instances very evanescent as compared with the fundamental. If, however, the fork is excited at a point near the centre of the ventral segment corresponding to the first upper partial, this partial will be generated with exceeding purity and intensity. In like manner the second partial may be brought out so as almost to quench all other tones. By means of the graphical method it is easy to show the co-existence

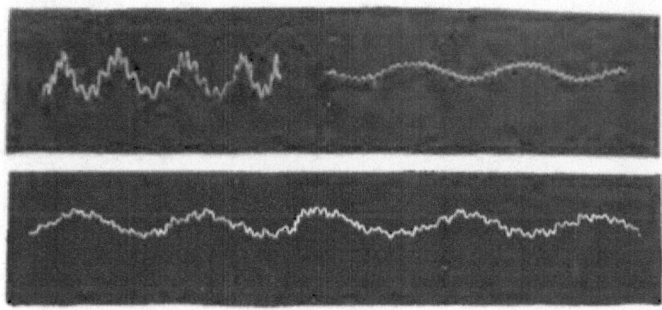

FIG. 52.

of these partial tones of a tuning-fork. In Fig. 52 we have traces corresponding to the fundamental and its first upper partial, as also to the fundamental and its first two upper partials.

The second case in which bars and rods are used in music is where they are free at both extremities. Fig. 53 shows how such bars may be supported. As will be noticed, the bar CD rests on two triangular pieces, A and B, which are ordinarily of wood or cork. The simplest division of the bar, corresponding to its gravest note, — its fundamental, — is here

FIG. 53.

represented. The two nodes, N and N', are situated at the points of contact of the two supports. Dotted lines indicate the ventral segments of the bar when in a state of vibration. As will be observed, the bar, when vibrating, divides itself into three segments of unequal lengths, the two extremities being a little less than one half as long as the middle segment, or 2:5. The two ends vibrate about the nodal points, N and N'. The intervening portion executes a movement of totality, as would a cord if attached at the points N and N'. Besides the one indicated, the bar can also assume other subdivisions, to each of which will correspond a higher partial tone. The number of nodes in such a vibrating bar, beginning with the fundamental note, are in the order of the numbers 2, 3, 4, 5, 6, 7, etc. Chladni was the first to determine the musical relation of the partial tones corresponding to the different modes of subdivision of a bar or rod. The following table gives the result of his investigations: —

Number of nodes.	2	3	4	5	6	7
Frequencies of the notes emitted — corresponding approximately to the squares of the odd numbers	$(3)^2$	$(5)^2$	$(7)^2$	$(9)^2$	$(11)^2$	$(13)^2$

The laws of vibration of a rod free at both ends, and of one free at one end and fixed at the other, are identical for all the partial tones except the fundamental. The prime of a rod free at both ends is higher than that of the same rod fixed at one end, in the ratio of 25 : 4.

Rods or bars free at both ends are used in the construction of an instrument called by the French a *claque-bois*.

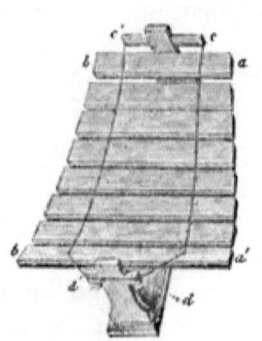

Fig. 54.

It is also known as a xylophone. Such an instrument (Fig. 54) is before you. It is, as you see, composed of a series of bars, $a b$ to $a' b'$, of wood of different lengths and thicknesses, and so tuned as to yield the notes of the gamut. The bars are held together by two cords, $c d$ and $c' d'$, passing through their two nodes. The notes which the bars are capable of yielding are educed by striking them with a small hammer.

Near by is a larger and more elaborate instrument, made of pieces of harder and more resonant wood. In this case the billets of wood are supported at their nodes on ropes made of straw, whence the name "straw-fiddle," which the instrument sometimes bears. Metal and glass rods and strips, and even bars of slate or other compact varieties of rock, are occasionally substituted for bars of wood. On the table are two instruments, in which the sonorous bars are made of steel. They are known as metallophones, and are sometimes employed to give brilliancy and color to band and orchestral music. When pieces of glass or rock are used as the vibrating material, the instruments are called glass or rock harmonicas.

The xylophone is apparently becoming more popular daily. It is frequently employed in orchestras for short solos with pleasing effect. Mozart introduced it into his opera of "Die Zauberflöte" to imitate the sound of bells. The metallophone, unlike the claque-bois, on account of the intensity and piercing character of its upper partials, could never be used alone; but when it is used with other instruments, these penetrating tones are so far quenched as to be no longer disagreeable, and the fundamental note, which has a bright, clear, bell-like tone, often contributes materially to the beauty and richness of the general mass of sound.

The partial tones of rods and bars are, as we have learned, of the kind denominated inharmonic. They do not all, by any means, form discordant intervals, but, unlike true harmonic intervals, their rates of vibration do not rise in the order of the natural series of whole numbers. Many of the intervals, it is true, are eminently discordant, and hence the unfitness of rods and bars for use in musical instruments, especially when played alone. But it must not be forgotten that tuning-forks, although vibrating as a bar fixed at one end, yield, as has been before stated, not only inharmonic partials, but also harmonic ones. So far, tuning-forks have never been used as musical instruments, although they may, as you know, be made to emit tones of exceeding purity and volume.

Let us now pass from the transverse to the longitudinal vibrations of a rod. An apparatus devised by Koenig (Fig. 55) enables us to demonstrate in a most striking manner the existence of longitudinal vibrations. A rod of brass mounted on a support is clamped at its middle point, and from the support an ivory ball is so suspended as just to touch the end of the rod. I now set in vibration the half of the rod farthest away from the ball, by rubbing it with a piece of resined leather. The point at the clamp is a node; but the vibrations imparted at the half of the rod which is being rubbed are at once communicated to the other end, as is evidenced by the tremulous motion of the ball. Rubbing the rod more vigorously, the vibrations become so intense that the ball is repelled violently whenever it touches the end of the rod.

By being clamped, the middle point of the rod is made a node. Here all the molecules are at rest. At the ex-

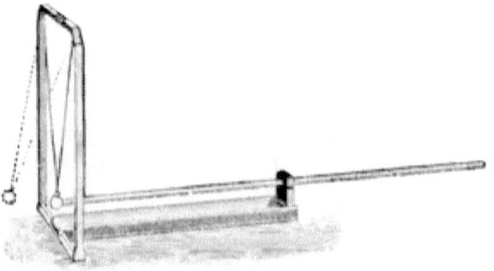

Fig. 55

tremities of the rod, on the contrary, the molecules have great amplitude of motion, as is attested by the experiment just made. By means of a spherometer, Savart measured the amount of elongation of a rod of brass, about an inch and a half in diameter and four feet long, under the influence of longitudinal vibrations. The strain, he found, was equivalent to that of a tensile force of over eighteen tons. The relatively feeble impulses thus communicated to the molecules of the rod may thus develop an enormous force. This is explained by the cumulative character of the motions imparted. A number of feeble impulses, properly timed, may, therefore, produce effects that a much superior force applied once could not effect. The elongations due to this vibratory motion frequently become so great as to cause the rupture of the strongest materials. Engineers and architects must take this fact into consideration in calculating the strength of materials. The cables of bridges are sometimes snapped by the longitudinal vibrations produced by the measured tread of soldiers crossing them. An accident of this kind befell a regiment of soldiers while crossing a bridge in France some years ago.

We owe to Savart an experiment which illustrates in a most striking manner the nature and intensity of the force developed by longitudinal vibrations. By clasping a glass tube with one hand, and rubbing it with a wetted cloth held in the other (Fig. 56), it is possible to develop such amplitude of motion in the molecules of the tube as to shatter its lower portion into fragments. The forms of the fragments are, as might be inferred from the character of the vibrations producing them, always annular, and the line of fracture is at right angles to the axis of the tube.

Fig. 56.

If a rod, ab, is held at its middle point, B, as in Fig. 57, and caused to vibrate by rubbing, as at A, one of its halves, it will emit its fundamental note. The rod in this case has a node at its centre, while the points of maximum vibration are at its extremities. If the same

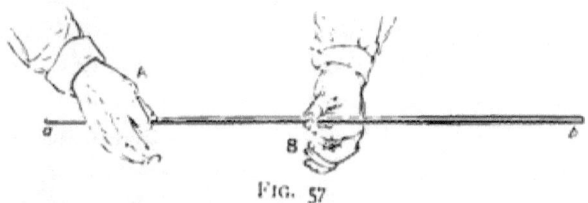

Fig. 57.

rod be held at N, I (Fig. 58), at a fourth of its length from the end A, and if the part $A\,N$ be then excited, a node is spontaneously formed at N', at a point such that $N'\,B = A\,N$. $N'\,N$, therefore, equals $A\,N$, and $N'\,B$ equals $\frac{AB}{2}$. The rod is thus divided into one whole ventral segment, $N'N$, and into two half ones, AN, NB. The note emitted is now an octave higher than it was before, and the number of vibrations is double what it was when there was only one node. The arrows in the figure indicate the direction of motion of the direct and reflected pulses.

If the rod be now fixed at N, II, of the adjoining figure, and caused to vibrate as before, it at once forms two other nodes, one at N and one at N',—points so situated that $N'B = AN$, and that $N'N' = N''N = AN + N''B = \frac{AB}{3}$. These four divisions vibrate in unison, and constitute three complete ventral segments of equal lengths. The number of vibrations executed in this case is three times that corresponding to the fundamental when the rod is fixed at the centre.

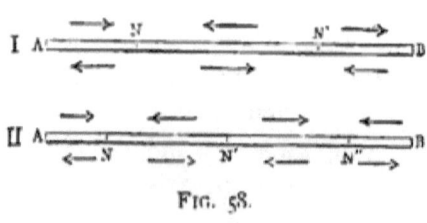

Fig. 58.

If the rod be divided into four complete ventral segments, it will produce a note whose pitch is four times that of the fundamental, and so on for higher subdivisions. Hence the notes emitted by a rod vary directly as the number of complete ventral segments, and inversely as the length of these segments. The frequencies of the notes yielded follow each other in the order of the harmonic partials and according to the series of the whole numbers 1, 2, 3, 4, 5, etc. The law is, therefore, the same as that which we have seen obtains for a string vibrating longitudinally, and the same, as we shall learn, as that which governs the vibrations of air in open organ-pipes. Another similarity between a rod free at both ends and an open organ-pipe is that in both cases the nodes occupy the same relative positions.

When the rod just used is fixed at one end and free at the other, the number of vibrations that it will execute in a given time is different, as is also the order of occurrence of the upper partials which may be produced.

Suppose the rod AB (Fig. 59), fixed at A, and free at B. When vibrating in its simplest way, so as to yield its prime tone, there is necessarily a node at A, and the centre of a ventral segment at B. I say the centre of a ventral segment because the rod, when vibrating so as to emit its fundamental note, is only a half ventral segment in length. Such rods, like those which are free at both ends, execute vibrations whose frequencies are inversely proportional to their lengths. A rod fixed at one end, and yielding its fundamental note, is different in length from a rod of the same length and material when free at both ends and emitting its prime tone. The note yielded by the former is an octave lower than that produced by the latter. In order that the notes may be in unison, the

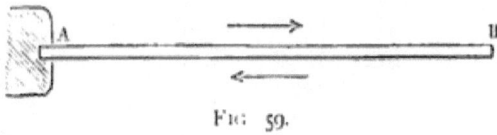

Fig. 59.

rod free at both ends should have twice the length of the one free at only one extremity.

Like rods free at both ends, those fixed at one end admit of subdivisions into segments while under the influence of vibratory motion. These divisions must always take place in such a manner that the fixed point is a node, and the free extremity the centre of a ventral segment.

When but one node is formed in the rod, it exists at N (Fig. 60), I, and divides the rod into two vibrating parts such that NB is one half AN, and one third AB. We have in this case a half ventral segment, NB, and a complete one, AN. The number of vibrations corresponding to the note emitted in this case is three times that executed by the rod when emitting its prime.

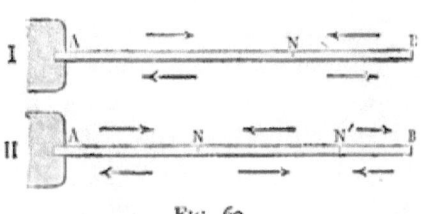

Fig. 60.

When two nodes are formed in the rod II of Fig. 60, the vibrating part $N''B$ is one fifth the length of AB. The rod is now divided into three vibrating parts, one half-ventral segment, $N''B$, and two whole ones, AN and $N''N$. The number of vibrations now executed is five times as great as when the rod sounds its fundamental.

From the foregoing it will be seen that the order of the notes developed in a rod fixed at one end is that of the unevenly numbered harmonic partials, — that is, they succeed each other as the odd numbers 1, 3, 5, 7, etc. The same law, as we shall learn later on, applies in the case of notes yielded by a stopped organ-pipe. Furthermore, rods fixed at one end and stopped organ-pipes have their nodes in the same relative position. The only instrument in music based on the longitudinal vibrations of bars is one devised by Marloye. Such an instrument (Fig. 61) is before you. It is, indeed, more of an acoustical curiosity than anything else.

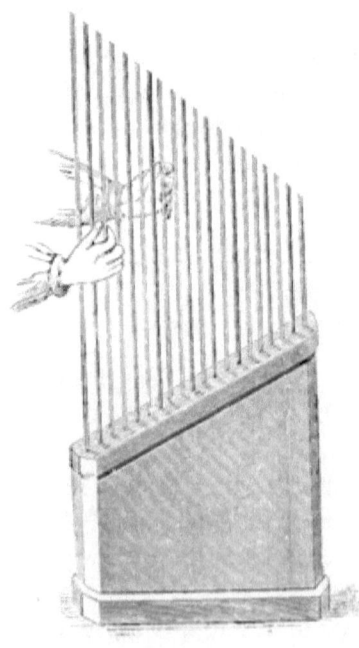

FIG. 61.

It is composed of twenty rods, firmly fixed at one end on a solid support. The white rods yield the notes of the diatonic scale, while the colored ones answer to the semitones of the chromatic scale. By rubbing them with resined fingers, a series of quite pure, sweet tones may be educed, and a simple melody might be played on them which the ear would find quite agreeable. Substituting rods of glass for those of wood, the smoothness and volume of the tones elicited would be considerably enhanced.

In elastic rods the number of longitudinal vibrations varies, as we have seen, inversely as the length of the rods, or the vibrating segments. The diameter and form of their transverse section have no effect on the number of vibrations executed by rods of the same length and material, provided their length is very great in comparison with their width and thickness. This is easily shown by experiment.

On a suitable support fixed to the table are clamped two steel rods (Fig. 62), each being one metre in length.

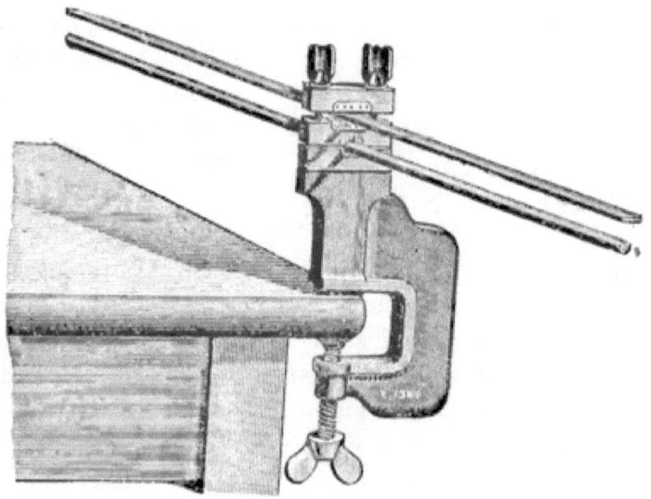

Fig. 62.

The lower one is cylindrical, the upper one prismatic. Passing a resined piece of leather in succession over the two, the same notes, as you hear, are elicited from both. I now replace the prismatic rod by a cylindrical one of greater diameter than that just used. We have now two cylindrical rods of quite different diameters, and yet, when they are thrown into vibration by rubbing them, they both emit the same note. Substituting a rod of one half metre in length for either one of those now clamped to the support, we have two rods, one of which is just twice the length of the other. Passing the resined leather over both of them, we find, as we have already learned should be the case, that the shorter rod yields a note which is just an octave higher than that produced by the longer one. Taking in place of the rod one half metre in length another one measuring one third of a metre, and causing it to vibrate with the rod below it, which is three times its length, we obtain notes whose frequencies are as 3:1. The short rod, as was to be expected, emits a note which is exactly a twelfth above that sounded by the longer one.

These experiments beautifully corroborate the results already obtained by causing rods to vibrate in segments and verify the law previously enunciated: namely, *the number of longitudinal vibrations is inversely proportional to the lengths of the vibrating segments, or, when rods of the same material but of different lengths are employed, the number of vibrations executed per second is inversely as the lengths of the rods*.

If now we use rods not of the same, but of different material, we shall find ourselves in a position to determine in a very simple way the velocity of sound in different solids. Fixing a rod of steel and one of copper in the support just used, and causing them to vibrate, you notice that the steel rod gives a more acute sound than that given by the copper one. The reason is found in the superior elasticity and lesser density of the steel, which permit the sound-pulse to travel through it more rapidly than it does in copper. If, instead of having rods of equal lengths as we now have, we were to use a steel rod seventeen inches long, and a copper one eleven inches long, we should, on causing them to vibrate, obtain notes that have approximately the same pitch. But the lengths of the rods employed are to each other very nearly as the velocities of sound in the two metals. The velocity of sound in steel and in copper is, in round numbers, 17,000 and 11,000 feet respectively. By simply making the rods of different materials of such lengths that they will yield the same note, we at once have an approximation to the relative velocities of sound in these materials, and knowing the velocity of sound in air, we can easily determine their absolute velocities.

Instead of steel and copper, let us take oak and fir. Cutting the rods to such a length that they both emit the same note, we find that the lengths are twenty-five inches for the oak, and thirty inches for the fir rod. But the ratio of the lengths of these rods, $25:30,=12.5:15$, is very nearly that of the relative velocities of sound in oak and fir. In the former the velocity of sound is a little more than 12,500 feet, and in the latter it is slightly in excess of 16,000 feet per second.

This method of determining the velocity of sound in solids was first suggested and applied by Chladni. The results he obtained for various substances correspond very closely with those arrived at by more refined methods of measurement. Its simplicity certainly commends it to the investigator who desires only approximate values.[1] It is applicable to all solids which can be fashioned into rods capable of executing longitudinal vibrations competent to yield a definite musical tone. Measuring the length of the sonorous rod, and estimating its pitch, both of which are exceedingly easy, are all that is required to enable one to calculate with a fair degree of approximation the velocity of sound in any given material.

A beautiful experiment, due to Biot, enables us to investigate, better than any other means at our disposal, the conditions of the molecules in various parts of a bar or rod when in a state of longitudinal vibration. It has been stated that the particles constituting the nodes of any vibrating body are quiescent, while those which compose the ventral segments are always in a condition of greater or less vibratory motion. In a rod free at both ends and emitting its prime tone, there is, as we have learned, but one node, which is at the centre, while on either side of the node there is a semi-ventral segment. In this case the

---

[1] According to recent investigations by Prof. A. M. Mayer, as yet unpublished, Chladni's method of determining the velocity of sound in solids is capable of giving more exact results than any other known method.

molecules that have the greatest amplitude of motion are at the extremities of the rod. At the node there can be no motion, because here the opposite sonorous pulses meet. There are, however, alternations of strain and pressure, and hence alternations in density. While, therefore, the node is characterized by absence of movement, and by variations of density due to pulses of condensation and rarefaction, which alternately meet at this point, the ends of the rod, corresponding to centres of ventral segments, are distinguished for great amplitude of movement, while the density remains always the same.

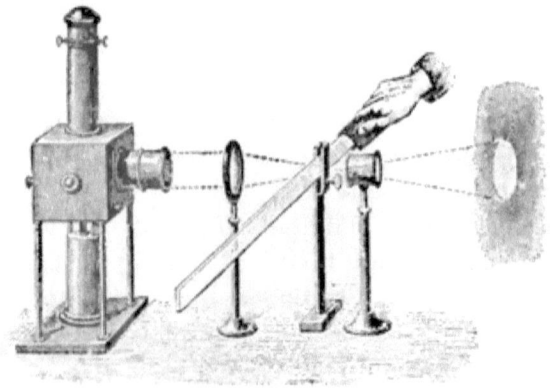

Fig. 63.

To the front of our lantern (Fig. 63) is attached a Nicol prism that gives a beam of polarized light. If now a second Nicol be placed in front of the first, in such a manner that the directions of vibrations in both are parallel, the beam will pass through the second prism also, as is evidenced by the luminous disk on the screen. But if the two prisms are so adjusted that their directions of vibration are at right angles to each other, the polarized beam from the first Nicol will not pass through the second, although both prisms are perfectly transparent. The light is quenched almost as completely as if it had been intercepted by a body perfectly opaque.

Light thus polarized is remarkable for its behavior with

respect to bodies in a condition of strain or compression. I take a narrow strip of plate glass and introduce it between the two prisms so that it is inclined to their direction of vibration. There is as yet no change on the screen. As soon, however, as the glass strip is bent, there is induced a condition of pressure on the concave and one of strain on the convex surface. The moment such change is effected, the light flashes out on the screen. If a similar condition of stress be caused by other means, by heat, for instance, or by sound-pulses excited in the molecules of the glass, a like result is obtained.

Adjusting the strip of glass in a vice in such a manner that the ray of polarized light can pass through its node, and sweeping over one of its halves a moist woollen rag, there is heard an acute note due to the longitudinal vibrations of the glass. Simultaneously with the production of the sound a brilliantly illuminated disk flashes out upon the screen. When the vibrations cease, the light is extinguished. But each time the cloth is passed over the glass the luminous disk is restored. Here, as is evidenced by the flashes of light on the screen, we induce changes of density — alternate states of condensation and rarefaction — in the node of the glass strip, precisely like those developed by heat or mechanical stress of any kind.

If now the glass strip is so placed that the beam of polarized light passes through it near either of its extremities, and it is thrown into vibration as before, no effect whatever is produced. The reason is that at these points of the glass bar there is no variation of density, due to alternations of strain and pressure, although the width of swing, or amplitude of movement, of the oscillating molecules is here at its maximum.

Like strings, rods may also execute torsional vibrations. If a rod be clamped at one end in a vice, and a violin bow be drawn around it, it will be caused to twist and untwist itself around its axis so as to execute vibrations that are as isochronous as transverse or longitudinal vibrations. According to Chladni, the pitch of a note due to the torsional vibration of a rod is about one fifth lower than that of a note produced by the longitudinal vibrations of the same rod having the same number of segmental divisions.

Like strings, rods may also execute very complex vibrations, in which transverse or torsional vibrations, or both, are compounded with longitudinal vibrations.

Savart was the first to elicit simultaneously from the same rod two notes, one of which is due to transverse, and the other to longitudinal vibrations. Since his time Terquem[1] and Koenig have studied these joint vibrations more closely, and, thanks to their investigations, we now know not only the laws which govern such compound vibrations, but also under what circumstances they may most easily be produced.

Clamping this steel rod, one metre long, in the support which we have just been using, I rub one of its halves vigorously with a piece of resinous leather. The rod is thrown into longitudinal vibration as in the preceding experiment, and a loud, clear note is the result. But in addition to the fundamental tone of the rod, you hear another note equally pure, and almost equally loud, which is exactly an octave lower. This is due to the transverse vibrations, which are developed simultaneously with and by those which are longitudinal. Such a grave tone is called by the French *son rauque*,—a raucous sound, and, as Terquem has shown, is produced only when the rod is of such a length that the note it emits when vibrating transversely is sensibly identical with a note that is an octave lower than that yielded when the rod vibrates longitudinally. Koenig has further found that the first upper harmonic partial due to longitudinal vibrations may, like the prime tone, excite transverse vibrations that will yield a note an octave lower than such partial. The vibrations thus developed in rods are, therefore, quite analogous to those which we have witnessed in Melde's experiments, in which a tuning-fork vibrating in the direc-

---

[1] See his "Étude de Vibrations longitudinales des Verges prismatiques libres aux deux Extrémités."

tion of the length of a string causes the string to execute transverse vibrations whose number in a given time is just one half that executed by the fork itself.

We are now prepared to pass to the vibrations of plates. They are far more complex than those of rods, but at the same time they are, by reason of the figures to which they may give rise, far more interesting. Chladni was the first to study experimentally the modes of subdivision of plates when under the influence of vibratory motion, and to him and F. Savart we owe most of our knowledge concerning the experimental part of this subject. Napoleon Bonaparte,[1] who had witnessed some of the experiments of the German philosopher, was so impressed by them that he had the French Institute offer a prize to the one who would offer a satisfactory theory of the phenomena observed. A lady mathematician, Mademoiselle Sophie Germain, gave a solution of the problem involved, for which she was especially honored by the Academy. Subsequently the theory of vibrating plates was discussed by the ablest mathematicians in Europe. Chief among these were Lagrange, Poisson, Cauchy, and Kirchhoff. And yet, notwithstanding the great work accomplished by these eminent analysts, much yet remains to be learned regarding the mode of vibration of plates, especially square plates whose edges are free. In the case of circular plates, theory and experiment are more concordant. The vibratory motions of such plates have been analyzed so thoroughly that the mathematician can now determine in almost any given case the number and kind of nodal lines, and calculate with the greatest exactness the series of sounds that will be produced.

By means of the vertical lantern and suitable plates, I shall now give some illustrations of the character of this vibratory motion. A square glass plate is clamped above the condensing lens of the lantern, and then strewn with

---

[1] On the dedicatory page of the French edition, "Traité d'Acoustique," of Chladni's great work is written, "Napoléon le Grand a daigné agréer la dédicace de cet ouvrage après en avoir vu les expériences fondamentales."

fine sand. The image of plate and sand is now distinctly focused on the screen. Placing my finger at the middle point of one of the edges of the plate, so as to form a node there, and drawing the bow along the edge near one corner, the sand immediately begins to dance about on the plate, and arrange itself along two nodal lines, which are at right angles to each other, parallel to the sides of the plate, and intersecting each other in the

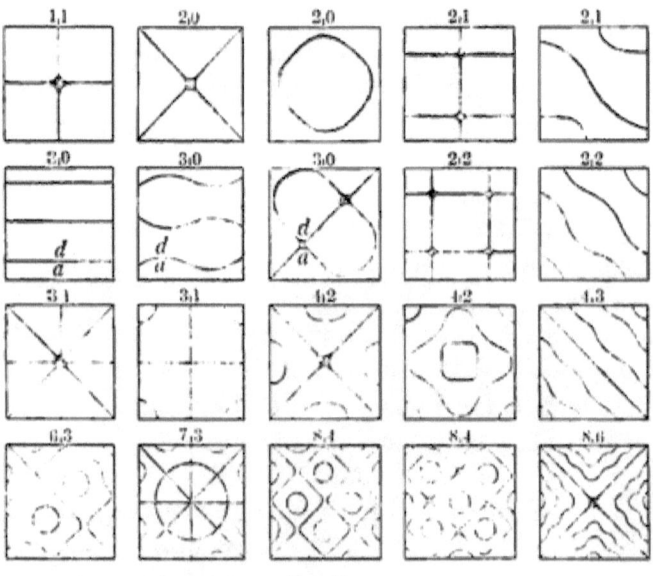

Fig. 64.

centre. These lines, in fact, constitute a cross, 1,1 (Fig. 64), dividing the plate into four equal rectangular segments. Placing my finger at the corner of the plate, and drawing the bow across the middle point of the edge, two nodal lines are formed as before, but their position is different, being along the diagonals of the plate as in 2,0 of the adjoining figure. Clamping the plate about midway between the centre and one of the edges, and bowing it at the proper point, we obtain a still different design, like 2,1 in the figure, composed of two parallel straight lines intersected by a third straight line at right angles.

These figures are named after their discoverer, and are known as Chladni's figures. They have been of invaluable service in studying the nature of vibratory motion in solid bodies, as they reveal at once the positions occupied by nodes and ventral segments. An almost indefinite number and variety of designs can be obtained from one and the same plate, and to most of these designs correspond sounds of different pitch.

A square plate yields its fundamental tone when it is divided into four equal squares, as in 1,1. The notes corresponding to 2,0 and 2,1 of Fig. 64 have a higher pitch. If the prime tone of the plate be C_1, the notes corresponding to the two diagonals will be a fifth higher, that is G_1, while the note corresponding to the third figure, 2,1, will be a major third of the octave above the fundamental, namely, E_2.

The pitch of the note emitted by a vibrating plate increases with the number of nodal lines formed, and the complexity of the figures developed. The designs in the accompanying diagram (Fig. 64) are a few of the multitudinous patterns that may be produced. Experiment shows that for plates of the same material, shape, and dimensions, the same figure always answers to the same sound. Different figures, however, under certain circumstances, may correspond to the same sound. With a little practice one can locate the position of the nodes, and determine the form of the figure that will be produced, with comparative ease and precision.

Wheatstone in 1833 was the first to give an explanation of these curious figures as formed on square plates. Koenig subsequently took Wheatstone's theory up and applied it to rectangular plates. Our knowledge of the transverse vibrations of rods will now be of use to us.

Suppose we have (Fig. 65) two rectangular plates of the same material and thickness, one having the length $abcd$, the other the length $efghk$; and let us further suppose that these are in unison when the former has two nodes, b and c, and the latter three nodes, f, g, and h.

194 SOUND AND MUSIC.

If we now superpose one on the other, we shall have a plate with a width *a b c d*, and a length *e f g h k*. Such a compound plate will admit both systems of nodes given by the plates separately, because the nodes are independent of the width of the plates, and will, while having the same system of nodes, emit the same sound. Knowing, then, the number and direction of the nodes given by two distinct plates, we can foresee what figures would result from

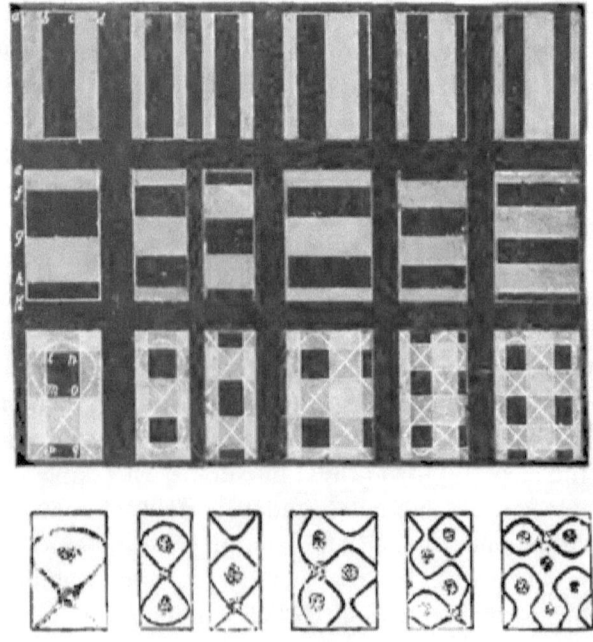

Fig. 65.

their superposition. The segments on the opposite sides of a nodal line, as is evident, must move in different directions, otherwise the formation of nodal lines would be impossible.

The parts of the plate that move upward are considered *positive*, those that have a downward motion, and are below the average position of the plate when at rest, are called *negative*. In the adjoining figure the negative parts are represented by dark spaces, while the positive ones are indicated by cross lines. In the first and second horizontal series of the figure are shown plates of various sizes and of different systems of nodal lines. In the third series are shown the nodal lines that theoretically should result from a superposition of the corresponding plates of the first two series. A little reflection will make it apparent that when the first two plates of the two upper series are superposed, the resultant nodal curve must pass through the points l, m, n, o, p, q, which are the points of intersection of the nodal lines of the plates taken separately. At these points only do the positive vibrations of one system neutralize the negative ones of the other system, and induce the condition of rest indicated by the nodal curve, — a condition that can result only from movements or vibrations which are equal and opposite in direction. In the various figures of the fourth horizontal series are exhibited some of the sand figures obtained by Koenig, showing the perfect agreement of theory and experiment.

Let us now study the effect of vibratory motion in circular plates. And in order to make the Chladni figures visible to all of you, I will, as before, project them by means of the vertical lantern. Clamping a glass circular plate above the condenser, and strewing it with sand, we throw it into vibration by bowing it. Damping any given point of the edge by touching it, and drawing the bow across the edge at a point forty-five degrees from the finger, two rectilinear nodal lines are formed, at right angles to each other and intersecting at the centre of the plate. There are now four equal segments, and the note emitted is the lowest note the plate is capable of yielding. Drawing the bow across the edge thirty degrees from the point damped, six vibrating sectors are formed, separated by as many nodal lines. Agitating the plate at points gradually approaching the one damped, we obtain in succession eight, ten, twelve, and more vibrating sectors, the number of sectors in all cases being an even one.

As in the case of square plates, the pitch of the notes evoked increases with the number of nodal lines that are produced. When these nodal lines are all rectilinear and intersect each other at the centre of the plate, thus making lines which are diametrical, the pitch of the notes emitted varies directly as the square of the number of diameters produced. Thus with 2, 3, 4, or 5 diameters, the corresponding notes would have frequencies represented by 2^2, 3^2, 4^2, 5^2. If then the prime tone of the plate corresponding to two diameters be C, that for 3, 4, and 5 diameters will be respectively D_2, C_3, $G_3^\sharp$.

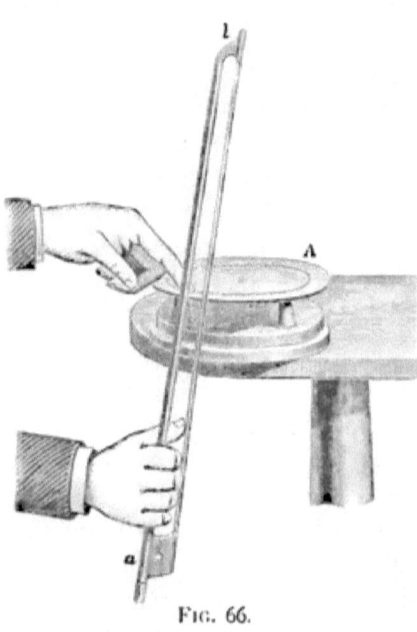

Fig. 66.

By supporting a plate at three points equidistant from the centre, as in Fig. 66, and drawing the bow across the edge, we get a single nodal curve, which in the present instance is a circle. Exciting the plate AB by drawing a resined string $b\,c$ through its centre, we obtain two circles, as in Fig. 67. Supporting a plate as in Fig. 68, and damping and bowing it at appropriate points,

Fig. 67.

we elicit a much more complex figure, composed both of diameters and circles, as p, i, c; g, n, i; and p, g, a; m, n, b.

If the fundamental note of the plate, corresponding to its division into two diameters, be C_1, theory gives for a figure answering to one circle and no diameter G_{2+}. A circle with one diameter yields B_2, with two diameters G_{3-}, and with three diameters D_{4-}. The signs + and − indicate, as previously, that the results given do not correspond exactly with any musical notes, + or − showing that they are to be slightly sharped or flatted. Two

FIG. 68.

circles with no diameters would, under the same circumstances, give G_{3-}.

The pitch demanded by theory, and that obtained by Chaldni for the different figures, approximate very closely. But, as will appear on inspection, many of the partials are inharmonic, and hence the discordant character of the sounds of cymbals, tom-toms, and different kinds of plates.

Damping the plate at certain points in the circumference, and exciting it at the centre, we may obtain the so-called "festoon figures" (Fig. 69), which have been known since the time of Chladni. The theory of such figures is imperfectly, if at all, understood. Employing larger plates, there may be produced simultaneously several different sonorous figures. Sometimes the circumference is divided into a greater number of parts than the central portion. In such a case, several tones, some of which may be in unison, are produced. Fig. 70 shows a complicated subdivision of this character.

If in lieu of sand a very light powder, like lycopodium, be strewn on a vibrating plate, the aspect of the figures produced will be entirely unlike those given by sand. The powder, instead of arranging itself along the nodal

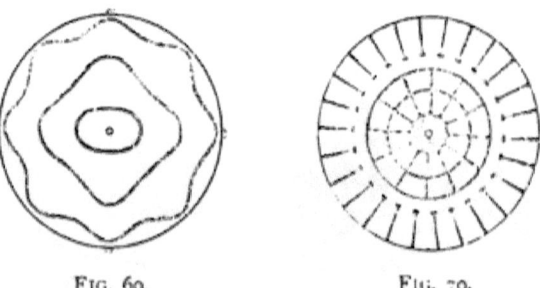

FIG. 69.   FIG. 70.

lines, as sand does, is collected in little heaps at the points of greatest agitation. Experimenters from the time of Chladni tried to account for the phenomenon, but it was reserved for Faraday to offer an explanation, as simple as it is natural. According to this illustrious physicist, the light powder is held in the centre of the ventral segments, where the motion is greatest, by little whirlwinds of air which are excited by the rapid and violent movements of the plate. The sand, on the contrary, in virtue of its greater density, is able to escape from these miniature cyclones, and hence if the plate be strewn with sand and powder at the same time, the two will be separated as soon as the plate is set in vibration. The sand collects along the nodal lines, and the lycopodium gathers at the points of greatest motion. That Faraday's theory is correct is proved by making the experiment *in vacuo* (Fig. 71). Here the plate is placed in a bell-glass from which the air has been exhausted, and is set in vibration by rubbing with a resined cloth the wooden rod to which it is attached. Immediately the plate is excited, sand and lycopodium alike are collected along the nodal lines and curves.

Before you (Fig. 72) is a large brass plate mounted on a strong support, and above it is fixed a resonant tube, so adjusted that it can be lengthened or shortened at will. Sprinkling the plate with lycopodium powder, and setting it in vibration, we get the same results as with the plate we have been using. Where the violin-bow is drawn across the edge of the plate is obviously the centre of a ventral segment, and the corresponding radial nodal lines are on either side of this point of maximum vibration. By shifting the bow to the right or the left of this point we evidently cause the nodal lines also to move in a similar manner. This is evidenced by the movements of the little heaps of lycopodium powder, and also by variations in the intensity of the tones emitted by the plate; for if the resonant

FIG. 71.

tube is adjusted, as it now is, so that its note is in unison with that yielded by the plate, an augmentation of sound is produced every time a ventral segment passes under the tube. When, on the other hand, a node passes under the tube, there is a corresponding diminution of sound.

These oscillations and turnings of the ventral segments and nodal lines, and the consequent variations in the intensity of the tone, produced in the manner indicated, are what might have been predicted without making the experiment. But Savart discovered that a similar displacement of the nodal lines may take place when the vibrating plate is left to itself. When, after the plate is excited, the violin-bow is quickly withdrawn, the nodal lines are observed to oscillate on either side of their original position. If now the plate be bowed strongly, and always at the same point, the amplitude of these oscillations may become so great that the nodal lines may be carried to the middle of the segments which separate them in their primitive position. Under such circumstances, an additional stroke of the bow will cause the nodal lines to pass this point and to assume the positions at first occupied by contiguous lines. A vigorous application of the bow, always at the same point, will now enable us to keep up this displacement, and to cause the nodal lines to travel around the entire circumference of the plate. But such a displacement can take place only in circular plates in which the pitch of the note emitted is independent of the position occupied by the nodal lines.

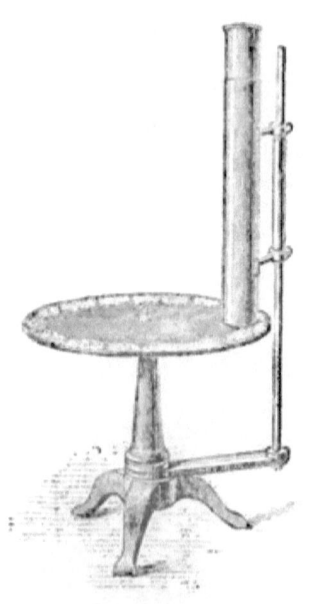

Fig. 72.

Instead of using lycopodium to show the movements we have been studying, we may, like Savart, employ a beam of light. Our lantern is now so adjusted that a beam from it is reflected from the polished surface of the plate, and we thus have an enlarged image of the plate on the screen. Setting the disk in vibration as before, we see the image on the screen transformed into a species of star, the rays of which correspond to the nodal lines of the plate. If the nodal lines on the plate are made to oscillate or to turn, the rays of the image on the screen oscillate or turn in a similar fashion. By means of a very vigorous use of the bow it is possible to make these rays turn so rapidly that, owing to the persistence of vision, they will coalesce and give a luminous image on the screen like that which is afforded when the disk is at rest.

Savart attributes this curious phenomenon to the lack of homogeneity in the plate employed. No matter how carefully the plate may be wrought, it is nearly, if not quite, impossible to fashion it so that it will be perfectly homogeneous. It will therefore, according to Savart, have two diameters, corresponding respectively to its maximum and its minimum resistance to flexure. If the point of excitation by the bow be properly chosen, the nodal lines will arrange themselves along these diameters, and remain stationary. If, on the contrary, the disk is attacked at some other point, the amount of flexure on either side of the bow, by reason of the difference of elasticity in these two points, will not be the same in both cases. The nodal lines will accordingly oscillate about the point of excitation, or, if the amplitude of oscillation be sufficiently great, they will, as we have witnessed, make an excursion around the entire circumference of the plate.

Although much yet remains to be learned regarding the laws of vibrating plates, Chladni has made us acquainted with those which depend on the thickness and diameter of the plates employed. Before you (Fig. 73) are six brass plates, three of which are circular, and three square. In these plates those of the same size have their thicknesses in the ratio of 1:2, while those of the same thickness have diameters which are likewise in the ratio of 1:2. Exciting two of the circular plates of the same diameter, one of which is twice as thick as the other, you will observe that two sounds are produced, that due to the thicker plate being an octave higher than the other. Hence Chladni's first law, which says that *for two plates of like form and* similar subdivision, as disclosed by the figures produced, the numbers of vibrations are directly proportional to the thickness of the plates.

Exciting another pair of plates, either square or circular, of the same thickness, but having diameters which are as 1:2, we find that the smaller plate yields a note just a double octave above that emitted by the larger plate. Hence the second law, which declares that *for two plates of the same thickness, but of different diameters, the figures produced being the same, the numbers of vibrations vary inversely as the squares of their diameters.*

From these two laws we may deduce a third. *If the thicknesses, as is here the case with two of the plates, are*

FIG. 73.

proportional to the other dimensions, that is, if the plates are similar solids, the numbers of vibrations are inversely as the homologous sides. Taking a plate, either square or circular, having twice the thickness and twice the diameter of another, the larger plate will emit a note that is an octave below that given by the smaller plate.

The last law holds true equally for solids, liquids, and gases, and must, therefore, be considered as a general expression for the laws of vibratory movement. Savart has shown that for bars of the same material and of similar form, the number of vibrations, as in plates, is inversely as the homologous sides. For spheres of the same substance, or cubes, or cylinders, or other solids of comparable dimensions, the law is equally true. Before you are suspended two spheres of iron, — one six inches, and the other three inches in diameter. Striking them so as to elicit their fundamental notes, we find that the larger sphere yields a note an octave below that emitted by the smaller.

Mersenne discovered that the number of vibrations executed by drums of similar form, but of different sizes, is inversely as their homologous dimensions.[1] This philosopher, as we shall see in our next lecture, also remarked that the same law obtains for sonorous tubes, both open and stopped. It was reserved for Savart, however, to give an experimental proof of the law. This he did by exciting vibratory motion in masses of air contained in cases and tubes of various forms and sizes.

Causing two cubical boxes, whose linear dimensions are in the ratio of 2:1, to speak, we shall find that the note emitted by the larger box is an octave below that emitted by the smaller one. Employing sonorous cases of spherical, cylindrical, or tetrahedral form, the result would be the same; namely, *that the notes emitted by masses of air in vibration are in all cases inversely as the linear dimensions of the cases in which the air is contained.* We shall reserve the experimental illustration of this law for our next lecture, where it will find an appropriate place.

It is but a step from plates to bells. A disk is to a bell, essentially what a rod is to a tuning-fork. In both disks and bells the mode of subdivision is the same. The number of vibrating segments is always even, and the prime note, in both instances, always corresponds to a division into four segments. As in disks, so in bells, the movements of adjacent segments must at any given time be in opposite directions. Under no other circumstances could the intervening node be formed.

The existence of nodes and ventral segments in bells is beautifully shown by this large glass bell (Fig. 74), around the edge of which are suspended four ivory balls. When the bell is excited by a violin-bow in such a manner that the balls touch the nodes, the motion is very slight.

---

[1] Harm., lib. xii. Prop. 18.

When, on the other hand, they are near the centre of ventral segments, they are forcibly repelled.

Filling a similar glass bell, A (Fig. 75), with water, and exciting it, as before, so as to yield its fundamental tone, the mode of vibration of the bell is disclosed by the condition of the water within. The surface of the liquid shows two nodal lines, fe and gh, which cut each other in the centre at right angles. Between these nodal lines the water is more or less agitated, as is evidenced by the ripples and crispations that play over its surface. The centres of the ventral segments — where the motion of

FIG. 74.   FIG. 75.

the bell, as well as of the water, is at a maximum — are at the points a, b, c, d. A few vigorous sweeps of the bow across the edge of the bell would develop vibrations of such amplitude as to shatter it into fragments.

The least number of segments in which a bell can vibrate is, as has been stated, four; and this division always obtains when the bell is yielding its lowest, or ground, tone. The next subdivision would be into six segments, and then into eight, ten, twelve, etc.; the number of segments, as in disks, being always even.

If a bell were perfectly regular and homogeneous throughout, the frequencies of the notes corresponding to 2, 3, 4, 5 meridianal nodal lines would be as the squares of these numbers; that is, as 2^2, 3^2, 4^2, 5^2. Supposing the prime note of the bell to be C_1, its first three upper partials would be D_2, C_3, $G\sharp_3$. The vibration numbers would thus follow the same law as governs circular plates having similar subdivisions. Such a bell would, like a disk, be characterized by many inharmonic partials, and would not answer the purpose for which bells, especially large ones, are ordinarily employed. Hence the empirical form — a sort of truncated conoid — in which large bells are now always cast.

The best form was found only after many ages of study and experiment, and the form aimed at was one that would bring out the fundamental tone and such of the upper partials as would harmonize with the prime. The diameter and height of the bell, the thickness and width of the sound-bow, its weight and size as compared with the rest of the bell, the material used (ordinarily copper and tin, in varying proportions), the relative weight of the clapper, — all these are problems that must be worked out, not theoretically, but experimentally, before the casting of your modern large, harmoniously toned bells can be attempted. Van den Gheyn (1550) and Hemony (1650) are the princes of the art of bell-founding. To them we are indebted for the types and models that are now followed by all bell workers. They have done for bells what Amati and Stradivarius did for violins. They have not only supplied us with models, but they have produced the most perfect work of their kind that the world has yet seen.

According to Hemony, a good bell should have three octaves, two fifths, one major and one minor third. The great bell of the cathedral of Erfurt, celebrated, not only for its size, but also for the fine quality of the metal from which it was cast, has E_1 for its prime, and this is accompanied by the following upper partials: E_2, $G\sharp_2$, B_2, E_3, $G_3\sharp$, B_3, $C_4\sharp$. I give in musical notation the approximate pitches of the compound note of three large bells that are widely celebrated: —

St. Paul's, London. Large Hour-Bell.

Big Ben of Westminster.

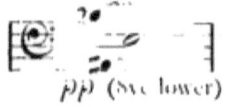

pp (8ve lower)

Great Tom of Oxford.

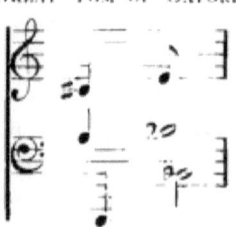

The loudest notes are indicated by minims, the weaker ones by crotchets. The wavy lines following some of the notes are to show that the notes vary in pitch.

Two of the bells of the peal at Terling, examined by Lord Rayleigh, give partials that are more inharmonic than those we have been considering. In musical notation the partials of the compound tones of these two bells would be written as follows:—

The signs + and —, as in the previous instances, signify that the notes after which they occur are to be slightly sharped or flatted.

It is rarely, if ever, that a bell can be cast so as to be perfectly symmetrical and homogeneous throughout. When, therefore, it is set in vibration, it frequently, by reason of its lack of homogeneity, divides itself into segments that emit two distinct sounds differing from each other slightly in pitch. This difference in pitch gives rise to the beats, or the risings and fallings of sound, that are noticed in most bells, especially when their tones are dying out.

Small bells do not yield such pure tones as larger ones, because of the presence of many inharmonic upper partials. In large bells, as we have seen, such inharmonic partials are weakened or entirely eliminated by the form in which the bells are cast. For this reason small bells, like hand-bells, and even such as are ordinarily used for carillons, are poorly adapted to purposes of music. They are frequently employed, it is true, but the inharmonic partials, which are always prominent in greater or less numbers, render the music produced by them dissonant in the highest degree, and all but unendurable.

The number of vibrations of bells of similar form varies inversely as their homologous dimensions. Thus bells of the same form, but of different sizes, will vary inversely as their diameters. Two bells, whose diameters are as $2:1$, would consequently yield notes an octave apart, the smaller bell emitting the higher note. It has also been found that the notes emitted by bells vary inversely as the cube roots of their weights. Working in accordance with these two laws, the bell-founder can cast a peal of bells that will approximate to any intervals that may be required. I say approximate to, as it is impossible in this instance, as in so many others, to carry out in practice exactly the indications of theory.

Membranes are closely related to plates in their modes of vibration. The chief difference is that the former are thinner and more flexible than the latter. They are ordinarily of paper, sheet rubber, or gold-beater's skin, and are stretched on a wooden frame with a tension uniformly distributed in all directions. They, like plates, have been carefully studied both theoretically and experimentally. They may be caused to vibrate either by percussion or by sounding near them a note in unison with their proper period of vibration. They exhibit Chladni's figures readily, and the resemblance of these figures to those excited on plates of the same form and size is very marked. The laws which govern the formation of the figures are apparently different in the two cases, and in some respects. indeed, these laws are as yet but imperfectly understood.

The mathematical researches of Poisson, Euler, Kirchhoff, Clebsch, and Mathieu, and the experimental investigations of Savart, Bourget, and Bernard, show that for the order of succession of the nodal lines of membranes, and their successive transformations calculated for the same sound, there is a striking agreement between the results of theory and experiment. The law governing the intervals between the various possible notes of a membrane requires further examination. So far the intervals given by experiment are always greater than those required by theory, and the difference is more pronounced as the membrane is thinner, and as the sounds approach more nearly to the fundamental.

In the following table, taken from the memoir of M. Bourget, are given the theoretical notes corresponding to the simpler nodal lines of circular membranes. In the illustrations given, Fig. 76, the nodal lines are either circles, or diameters including equal angles, or combinations of circles and diameters equally inclined towards each other, according to theory. When the membrane is properly stretched, the figures are perfectly regular, and present exactly the dimensions required by theory. The first figure represents a membrane vibrating as a whole, and yielding its prime. Supposing its fundamental to be C_1, its first upper partial with one diameter will be G_1, the ratio of whose vibrations to those of the prime is, as the numbers show, 1.594: 1.000. When the membrane vibrates so as to form two diameters, it emits the note C_2, whose frequency is 2.136 times that of the fundamental; and when it develops three diameters, the note yielded is F_2, with a frequency 2.653 times that of its prime. By inspecting the table, one can tell at a glance the notes and rates of vibrations that appertain to the different figures

		0 Diameter		1 Diameter		2 Diameters		3 Diameters		4 Diameters
		Radii of Nodal Circles.	Corresponding Sounds.	Radii of Nodal Circles.	Corresponding Sounds.	Radii of Nodal Circles.	Corresponding Sounds.	Radii of Nodal Circles.	Corresponding Sounds.	Radii of Nodal Circles.	Corresponding Sounds.
0 CIRCLE		—	$1.000\ C_1$	—	$1.594\ G_1 =\!-$	—	$2.136\ C_2 =$	—	$2.653\ F_2 -$	—	$3.156\ G_2 =\!-$
1 CIRCLE		0.436	$2.296\ D_2 \div$	0.546	$2.918\ G_2 -$	0.610	$3.501\ A_2 =\!-$	0.654	$4.060\ C_3 +$	0.686	$4.602\ D_3 +$
2 CIRCLES		$\{0.278,\ 0.638\}$	$3.600\ A_2 =\!+$	$\{0.377,\ 0.690\}$	$4.231\ C_3 =$	$\{0.442,\ 0.724\}$	$4.833\ D_3 =\!+$	$\{0.499,\ 0.750\}$	$5.414\ F_3 +$	$\{0.528,\ 0.770\}$	$5.979\ G_3 -$
3 CIRCLES		$\{0.204,\ 0.468,\ 0.734\}$	$4.095\ F_3 -$	$\{0.288,\ 0.527,\ 0.764\}$	$5.542\ F_3 =\!-$	$\{0.348,\ 0.569,\ 0.785\}$	$6.155\ G_3 =\!-$	$\{0.393,\ 0.602,\ 0.802\}$	$6.748\ A_3 +$	$\{0.431,\ 0.627,\ 0.816\}$	$7.328\ A_3 =\!-$
4 CIRCLES		$\{0.161,\ 0.370,\ 0.580,\ 0.790\}$	$6.211\ G_3 =$	$\{0.233,\ 0.426,\ 0.618,\ 0.809\}$	$6.851\ A_3 +$	$\{0.287,\ 0.469,\ 0.647,\ 0.824\}$	$7.471\ F_3 -$	$\{0.329,\ 0.503,\ 0.671,\ 0.836\}$	$8.074\ C_4 +$	$\{0.364,\ 0.531,\ 0.691,\ 0.846\}$	$8.663\ C_4 =\!+$

given. The signs + and — have the same signification as in other parts of the lecture.

On examining the preceding table it will be found that the higher upper partials succeed each other very closely, and that the interval separating them is in some cases less than a semitone. Hence we infer that within certain determinate limits a membrane is capable of vibrating in unison with any note whatever. This is especially true of the tympanic membrane of the ear. Here, however,

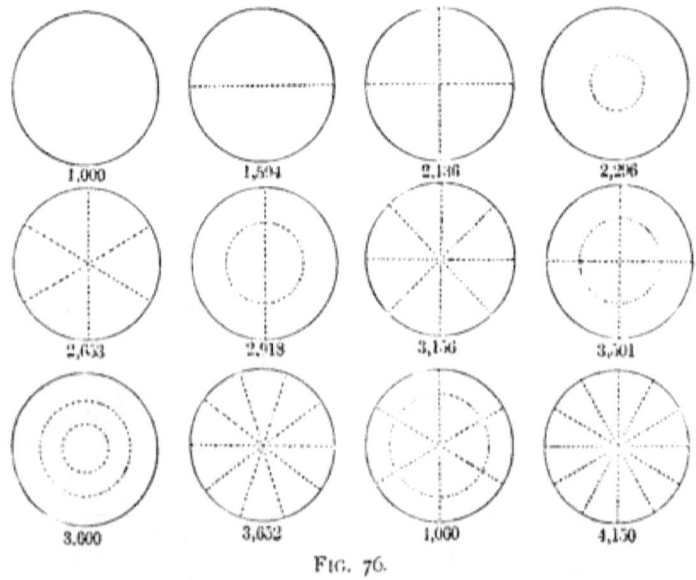

Fig. 76.

owing to the chain of ossicles connected with the tympanum, and the ligaments which bind the ossicles together, the tension of the auricular membrane can be varied within quite wide limits. For this reason the tympanum responds with such readiness to all notes, from the most grave to the most acute.

The same phenomenon is observed in the disks and diaphragms of telephones and phonographs. Such diaphragms, in addition to responding to vibrations of a certain determinate period, depending on the nature and form of the disks, have also a general resonance in virtue of which they are sensitive to any vibratory motion whatever. By reason of this general resonance, which they possess, and their competency to respond to vibrations of different periods, the telephone and phonograph are capable of transmitting and recording all sounds within the limits of ordinary audition.

The audiphone is another illustration of the same fact. As shown in Fig. 77, it is a fan-shaped sheet of hardened india-rubber, the upper part of which is held against the teeth of the upper jaw. Owing to its general resonance, it vibrates in unison with all sounds. The sounds thus collected, as it were, are transmitted by the teeth and

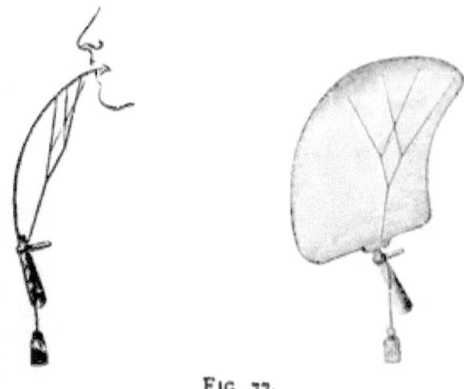

FIG. 77.

bones of the head to the auditory nerve. By this means, deaf persons who suffer from some disease or malformation of the external ear, but whose auditory nerves are intact, are able to hear with comparative ease and satisfaction. Chladni's figures excite our admiration and wonder. But these designs, complicated as some of them are, are excited by comparatively simple vibrations. The vibratory motions induced in the audiphone and in the disks of the telephone and phonograph are infinitely more complex and varied, and calculated, when we reflect on the matter, to excite our sense of wonder far more than anything disclosed by the experiments of Chladni, Savart, or Bourget. And yet further. The equations of the mathematician, and the experiments of the physicist, may tell us something about the laws governing the simpler vibrations of plates and membranes, but no mathematical *tour de force*, however transcendent, no experiment, however ingenious or refined, will ever be competent to unravel the infinitude of motions — changing as they do with the slightest modifications in pitch, intensity, and quality of tone — which characterize that most marvellous and most sensitive recipient of vibratory movement, the tympanic membrane of the human ear.

CHAPTER VI.

SONOROUS TUBES.

IN the two preceding lectures we studied sounds generated by solid bodies. In all the instances considered, the air served simply as a medium for the transmission of the sonorous waves to the ear. To-day we shall devote our attention to the investigation of sounds which have their origin in the vibrations of the air itself, and for which the air, as in the case of solids, serves also as the medium for transmission.

All musical instruments in which a vibrating column of air serves as the sonorous body are known by the general name of wind-instruments. They, like the other instruments we have been studying, are of great antiquity. This is especially true of some of the simpler forms of wind-instruments, such as the syrinx, or pandean pipes, the flute, and the trumpet.

According to Diodorus Siculus, their invention is to be ascribed to some shepherd who had studied the whistling of the wind among the reeds, and who endeavored to reproduce what he found in nature. Lucretius expresses the idea beautifully when he says, —

> "And Zephyr, whistling through the hollow reeds,
> Taught the first swains the hollow reeds to sound;
> Whence woke they soon those tender-trembling tones
> Which the sweet pipe, when by the fingers prest,
> Pours o'er the hills, the vales, and woodlands wild,
> Haunts of lone shepherds and the rural gods."[1]

---

[1] Et Zephyri, cave per calamum, sibila primum
 Agresteis docuere cavas inflare circutas.
 Inde minutatim dulceis didicere querelas,

That a sound can be produced from a vibrating column of air independently of the material of which the pipe enclosing the air is made, may be shown by a very simple experiment.

I have here a brass tube about twenty inches long and an inch and a half in diameter. Holding it longitudinally with one hand, and striking one of its open ends with the palm of the other hand, the enclosed air is set in vibration with sufficient force to yield a distinct musical note. If now the hand is quickly withdrawn from the end of the tube, another note is heard; but its pitch is an octave higher than that first emitted. In the former case the air vibrates as it does in a stopped pipe; and in the latter case it obeys the laws governing the vibrations of aerial columns in open pipes. We shall study these laws subsequently. In both instances, it must be remarked, it is the air that vibrates and produces the sound heard, and not the material of the tube which encloses the air.

That such is the case, is easy of demonstration. Striking the tube with my finger, or with a small billet of wood, so as to evoke the prime tone of the metal, we have a note that is much more acute than either of those produced when the enclosed air was in a state of tremor. We thus learn that the air-column within a tube may be caused to vibrate independently of the tube itself, and that the notes emitted by the former are entirely different in pitch from those that may be elicited from the latter.

We may vary the experiment by using pipes of different materials. Here are three different pipes, — one of brass, one of wood, and one of cardboard. Causing them to "speak" successively, you perceive that the pitch of the note in the three cases is identical. If the materials of which the pipes are made had any influence on the

> Tibia quas fundit, digitis pulsata canentum,
> Avia per nemora ac sylvas saltusque reperta,
> Per loca pastorum deserta, atque otia dia
>
> *De Rerum Natura*, lib. v. 1381 et seq.

See also Ovid, Fab. xv., "Syrinx changed into Reeds," and Virgil, Eclogue ii. 32, 36.

number of vibrations, the pitch in these three instances would be different. But the pitch of the three pipes being the same shows that the frequency of the notes generated is independent of the materials of the pipes, and is due solely to the length of the enclosed column of air, which in the instances now under discussion is itself the true sonorous body.

If instead of air the three pipes just used were filled with gases of different densities, the result would no longer be the same. If we were to fill one with air, another with hydrogen, and the third with carbon-dioxide, we should find that there would be a very marked difference in the pitch in the three cases. We saw in our first lecture that the velocity of sound varies for the different gases, and that it is less for carbon-dioxide and greater for hydrogen than it is for air. As pitch varies directly as velocity, and as the velocity of sound in hydrogen is almost four times as great as in air, the note emitted by the pipe filled with this gas would be very nearly two octaves above that produced with the pipe containing air. For a similar reason, the note yielded by the pipe containing carbon-dioxide would be graver than that in which air is the sonorous body.

There are many ways of exciting an air-column so as to make it yield a musical note. A simple and instructive way is by means of a tuning-fork. The column of air in the glass cylinder, C (Fig. 78), is thus acted upon by a tuning-fork, D, to one of the prongs of which is attached a disk, A, of the same diameter as the cylinder. By means of the disk the vibrations of the fork are communicated to all the particles of air at the opening of the tube. By pouring mercury into the tube, the proper sound of the air-column can be made to synchronize with that of the tuning-fork.

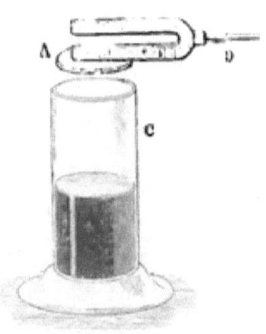

Fig. 78.

The moment when the two notes are in unison is declared by a remarkable augmentation of sound. We shall study this phenomenon more attentively when we come to investigate the nature and cause of resonance. Suffice to say now that a column of air is always most strongly reinforced when its period is perfectly isochronous with that which throws it into vibration.

Wind-instruments used in music are rendered sonorous by mouthpieces or by reeds. Hence their division into mouth-instruments and reed-instruments.

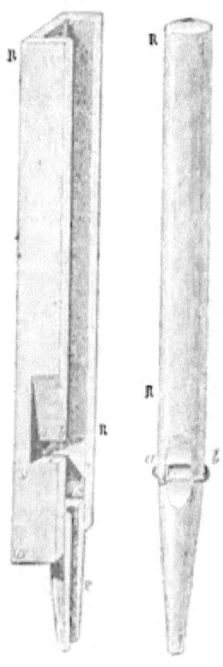

Fig. 79.

Here (Fig. 79) are two organ-pipes, one made of wood and prismatic in form, the other of metal and cylindrical in form. The first is open at the top, and the latter closed. Hence the names used,—open pipes and stopped pipes. The air is admitted through the foot, P, into the chamber, K, whence it escapes through a slit, c. The sharp bevelled edge, $a\,b$, is called the lip. The space between the slit, c, and the lip, $a\,b$, is called the mouth, or embouchure.

The precise manner in which vibrations in such pipes are executed seems still to be but imperfectly understood. According to the view which generally obtains, when a current of air enters the embouchure a fluttering or hissing noise is produced. This fluttering, like most noises, is made up of a large number of discordant sounds. From the mass of confused sounds the tube $R\,R$ selects one which it strongly reinforces. It can, however, reinforce that note only whose period synchronizes with its own. We have, then, repeated here, but in another form, the experiment of the tuning-fork and the glass cylinder. In the cylinder the air-column was excited by a tuning-fork vibrating in unison with it. In the organ-pipe the vibrations are set up by the current of air which issues intermittently from the embouchure.

According to a more recent theory, advocated especially by M. Cavaillé-Coll, Herr Schneebeli, and Mr. Hermann Smith, the vibrations excited in the aerial column within the pipe are produced by the sheet or blade of air issuing from the slit acting as a reed. Cavaillé-Coll styles this air-blade a free aerial reed ("anche libre aerienne"); Herr Schneebeli calls it a "Luft-lamelle," an aerial lamina; while Mr. Smith denominates it an "aero-plastic reed," or simply an "air-reed." Novel as it may appear, this view seems to have a solid foundation in fact, and the many and ingenious experiments made in support of the theory are apparently inexplicable on any other assumption. According to Mr. Smith, the air-reed, on issuing from the slit, does not strike the edge of the lip, as the old theory maintains, but passes very near its outer surface. Like a metal reed, whose action we shall study presently, the air-reed oscillates backwards and forwards, and generates in the air-column within the pipe the alternate condensations and rarefactions which are essential to the production of a musical note. Judging by the experiments appealed to in corroboration of it,—time forbids our discussing them here,—it would appear that the new theory is virtually established, and on a basis that is unassailable. As a working hypothesis, I think we are justified in regarding it the more probable of the two theories which now generally prevail.

Organ-pipes like those which we are now using are called, indifferently, mouth-pipes, flute or flue pipes. All parts of the mouthpiece are fixed, and ordinarily the pipe is designed to yield but one note. For this reason they are said to be of constant pitch. In instruments, however, like the flute or flageolet, which act on the same principle as an ordinary organ-pipe, a number of notes may be produced, and hence they are said to be of variable pitch.

The locomotive whistle is but a modified form of the organ-pipe. Inspection of Fig. 80 will show that the former differs from the latter in having a circular instead of a rectilinear embouchure, $a\,a$, above which is placed the sharp edge, $b\,b$, of the bell, T. The mode of action in both cases is essentially the same.

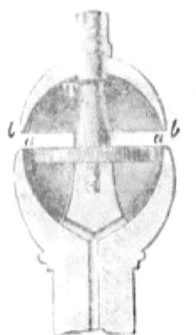

Fig. 80.

Daniel Bernouilli was the first to establish the laws which govern the notes emitted by organ-pipes. For their more elaborate experimental verification we are indebted to Mersenne, Savart, Wertheim, and Koenig.

The first law is that the pitch of the note is inversely as the length of the tube. Placing three similar tubes, K, K'', K''', on the wind-chest, $A\,B$, of the acoustic organ (Fig. 81), and admitting air into them, they are found to give notes that are separated from each other by an exact octave. The largest tube sounds the note C_2, the next C_3, and the shortest one C_4. By selecting tubes, with diameter of cross section very small compared to the length of tube, whose relative lengths are as the numbers $1, \frac{4}{5}, \frac{2}{3}$, we should, as in the case of vibrating strings, obtain notes constituting the perfect major

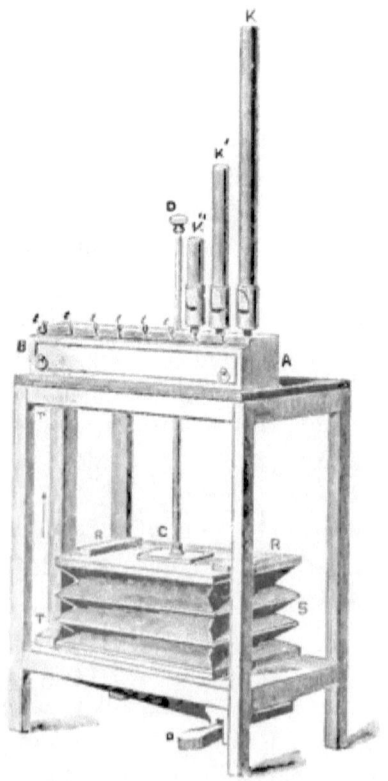

Fig. 81.

chord. Supposing the lowest note to be C_3, the other two would be respectively E_3 and G_3.

Let us now choose eight pipes whose lengths are to each other as the wave-lengths of the different notes of the diatonic scale, beginning with C_2. Placing them in the apertures t, t, t, etc., and forcing air into them, we find on touching in succession their corresponding keys that we have all the notes of the gamut between C_2 and C_3. The result obtained here is identical with that obtained with vibrating strings. As with strings, the number of vibrations varies inversely as the length of the string, so with tubes the number of vibrations varies inversely as the length of the columns of air which they enclose.

But a mass of air in vibration may, like solids, generate several partial tones in addition to its fundamental. Mersenne remarked that one may easily elicit from a harmonic trumpet the tonic, the octave, the twelfth, and the double octave, but no intermediate notes. Sauveur made a similar observation; but it was Daniel Bernouilli who first discovered the law governing the succession of harmonic partials both in open and in stopped pipes.

The experimental illustration of these laws is quite simple. For this purpose we require a long tube of small diameter (Fig. 82), provided at the bottom with a stopcock, R. The tube, which is open at the top, is placed in one of the apertures of the wind-chest of the acoustic organ, and the air is allowed to enter through $T T'$, from the bellows, $R R S$. When the stopcock is partially open and the pressure is suitably regulated, a deep, pure tone is produced. The note you now hear is the fundamental, the lowest the tube is capable of yielding. But by admitting more air, and especially by increasing the pressure, — which is effected by bearing down on the rod $D C$, or the pedal D, — we obtain a note an octave higher than the one you have just heard. Augmenting the pressure, a still higher note is produced.

FIG. 82.

The musicians present will recognize this as the third harmonic partial, or the fifth of the second octave. By increasing the pressure still more, and turning the stopcock so as to admit a full blast of air, we elicit still higher notes. We now have the second octave above the fundamental, — now the third of the second octave, — and now the fifth. You are familiar with the order of occurrence of these notes; we have adverted to them many times before. They are, in fact, the harmonic partials which succeed each other as the numbers 1, 2, 3, 4, 5, 6.

With the pipe before us, we have readily obtained six partial tones, and might, if it were desirable, elicit several others. The theoretic number of such partial tones has, indeed, no limit. Experimentally it is possible to demonstrate the presence of at least twenty. But to do this, special appliances are required.

The experiments just made enable us to formulate a second law for sonorous tubes; namely, that an open tube is competent to execute vibrations whose relative numbers are to each other as $1:2:3:4:5:6$. The notes thus generated constitute the complete series of harmonic partials. As you will remember, we have the same order of succession of notes for the transverse and longitudinal vibrations of strings, and for the longitudinal vibrations of rods that are free at both ends.

We now replace the tube just used with a stopped pipe of the same length and diameter. Proceeding as before, we educe the fundamental and a series of higher notes. But now the order of succession of the upper partials is different. The first note above the prime is not the octave, as in the open pipe, but the fifth of the second octave. We thus have, as the first note heard above the fundamental, the third instead of the second partial. The next higher note audible is not the fourth partial, as before, but the fifth; and the one following, as is found by experiment, is not the sixth, but the seventh in the order of the harmonic series. Hence the partials in stopped pipes succeed one another in the order of the odd numbers 1, 3, 5, 7, etc., and not as they do in open pipes, where the whole series of partials is found. This fact, as we shall learn later on, will account for the marked difference of quality which distinguishes the two classes of pipes.

We now fix in the wind-chest, side by side, the two tubes with which we have been experimenting, and upon causing them to speak, we observe another fact which distinguishes an open from a closed pipe. Although both pipes are of the same size, the pitch of the notes is not the same. The sound yielded by the open pipe is just an octave higher than that produced by the closed one. This is a general law, — an open pipe yielding its prime tone is always an octave higher than a stopped one of the same length and diameter.

You cannot fail to remark the difference in the quality of sound which characterizes the pipes. That of the open one is full, rich, and brilliant; that of the stopped one is, in comparison, jejune, poor, and dull.

Like solids, vibrating air-columns admit of subdivision, as is evidenced by the formation of upper partials, which we have been studying. They have, consequently, nodes and ventral segments, or points of maximum and minimum motion. The vibrations of the air particles as to their direction of motion follow the same laws as govern the longitudinal vibrations of strings and rods. They make their excursions to and fro parallel to the axis of the tube in which the air is enclosed. Their nodes are, therefore, points of no motion, but of varying density; the centres of their ventral segments are points of maximum motion, but of a density which is constant, being the same as that of the air external to the tube.

In Fig. 83, I, II, III, IV, we have represented the subdivisions of an open pipe when emitting its fundamental and first three upper partials. In I, corresponding to the prime tone of the pipe, there is but one node, N, which is at the centre. At both ends of the pipe are centres of ventral segments, VV. It is obvious that such must be the case, as the air at these points, being in communication with the external atmosphere, must be always of the same density. The arrows indicate that the paths of movement on opposite sides of a node are always in opposite directions, and the perpendicular lines reveal the position of the nodal planes. The symbolic wave-forms show that when an open tube yields its prime tone, it divides into two semi-ventral segments, making thus one complete ventral segment for the fundamental. When the pipe emits its first upper partial, as the wave-form indicates, it

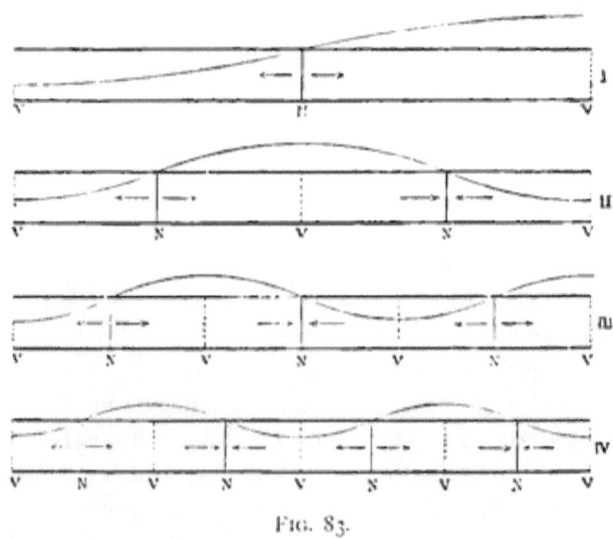

Fig. 83.

is divided into four semi-ventral, or two complete ventral segments. Similarly, for the second and third upper partials, there are six and eight semi-ventral or three and four complete ventral segments. The nodes increase in number according to the same ratio. There is one node, which is in the middle of the pipe, for the fundamental. For the first upper partial, or second partial simply, we have two nodes, each of which is one fourth the length of the pipe distant from its corresponding extremity. Similarly for the third and fourth partials there are respectively three and four nodes. The pitch of notes in open pipes is, consequently, directly proportional to the number of nodes, or the number of complete ventral segments.

In the case of stopped pipes it is different. Instead of yielding notes according to the order of the natural numbers, they emit, as we have seen, notes corresponding only to the odd numbers. Inspection of Fig. 84, I, II, III, IV, will make apparent the reason for this difference.

The open end of a stopped pipe, for the same reason that obtains in an open pipe, must be the middle of a ventral segment. It is here that the direct pulses are

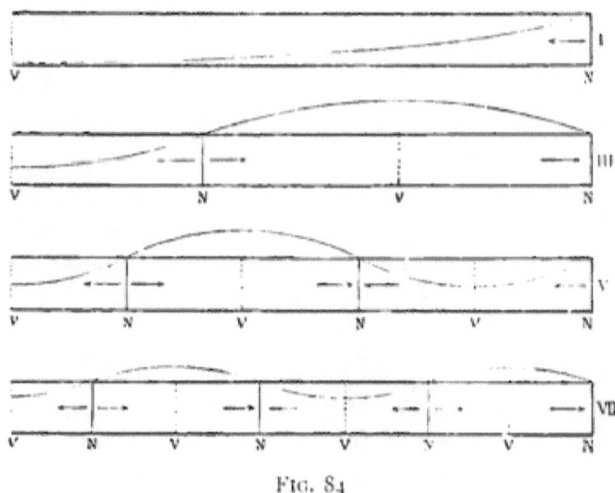

FIG. 84

originated, and for this reason it must be a point of maximum vibration. At the closed end, on the contrary, there must necessarily be a node, because longitudinal vibrations of the air-particles are here impossible. The simplest way, therefore, in which a stopped pipe can vibrate is that indicated in I, in which the open end answers to the middle of a ventral segment, V, and the closed end to a node, N. The pipe in this case, as is evident, forms only a semi-ventral segment, and is one half the length of an open pipe yielding the same note. In an open pipe the wave-length corresponding to the prime tone is, as the symbolic curve shows, twice the length of the pipe. In a closed pipe, however, the wave-length is four times the length of the pipe.

A little reflection will show why this is so. A condensed pulse, starting from the mouthpiece of an open pipe, is reflected from the other end as a rarefied pulse. This change from condensation to rarefaction is due to the lesser density of the air on the outside of the tube as compared with that of the condensed pulse within. When a condensation arrives at the open end of the tube, there is a sudden expansion, which gives rise to a rarefaction that is propagated back through the pipe. A condensation, accordingly, is reflected as a rarefaction, and a rarefaction, for a similar reason, is reflected as a condensation. A condensed pulse, starting at the mouthpiece, and reflected at the opposite end as a rarefied pulse, will, on its return to the mouthpiece, be reflected a second time, and will, for the same reason as before, undergo a change of density. It accordingly starts forward a second time as a condensed pulse, and is therefore in its initial state. A complete wave-length, then, in an open pipe is equal to twice the length of the pipe, and the period of vibration required for such a pipe is the time required for propagating a pulse through twice its length.

In a stopped pipe the propagation of the sonorous pulse follows a different law; for if a condensed pulse excited at the embouchure be propagated to the closed end, it will there, owing to the resistance offered, be reflected unchanged. It will accordingly return to its starting-point as a condensed pulse, but on arrival there will be reflected a second time. This time, however, the condensed pulse will be changed into a rarefied one, and for the same reason as a similar change is effected in an open pipe. On reaching the closed end the rarefied pulse will be reflected again, but reflected as a rarefied pulse. Arriving at the mouthpiece a second time, another change of density occurs, and the rarefied pulse once more becomes a condensed pulse. It is now in its initial condition. We have a complete vibration, but only after the pulse has travelled four times the length of the pipe. In pipes of the same length, therefore, the wave-length of a stopped pipe is twice that of an open one, and the pitch of the former is an octave lower than that of the latter.

The vibrations of the air-columns of pipes, like the vibrations of strings, give rise to stationary undulations. In both instances they are produced by the combination of direct and reflected waves, which are equal and similar to one another. In the production of upper partials the air-column always subdivides itself into a greater or less number of such stationary undulations, separated by a corresponding number of nodal surfaces. At equal distances on opposite sides of the nodal plane the air-particles have equal and opposite velocities. For this reason the air at a node is always subjected to equal and opposite forces, and hence remains unchanged in position.

As the air of a vibrating segment sways to and fro, and as the motions of any two adjacent segments are opposite in direction, it follows that any two consecutive nodes must always be in opposite conditions of condensation and rarefaction. As in the stationary undulations of strings, so also in those of air-columns, the middle points of ventral segments are where the amplitude of motion is greatest. But while the amplitude of motion at these points is greatest, the variations of density, as has been observed, are least. The density of the air at these points is the same as it is at the open ends of pipes, where variations of density are precluded by free communication with the atmosphere outside.

These considerations follow naturally from the demands of mathematical theory. But the conditions which theory demands can all be shown by experiment to have an actual existence.

Savart has taught us a simple method of determining experimentally the position of nodes in sonorous pipes, whether open or closed. A little wooden ring, S, to the bottom of which is attached a thin membrane, is suspended by a string inside an open organ-pipe, T (Fig. 85), when emitting its fundamental tone. A little fine sand is strewn over the membrane, and as soon as it is introduced into the pipe, you hear the sand dancing about on the membrane; and if you were near enough you could also see, through the glass side of the pipe as the ring descends, that the agitation of the sand becomes less and less until it reaches the centre of the pipe, — which, as we have learned, is a nodal point, — where it becomes entirely quiescent. On lowering the membrane still further, the sand becomes more and more agitated until it approaches the embouchure, when the agitation, as at the upper end of the pipe, attains a maximum. This, as we have seen, is what should occur. The two ends of an open pipe yielding its prime are centres of ventral segments, and consequently places of maximum movement, while the middle of the pipe, where the direct and reflected pulses cross each other, must be a point where there is no motion whatever.

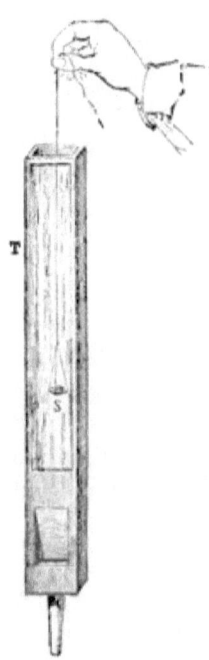

Fig. 85.

By increasing the pressure of the air so as to elicit from the pipe some of its upper partials, we should by the same simple means be able to locate the positions of the nodes and ventral segments of such partials as readily as we have found those corresponding to the fundamental.

Fixed in the wind-chest are two organ-pipes, one stopped and the other open. The former is one half the length of the latter. But, as we have learned, they should both emit notes of the same pitch. Causing the pipe to speak, we find that such is the case.

The same fact may be more strikingly illustrated by the pipe, T, Fig. 86. By means of the slide, A S, which has a large hole in one end and moves in a groove in the middle point of the tube, the pipe may be made to speak as an open pipe or as a closed one of half the length of the open pipe. Arranging the slide so that the hole in it permits the two semi-ventral segments corresponding to the prime tone of the pipe to be in communication with each other, the pipe is caused to yield its fundamental. The slide is now moved in so as to make a stopped pipe of one half the length of the open one. The note is still the same. Keeping the pressure of the air the same, the slide is moved to and fro several times in rapid succession, and the pitch of the notes corresponding to the open pipe and the closed one of one half the length, remains unchanged. You note, however, a difference in the quality of the sound, that yielded by the open pipe being brighter and richer than that emitted by the stopped one.

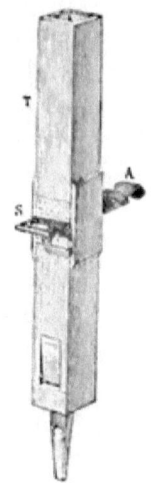

FIG. 86.

If a hole is made in the side of a pipe at a point occupied by a node, such a point is thereby changed at once into the centre of a ventral segment. This is well illustrated by the open pipe, Fig. 87, in one of the sides of which, at the middle point, is a hole which can be opened or closed by a small button. When this opening is closed and the pipe emits its fundamental note, there is a node at this point. As soon, however, as the button is turned to one side, this point becomes the centre of a ventral segment, as is evidenced by the change in the pitch of the sound now yielded. The reason is obvious. The middle point of the pipe is now in free communication with the external air, and hence there can be no variation in density, and consequently no nodal point where before there was one. But instead of one nodal point we now have two,— one midway between the aperture and the upper extremity of the tube, and the other at the same distance on the opposite side of

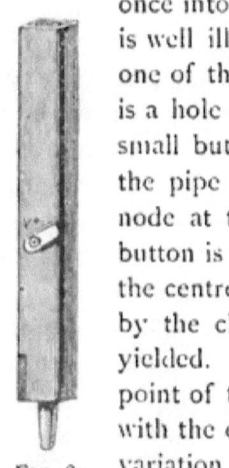

FIG. 87.

the opening. The note emitted under these circumstances should be an octave higher than that yielded by the pipe in the first instance. The musicians present can vouch for the fact.

A simple experiment will remove all doubt regarding the matter. A second open pipe, one half the length of the one with the aperture in it, is now mounted on the wind-chest, and both pipes are made to speak simultaneously. As was expected, the notes are in unison. Under the conditions of the experiment the small pipe yields its prime, and the larger one its first upper partial. This shows conclusively that the wavelength, and consequently the pitch, of the first upper partial of a pipe, A, is the same as that of the fundamental of a pipe, B, of one half the length of A.

Fig. 88.

But we may carry our illustration still farther. Instead of using a tube with but one aperture in the side, let us take one in which there are four such openings. Fig. 88 shows such a tube. If the pressure of the air in the bellows be now so regulated that the pipe shall yield its third partial, the middle points of its corresponding ventral segments will be, as indicated, at the points v and v. These points may be put in communication with the external air by opening the holes at v and v, and the pitch of the note will remain unaffected. If, however, the apertures at a and b are uncovered, the nodal points are changed, and there is immediately produced a note of higher pitch. This same method is applicable in determining the positions of nodes and ventral segments in stopped as well as in open pipes.

From what has been said it is manifest that when a tube yields one of its upper partials the air-column within undergoes spontaneous subdivision into aliquot parts, each of which vibrates independently, but in unison with each of the others.

Let us, for instance, cause the long open pipe, called

the flute of Bernouilli (Fig. 89), to emit its fourth partial. The air-column within must now, according to what has been said, be subdivided into four columns of equal length, each of which, vibrating separately, would give the fourth partial, which you all hear. The centres of the ventral segments corresponding to the partials now sounding, are at v, v, v. If now the first, second, and third upper sections of the pipe are detached in succession, you will remark no change in the pitch. The lower section of the pipe alone yields the same note as was emitted by the whole pipe, or by a pipe whose length is twice or thrice that of each section taken separately. To show that this is the case, we may reverse the order of the experiment just made. While the lower section is yielding its fundamental note, we add in succession the three upper sections, and if the pressure of air is properly regulated, the pitch of the note will remain unchanged throughout.

FIG. 89.

The same fact can be shown in another manner. If we take, as did Bernouilli, a long tube, T (Fig. 90), and close its upper extremity by the piston, p, we shall have a stopped pipe. If now the tube is made to yield one of its upper partials, and the piston is slowly moved downward, you will observe a gradual change of pitch. But when the piston reaches one of the nodes corresponding to the partial first produced, the original note comes out loud and clear. We thus show that the same law obtains for the partials of stopped as for those of open pipes.

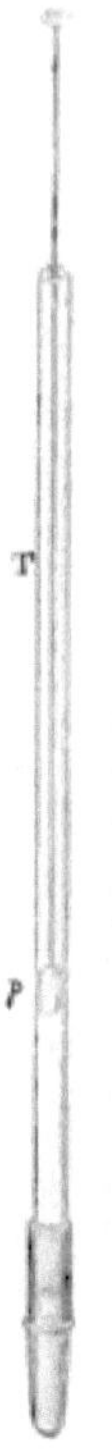

We are indebted to Dr. Koenig for a still more beautiful and delicate method of analyzing the condition of the air in sonorous tubes. For this purpose we use what is called a manometric flame. The apparatus for producing such a flame consists of a small wooden capsule (Fig. 91), one side of which is

FIG. 90.

closed in with gold-beater's skin or a thin sheet of caoutchouc. Two openings are made in the capsule, — one at
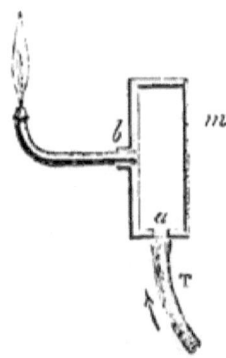
a, and the other at b. To the aperture a is attached a rubber tube, T, through which is admitted illuminating gas. At b is fastened a small gas-burner, at the end of which the jet of gas may be ignited.

If now the gas be maintained at a uniform pressure, it is evident that its escape will be modified by any motion that may be imparted to the membrane, m. If the membrane is forced inwards, the gas will escape more rapidly, and the flame will be proportionally elongated. If the membrane move outwards, the gas will escape more slowly, and the flame will be correspondingly shortened. If the membrane be very suddenly and violently agitated, the flame will be extinguished. Such

Fig. 91.

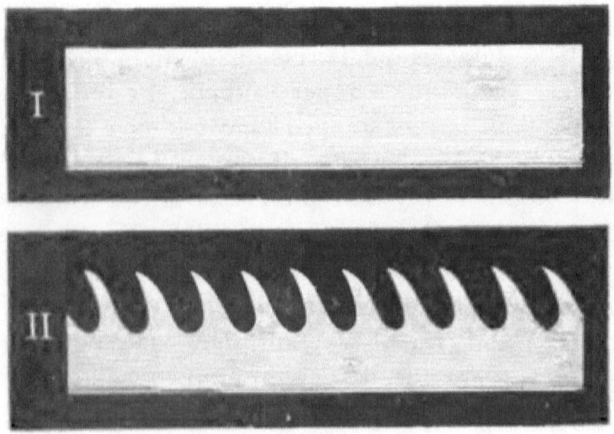

Fig. 92.

being the case, it is evident that this little apparatus affords a very delicate means of rendering visible the variations of pressure to which the gas within the capsule may be subjected. To render the device still more delicate, the flame is looked at in a cubical mirror which revolves in front of it. The use of such a revolving mirror in observing vibratory flames is due to Wheatstone.

As long as the pressure in the capsule is uniform, the image of the flame reflected from the mirror is in the form of a luminous ribbon, I (Fig. 92), of constant width and equal to the height of the flame. With rapid variations of pressure, however, the image becomes indentated, like II of the adjoining figure, each denticulation indicating an augmentation of pressure within the capsule.

To an open organ-pipe, AB (Fig. 93), mounted on the wind-chest, are attached three manometric capsules, b, a, c, communicating with a common reservoir, DD, into which illuminating gas is admitted through the tube, T. The capsule a is nearly at the middle of the pipe, and at the nodal point, therefore, of the pipe when sounding its fundamental. The capsules b and c are at the nodes corresponding to the second partial, or octave of the fundamental.

When air from this wind-chest is admitted into the pipe and the pipe yields its prime, there is, as we have learned, a variation of pressure in the vibrating air-column. This pressure is greatest at a, and diminishes on either side towards b and c, becoming zero at the open extremities. When the light from a is reflected from the revolving mirror, you observe a luminous band with deep indentations. Here the pressure is at a maximum. The indentations afforded by b and c are, by reason of the less pressure at these points, much less strongly marked. When the jet is small and the sound very intense, the agitation is sufficient to extinguish the flame.

If we cause the pipe to yield the octave above the fun-

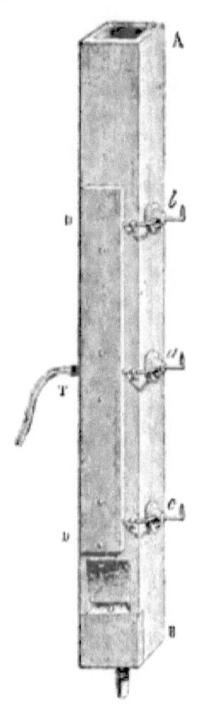

FIG. 93.

damental, the nodes are changed. They are now at b and c, a being the centre of a ventral segment where there is no variation of pressure whatever. This is indicated clearly by the action of the flames, that belonging to the capsule a being perfectly quiescent, whereas those at b and c give the same strong indentated ribbons as were seen at a when the pipe sounded its fundamental.

Let us now try a stopped pipe, AB (Fig. 94), provided with manometric flames. It is similar to the open one we have just employed, but, for reasons you are already familiar with, the nodes in this case occupy different positions from those of an open pipe. The stopped end of a pipe being always a node, one of the capsules is fixed at b. When the pipe yields its second partial it has a node both at b and at c, while a is then the middle of a ventral segment.

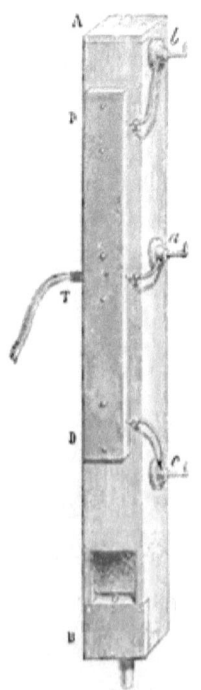

FIG. 94.

Causing the pipe to speak its fundamental, we observe in the reflected images that all the three flames are in a state of vibration. That at b, the nodal point corresponding to the prime tone, is most agitated; the agitation at a is less, and that at c is less still. At the embouchure, o, where the vibrating column is in contact with the external air, is the centre of a ventral segment, and here, consequently, a manometric flame would show that the pressure is constant, being always that of the atmosphere.

When the pipe sounds its second partial, a becomes the centre of a ventral segment. Here again, as declared by the motionless flame, the air is quiescent, because there are no variations of density. At b and c, on the contrary, the flames vibrate strongly, because at these points are the nodes corresponding to the second partial, which is now sounding.

Desiring to secure more accurate results than those afforded by the manometric pipes with which we have been experimenting, Dr. Koenig constructed one on a much larger scale. Such a one is now before you (Fig. 95).

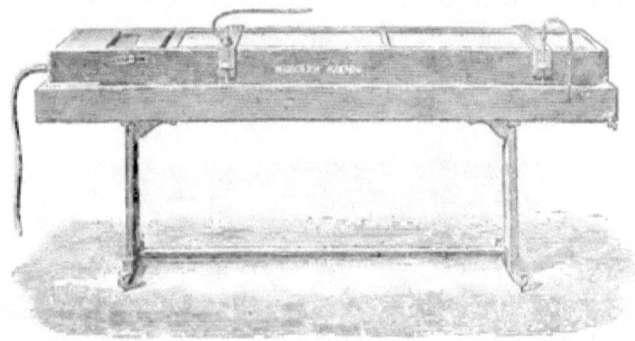

Fig. 95

It is over seven and one half feet in length, and about five inches in depth and width. It is brought to a perfectly horizontal position by means of levelling screws in the feet of the support. Its prime note is C_1. Figure 96 exhibits a cross section of the pipe. A narrow, cleft-like opening extends the whole length of the bottom of the pipe. This is to permit the exploring tube, $a\ c\ d\ b$, attached to the support, $m\ n$, to be moved at will to any point along the axis of the pipe. The opening of the pipe is closed by partially filling the trough, in which it rests, with water. The upper side of the pipe is made of glass, so that the observer can see what is going on within.

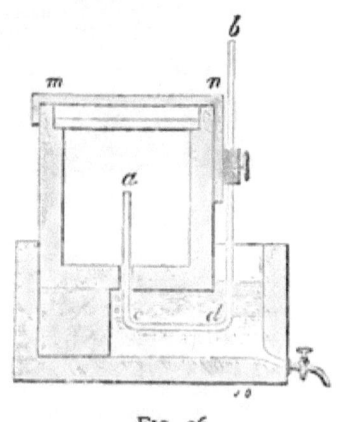

Fig. 96.

Passing the exploring tube along the length of the pipe, while it is emitting a note, and bringing the end, b, of the tube into communication with the ear, we are apprised of an augmentation of sound at the nodes, and of a diminution of it at the middle of the ventral segments. What is surprising is that it is easier to locate exactly the centre of a ventral segment than the position of the nodes. At the former points the sound disappears suddenly, so that we can determine the middle points of the ventral segments with the greatest ease and exactness.

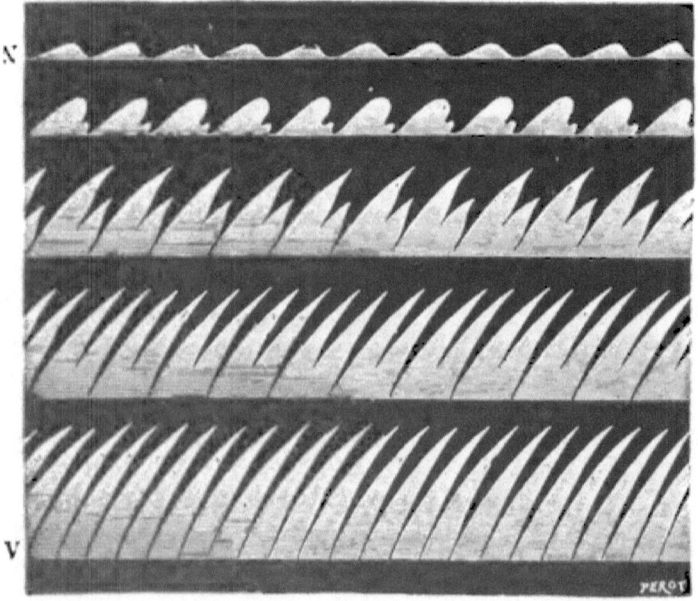

FIG. 97.

Connecting a manometric capsule with the end, b, of the exploring tube, and employing a short flame, we get results, if anything, more exact than those afforded by observations with the ear. At the centre of each ventral segment the flame suddenly becomes very luminous, while at all other points it is quite bluish and but faintly visible. Fig. 97 shows the appearance of the flame at the node, N, at the centre V, of a ventral segment, and at intervening points.

With this pipe Koenig showed, as Wertheim had demonstrated by other means, that the indications of theory as regards the vibrations of pipes are not realized by experiment. It is the old story over again, — the discrepancy between the observations of the experimenter and the demands of the mathematician.

The length of a pipe, whether open or stopped, emitting its fundamental note is less than that assigned by theory. Again, when a pipe yields one of its partials, it is found that the nodes next the embouchure, and the end opposite, in an open pipe, are nearer the extremity than theory calls for, and that the same discrepancy obtains for the middle of the ventral segment next to the closed end of a stopped pipe. It is nearer the end of the pipe than it should be according to theory. These variations are due to what are called terminal perturbations. For these reasons the prime note of a pipe is graver than that which the length of the pipe calls for.

Again, as Koenig has demonstrated, the partial sounds of an ordinary pipe do not follow the law of harmonic partials. According to his observations, the eighth partial may in any moderately large pipe have very nearly the same pitch as the ninth partial. Wertheim had previously remarked that in endeavoring to determine the fundamental of an organ-pipe by means of one of the upper partials he always obtained a value that was greater than that indicated by theory, in proportion as he employed a higher partial.

Savart has shown, however, that when the pipe is long and of very small diameter, and set in vibration by an oscillating plate, the number of vibrations is, as theory indicates, inversely proportional to the length of the pipe. In each case, too, the node corresponding to the fundamental is sensibly at the middle of the pipe, and the proper sounds of the pipe are true harmonic partials of the fundamental.

When, as in the case of ordinary pipes, the length is between six and twelve times the diameter, there is a slight divergence of experimental from theoretic values;

but as the transverse section increases, this divergence augments very rapidly.

By simply increasing the diameter of a pipe, and leaving its length unchanged, Mersenne succeeded in lowering the fundamental by seven whole tones. Taking a pipe seventy-two lines[1] in length, which we will suppose yielded the note C, — the note in fact would be many octaves higher, — and varying the diameter, he was able to get the results indicated in the following table:[2] —

Diameter in lines,	3	6	12	18	25	51
Notes emitted,	C	A_{-1}	G_{-1}	E_{-1}	$C\sharp_{-1}$	$A\sharp_{-2}$

The law governing the vibrations of similar pipes was discovered by Mersenne. It was afterwards verified by Savart, and extended to pipes of the most diverse forms. "If," says Mersenne, "we give to a pipe one foot in length a diameter of three digits, it will make exactly an octave with a similar pipe two feet in length and six digits in diameter."

The law of Mersenne and Savart may be expressed as follows: *Two similar pipes having similar embouchures emit notes whose pitch is inversely proportional to their lineal dimensions.* Thus, for instance, the prime tone of a square prismatic pipe twelve inches long and four inches wide will yield a note an octave lower than a similar pipe six inches long and two inches wide.

On the wind-chest of the acoustic organ are fixed eight pipes, of the forms shown in Fig. 98, the larger of which is in each case just twice the dimensions of the smaller. Causing them to speak, you observe that the smaller one in each instance gives a note an exact octave above that emitted by the larger ones. The law just enunciated was adverted to in our last lecture. We then learned that it was universal, and applied to all vibrating systems, solid, gaseous, or liquid.

In the manufacture of organ-pipes this law is of special practical value, as it enables the artisan to produce pipes

---

[1] A line is the one twelfth of an inch. [2] Harm. lib. xi. Prop. 9.

which are in perfect accord. Their consonance is not changed by variations of temperature, inasmuch as pipes of different dimensions would be equally affected in proportion to their size.

Owing to the difference between the observed and the theoretic length of an organ-pipe for any determinate note, organ manufacturers have recourse to an empirical law which meets their wants and is found to hold true within quite wide limits. M. Cavaillé-Coll, the celebrated organ-

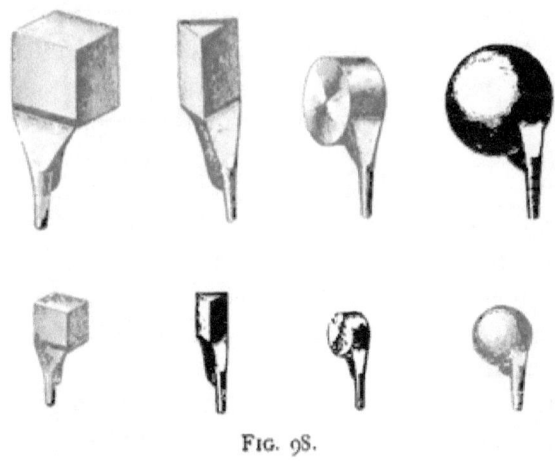

FIG. 98.

builder of Paris, employs in the construction of open pipes the following formula: —

For rectangular pipes of a depth p, $L' = L - 2p$
For cylindrical pipes of a diameter d, $L' = L - \frac{1}{3}d$.

In both these formulæ L' denotes the actual, and L the theoretic length of the pipe for any given note. Similar empirical laws govern the manufacture of stopped pipes, and of pipes of varying depth, but of the same length. It is found that in pipes of the same length but of different widths, the pitch of the note is the same, — provided the embouchure extends across the entire width of the pipe. The only difference then observed in notes yielded by pipes of the same length and depth, but of different width, is one of intensity, the wider pipe emitting the louder note.

Two pipes of equal length and depth, but of different widths, are now mounted on the wind-chest, and when they are made to speak, you are unable to distinguish any difference in the notes emitted, save the one mentioned. The larger pipe yields a note considerably louder than that emitted by the smaller one, but the pitch in both cases is identical.

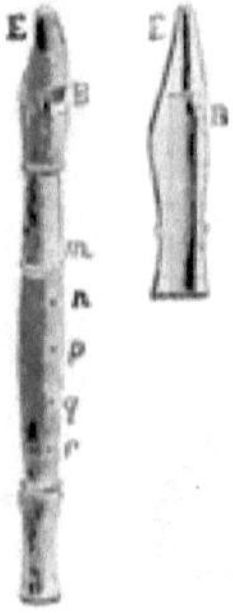

Instruments like the flute, fife, piccolo, and flageolet yield, in addition to the harmonic partials, a number of intermediate notes. The former, as we have learned, are produced by varying the pressure of the wind, thereby subdividing the air-column within the tube into a greater or less number of segments. The latter are obtained by a number of lateral orifices closed or opened by the fingers or suitable keys.

Fig. 99.

The flageolet (Fig. 99) has, as you see, a mouthpiece, $E B$, like an ordinary organ-pipe. The lateral openings are shown at m, n, p, q, r.

In the flute (Fig. 100), the embouchure is an oval opening, A, at the side. The player places his lips above the orifice, and at a short distance from its sharp edge, which answers to the lip of a mouthpiece.

Taking, then, an instrument like the flute, whose fundamental is C_2, and which has six lateral openings between its open extremity and its embouchure, we produce by opening the holes in succession an effect analogous to that which would result from shortening the tube by cutting off in succession those portions between its open end and the different apertures, beginning with that which is farthest away from the embouchure. Thus, the prime tone being C_2, we obtain by opening in succession the six holes, beginning with the one nearest the

Fig. 100.

open end of the tube, the notes D_3, E_3, F_3, G_3, A_3, B_3. By closing all the lateral orifices and increasing the pressure of the wind, we get C_4, an octave above the prime, and by opening the holes as before, we get the notes of the second octave. In a similar manner we elicit those of the third octave. The flats and sharps of the chromatic scale are obtained by suitable keys, which open and close holes intermediate between those yielding the notes of the diatonic scale. And what is here said of the flute applies to all instruments of its class.

We come now to the consideration of reed-pipes properly so-called. We have seen that flute-pipes may be considered as reed-pipes, and that the aërial column within them may be caused to vibrate by means of the "Luftlamelle," or air-reed; but it is probably better, in order to avoid confusion, to retain the old name of flute or flue pipe.

A reed-pipe may be defined as any kind of wind instrument in which the aërial column is excited by the vibratory motion of an elastic body called a reed. Under the action of this reed the air within the pipe forms pulses of condensation and rarefaction, as in flute-pipes. Nodes and ventral segments are also developed according to the laws which we have already considered.

In organs, harmoniums, concertinas, harmonicums, accordeons, and similar instruments the reed is made of metal, usually brass. The reeds of the clarinet, oboe, and bassoon are of thin cane. The vocal cords answer to reeds in the human larynx, while in such instruments as the horn, trumpet, trombone, and brass instruments generally, the work of reeds is performed by the lips. The vocal cords and the lips are, hence, frequently classed as membranous reeds. In the clarinet and organ and in all instruments generally in which metal reeds are employed, we have what are called single reeds; that is, there is only a single vibrating lamina for each pipe or note. The bassoon and the oboe have what are denominated paired or double reeds.

Again, reeds are distinguished as free or striking reeds. A and B (Fig. 101) show in perspective and in section a free reed such as is used in harmoniums. As you will remark, the reed zz, which is technically called a tongue, or vibrator, is attached to a metal block, aa, in which there is an opening a trifle larger than the tongue. When at rest, it occupies the position shown in A. When in motion the tongue occupies alternately the positions shown at z_1 and z_2 B. In the former position there is an opening for the admission of the air, as indicated by the direction of the arrow. In the latter, the stream of air is cut off entirely, when, in virtue of the elasticity of the tongue, it returns to its former position, z_1.

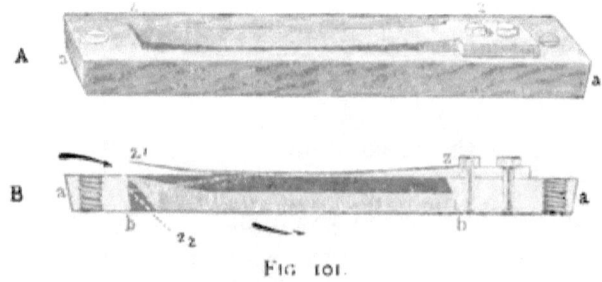

FIG. 101.

From the foregoing it appears that the action of a reed is essentially the same as that of a siren. The principal difference lies in the manner in which the orifice which admits the air is opened and closed. In the siren this is effected by the rotation of a delicately balanced disk. In the reed it is accomplished by the oscillatory movement of the tongue. The function of the reed is purely mechanical. It merely serves the purpose of determining the period of vibration of the air, which is itself the sonorous body, and not the reed, as is sometimes supposed.

A and B (Fig. 102) show the kinds of reeds used in connection with organ-pipes. In the former is a free, and in the latter a striking reed. The length of the tongue, and consequently its pitch, is in both cases adjusted by a movable wire, d, called a tuning-wire. The note of A is reinforced and its quality modified by a conical tube.[1] The wind is driven into an air-chamber, pp. Thence it passes into the semi-cylindrical tube, rr, fastened to the block, ss. The

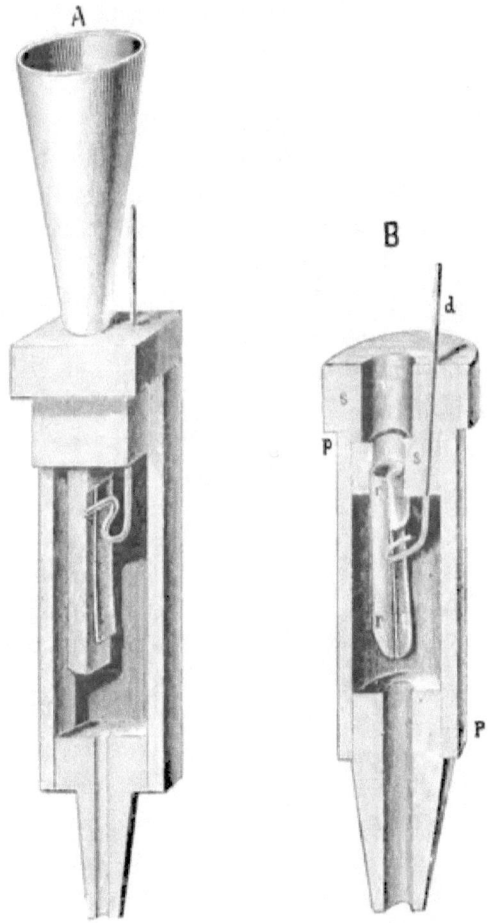

FIG. 102.

tongue is thus caused to execute a series of oscillations which determine the pitch of the vibrating air-column. Pushing down the tuning-wire would, as is obvious, shorten

---

[1] In organs, the reed-pipes are made to yield notes of different qualities according to the form and length of conical and pyramidal pipes. — "cornets," — with which they are connected.

the tongue, and consequently heighten the pitch. Raising the wire would lengthen the tongue and lower the pitch.

Helmholtz has demonstrated that the point of a pipe at which a reed is inserted is to be considered a node. This is readily understood when we reflect that the variations of air-pressure, by reason of the peculiar vibratory motion of the tongue, are here at a maximum. A pipe, therefore, with a reed at one of its extremities is to be considered in the light of an ordinary stopped pipe of the same length.

FIG. 103.

The law governing the production of the fundamental and the upper partials is in both cases the same. For this reason a cylindrical tube, like the clarinet (Fig. 103), is competent, when emitting its proper notes, to yield only the odd partials of the prime tone. By orifices made in the side of the tube, and opened and closed by the fingers or keys, all the notes of the chromatic scale may be obtained. The annexed figure shows how the reed, C, is attached to the mouthpiece, B. The lips of the performer regulate the length of the reed here, as does the tuning-wire in the case of the ordinary reed-pipe.

The oboe and bassoon, as has been stated, differ from the clarinet in having a double, instead of a single, reed. But there is, besides, a more important distinction. Owing to their conical form,[1] they are competent to yield all the upper partials of the fundamental, — the even as well as the odd. The bassoon differs from the oboe in that the tube of the latter is of greater volume than that of the former. The lowest note of the bassoon is a twelfth below

---

[1] Mr. Ellis says, "Too much has been attributed to the cylindrical bore for producing only the unevenly numbered partials." He quotes Mr Hermann Smith, who, having given the subject special study, states that "an oboe reed fixed on the clarinet tube gives oboe pitch of tone and oboe partials." (Ellis's Helmholtz, p. 553).

the gravest tone of the oboe. For this reason the bassoon is to the oboe what the violoncello is to the violin.

In the heavy metal tongues of the harmonium and the organ, the notes emitted have sensibly the same pitch as would be yielded by the isolated vibrating tongues. There must, therefore, in these cases be at least one tongue for each note.

The lighter reed-tongues of the clarinet, oboe, and bassoon, on the other hand, are capable of yielding a large number of notes. The reason is that the vibrating column of air in these instruments has sufficient force to control the vibration of the tongue, and compel it to yield notes corresponding in pitch to the proper notes of the tube. As a consequence, the tongue is made to execute vibrations whose period is much greater than those which it would make if isolated. As a matter of fact, the proper notes of the tongue are never used in music, because they are too high and piercing, and because it is impossible to give to them any degree of steadiness.

Instruments like the French-horn, cornet, ophicleide, and other brass instruments of this class, differ from those of which we have been speaking, not only in their form and in the quality of the tone that characterizes them, but especially in the form of mouthpiece employed. As is seen from those I have in my hand (Fig. 104), they are conical, or cup-like, in shape. Such mouthpieces are known as *embouchures de cor*, or horn mouthpieces.

Fig. 104.

Connected with resonant tubes, they are applied to the lips, which then act just as reeds. The air from the lungs sets the lips in vibration, and with them the column of air in the instrument. The rapidity of oscillation depends on the pressure of the air and the tension of the lips, or the force with which the performer presses them against the embouchure. It is the proper adjustment of the wind pressure and the tension of the lips that make playing on these instruments so difficult.

According to Mr. D. J. Blaikley, quoted by Ellis, "the lips do not vibrate throughout their whole length, but only through a certain length, determined by the diameter of the cup of the mouthpiece. Probably also the vibrating length can be modified by the mere pinch, — at least this is the sensation I experience when sounding high notes on a large mouthpiece. The compass — about four octaves — possible on a given mouthpiece is greater than that of any one register of the voice, and the whole range of brass instruments played thus with the lips is about one octave greater than the whole range of the human voice, from basso profundo to the highest soprano."

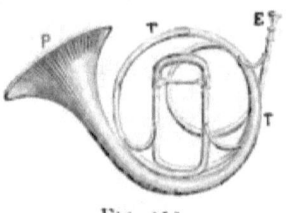

Fig. 105

Before you (Fig. 105) is one of the older forms of the French-horn, which corresponds to the Waldhorn, or German hunting-horn. As you see, it is a long coiled conical brass tube, ETT, terminating in a wide "bell," P. As it has no side-holes, or keys, it can yield only its prime and the corresponding harmonic upper partials. According to Zamminer, the tube of such a horn is 13.4 feet long. Its fundamental note is $E\flat_{-1}$. This, and the first upper partial $E\flat_1$, are never used. Only the higher partials are employed in music. These, beginning with the third partial, are $B\flat_1$, $E\flat_2$, G_2, $B\flat_2$, $D\flat_3$, E_3, F_3, $A\flat_{3+}$, $B\flat_3$, etc., and supply most of the tones of the scale. Those which are missing are partially elicited by placing the closed hand in the bell of the horn, thus more or less closing it at this point. For this reason such notes are sometimes called "hand-notes."

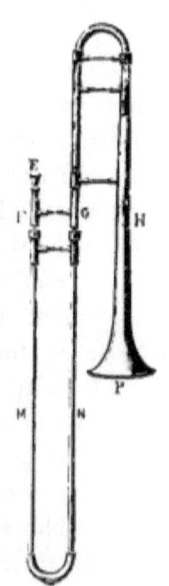

Fig. 106.

The trombone (Fig. 106) is a modified form of the horn. It is composed of a fixed part, $EFGHP$, and a movable part, MN, by means of which the player can vary the length of the aërial column, and thus, also, the pitch of the notes emitted.

The trumpet belongs to the same class as the trombone; indeed, the latter is the natural bass of the former. The trumpet speaks in an octave higher than the French-horn, of which it possesses the first eleven open notes. On all these instruments, owing to the absence of fixed notes, it is possible, as with instruments of the violin family, to play in pure intonation. For this reason, they are capable, in the hands of expert players, of yielding musical effects that, with keyed instruments, are quite impossible.

The ophicleide, EP (Fig. 107), is also a long conical tube, but it differs from the French-horn and the trombone in having a certain number of openings along its side. These can be closed and opened by means of keys, and thus the number of notes which the instrument is capable of yielding is greatly augmented.

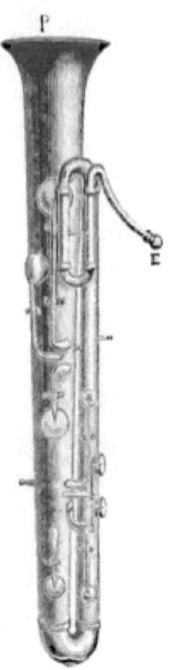

FIG. 107.

The cornet-a-piston (Fig. 108) is an improved form of the trombone, just as the trombone is a modification of the French-horn. Like its prototypes, the cornet-a-piston is provided with a bell, P, and an embouchure, E. Parallel to the principal tube of the instrument are placed smaller tubes. B, C, D. These latter are put into communication with the former

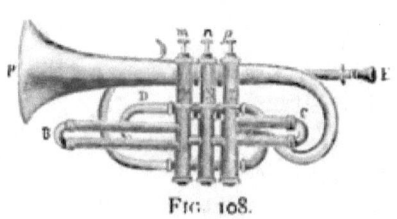

FIG. 108.

by means of the cylinders, M, N, P, in which pistons connected with the rods, m, n, p, are made to open valves. This is equivalent to lengthening the tube so as to make it yield notes one, two, or three semitones flatter. The valve-action in the cornet thus serves the same purpose as the sliding-tube in the trombone. These instruments, like clarinets, are made of various sizes and pitches, and are especially employed in military bands.

In instruments like the flute, clarinet, and similar keyed instruments, the acoustic length of the tube — that is, the portion which chiefly determines the pitch of the note emitted — is that part between the embouchure and the nearest open aperture. Opening or closing the six holes in such an instrument is tantamount to lengthening or shortening the tube, and, consequently, to raising or lowering the pitch of the notes emitted. In brass wind instruments, on the contrary, the acoustic length of the tube is, as we have seen, more generally regulated by valves and sliding-tubes, which determine the length of the aërial column actually in vibration. It would, however, be a misstatement of fact to say that the opening of the side-holes of wind instruments has precisely the same effect as shortening the tube. Such is not the case; and for the simple reason that the reflection of the sonorous pulses from such lateral opening is not exactly the same as that at the open end of the instrument. The theory of the side-holes of wind instruments is very complicated, and strange as it may appear, there is much about it that still requires explanation.

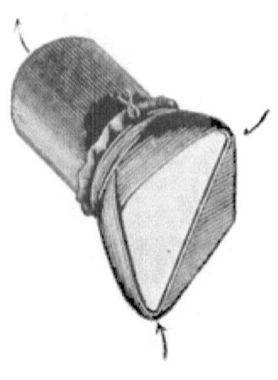

FIG. 109.

In the human larynx we have the most perfect of all musical instruments. It yields the sweetest and richest tones, and admits of variations of pitch, intensity, and quality that in other instruments are quite impossible.

A model of the larynx in its simplest form is shown in Fig. 109. This is a modified form of that first devised by the illustrious comparative anatomist, Johann Müller. It is nothing more than a short glass tube, across one of the ends of which are stretched two bands of india-rubber so as to form a narrow slit through which air may be urged. When in vibration each of the strips of rubber acts as a reed, and as there are two of them, this simple device is nothing more than a double-reed instrument.

The same may be said of the organ of the voice; it is nothing more than a double-reed instrument. The trachea, or windpipe, corresponds to the glass tube in the model in my hand, and the vocal cords to the strips of india-rubber.

The vocal cords are caused to vibrate by air issuing from the lungs, and the variations in the pitch of the notes emitted are determined by modifications in the tension and length of the cords, as well as by the length and width of the intervening aperture called the glottis.

The quality of the tone depends partly on the structure of the larynx itself, and on the form and size of the vocal cords, and partly on the form and size of the oral and nasal cavities, which perform the office of resonators. As all parts of the larynx, and its adjoining resonant cavities, are perfectly and readily adjustable, we have in the organ of the voice an instrument that is susceptible of every shade of modulation, and of the most marvellous variations of quality and power.

So far we have been speaking of sonorous tubes which are set in vibration by a blast of air from a bellows, or that which serves the same purpose, the lungs. The air-columns of tubes may, however, be excited by other means. Anything competent to impart a periodic impulse to the air within a tube, is sufficient to cause the generation of a musical note.

A jet of ignited gas may, under suitable circumstances, give rise to a loud, pure tone. A simple means of illustrating this fact, as we saw in our first lecture (Fig. 10), is afforded by the chemical harmonicon. The apparatus used consists, as you remember, of a Woulfe bottle, in which are placed the materials for generating hydrogen gas. In one of the openings of the flask is fixed a safety tube, and in the other a small glass tube drawn to a fine point, through which the hydrogen issues. On igniting the gas, and holding over the flame a glass tube of suitable size, you at once hear a clear, musical note.

Faraday was the first to demonstrate that the note is due to a series of rhythmic explosions whose periods synchronize with the rate of vibration of the aerial column enclosed by the tube. Chladni showed that the glass tube in this case acts exactly like an open organ-pipe, and that by properly adjusting the size of the flame and its position in the tube, one can not only get a note corresponding to the fundamental of the pipe, but also elicit at least two of its upper partials.

With a larger apparatus than the one just used we evoke much louder tones and a greater number of partials than were obtained by Chladni. We have here a large copper cylinder, in which hydrogen is condensed under high pressure. Near by is a number of glass tubes of various sizes, from two to six feet in length, and from one to two inches in diameter. Among these are eight which are of the same diameter, but whose lengths are so adjusted that they give, when placed in succession over the flame, the eight notes of the diatonic scale. Measuring the length of these tubes, we find that they are inversely as the pitch of the notes they respectively emit. They therefore conform to the same law as the other forms of sonorous tubes which we have been investigating.

Taking one of the larger tubes, and holding it over a larger flame, we get a louder and deeper note than any we have yet heard. The tube is now yielding its prime tone. Lowering the flame, a note of higher pitch is heard. This is the octave of the fundamental. Diminishing still more the size of the flame, we obtain the twelfth, or the third partial. In a similar manner, by regulating the size of the flame and its position in the tube, we should be able to elicit a number of higher partials.

It has been said that the notes produced by such flames are due to a series of explosions. Wheatstone has shown us how we can prove this experimentally. Taking the cubical mirror, which we have used in studying Koenig's manometric flames, and rotating it before the singing flame, we see that it is immediately resolved into a chaplet of luminous images. The images are at a greater or less distance from each other according to the greater or less velocity of rotation of the mirror. Reducing the flame to silence, we have reflected from the mirror a continuous band of light. The band remains continuous as long as the flame is in a state of quiescence. But as soon as it is made to sing, the ribbon of light seen in the mirror becomes discontinuous as before.

It is an easy matter to determine the number of explosions per second corresponding to the note which is being produced. All that is necessary is to obtain the pitch of the note. This can be done approximately by measuring the length of the sonorous tube, and dividing this length, multiplied by 4, into the velocity of sound per second. It would obviously be necessary in this case, in order to have anything approaching an exact result, to make corrections for the high temperature of the aërial column, and for the amount of aqueous vapor present. We can, however, estimate approximately the pitch of the note by ear. But our tuning-fork tonometer stands us in good stead now. A few trials will enable us to determine almost exactly the pitch of the note now sounding. We find that it approximates closely that of the fork I now hold in my hand, F_2, which executes 348 vibrations per second. As, therefore, each explosion is equivalent to a single vibration, we conclude that the tone of the flame now singing is produced by a series of rhythmic explosions which number about 350 per second.

Instead of using glass tubes, let us take this brass tube supported on a solid stand. The tube is over three inches in diameter, and about eight feet long. And instead of the small jet hitherto employed, we shall use that issuing from a large rose burner. The gas is now ignited, and placed in position within the tube. Regulating the pressure so as to secure a large flame, we obtain the fundamental tone of the tube, which, as you perceive, is one of extraordinary volume and power. So intense are its vibrations

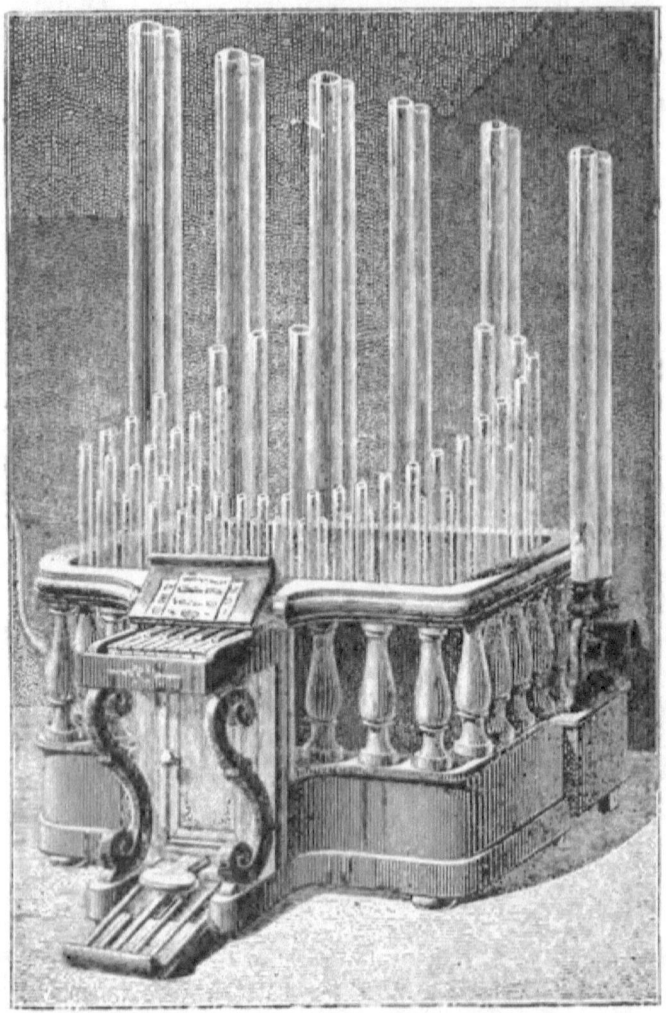

Fig. 110.

that they excite corresponding tremors in the floor and the windows and the furniture of the room. Ordinary illuminating gas might be used instead of hydrogen, but it cannot be made to sing so readily, and requires more care in securing the right pressure. The experiments of Count Schaffgotsch and Tyndall have greatly extended our knowledge of the origin and nature of singing flames of all kinds.

Singing flames so far have been of no practical value in music, although several instruments have been devised in which such flames were used. The first of these was constructed by Wheatstone. More recently M. Kastner has made a much more elaborate instrument, which he calls a pyrophone. A picture of this quaint instrument (Fig. 110) is projected on the screen. It is, as you see, a sort of pipe organ, which has twin singing flames in each pipe.

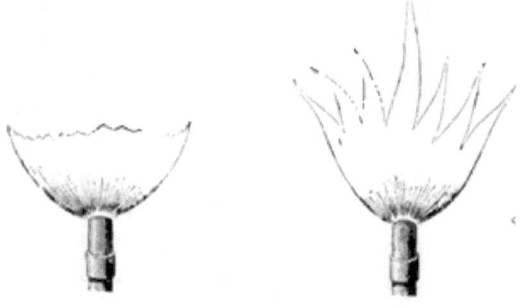

Fig. 111.

The notes are elicited by placing in each of the tubes at a point one third of their length from the lower extremities two small flames in contact. As long as the flames are together they are quiet, but when separated they begin to sing. By the use of suitable keys it is possible to unite and separate the flames so that a simple melody can be played with comparative ease.

Closely allied to singing flames are what are known as sensitive flames. They were first observed by Professor John Le Conte in 1857. But it is to the researches of Govi, Tyndall, Barry, and Geyer that we owe the very sensitive flames we now have at our disposal.

When ordinary illuminating gas is allowed to issue from a common bat-wing burner at the usual pressure, it burns with a steady flame of the form shown in the left of Fig. 111. In this condition it remains unaffected by any sounds that might be produced. If, however, the pressure is so increased that the flame is just at the point of flaring, it is sensitive to certain sounds, although uninfluenced by others. When more gas is turned on, and the flame is on the point of roaring, it is very sensitive indeed. A sound of proper pitch from an organ-pipe or a flageolet will at once cause it to assume the tongued appearance exhibited at the right of the adjoining figure.

The degree of sensibility of a flame depends on a variety of circumstances. It is modified by the size and form of the nipple employed, by the diameter of its orifice, and by the diameter of the tube connected with it. It is likewise affected by the pitch of the notes that are sounded; for it has been discovered that such a flame is most sensitive to notes that it is itself competent to yield, or is on the point of emitting.

FIG. 112.

Before you (Fig. 112), and issuing from a steatite burner, is a much more sensitive flame than the one we have just been using. It is upwards of twenty inches long, and is sensitive to the slightest noise. Walking across the floor, tearing a sheet of paper, shaking a bunch of keys, or whistling, will set it in commotion. Certain sounds cause it to change its length and form, others will make it roar, while others still will cause it to drop down to a short non-luminous flame like that shown on the right of the accompanying figure. It is particularly sensitive to acute notes and to noises that contain acute notes. It is also affected in varying degrees by the different vowel-sounds. Those which, like *a*, *e*, and *i*, are characterized by high upper partials, agitate it much more than *o* and *u*, in which the higher partials are totally absent.

By interposing a wire gauze between the burner and the flame, Mr. Barry, of Ireland, was able to get a more sensitive flame than any we have yet seen. Mr. Geyer, of Stevens' Institute of Technology, greatly enhanced the delicacy of Barry's experiment by covering the flame with a tube of suitable size, which rests on the gauze. Such an apparatus stands before you (Fig. 113).

We have now a luminous flame about seven inches long, which is specially sensitive to acute sounds. By elevating the gauze and tube, the flame is gradually shortened and rendered less luminous, until it finally becomes violently agitated and breaks forth into song. The note it at present emits may be maintained indefinitely. It is not now affected by external sounds. By gradually lowering tube and gauze until the flame just ceases to sing, it becomes a sensitive musical flame of extraordinary delicacy. It is at present quiescent, but the least noise will start it into song. Tapping on the table, whistling, hissing, crumpling paper, causes it to sing and to continue its note as long as the noise endures. Indeed, so sensitive may it be made by careful adjustment that it is affected by sounds that are almost, if not quite, inaudible. For this reason, a flame like this, as well as the others which we have been studying, can be used as detecters of sonorous vibrations whose presence could not be discovered by other means.

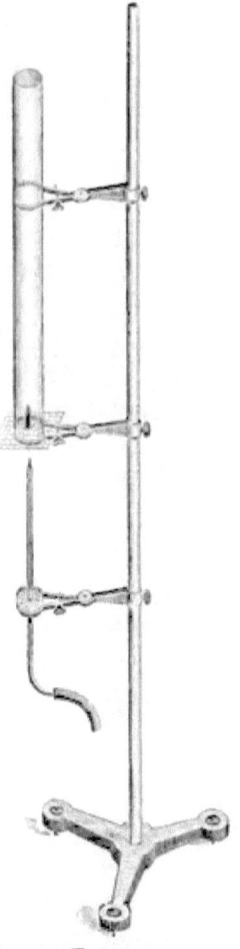

Fig. 113.

The seat of sensitiveness of the flames we have been examining is, as has been demonstrated, at their root, or the points at which they issue from the burner. The gas in passing through the orifice of the burner suffers friction, which, when the pressure of the gas is properly regulated, sets the flame in vibration, and induces flaring. But when the flame is just on the point of flaring, external vibrations, if properly timed, are competent to produce the same effects as an increase of pressure. The action in this case is analogous to that which obtains in sympathetic vibrations generally, of which we shall see more in our next lecture. We shall then learn that bodies in a state of vibratory motion, whose periodicity is the same, are capable of yielding results which, under other conditions, are impossible.

If the sensitiveness of a flame does not depend on the flame itself, but on the friction of the gas as it issues from the orifice of the burner, it is obvious that the same phenomena should accompany gases which are unignited as well as those which are burning. Such has been found by experiment to be the case. Unignited coal-gas, hydrogen, air, and carbon-dioxide may be made to yield the same results as does the most sensitive flame. By associating smoke or the fumes of sal-ammoniac with the gas as it issues from its orifice, we can render the jet and its motions visible, and thus experiment with it as well as with a flame.

A long, delicate smoke-jet (Fig. 114) is now issuing from the orifice of our steatite burner. The slightest noises disturb it, and cause it to assume different forms and lengths. But the pitch which will most strongly agitate this smoke-jet is lower than that which depressed our long flame. By sounding a note of the proper pitch the jet now so long becomes at once short and bushy at the top, as shown at the right of the figure.

But this marked sensitiveness to vibrations of notes of certain pitch is not confined to gaseous jets only. Savart has shown that liquid veins, or jets, are equally sensitive, and the effects produced on such veins are fully as interesting and remarkable as anything we have yet witnessed. Lack of time, however, precludes our giving any illustration of the action of liquid veins under the influence of sonorous vibrations. Suffice it to say that the cause which gives rise to the phenomena observed is the same in one case as in the other; viz., an equality of periodicity on the part of the sonorous body, and the jet or vein which is affected.

Having made ourselves familiar with the laws of vibration of sonorous tubes, we are now able to appreciate a very interesting method of determining the velocity of sound in air and in various gases. We have learned that owing to terminal perturbations there is a difference between the theoretic and the actual length of an organ-pipe of a determined pitch. But by a series of very careful experiments Wertheim has been able to ascertain the constant quantity by which the length of a pipe yielding its fundamental is to be augmented in order that it may equal the theoretical length. Once knowing the theoretical length of any given pipe, we may determine the velocity of sound in any gaseous medium by the simple formula $L = \frac{V}{N}$. L here equals the wave-length of a given sound, N the number of vibrations per second, and V the velocity of sound in the medium employed. If we take an open organ-pipe emitting its prime tone,

FIG. 114.

the length of the pipe increased by Wertheim's constant gives one half the theoretical wave-length. The full wave-length is, therefore, equal to $2L$. The value of N may be ascertained by any of the various methods employed for determining the pitch of sounds. This gives us the two known quantities, $2L$ and N, from which the third, V, is easily deduced.

By the application of the formula $V = 2LN$, Dulong and Wertheim were able to determine very accurately the velocity of sound in the various gases on which they experimented. Indeed, the values usually given for the velocity of sound in different gases have been obtained by this method.

Kundt has greatly extended and elaborated the method just indicated by rendering visible the subdivisions of a tube corresponding to any given note. He has, in fact, accomplished for sonorous tubes what Chladni did for vibrating plates.

If a light powder, like lycopodium, amorphous silica, or finely sifted cork filing, be distributed over the inner surface of a glass tube, and the tube be set in vibration by rubbing it with a moist cloth, we shall see the powder within arranging itself as in Fig. 115. At the nodes, $N N N N$, as you perceive, are small circles, and along the ventral segments are transverse lines. A glass tube filled with air and yielding its fundamental note would exhibit sixteen such segments; only four are shown in the figure, showing at once that the velocity of sound in glass is sixteen times as great as it is in air.

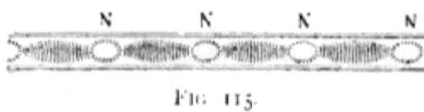

Fig. 115.

We have here a series of four tubes of the same size, and filled with air, carbon-dioxide, illuminating gas, and hydrogen. When rubbed with a moist cloth so as to yield their octave, the powder within forms like figures, but the number of segments is different for the various gases. For air we have 32, for carbon-dioxide 40, for illuminating gas 20, and for hydrogen 9. The velocity of sound in the gases named is inversely as the numbers. Taking air as unity, the velocity of sound in the four gases in the order given would be 1, .8, 1.6, 3.56. Thus with a single sweep of the cloth we are able to tell the relative velocity of sound in the different gases, and knowing the velocity of sound in air, we can readily calculate the absolute velocities.

But in order to secure more accurate results, Kundt found it necessary to modify somewhat his method of procedure. Instead of rubbing the tube containing the powder to be excited, he excited the air within by means of a smaller tube.

Before you is a glass tube, AB (Fig. 116), six feet long and nearly two inches in diameter. The end, A, is closed by a movable stopper, while the end, B, is closed by a cork, through the middle of which passes the small glass tube, CD. This tube is held at its centre, E, by a vice. The end, C, of the small tube is closed with a cork, a part of which is just large enough to fill loosely the bore of the larger tube. The interior of the larger tube between A and C is coated with siliceous powder. When now a moist

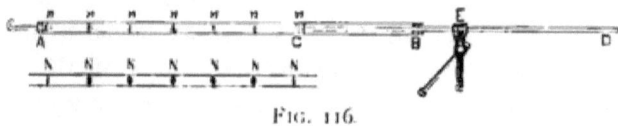

Fig. 116.

cloth is drawn along the smaller tube between E and D, it is thrown into longitudinal vibrations, and yields its fundamental note.

But in order that the vibrations of the air between A and C may synchronize with those of the small glass tube, it must subdivide itself into segments whose lengths will be to those of the glass tube inversely as the velocity of sound in these two substances. This is exactly what is seen to occur. If the length of the glass tube from C to D were equal to the aërial column, AC, the number of ventral segments formed between A and C would be sixteen. This would show that the air-column, in order to accommodate itself to the rate of vibration of the glass tube, must divide itself into segments which are sixteen times shorter than the vibrating segments of glass. This means that the velocity of sound in glass is sixteen times as great as it is in air.

Instead of using glass to impart vibrations to the aerial column within the larger tube, we might substitute rods of wood or metal. The results would be the same, with this difference, that the number of segments formed by the powder would vary with the velocity of sound in the materials employed.

The result given for the velocity of sound in glass in the experiment just made is only approximate. It will of course vary with the quality of the glass used. Instead of being, as stated, exactly sixteen times as great as in air, the velocity of sound in glass has been found by the very careful experiments of Kundt to be 15.25 times greater in the latter than in the former medium. Similar experiments with steel, brass, and copper rods give for the velocity of sound in these metals — that in air being taken as unity — the numbers 15.34, 10.87, and 11.96. These values, however, are only approximately correct. Kundt's method does not give exact measures of velocity because the rod is loaded, the cork rubs against the sides of the tube, and finally because the velocity of sound in tubes of small diameter is unknown. Old Chladni's method is the best, now that we have, thanks to Koenig, the means of getting the absolute number of vibrations of a tuning-fork at any given temperature.

In order that there may be perfect synchronism between the vibrations of the smaller glass tube, CB, and the segments of the air-column, AC, it is necessary that the length of the air-column, CA, be an exact multiple of the half-wave-length of the sound in air. When the tube CD yields its fundamental, the wave-length of the corresponding note is, as you know, equal to twice the length of the tube. The wave-length corresponding to this note in air will therefore be equal to twice the length of one of the dust segments in the interior of the tube, as one of these segments is but a half wave in length. The proper adjustment of the length of the aërial column is made by means of the movable stopper at A. The aspect of the dust figures tells us when the cork is in the right position. The powder seeks the nodes, n, n, n, etc., and N, N, N, etc., more completely, and the nodal lines are more perfect, in proportion as the adjustment is more exact. When the air-column is an exact multiple of a half-wave length, the silica leaves the ventral segments entirely, and collects in tiny well-defined heaps at the nodes N, N, N, N (Fig. 115). By measuring the distance between any two of these heaps we have at once the value of a half-wave length of the note in air. The length of the tube, CD, when sounding its fundamental, is equivalent to the half-wave length of the same note in glass. A simple proportion, then, $\frac{l}{L} = \frac{v}{V}$, gives the ratio of the velocities of sound in air and glass. The same proportions, as is obvious, would apply to any other solid as well as glass.

Inasmuch as the vibrations of liquid columns obey the same laws as the vibrations of columns of gas, several attempts have been made to determine the velocity of sound in liquids by enclosing them in suitable tubes, and applying to them the same mode of procedure as we have found to be so effectual with gases and solids. So far, however, notwithstanding the many ingenious contrivances resorted to in the experiments made, the results attained have been unsatisfactory. But the difficulties encountered seem rather to exist in the apparatus employed than to be inherent in the method itself. Whether or not these difficulties can be overcome by other and improved forms of apparatus, or by experiments conducted under different and more favorable conditions, time alone can disclose.

CHAPTER VII.

RESONANCE AND INTERFERENCE.

SO far we have been dealing with single, individual sounds. We have, it is true, had occasion to listen incidentally to two or more sounds simultaneously produced; but I have reserved a more detailed account of such concomitant sounds for the present lecture. To-day I shall speak of what is known as resonance, and its correlative, called interference, of sound. Some of the most practical and important consequences to musicians follow from the first of these phenomena, and some of the most interesting and paradoxical results arise from the second.

To understand the nature and effect of resonance, it is important at the outset to appreciate properly the cumulative effect of feeble impulses, when suitably timed, in moving comparatively large masses of matter. We have before had occasion to employ various contrivances to illustrate by slow mechanical motions the much more rapid movements of sonorous bodies; and a similar procedure now will enable us better than anything else to comprehend the full import of the various and striking phenomena embraced under the general head of resonance.

On a strong wooden frame is suspended by a cord a good-sized cannon-ball. Attached to the ball is a fine cambric thread, which is capable of supporting only a small fraction of the weight of the ball. I give the string a very gentle pull, and by this means there is imparted a slight, almost an imperceptible, motion to the ball. By properly timing these slight pulls, always pulling when the ball is coming towards me, and never when it is moving in the opposite direction, I can cause the ball to swing through quite a large arc. The pulls, however, must be isochronous; that is, they must be of the same period as the ball which oscillates as a pendulum. Should I attempt to pull the string when the ball is moving away from me, it would at once snap in twain. The force now stored up in the moving ball is so great that it can only be overcome by using a much stronger cord, or by gradually counteracting it by slight periodic pulls with the cambric thread when the ball is receding. This experiment shows us that quite large masses of matter can be put in motion by very slight impulses, and that these same slight impulses, when periodically applied, are sufficient to bring again the moving mass to a standstill.

We may vary the experiment by imparting gentle impulses in a different manner. Instead of using fine thread, we have recourse to slight periodic puffs of air from the mouth. "But," you will exclaim, "such an insignificant force is utterly inadequate to move such a heavy mass." So it seems. But let us try.

Having found out by the foregoing experiment the period of the ball, I know how to direct my breath against it. I blow against it once, and again, and still again, and there is scarcely any perceptible movement. I continue to direct little puffs of air against it, and in a few moments the motion becomes very considerable. Should the impulses directed against the ball be improperly timed, the effect produced would be little, if anything at all. And, as in the first experiment, I can bring the ball to rest by little puffs of air impinging against it every time it comes towards me.

Allow me to modify the experiment still further. Instead of the cannon-ball we may now use a smaller ball, also of iron, as a pendulum. Close to it, and from the same support, is suspended by the same length of string another ball identical in size and material. But the size and material of the balls is not of so much importance as that the strings supporting them should be of exactly the same length. We have here what are in reality two pendulums whose periods of vibration are isochronous. When one of them is made to swing to and fro, observe what takes place. The other one remains at rest for a moment; but soon you perceive a slight oscillation, which eventually becomes as great as that of the first ball.

How do we explain this? Is there an invisible string or breath of air to cause the first to act on the second? No; but the vibratory movement of the one is communicated to the other in a no less effective manner. In this case the vibrations -- they are very slight, it is true — are conveyed through the beam that acts as the common support. The vibrations are so slight as to be imperceptible to sight or to touch, but they are none the less real and operative.

Clock-makers have long known of these forced vibrations. They were first observed by the famous Huygens, the inventor of the pendulum clock, over two hundred years ago. It is well known, for instance, that two clocks, whose rates are slightly different, will, when brought near together on the same table or other support, keep the same time. The pendulum of the more rapid clock forces up the speed of the slower one, and compels it to move at the same rate. But while the speed of the latter is advanced, that of the former is retarded correspondingly. If, however, there is any material difference in the rates of vibration of the two clocks, this effect will not take place. This fact can be easily illustrated by means of the two pendulums with which we have been experimenting.

We will lengthen the string of one of them, and then set it in vibration. As you perceive, it has no effect on the other. But if the string be still more elongated, and made twice or three or more times as long as the string of the other pendulum, the result will be different. By setting the longer pendulum in motion, it will after some time cause the shorter one to vibrate also. In this case the former imparts an impulse to the latter, not at every swing of the latter, but at every second or third swing, according to its length. The number of impulses communicated being then only one half or one third as numerous as when the pendulums were of equal length, the amount of motion set up in the shorter pendulum will be proportionately less.

In the preceding experiments a large ball was moved by a small string or by small puffs of air. A similar effect to that just produced by one pendulum acting on another of different length, would be obtained by pulling the ball or blowing against it every second or third vibration. But the result secured would obviously be correspondingly less than when the motion is accelerated at each vibration. In all these experiments, however, the important fact to bear in mind is that the impulses communicated, whatever their nature, and whatever their number, must be of the same period — or multiple or submultiple of the period — as that of the vibrating bodies themselves, and must take place in the same phase.

There are many familiar instances of synchronous motion produced by regularly recurring impulses. The aërial pulses generated by certain organ pipes shake the windows and pews and columns of a church. A large bell set swinging by the properly directed efforts of a single boy will in turn convey a very marked vibratory movement to a massive tower or belfry. We have all observed how a six or seven story building may be caused to vibrate from cellar to garret by the passage of a carriage over the cobble-stones of the street. A company of soldiers in crossing a bridge is made to break step, in order to prevent the injurious results that might follow from forced vibrations. Hence also the reason of the prohibition to drive over a bridge "faster than a walk."

Lord Rayleigh, in his admirable *Theory of Sound*,[1] remarks that "illustrations of the powerful effects of isochronism must be within the experience of every one. They are often of importance in very different fields from any with which acoustics is concerned. For example, few things are more dangerous to a ship than to lie in the trough of the sea under the influence of waves whose period is nearly that of its own natural rolling." Indeed, so great

[1] Vol. i. p. 61.

may be the cumulative effects of periodic impulses, however feeble, that a distinguished English physicist has not hesitated to declare that he could, with a suitable appliance, break an iron girder by projecting against it ordinary pith-balls.

We are now prepared to pass from the visible mass-motions with which we have been dealing, to the invisible molecular motions, and the almost invisible segmental mass-motions which generate sound.

On the table are two tuning forks, A and B, on a resonant case, each fork giving exactly the same number of vibrations per second, 512. The forks are placed a foot apart, with the openings of the resonant boxes facing each other, and one of the forks is then excited by a violin-bow. But no sooner is one, A, set in vibration than we hear the other, B. This is a most startling result; and yet only what should have been expected after our experiments with pendulums.

But how does one fork convey its tremors to the other? Not through the material of the table, as the vibrations of one pendulum were conveyed to the other through their common support, because, as you will notice, the resonant cases are so constructed that this is impossible. Attached to the bottom of each case are two caoutchouc tubes that effectually destroy any vibrations that might otherwise pass from one fork to the other through the material of the table. The only means of communication therefore is the air. But can the air transmit impulses with such force as to give rise to the loud sound you have just heard in the second tuning-fork, B? Yes; but only under the same conditions under which one pendulum can cause another to oscillate.

The first condition is that the two forks must be in unison. When A, then, is set in vibration it generates a series of air-pulses which are conveyed to B, and these, impinging against it, throw it into vibration. From the fact that the forks are isochronous, each impulse from A strikes B when it is in the same phase; that is, in the same position and moving in the same direction with reference to its point of departure. A then generates in the air waves of condensation and rarefaction, and the air-pulses thus formed impinge against B at the rate of 512 per second. These aerial impulses taken separately are very feeble; they may be all but infinitesimal; but the number and absolute periodicity of the impulses are capable by their cumulative effect of producing results that would be deemed incredible, if not impossible.

The forks are separated still more, one of them now being full twenty feet away from the other. The bow is again drawn across A, and its distant companion at once responds. Indeed, so quick is the answer that B is heard almost as soon as A. We might separate them a hundred feet or more, and the result would still be the same.

With two similar tuning-forks executing 128 vibrations per second, and placed with the open ends of their resonant cases facing the opposite ends of the conduit of St. Michel, in Paris, Dr. Koenig was able, by exciting one, to cause the other to resound very distinctly, although more than a mile distant. When we reflect that the density of steel is more than six thousand times that of air, the fact that it can be thrown into sonorous vibration, and at such a distance, by such insignificant impulses as are brought to bear on it, is truly marvellous.

But one fork will not only set another into vibration, it will also communicate its vibratory motion so completely that the latter can be made to resound as loud as the former, and in some cases even louder. This, however, will take place only when the two forks are perfectly isochronous.

Retaining the two forks, A and B, which we have been using, it is easy so to vary the experiment we have just made as to secure a more surprising result than any we have yet witnessed. I cause A to vibrate as before, and then immediately damp it by placing my fingers on the prongs. You now hear B vibrating alone. I take my fingers off A, and it is again excited by the vibrations of B. I damp B, and A is now heard vibrating as before, but with diminished intensity. I again damp A, and once more B is heard. I can thus cause A and B to communicate to each other their vibratory motion several times in succession, the sounds continuing quite audible, though the two forks may be at different ends of the room, or at even more considerable distances from each other.

This remarkable property that one sonorous body has of impressing its vibratory motion on another sonorous body is called *resonance*, or *consonance*. Resonance is the term more generally employed, as consonance is also used to designate the harmonious effect produced by the simultaneous sounding of two or more musical notes. When the notes produced are in perfect unison, as is the case in those generated by the tuning-forks A and B, the sound excited in B by A is sometimes spoken of as a *sympathetic sound*, being caused by what are called *sympathetic vibrations*. The German word *Mitschwingung*, co-vibration, expresses admirably the character of the vibratory motion that gives rise to resonance, or sympathetic sounds.

I would not, however, have you conclude from what has been said that resonance requires absolute periodicity in the source of sound and in the body in which the sound is originated by influence or co-vibration. To obtain such marked responsive effects as you have just witnessed in the forks A and B perfect periodicity is of course essential. But if these forks differed from each other by a very few vibrations, resonance could still be excited in B by sounding A. The response, however, would be much slower and much feebler. Any great difference in the frequency of the forks, barring an exception I shall presently speak of, would destroy resonance entirely.

Let me illustrate. Before you is a glass jar (Fig. 117) twenty inches in depth. I hold over it a tuning-fork, C_2, making 256 vibrations per second, but as yet no sound is audible. Water is slowly poured into the jar, and soon you perceive a gradual augmentation of sound. When, however, the water reaches a certain height the note of the fork attains its maximum intensity. If now more water is poured into the jar the sound rapidly dies away, until it becomes quite inaudible. Pouring out some of the water, and thereby lengthening the air-column, the sound is again reinforced. It is found, however, that for this particular fork the water must always be at the same height in the jar in order that the reinforcement of sound may be at its maximum, or, what amounts to the same thing, in order that we may have the most perfect resonance. If we diminish or increase the amount of water, we do not at once destroy resonance completely, as is so often asserted, but we lessen it in a very marked manner. Beyond certain limits it entirely disappears.

By means of a series of carefully made experiments Koenig has shown that the limit of departure from unison at which the reciprocal action of two tuning-forks ceases to be perceptible is proportional to the frequencies of the forks. Thus the intensity of resonance for the forks C_3, C_4, C_5, C_6, C_7, was about the same when they differed from unison by 2, 4, 8, 16, 32 vibrations per second, — that is, when they differed from unison by 1 vibration to every 128 vibrations per second.

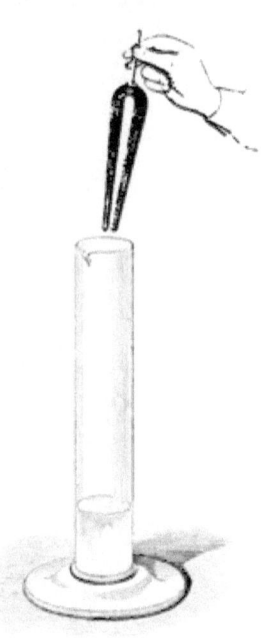

FIG. 117.

Let us now try another fork, C_4, making 512 vibrations per second. Bringing it over the mouth of the jar, we find that the greatest resonance is obtained when the air-column is just one half the length of that which responded with greatest intensity to C_3. Trying C_5, whose frequency is 1024, the vibrating air-column must again be divided by 2 in order to secure the greatest augmentation of sound. We might try any number of forks with different rates of vibration, and we should find that in each case only one certain length of air-column in the jar would be capable of exciting the maximum of sympathetic resonance.

Measuring the lengths of the air-columns resounding the loudest to the forks C_2, C_3, C_4, we find them to be 13, 6½, and 3¼ inches, respectively. These measurements agree very closely with what calculations, based on the known rates of vibrations of the forks, and the velocity of sound in air at the temperature of this room, should lead us to expect. They show also that the lengths of the most effective resonating air-columns are inversely proportional to the frequencies of the tuning-forks used in our experiments.

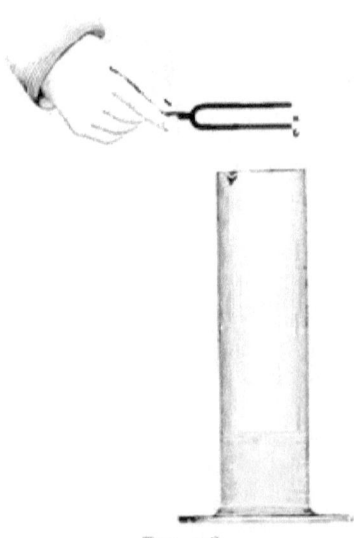

FIG. 118.

If we examine the matter with a little attention, we shall find that we have here exactly the same condition of things as obtained with the two unisonant tuning-forks. The air-columns in the glass jar resound most perfectly to the different tuning-forks only when their periodic vibrations are the same as those of the forks.

While the prong of the fork is moving from a to b (Fig. 118), the condensation produced runs down to the surface of the water, and is reflected back to a just as the fork is ready to return to b. The accompanying rarefaction follows the condensation in the same manner, but in a reverse order; viz., going downwards while the condensation is coming upwards. The waves both of condensation and rarefaction are so timed that their upward and downward motion are in perfect unison with those of the fork. If there should be a slight difference in the periods of the air-column and the fork, a consequent diminution of resonance would be the result, just as we saw is the case when two tuning-forks differ from each other by a few vibrations.

The foregoing experiment affords an explanation of the office of the resonant boxes attached to many of the tuning-forks before you. It is to heighten resonance, and it does so the more effectually the more nearly the periodic times of fork and box are in unison. As a matter of fact, the resonant chamber is not, as a rule, constructed so as to be perfectly in unison with its accompanying fork, for the

FIG. 119.

reason that when perfect resonance exists, the sound of the fork dies away much more rapidly than when there is a slight difference in the periods of vibration.

The cause of this is obvious. When the resonant case and the air contained within it vibrate in perfect unison with the fork, the amplitude of the vibratory motion both of air-particles and box is at its maximum. But this intensity of vibration is kept up only in virtue of the energy imparted to it by the vibrating fork. The greater the resonance, therefore, and the closer the approximation of the periods of fork and resonant case, the greater the amount of energy required, and the shorter the duration of the sound produced.

Savart has devised a very beautiful apparatus for exhibiting the phenomena of resonance. It consists of a bell, T, P, mounted on a stand, D, F, C (Fig. 119), accompanied by a resonant tube, A, B, in which there is a movable piston. Agitating the bell by means of a resined bow, it at once bursts forth into sound. When the opening of the resonator is brought close to the rim of the bell, the sound is considerably intensified. By moving the piston in the tube, the sound is made to vary in loudness according to the position which the piston occupies. When it reaches one certain point, however, the sound comes forth with extraordinary volume and power, and then resonance is most complete. This climax of sonorousness indicates, as you are now aware, that the vibration periods of bell and resonator are equal.

FIG. 120.

Vibrating plates can also be made to illustrate very beautifully the phenomena of sympathetic vibration.

Before you are two square brass plates (Fig. 120), one of which is mounted on a cast-iron support, while the other is attached to a simple handle. They are so constructed that when they give the same figure the notes emitted are as nearly as possible in unison. Fine sand is strewn over both plates, and grasping the one with the handle, I excite it with the bow. At once a characteristic Chladni figure is formed. Holding this plate, while yet in vibration, above the other, a figure is designed on the lower plate that is an exact duplicate of the one on the plate in my hand. The periods of the two plates being the same, one takes up the vibrations of the other even when some distance apart.

Membranes are particularly susceptible of co-vibration, on account of their lightness, extent of surface, and facility of subdivision. They are especially sensitive to shrill sounds. The note of a whistle or of a small bell will throw a membrane into violent agitation even when several yards distant. Sand strewn on the membrane at once shows the existence of vibrating segments similar to those exhibited by vibrating plates.

Fig. 121.

An elliptical bell, like Fig. 121, emitting a very strident note, is a most convenient instrument for the production of figures on membranes. Thus a circular India-rubber membrane (Fig. 122), which can be readily adjusted to various degrees of tension, is now tuned to the note given by the bell. On strewing the membrane with sand, and drawing the bow across the edge of the bell, a harsh, creaking sound is heard, which causes the sand immediately to arrange itself in the most complicated patterns.

Fig. 122.

Mr. Sedley Taylor has devised a clever method of showing the manner in which sound affects liquid films. The apparatus used consists of an air-chamber (Fig. 123) that may be covered with metal plates, in which are circular, square, or triangular openings. A tube through which sound-pulses may enter is attached to the side of the air-chamber. If now a soap-film be stretched over the openings in either of the plates, and projected on a screen, we obtain, by speaking or singing into the resonant cavity of the apparatus, the most gorgeous kaleidoscopic effects conceivable. Every note, and

Fig. 123.

every vowel sounded on the same note, instantly evokes the most marvellous figures, tinted with all the delicate hues of the rainbow. There is nothing in the whole range of physics more beautiful than the phenomena here exhibited, — nothing that discloses more strikingly the complicated nature of sonorous vibrations, and portrays more clearly those infinitesimal differences of quality of sound that entirely elude even the most sensitive ear. The forms and patterns that rapidly succeed one another, with all the varying changes of tone, are as exquisite in design as they are magnificent in chromatic display; and the agent employed in the experiment, an ordinary soap film is as simple as the exhibition is superb.

It is resonance that gives to musical instruments all the value they possess. Without a resounding body in connection with the origin of sound, the note produced would be scarcely audible. In violins, harps, and pianos, for instance, the sounds are excited by vibrating strings; but as they come forth from the strings alone, they are almost, if not entirely, imperceptible. It is only when they are reinforced by suitable sounding-boards that they acquire sufficient volume for the purposes of music.

You will observe, however, that the resonance of the sounding-boards of musical instruments has a much wider range than that of the resounding bodies of which we have been speaking. Unlike the glass jar, and the resonant case of the tuning-fork, which respond to only one note, the sounding-boards of musical instruments reinforce all the notes within their compass. But besides this general resonance for all notes there is a particular resonance corresponding to some one special note. And, strange as it may seem, this special resonance in musical instruments is something that is, as a rule, passed unnoticed even by the most accomplished musicians.

Thus the proper tone of the violin is C_2, as can be shown by blowing across the "f holes," or by sounding in their widest part a properly tuned fork. The viola and the violoncello have likewise proper tones, which can be evoked in the same manner. Fortunately, however, these proper notes, on account of the peculiar construction of these various instruments, are not so prominent as one would expect them to be. If they were, they would very seriously affect the quality of the scale, as played on stringed instruments. As it is, special attention must be directed to them in order that they may be heard at all.

Sounding-boards enhance the volume of sound emitted by musical instruments by exposing a larger vibrating surface to the air, and, in many instruments, by simultaneously throwing into vibration a large mass of air contained within the resonant body. The process in all cases is somewhat complex. In the violin, for instance, the string is first excited by bowing. Its vibrations are then communicated by the bridge and post to the belly and back of the instrument, and to the mass of air intervening between these two highly sonorous pieces of wood. The body of the violin and the contained air being thus agitated as a whole, the vibratory motion superinduced is finally communicated to the circumambient air.

There are still other instances of resonance as illustrated by musical instruments to which I must advert. They are as interesting as they are instructive, and so simple that they can be studied by any one.

Press down gently one of the keys of a pianoforte so as to raise the damper, without, however, causing the hammer to strike the wires, and sing loudly the corresponding note. At once the note is echoed back with surprising distinctness. That it has been generated by the sympathetic vibration of the uncovered string is proved by allowing the damper to fall back, when the sound is immediately extinguished. Raise the damper again, and pluck sharply one of the three strings that combine to produce the note before sounded. After a few seconds damp this wire with the finger, and you will hear the other two continuing the same sound. They have been thrown into sympathetic vibration by the first, which has been tuned in unison with them. We can easily assure ourselves of this fact by touching them with our fingers, when we may feel the motion, or by putting little paper riders on the wires, when those not occupying nodes are thrown off forthwith. Similarly, if any two strings of two violins, M and N, are in unison, it is easy to excite sympathetic vibrations in the string of N by sounding that of M.

This fact can be beautifully illustrated by the monochord. On it are stretched two wires in perfect unison. As soon as one of them is plucked, sonorous vibrations are excited in the other. If the unison of the wires is disturbed by changing, even slightly, the tension of one of them, the resonance is less marked. By varying the tension a little more, the resonance disappears entirely.

Instead of thus producing resonance in a wire by agitating another in proximity to it, we can do it just as well by means of a tuning-fork. If the wire should be in unison with the fork employed, we have only to bring the foot of the fork down on one of the nodes of the wire, when sympathetic vibration will at once be established. If the wire and the fork are not unisonant, they can be made so by changing the tension of the wire.

But even this is not necessary. If the wire should give a note that is graver than that of the fork, we can easily find one in unison with it by placing the foot of the fork on the wire, and moving it along it until a point is found at which a part of the wire is heard to respond most loudly. This part of the wire, measured from the foot of the fork to its point of attachment, will give a note exactly in unison with that yielded by the fork. The same result could be obtained with a violin or any other stringed instrument.

Professor Helmholtz has availed himself of this property of sonorous bodies in the construction of his resonators for analyzing sound, or for detecting the existence of sounds that would otherwise be inaudible. They are generally made of metal, but glass or any other rigid material would answer. The one I hold in my hand is, as you observe (Fig. 124), a spherical shell, R, with two projections opposite to each other, one of which, a, is somewhat larger than the other, b. In each projection is an aperture corresponding in diameter to that of the projection itself. By means of the smaller opening, the resonator is connected with the ear, while the other serves for the admission of sonorous vibrations.

On the table is a series of ten resonators similar to the one first examined, and accurately tuned to as many

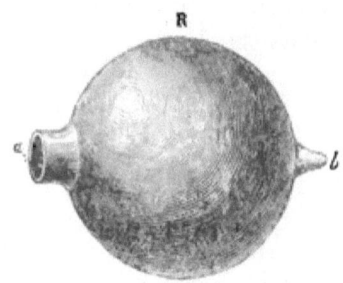

FIG. 124.

different notes. Like all resonators, they vary in size inversely as the pitch of the sounds they are intended to reinforce. If the nipple of the resonator accorded to the note C_3, for instance, be inserted in the ear, and the corresponding fork be set in vibration, one should at once hear a note that would sound much louder than it could without the resonator.

In the case of weak sounds thus reinforced, the results are still more striking. Even when there is apparently perfect silence, we can hear, by means of these wonderful sound-collecting globes, a whole series of musical notes, corresponding to those to which the resonators are attuned. The atmosphere is always in a condition of tremor, the result of countless vibrations proceeding from every conceivable source. Occasionally these tremors are apprehended by the unaided ear as a noise or as a gentle hum; but more frequently, especially at night, they are, for most persons, at least, entirely inaudible.

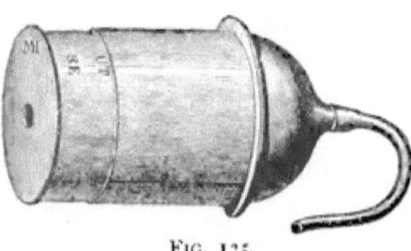

FIG. 125.

Sometimes a resonator is so constructed that it is capable

of reinforcing several distinct notes. As constructed by Koenig, it is made of metal and is almost cylindrical in form (Fig. 125), and is composed of two tubes, one of which is accurately fitted into the other. The resonator is thus capable of being adjusted for several notes, which are stamped on the inner tube. The compass of such a resonator admits of considerable extension, as the notes which will be reinforced depend almost solely on the length of the tube.

Here is another adjustable resonator (Fig. 126), of still different form, due to M. Daguin. It is designed for reinforcing a greater range of sounds than any we have yet seen, and for this reason is better adapted for certain classes

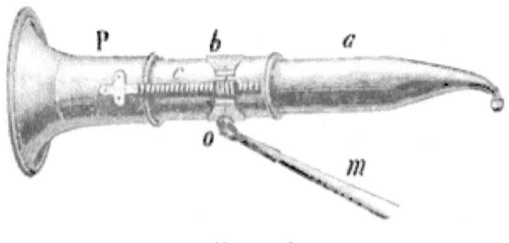

FIG. 126.

of experimental work. It is composed of three parts, P, b, a. The last of these parts, shaped so as to fit into the ear, may be made to slide into b, and b in turn may be made to slide into P by means of a rack and pinion, m, o, c.

Such an instrument is admirably adapted for singling out the notes, which, as we have learned, constitute those confused and disagreeable sounds ordinarily denominated noises. By its use we can resolve into elementary tones the sound of a waterfall, the whistling of the wind, the rumbling of a carriage over the pavement, and the confused murmur of the multitude speaking with every variation of pitch and quality of voice. More than this, we can show that the quiescent atmosphere, even during the still hours of night, is always more or less vocal, and that, without knowing it, we are ever in a medium in which

"A thousand trills and quivering sounds
In airy circles o'er us fly."

Coleridge, then, spoke more wisely than he knew when he said, —

"The mute, *still* air
Is music slumbering on her instrument."

M. Daguin has also designed an instrument similar in form to the foregoing, and although nothing more than a special form of resonator, it gives what at first would appear to be very paradoxical results It is a simple straight cornet (Fig. 127), in the side of which are three small apertures that may be opened or closed with the fingers. This instrument M. Daguin calls a melodiaphone, which, in the language of the inventor, "permits one to obtain the singular result of hearing a melody that does not exist, by means of an instrument that emits no sound."

When, however, one understands the function of one of Helmholtz's resonators the mystery of the melodiaphone disappears. The melody that does not exist is then found to have its origin in the almost inaudible noises that continually fill the air, and the instrument that emits no sound is so designed that certain of the notes that go to make up these noises are reinforced, to the exclusion of all others. The instrument is used by inserting the small end, *o*, in the ear, when, on closing and opening the apertures with the fingers, one will hear in musical sequence the notes that correspond to the different lengths of vibrating air-columns in the tube. The instrument is, in fact, a resonator that is adjusted, not by changing its length, but by opening or closing one or more of its apertures, thereby changing the length of the aërial column that resounds to correspond with some note in the confused

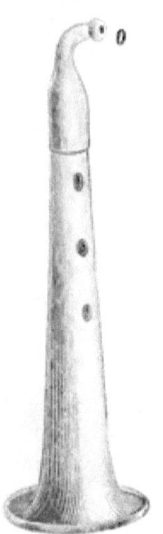

FIG. 127.

maze of very feeble sounds which unceasingly keep the atmosphere in a state of greater or less perturbation.

The singular power possessed by the melodiaphone cannot fail to recall to one's mind the story of the "Lost Chord." Here, as in so many other cases, fact and fancy, science and fiction, may find a common trysting-place.

Most persons are familiar with many similar phenomena, without, however, having any knowledge of their cause. A common instance is afforded by an ordinary conch or cowry shell. One can always hear a characteristic sound on bringing either the one or the other close to the ear. Such shells are popularly supposed to re-echo the sounds of the sea; but, as is evident, they are nothing more than peculiarly shaped resonators, which sift out and intensify some one of the many tones existing in the atmosphere.

Some of the most beautiful verses Wordsworth ever wrote have reference to these curious shell-tones; and I must ask your permission to quote from them. I would fain introduce a few lines here, if for no other reason than to give a little color to the plain and unvarnished facts of science: —

> "I have seen
> A curious child, who dwelt upon a tract
> Of inland ground, applying to his ear
> The convolutions of a smooth-lipped shell,
> To which, in silence hushed, his very soul
> Listened intensely; and his countenance soon
> Brightened with joy; for from within were heard
> Murmurings, whereby the monitor expressed
> Mysterious union with its native sea." [1]

The external auditory passage of the human ear has the same power which ordinary resonators possess of selecting certain sounds for reinforcement. The sounds thus specially intensified are, according to Helmholtz, those that lie between E_6 and G_6, and embrace between 2,640 and 3,168 vibrations. This fact explains a phenomenon that musicians are often at a loss to account for; namely, the peculiar sharp, cutting effect of certain notes

[1] The Excursion, book iv.

in the neighborhood of F_6. The note producing such an effect is the one whose frequency is most nearly in unison with that of the aural passage, and which, consequently, is more strongly reinforced than any other note within the whole range of the instrument. If we lengthen this passage by inserting a small tube in the ear, the cutting effect at once disappears for this particular note, but some lower note more in tune with the elongated auditory passage breaks forth instead with the same cutting effect. The chirp of the cricket is so grating on the ear because it is so nearly the proper tone of the air passage. A small tube applied to the ear weakens this strident sound at once. Dogs also, as most persons may have remarked, are extremely sensitive to certain sounds. In their case, too, the notes that most affect them are those which are most strongly reinforced by the auditory canal. According to Madame Seiler, they are especially sensitive to E_6 of the violin.

So far I have been giving examples of resonance in which the responsive vibration is of the same period as that which excites it. But there are other cases of sympathetic sounds that are even more interesting than those which obtain when both notes are in unison. When experimenting with pendulums, we found that a pendulum was capable of imparting motion, not only to another pendulum of the same period, but also to pendulums whose rates of vibration were two or three times as great.

The same thing precisely holds good in the case of musical sounds. Any given note, will excite not only one in unison with it, but also other notes whose rates of vibration are some multiple of its own. Thus, take a fork A, and it will cause, not only one of the same frequency to resound with it, but also several of its upper partials.

Let me demonstrate experimentally the truth of this statement. On the table is a series of twelve perfectly tuned forks mounted on resonant cases. The fundamental is C_2, with 128 vibrations per second. The others have the same number of vibrations multiplied by the whole numbers 2, 3, 4, etc., up to 12, respectively.

The smaller forks are placed in close proximity to the larger, C_2, and then the latter is strongly bowed. After allowing it to sound for a few seconds it is damped, when you hear a very pleasing sound of higher pitch. Some of the other forks are vibrating, but it is impossible to distinguish by the unaided ear just how many and which particular forks are sounding. By exciting C_3, C_4, and the other forks in succession by the large fork C_2, we can easily determine exactly how many of the upper partials respond to their fundamental. By experimenting in this manner it could be shown that C_2 is capable of exciting all its upper partials as far as C_5 inclusive. This means that C_2 is capable of impressing its motion, not only on another fork in unison with it, but also on seven others whose frequencies are in the ratio of its first seven multiples.

The resonance that a fundamental calls forth from its upper partials is, however, by no means so strong as that which it evokes from one with which it is in unison. According to Koenig, the amplitude of C_2 when in vibration, being taken as 1, that of its first upper partial, C_3, will be $\frac{1}{4}$. Above this the amplitude decreases in succession by one half, being for G_3 $\frac{1}{8}$, for C_4 $\frac{1}{16}$, and so on to $\frac{1}{256}$ for C_5. Now, the intensity of sound, as we know, is proportional to the square of the amplitude of vibration. There is, therefore, a very rapid and marked diminution in the loudness of the resonance as we pass from the lower to the higher upper partials. The octave responds loudly and clearly; the twelfth and the second octave are also distinctly heard, whereas the notes above these, although perceptible, require, especially for the last two, all the attention the ear is capable of bestowing.

But tuning-forks are not the only means we have of exciting sympathetic resonance in upper partials. Many other sonorous bodies are capable of doing this equally well, and some of them in an equally striking manner. Stringed instruments are particularly well adapted for this purpose.[1]

---

[1] Mersenne was quite familiar with the principal facts of sympathetic resonance. He gives them detail in Props. 37, 38, and 39. "Harm. Lib." iv.

A simple and instructive illustration is afforded by raising all the dampers of a pianoforte and singing loudly any given note, when a whole series of notes will be returned, by way of response. If C_2 is sung, the upper partials will answer in the same order as did those emitted by the tuning-forks. The number and intensity of the partial tones in this case will depend on the voice, — its loudness, the tuning, and the resonant qualities of the pianoforte itself; both voice and instrument, as is obvious, being, according to circumstances, of varying degrees of strength and perfection.[1]

Before dismissing the subject of sympathetic vibrations I must introduce to your notice a novel little instrument, devised independently and almost simultaneously, by Prof. A. M. Mayer and Dvořák.[2] Professor Mayer calls it a sound-mill. It is also known as a sound-radiometer, or an acoustic reaction-wheel. As made by Koenig, it is composed of four small resonators, Fig. 128, open at one end only, and attached to the ends of a small cross.

FIG. 128.

This cross is carefully balanced, and supported at its centre on the point of a vertical stand. The resonators are made of aluminum, on account of the lightness of this metal, and each is very accurately tuned to C_4. When this apparatus is placed, as it is now, before the opening of a resonant box of a fork sounding C_4, the wheel at once

---

[1] The reader will not fail to note that there is a difference in the way in which sympathetic notes are excited by the human voice and by a tuning-fork. The former, yielding a compound note, would evoke from the piano those notes which are in unison with the partial tones of the voice, even if the fundamental tone did not possess the power of exciting upper harmonic partials.

[2] Professor Mayer read a paper on the sound-mill, and exhibited the instrument before the New York Academy of Sciences, May 22, 1876. A description of it was published in a report of this meeting in the "Scientific American," July 8, 1876. Dvořák's account of a similar instrument was published in "Pogg. Annalen," Band III., No. 3, Nov. 10, 1877.

commences to rotate, and continues in motion as long as the sound lasts.

In most other sonorous bodies we see how mechanical movement is transformed into sound. This little contrivance shows us that it is possible to reverse the process, and cause sound vibrations to generate mechanical motion.

Does not this experiment remind you of the stories told of Orpheus and Amphion? We have not, indeed, the power of Orpheus, because, we are told, he, —

> "With his lute made trees,
> And the mountain tops that freeze,
> Bow themselves when he did sing;
> To his music plants and flowers
> Ever sprung; as sun and showers
> There had made a lasting spring."

We cannot, like "Amphion the divine," by the magic power of sound alone, build the walls of a great city like Thebes; for at the sound of his lyre, it is said, the stones came together and placed themselves one upon another.[1] But we can show that sound is indeed competent to put matter in motion, and that there is in the Greek legend just quoted an element of truth, slight though it be, that may not be disregarded. We have here another instance of truth and fiction meeting upon a common ground, — a striking illustration of the fact so frequently commented on, namely, that poets often have visions of things that are revealed to men of science long generations after they have been embalmed in immortal verse.

The experiment with the sound-mill is a most interesting one, and shows better than anything else the absolute necessity of perfect periodicity to secure the maximum effect of which the instrument is capable; for if the resonators are not perfectly tuned to the fork there will be no rotary motion whatever. A sound from any other source, if sufficiently intense and in perfect unison with the resonators, will cause the wheel to revolve as well as

---

[1] ". . . Agitataque saxa per artem
Sponte sua in muri membra coisse ferunt."

a tuning-fork. By means of a fork actuated by electricity (Fig. 129), the motion of the wheel can be kept up indefinitely. Turning on the current from a single Grenet cell, the wheel at once begins to revolve, and after it is once started, the motion will remain uniform as long as the electric current retains the same strength.

The explanation of the singular performance of this reaction wheel is to be found in the fact that the mean pressure of the air at the node of a stationary vibration in a column of air is superior to the pressure of the air in a state of rest, provided the vibrations be not infinitesimally small. In the resonators employed in this instance the nodes are found at their closed ends, as is the case in a stopped organ-pipe. If then the air in the resonators vibrate with sufficient force to produce in their interior, at the closed end, a mean pressure that is greater than that of the free air at the end opposite, rotary motion will, under the circumstances, be the natural result.

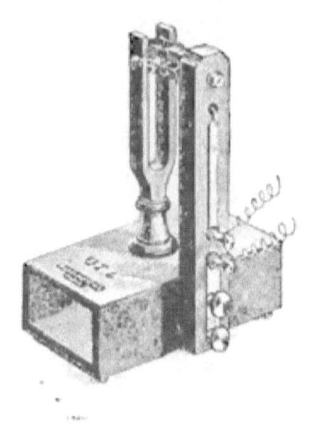

FIG. 129.

We come now to the opposite of resonance; namely, interference of sound. We can best elucidate this subject by constructing curves representing wave-systems of different periods, amplitudes, and phases.

In Fig. 130, *A* and *B*, let the two dotted curves represent two wave-systems of the same period and phase, but of different amplitudes. The resultant of these wave-systems will be indicated by the heavy lines. In this, as in all cases where two curves corresponding to two or more wave-systems are combined, the perpendiculars of the resultant curve are equal to the algebraic sum of the ordinates of its constituents. In *A*, the two wave-systems acting in the same direction, and having consequently the same phase, tend to reinforce each other. In B, on the contrary, the wave-systems are in opposite phases, and one of them, therefore, as indicated by the resultant curve, partially annuls the effects of the other. In C we have represented two wave-systems of equal period and amplitude, but of opposite phase. When one forms a crest, or

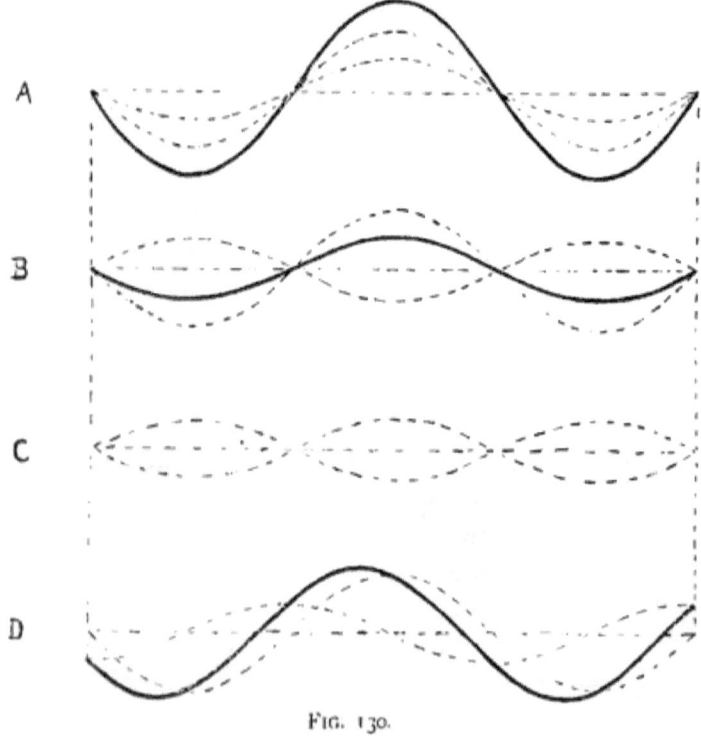

FIG. 130.

a condensation, the other forms a trough, or a rarefaction. Their joint effect, therefore, is zero. One wave-system entirely destroys the effect of the other. This is an illustration of a case of complete interference of wave-motion.

If, as in D, the two wave-systems indicated by the dotted lines do not cut the horizontal line at the same point, but differ from each other by a quarter of a wave-length, the resultant wave-system will be represented by the heavy line. The two wave-systems in this case do not start off from the same point at the same time, and the resulting difference in phase, as shown in the figure, may be considered as due to the horizontal displacement of one of the curves, which, in this instance, is the one of lesser amplitude. D differs from B only in the fact that in the former there is a displacement of the smaller

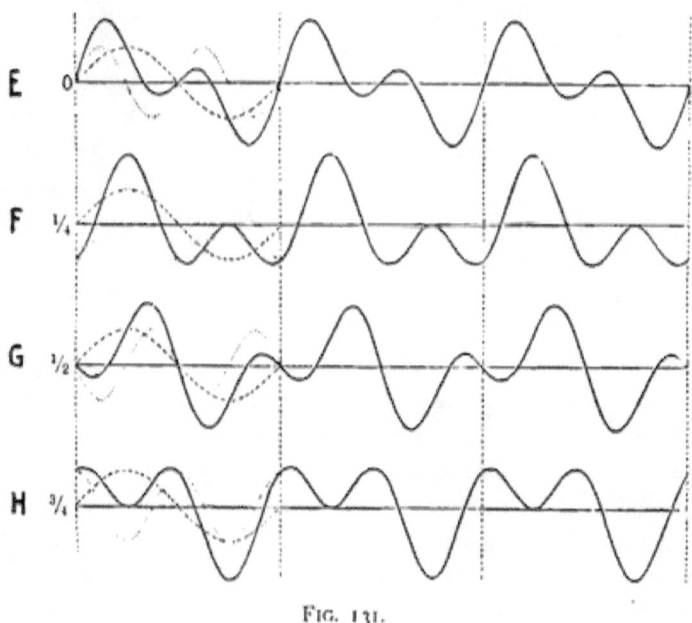

FIG. 131.

curve by a quarter of a wave-length, while in the latter it amounts to a half wave-length. In each case partial interference is the result.

If two wave-systems, whether of the same or of different amplitudes, differ from each other in point of departure by anything less than a half wave-length, we shall always have a corresponding difference of phase, and a consequent partial interference. When they differ from each other by a half wave-length, or any odd number of half wave-lengths, and the waves are of equal periods and amplitudes, there will always be complete interference, and the body acted upon will remain in a state of rest.

If the periods should be different, — that is, if the waves should be of different lengths, — then the resultant wave would be represented by a curve obtained in the same manner as the foregoing; namely, by taking the algebraic sum of the ordinates of the component curves to form their resultant. But we should find that the form of such curve would be quite different from that of those we have been examining. This is shown in Fig. 131, *E*, where the wave-lengths of the two systems are as 1 : 2, and where they are regarded as originating at the same point. In *F* of the adjoining figure we have the same wave-systems represented in which the shorter wave shows a horizontal displacement of one fourth of a wave-length. In *G* and *H* the horizontal displacement amounts to one half and three fourths of a wave length respectively, — equivalent, therefore, to a difference of phase of one half and three quarters of a wave-length.

The difference in the forms of the resultant curves in these four cases is very marked. Any similar variation in period, amplitude, or phase of wave-systems would give rise to correspondingly different resultant curves. By taking three or more curves of varying period, amplitude, and phase, we could obtain an endless variety of curves corresponding to the endless variety of complex wave systems.

The curves we have been studying are graphical representations of what takes place in the formation of water and other liquid waves, and likewise of what obtains in the compounding of simple sound and light waves.

If a pebble be thrown into a body of still water, a series of expanding waves is at once formed, which are equidistant from each other, and which decrease in amplitude as they recede from their centre. If a second pebble be thrown into the water so as to strike its surface some distance from where the first pebble fell, a similar set of waves will be set up around the second centre of disturbance, and will eventually meet those generated at the first centre. At some points where the two wave-systems meet, crest will be superposed upon crest, and the resultant wave will be equal to the sum of its component waves. In other places trough will meet trough, and there will be a correspondingly greater depression. In still other places crest will coincide with trough, and if the two waves are of equal size, the result will be total interference, and the water will remain undisturbed. If, on the contrary, the waves are unequal, the interference will be only partial, and the amount of disturbance will be equal to that produced by the difference of the two opposing forces. This is an experiment any one can make, and it is as instructive as it is simple.

Observations on water waves, then, teach us that motion added to motion may produce rest. The question now arises, have we anything comparable to this in the case of sound? In other words, can sound added to sound ever give silence?

If you will recall what has been said about the origin and nature of sound, you will be able to answer the question without hesitation. Sound, mechanically considered, is, as we have seen, in all cases, due to vibratory motion, and if the vibrations generating two sounds be of equal intensity and period, but of opposite phases, silence will invariably be the natural result.

Partial interference of sonorous vibrations is quite common, as we shall see in our next lecture, but total interference is more rare, and, except in a few cases, more difficult to illustrate experimentally. And yet one of these few cases enables us to show the phenomenon of complete interference most satisfactorily. The only instrument needed in this instance is an ordinary tuning-fork. But I have known musicians to use tuning-forks for years, and, strange as it may appear, never be aware of this fact of interference until their attention was especially directed to it. This shows how very striking phenomena, that daily appeal to our senses, may sometimes escape our mind, unless our attention be particularly drawn in their direction.

I hold a tuning-fork in my hand, and on turning it round near my ear I find that there are four positions of maximum loudness, and four positions in which no sound whatever is audible. Sounds are heard when the faces of the fork or the sides are turned towards the ear, and silence interference — ensues when the intermediate points or edges of the fork are directed towards the auditory passage. At the points between those where sound attains the maximum of intensity and those where it entirely ceases, there is partial interference, and consequently a variation of sound from its maximum to zero.

These phenomena, first remarked by the celebrated Dr. Thomas Young, can be shown more strikingly, and in such a manner as to be audible throughout the room, by reinforcing the sound by means of a resonator accurately tuned to the period of the fork. As the fork I hold in my hand is revolved before the large aperture of this resonator, you notice the varying changes in the intensity of the sound, now loud, now medium, now quite imperceptible. During each revolution, as you observe, there are four periods of maximum intensity of resonance, and similarly four periods of absolute silence.

It is easy to show that this variation of intensity is produced by interference of sonorous vibrations. All that is necessary to do this is to cover one of the prongs of the fork with a small paper tube, which partially destroys the undulations from that prong, and consequently prevents their interference with the vibrations of the other prong. At once the sound bursts forth loudly, where before there was no sound at all. Uncovering the prong, the sound immediately dies away, and all is silence. Experimenting in a like manner with the other prong, we should obtain a similar result. Thus we demonstrate the existence of a most paradoxical fact, — the fact that under certain conditions sound added to sound gives silence. The demonstration in this case is complete. Sonorous vibrations in different phases are mutually destructive, and when of equal period and intensity have no effect on the tympanum of the ear, and consequently excite no sensation in the brain.

In the experiments hitherto made you have observed that the sound is very feeble when the fork is made to vibrate alone. This is, in part, due to interference, as an examination of Fig. 132 will make evident. This pictures the tuning-fork as seen from above, the extremities of the prongs being represented by a and b. During their outward swings towards c and e, waves of condensation are formed by the prongs at a and b, which move in opposite directions. At d and f the sonorous impulses are always in the same phases, and sound here is at a maximum. The arrows indicate the alternate and the opposite movements of the prongs of the fork. Waves of rarefaction are generated in the space between the prongs of the fork; and as

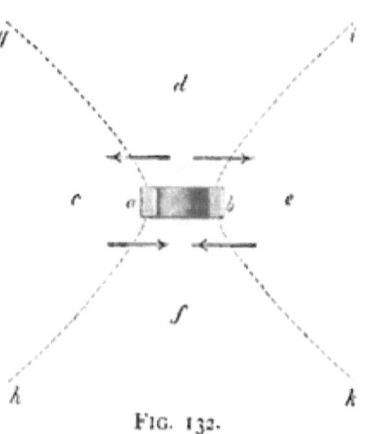

FIG. 132.

both the condensed and the rarified waves have the same velocity, they will meet along the dotted lines g, h, i, k; and since they are of equal period and intensity, one will exactly annul the effect of the other. Hence along these lines, which Weber has shown to constitute equilateral hyperbolas, there is total interference, and no effect whatever is produced in the organ of hearing.

That the air under such circumstances remains in a state of rest can be most conclusively proved by several cleverly devised experiments.

As one of the proofs, I shall first show you a very striking experiment devised by Hopkins. For this purpose we may employ one of the round brass disks used in exhibiting Chladni's figures, and a forked metal tube, Fig. 133, which is supported above the disk. The tube C is adjusted to a given note produced by the disk, and as soon as the disk is set in vibration we obtain, on strewing it with sand, a characteristic figure. When the prongs, $D E$, of the fork are above two alternate sections, like A and A', or B and B', the air in the tube is violently agitated, as is shown by the action of the sand strewn on the membrane on the top of the tube. When, however, the two branches of the tube are over adjacent sectors, as

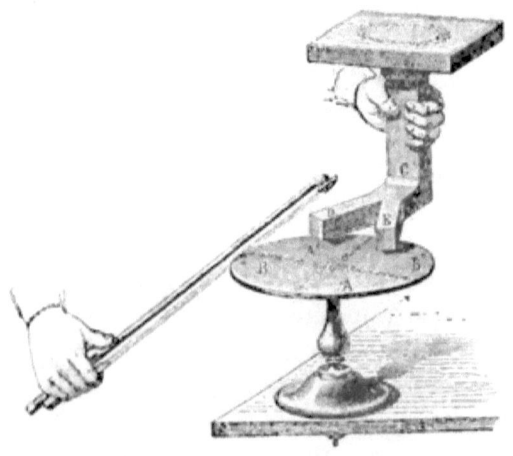

Fig. 133.

A and B, or A' and B', the air in the tube is at rest, for in this case there is not the slightest vibration imparted to the membrane, as the sand remains undisturbed.

The reason for these opposite effects is obvious. When the branches of the fork are over alternate sectors the vibrations excited in them are in the same phase, and the vibrations of the air-column in the tube are equal to the aggregate vibrations of the two branches. But when the fork is so placed that its branches are over adjacent sectors, the vibrations excited are in opposite phases. One sector of the plate moves upward, while the other moves downward; hence a condensed and a rarefied pulse enter the tube simultaneously,—one neutralizing the effect of the other. Thus the result, as might have been expected, is total interference.

Lissajous, to whose ingenuity we are indebted for so many beautiful experiments in acoustics, illustrates the same phenomenon in an equally interesting manner. Instead of a forked tube, he employs a disk (Fig. 134 B), cut into sectors, the number of sectors being one-half as great as those formed by the vibrating plate, A, used in connection with it. If the upper disk, for instance, has three sectors, and the one underneath, as indicated by the sand figures, is divided into six, then the pulses emanating from three of the alternate sectors of the lower disk will be quenched by the corresponding sectors of the upper disk. In this wise, condensations and rarefactions are prevented from neutralizing one another, and a strongly reinforced sound is the consequence. Only vibrations in the same phase are permitted to enter the ear, those of the opposite phase being suppressed. By rotating the upper disk, we at once hear risings and fallings of sound, according as the proper ventral segments of the vibrating plate are covered or exposed.

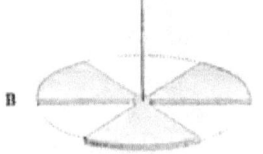
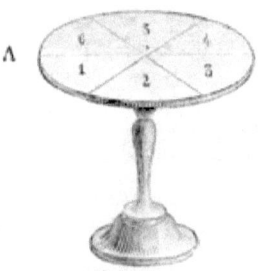

FIG. 134.

Interference can also be shown by means of organ-pipes. On a small wind-chest are mounted two unisonant pipes (Fig. 135), giving the note C_3. When the wind-chest is connected with the bellows, and air is admitted into one of the pipes, you hear a full mellow note. I next allow air to pass into the second pipe also. Now, it would seem that when both pipes are connected with the wind-chest, we should have a sound of double the intensity of that emitted by either pipe alone. Such, however, is not the case. The fundamental note of each pipe has been so weakened that at a short distance they are inaudible. All that you now hear is a rustling noise due to the escape of air from the embouchures of the pipes, and the octave of the fundamental, which still remains unaffected. The cause of this is that the wind in the wind-chest, by reason of the varying pressure in the pipes, passes into the two pipes alternately, and thus produces condensation in the one, and rarefaction in the other. These condensations and rarefactions being equal in intensity and opposite in phase, neutralize each other as respects their action on the surrounding air, and the result is that it remains at rest, and no sound is heard.

By means of Koenig's manometric flames we are able to prove beyond a doubt the existence of these conditions of condensation and rarefaction which alternate with each other in the pipes. The two pipes just used are replaced by two similar ones (Fig. 135), provided with manometric capsules at their middle nodes. These capsules are connected by rubber tubes to two jets placed one above the other in a vertical line and arranged in such a manner that when the gas is ignited, both flames will be reflected from an adjacent revolving mirror. When the mirror is rotated, and no sound is issuing from the pipes, we perceive two continuous bands of light, one above the other. As soon, however, as air is admitted into both pipes, these bands become at once similarly serrated, except that the elevations and depressions of the two bands alternate, the tooth of one corresponding exactly to the indentation of the other. Thus the evidence of the existence of pulses of condensation in one pipe, while opposite pulses of rarefaction prevail in the other, is as conclusive as the experiment on which it reposes is beautiful.

But supposing that while air is forced into both pipes, as in the preceding experiment, we connect the two capsules with a common jet, what will take place? A little reflection will tell us that there will be no agitation of the flame, for the simple reason that the pulses reaching the jet are in opposite phases, and therefore neutralize one another. We make the necessary changes in the connections, and on admitting air, as before, into the two pipes, and revolving the mirror, the result is just as was anticipated, — perfect quiescence on the part of the flame, as indicated by the continuous band of light pictured in the mirror. The physical basis of sound, as we have learned,

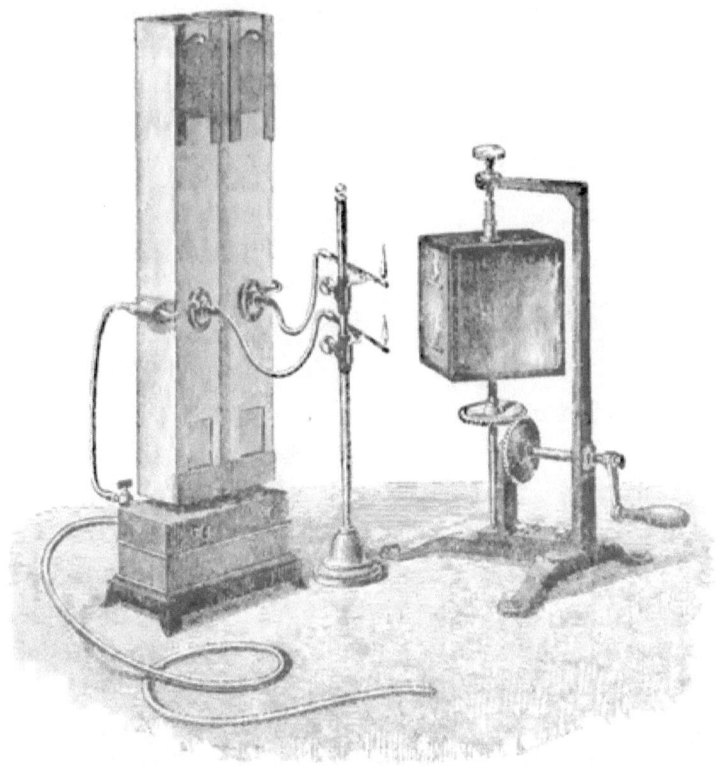

FIG. 135.

is motion. Here, as is evidenced by the aspect of the flame-image, there is no motion, therefore no sound.

Norremberg, acting upon a suggestion given by Sir John Herschel, demonstrated the existence of interference in a still different manner. He caused sonorous vibrations to enter a tube with two branches of different lengths, which afterwards reunited. Here is shown a simple form of this apparatus (Fig. 136), as modified by Quincke. A sound-wave enters one end, *o*, of the apparatus, and on reaching the two branches of the tube at *b*, is divided, to be again united on reaching the other end, *c*. If the branches are of equal length, the ear placed at one end, *s*, will hear undiminished any sound emanating from the other end. If, however, one of the branches, *c p q f*, is longer than the other, *a d*, by a half wave-length of the sound passing through it, then the sonorous waves, on reuniting at *c*, will meet in opposite phases, and the ear placed at the end, *s*, of the tube, *n r*, opposite that at which the sound enters, will hear nothing.

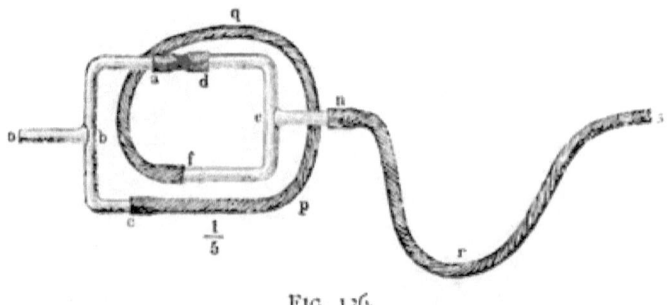

FIG. 136.

One may have a pleasing modification of this experiment by availing himself of Kundt's device, with which you are familiar, of showing, by means of a light powder, the presence of sonorous vibrations in tubes. The instrument employed for this purpose is before you (Fig. 137). It is essentially a combination of Kundt's tube with Quincke's apparatus. If the branches, *h g e* and *h o f n e*, of the tube are so adjusted as to differ from each other by exactly a half wave-length, or some odd multiple of a half wave-length, a sound excited by friction of the rod, *b a*, in one end, *d*, of the instrument will not give rise to any disturbance of the light powder in the other end, *h k*, of the tube. But should they, by sliding the tube *f* from *o n* to *o' n'*, be made to differ from each other by more than a half wave-length, or some even multiple of a half wave-length, the characteristic dust segments will at once appear, with greater or less distinctness, at the end of the tube opposite to that at which the sound-vibrations are generated.

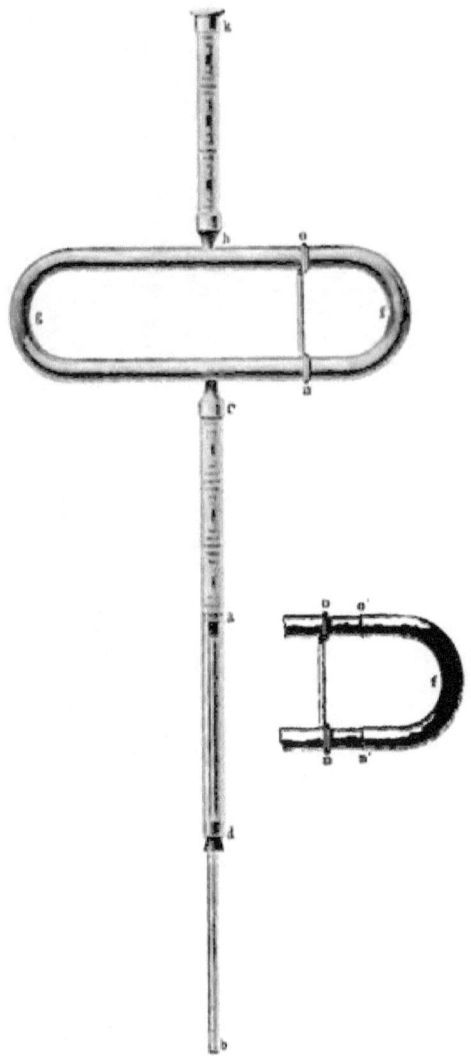

Fig. 137.

But probably the most elaborate and comprehensive method of exhibiting interference is that employed by

Koenig. It is essentially the same in principle as that proposed by Herschel, but in accuracy of results obtained is immeasurably superior to anything of which this great philosopher ever dreamed. Such an instrument is before

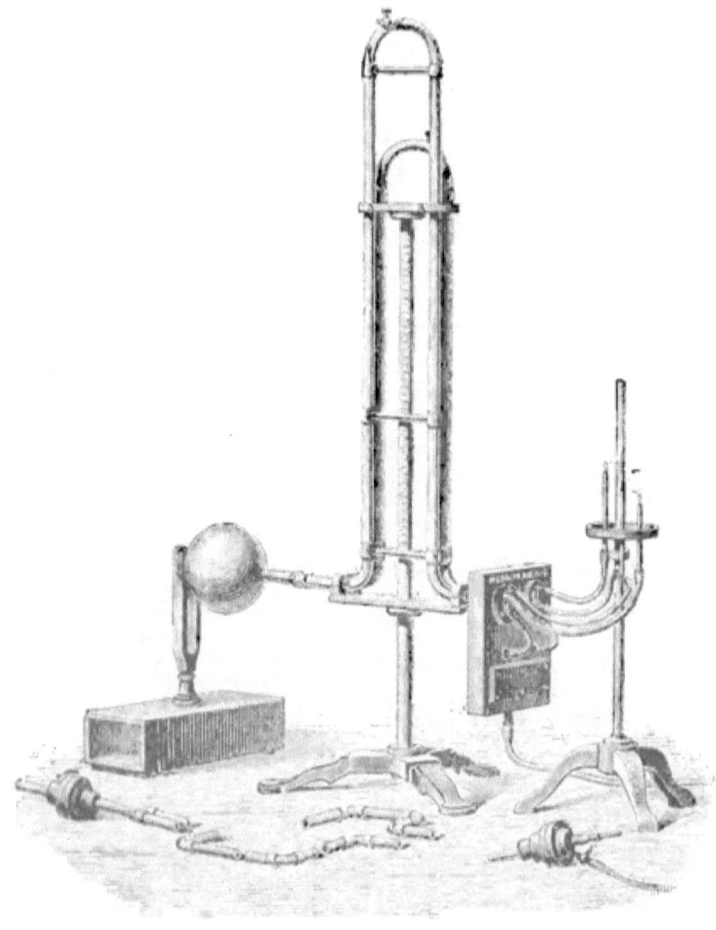

Fig. 138.

you (Fig. 138). With it the manometric flame fulfils the same function that is assigned to the ear in Quincke's apparatus, and subserves the purpose of the powder in Kundt's tube; but its indications are far more delicate than either ear or powder.

The tube and its branches are of metal, and divided into millimetres, *i. e.* twenty-fifths of an inch. By means of a draw-tube at its topmost part one of the branches is capable of being lengthened or shortened at will. In order to procure a proper tone, a tuning-fork with its resonator is used as the source of sound. To the end of the tube opposite to that at which the fork is stationed, is attached a manometric capsule. This, in turn, is connected with a gas-jet, which is supported before a revolving mirror. When both branches of the tube are of equal length, the sound issuing from the fork and passing through the tube declares its presence at the capsule end by the beautiful serrated band of light, which is seen when the mirror is rotated. But if one of the branches of the tube is made longer than the other by just a half wave-length of the sound emitted by the fork, then we have complete interference of the sound-waves, as is evidenced by the quiescent state of the manometric flame. For now, when the mirror is rotated, you no longer see a serrated band of light, indicating the existence of vibratory motion in the capsule, and the end of the tube to which it is attached, but we have, instead, a continuous ribbon, which is proof positive of total interference.

In order to render simultaneously visible the condition of vibratory motion at the end of each branch taken separately, and the result produced when the two tubes are combined, we may, after Koenig, attach a capsule to the end of each branch, and provide each capsule with two rubber tubes. These tubes are connected with three separate jets, all mounted on the same stand, and one placed immediately above the other. The middle jet is connected with both capsules as in the foregoing experiment, while the lower and upper jets are joined one to each capsule independently.

If now the sound of the tuning-fork be made to act on the three flames, when the branches of the tube are of the same length, the upper and lower jets, as viewed in the revolving mirror, are seen to give two similar indentated bands of light, *a* and *b* (Fig. 139), whilst the central jet gives a like serrated ribbon. But the latter being acted upon by the sum of the pulses affecting the upper and lower flames, its indentations, $a + b$, of the same figure, are correspondingly deeper. By so lengthening one of the branches that it differs from the other by an exact half wave-length, the result manifests itself instantly. The upper and lower flames, being, as before, under the influence of like but separate vibratory motions, remain unchanged, as is shown by the upper and lower flame-images at the right-hand side of the figure. The middle flame, on the contrary, as the middle image on the right of Fig. 139 declares, does not betray the slightest quiver. The contrast

FIG. 139.

presented shows most strikingly the perfect interference that now prevails.

The same ingeniously fashioned apparatus is available for exhibiting interference of sonorous waves proceeding from other sonorous bodies as well as from those generated by tuning-forks.

It can also be utilized for measuring the velocities of sound in air and in gases. When we wish to employ it for determining the velocity of sound in air, we have only to secure perfect interference by properly adjusting the branches of the tube when a simple tone of a given number of vibrations is passing through it. The wave-length is twice the difference of the lengths of the paths travelled by the divided sonorous pulses. This, multiplied by the known rate of vibration of the fork, is the velocity of sound in the air at the temperature of the atmosphere at the time of the experiment.

By means of the little stop-cocks fitted into the top part of the branches we can fill the tube with any gas we choose, and determine its velocity in the same manner as we find that of air. In this instance, however, we shall have to take the precaution of preventing the escape of gas at the ends of the tube, or at the joints, — an emergency that is neatly provided for in the construction of the instrument. Having done this, we shall find, in adjusting the branches so as to insure total interference, that the difference in the lengths of the branches of the tube will vary according to the gas with which the tube is filled, and, as a consequence, that as the length of the branches for the different gases varies, so will the velocity of sound in these gases vary.

It may be stated, in conclusion, that the phenomena of reinforcement and interference of vibratory motion apply to all kinds of wave-systems. They obtain in heat and light as well as in sound. Our experiments have shown us that sound added to sound may produce silence. Similarly, light added to light may cause darkness, and heat rays may interfere with each other in such wise as to cause a diminution of temperature. All that is necessary in either case is that the heat or light vibrations should meet each other in opposite phases.

More than this. According to Hertz's experiments, electric and magnetic vibrations may similarly interfere with each other as completely as those of light or of sound.

Nothing shows better than the experiments we have just witnessed the nature of these various forces, or proves more conclusively that they are, one and all, simply modes of motion. The germ of this grand generalization, — a generalization demonstrated experimentally, step by step, — is to be found in an experiment on the diffraction of light made by a Jesuit philosopher, Grimaldi, over two hundred years ago. This germ has been developed by the researches of Huygens, Young, Arago, Dr. Lloyd, Sir

William Hamilton, Maxwell, Hertz, and others, but above all by that brilliant young French physicist, Augustin Jean Fresnel. It was he that put the truth of the wave-theory of light beyond further question by his celebrated *experimentum crucis*, in which he obtained total interference of luminous rays both by reflection and refraction.

CHAPTER VIII.

BEATS AND BEAT-TONES.

IN our last lecture we dealt with vibrations that are so related to each other that their resultant effect is either resonance or total interference. We found that when two sounds are in unison, and in the same phase, they tend to reinforce each other; and that when the same sounds are in opposite phases, — their intensity being equal, — one cancels the other, and silence is the result. Under these conditions we discovered that the result must always be either augmentation or annihilation of sound, — no other result being possible.

It is, however, comparatively seldom that we deal with two sounds that are exactly in unison. We are more frequently called upon to consider notes whose rates of vibration differ from each other by a greater or less amount. What, then, is the result, when two notes differing more or less from each other in pitch are sounded simultaneously? This question — one that is of special interest to musicians — I shall endeavor to answer in to-day's lecture. What we have learned about resonance and interference has paved the way for our work to-day, — for the discussion, namely, of what we shall, after Koenig, designate as beats and beat-tones.

Before you are the two C forks used in our last lecture. I damp one of them by attaching a small pellet of wax to one of its prongs. On exciting it with the bow, you perceive that it gives a slightly lower note than it did before. The extra load it has to carry retards its motion, and it executes, in consequence, a smaller number of vibrations than previously, and a smaller number, too, than is made by its unencumbered companion.

If now both forks are sounded simultaneously, what will be the result? Something entirely different, apparently, from what was considered in our last lecture, and yet, as we shall see, something closely related to the phenomena then discussed. You hear peculiar risings and fallings of sound, peculiar throbbing notes, disclosing an augmentation of sound resembling resonance, and a diminution that approaches interference. This, in fact, is what we actually have,—alternate conditions of resonance and of total interference. As, however, the totality of interference lasts but a very small fraction of a second, the sound seems to be continuous and to vary only in intensity.

That extinction of sound actually occurs, can be demonstrated in various ways. For the present, however, we shall simply consider the phenomena in the light of sinuous curves representing the sounds produced. As before, we shall call the two forks A and B. Suppose now that A, which we shall consider as the loaded fork, makes eight vibrations, while B executes nine. The difference in their frequencies, as a matter of fact, is not so great; but this is immaterial. Viewing them as vibrating in the ratio of 8 : 9, we construct their curves accordingly. Let the light continuous curve (Fig. 140) represent the condensations and rarefactions originated at the fork A, and the dotted curve those proceeding from B. By combining these two curves, as in previous instances, and remembering that the perpendiculars of the resultant curve are always equivalent to the algebraic sum of those of its constituents, we have as a resultant in this case the curve a, b, c, d, e, f.

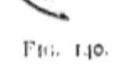

FIG. 140.

g, h. In the figure we notice that the two systems of waves commence and terminate at the same points. Hence, at a, b, c, d, e, f, g, h, the crests and troughs will be correspondingly larger. At M, however, crest meets trough, and at this particular point there can be no disturbance.

Translated into the language of sound, these curves signify that when waves of condensation concur, resonance is the result, and that when condensation meets rarefaction, silence ensues. Between the points of maximum resonance and total interference, — that is, between A and M, — there is a gradual diminution of sound; and between the positions of interference and greatest resonance — that is, between M and b — there is a corresponding augmentation. Hence the alternate risings and fallings of sound that are heard when two forks, such as A and B, are sounded together after their unison has been disturbed by so loading one of them as to lower slightly its frequency. Such alterations in the loudness of sounds are called beats, and, as we shall see, are of the utmost importance in acoustics, as well as in music.

When the frequencies of two notes differ from each other by one vibration, there is one alteration of intensity, and, consequently, one beat per second. If two notes differ from each other by two vibrations there will be two risings and sinkings, and, therefore, two beats per second. And, in general, the number of beats per second arising from two notes near unison, sounding at the same time, is equal to the difference of their frequencies.

Let us now apply this knowledge to the determination of the frequency of the loaded fork A. Unencumbered, it executes exactly 512 vibrations per second, as does also its companion B. Loaded, its vibration is something less. Let us see how much. Exciting A and B simultaneously, you hear the same loud distinct beats that were perceived in our previous experiment. Watch in hand, I count the number of beats heard in ten seconds. The number is twenty, and the number of beats for one second is, therefore, two. Subtracting this from 512, we have 510 as the frequency of the fork A as now loaded.

By means of a little wax, a small coin is attached to the fork A. It is thus damped still more. The number of beats audible per second is greater than before. Observation shows that we have thirty-five beats in ten seconds, and, consequently, three and a half in one second. The frequency of the fork A is now reduced to 508.5 vibrations.

Loading the fork A still more, the intervals of reinforcement and diminution succeed each other more rapidly, until finally the beats become so numerous that it is impossible to count them directly. We now become conscious of an unpleasant sensation, which musicians call discord. When two sounds near the middle of the scale give rise to thirty-three beats per second, the discord that ensues is, according to Helmholtz, at a maximum.

But tuning-forks are not our only means of exhibiting the phenomenon of beats. Any two sonorous bodies will, if slightly out of unison, manifest the same alterations in intensity when caused to sound simultaneously.

Let us try these two large open organ-pipes. They are now in unison, each emitting the note C_2. By moving downward the slider at the top of one of them, we diminish the length of the vibrating column of air, and at the same time change the pitch of the note emitted. On causing the two pipes to speak, you at once hear, as in the case of the dissonant tuning-forks, loud and very marked beats. If we move the slider upwards the beats succeed each other less frequently, until, finally, when the two pipes sound in unison, they disappear altogether.

We can, however, cause them to break forth again, without touching the slider. It is sufficient to bring the finger near the embouchure of one of the pipes, thus lowering its note, to evoke slow or rapid beats at will. The number of beats, in this case, will depend on how much the embouchure of the pipe is covered. Similarly, by placing the hand on the top of the pipe, and covering it more or less, we may lower the note, and thereby obtain beats of varying degrees of rapidity.

By means of the pipes furnished with manometric capsules used in our last lecture (Fig. 135), we can observe with the eye the character of these beat-producing tones. To this end, we connect the capsules of the two pipes to the same jet, and ignite the gas that is caused to issue from it. So long as the notes from the pipes are in unison, the flame is quiescent. But no sooner is unison disturbed by moving the slider of one of the pipes, or by putting the finger before the embouchure, than we have beats that cause the flame to dance in time with them. If the beats follow each other quickly, the flame dances with corresponding rapidity. If the beats are slow, as is the case when the two notes are near unison, the flame at once declares the fact.

If now the cubical mirror before the flame be rotated, we have an elongated image of the flame that exhibits most beautifully its intermittent action, and pictures clearly the alternations of resonance and interference. The luminous band seen in the mirror reminds us of the resultant curve given in Fig. 140; the serrated parts of the band correspond to the crests and troughs of the curve, and indicate greater or less coalescence and reinforcement of sound, while the continuous portion of the luminous ribbon, like the middle part, M, of the curve, is certain evidence of total interference.

A very pretty and striking method of observing beats is afforded by means of two singing flames. Before you are two singing flames (Fig. 141) in unison. By raising or lowering a telescopic slider attached to one of the tubes, we can easily change the pitch of the note emitted by the column of air vibrating within the tube. As soon as we thus disturb the unison of the two notes, you hear loud beats that succeed each other with more or less rapidity,— just in proportion as we increase or diminish the interval between the two tones. At the same time you observe a characteristic flickering of the flame. It dances to the beats and keeps perfect time with them.

Beats are very marked in pipe or reed organs tuned according to equal temperament. The so-called tremolo effects given by certain stops of these instruments are due to beats. But bells give rise to beats more readily, perhaps, than other forms of sonorous bodies. This is particularly the case with large bells, and, as we have learned, arises from the impossibility of casting them so that they will be perfectly symmetrical and homogeneous throughout. When ringing, the bell is divided into sections of different sizes, whose periods of vibration differ more or less from one another.

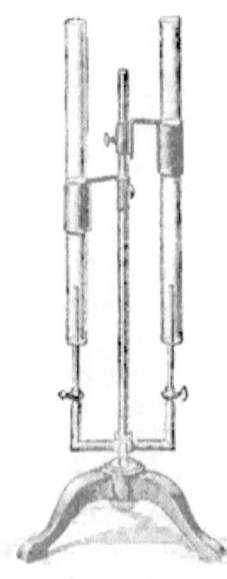

Fig. 141.

On the table are two rare antique Japanese gongs, which either singly or together give forth beats in a most remarkable manner. They are made of bronze, and are quite thin; but the purity and softness of the notes which they emit, and the length of time during which they continue to vibrate after being struck, are quite surprising. The sounding of a number of such bells, properly tuned, in the ancient temples of Japan, must have been productive of effects that were not only pleasing to the ear, but also conducive to solemn religious emotion. The gongs are placed on small, soft mats, to give mellowness to the tone; and for a similar reason they are struck, not with hard hammers, but with padded sticks. I now strike the large gong, and a delightfully soft and pure note is the result. The beats engendered succeed each other in such a way as to produce a tremolo effect rivalling that afforded by the most perfect musical instrument. On exciting the smaller gong we secure similar results, the only difference being that in this case the pitch is higher. Both gongs, as you observe, are especially rich in upper partials. By properly striking the gongs, their first upper partials can be made to sound quite as loud as their primes. The primes and first upper partials can now be heard distinctly in all parts of the hall.

When both gongs are struck at the same time, we get a most confused combination of sounds. And the fact that the gongs, when sounding their primes, are slightly out of tune, only intensifies the dissonance when their upper partials are brought out with any degree of force. When, then, both gongs are sounded simultaneously, we have the beats due to each taken separately, and the beats caused by the interferences not only of the primes with each other, but also of the upper partials with each other, and of these partials with their primes. Some of the beats, as you will perceive by listening closely, are very slow, others more rapid, and others again so rapid that they give rise to a rough, rolling noise that is quite painful to the ear. This harshness is observed in chimes of bells when not carefully tuned. It is more prominent in bells than in the gongs we have used, because the tones of the former are more piercing than those of the latter.

Beats furnish us the simplest and the most delicate means of determining when two notes are in unison. Let me illustrate. I take the sonometer and place the bridge as nearly as possible midway between the two supports of the wire. As nearly as I can judge by the eye, the two divisions of the string are equal in length. They should, therefore, give the same note. I excite one section of the string, and as soon as the note produced is extinguished, the other section is agitated. As far as the ear can estimate, there is no difference in the two tones. If we now sound the two divisions of the string together, we at once hear beats that declare the absence of perfect unison. The beats are not very rapid, it is true, because there is very little difference between the frequencies of the two notes. But this difference, slight as it is, manifests itself at once.

By means of beats we are able to distinguish from each

other notes that do not differ from each other in frequency by more than one fifth of a vibration in a second. Scheibler's marvellously accurate system of tuning is based on beats entirely. According to his system, there is no attempt made to bring the note of a string, pipe, or reed into unison with a standard of pitch directly. The work is done indirectly, but with a degree of accuracy that is well-nigh absolute. For this purpose a specially constructed set of forks is required, giving notes just four vibrations lower or higher than those which are to be attuned. To tune a piano, for instance, its note of A_3 is made to give just four beats per second with a fork that makes exactly that number with a standard A_3 fork, whose absolute number of vibrations is known. We are thus certain that the piano-string executes the same number of vibrations as the fork taken as the standard of pitch. By this method any one who can count beats is capable of tuning.

On the table are two sets of forks, — thirteen in each set, — one of which gives the tempered chromatic scale from C_3 to C_4, according to French pitch, — $A_3 = 435$ vibrations per second, — while the other furnishes the same notes heightened by precisely four vibrations, and generating, consequently, four beats per second.

Allow me to show you how such forks are used. I will take A of the second set of forks, — these are called *auxiliary forks*, — and adjust the string on our sonometer so that it will generate just four beats per second when sounded with the fork chosen. A few moments only are required for the adjustment. When it is once attained, as we know by counting the beats, we are certain that the string is executing exactly 435 vibrations per second, and emitting the note A_3 of the standard of pitch of the French Conservatory.

In a similar manner we could, by means of these forks, tune all the notes of an entire octave — from C_3 to C_4 — of any musical instrument whatever. Musicians, however, are not so exact. They are satisfied to get the pitch of one note right, — generally A_3, as above, or C_4, — and then proceed from this one note to tune all the others by ear, by estimation of the fifths. The accuracy of tuning in this manner varies, of course, with the delicacy of the tuner's ear. For this reason no two persons, except by chance, would tune exactly alike. And for a similar reason, no one, who is thus guided solely by his ear, could tune in succession two instruments that would be perfectly in unison.

For perfect tuning, one of Scheibler's tonometers is indispensable. The two sets of forks before you are sometimes called tonometers, because Scheibler's method is used in connection with them. But the tonometers which were devised and used by Scheibler consisted of a series of forks not only extending over a whole octave, as do those on the table, but also giving four beats for every possible note within the octave. Thus, one of his tonometers intended for the octave A_2 to A_3, German pitch, — that is, from 220 to 440 vibrations per second, — embraced fifty-six tuning-forks. Beginning with A_2 of 220 vibrations, each fork in succession of this tonometer was tuned exactly four beats higher than the one preceding.

Koenig makes, on Scheibler's principle, superb tonometers of sixty-seven forks for the octave from C_3 to C_4. In addition to this, he has, with the expenditure of infinite labor and skill, constructed a like tonometer, as we saw in our second lecture, for the entire compass of musical sounds. By means of this unique instrument one may determine with ease the absolute pitch of every note from C_{-2} to F_9.

By means of one of Lissajous' apparatus, as modified by Mercadier and constructed by Duboscq, I am able to give you a most telling optical illustration of the phenomenon of beats. The apparatus consists of two tuning-forks (Fig. 142), one of which is provided with a coil so that it may be kept in vibration electrically. The fork A carries a style on one of its prongs, while one of the prongs of the fork B bears a piece of smoked glass. This latter fork is also furnished with sliding weights, by means of which it may be made to give various intervals with the fork A.

The ends of both forks, with style just touching the smoked glass plate, is adjusted over the condenser of the lantern. The fork B is now set in vibration by passing an electric current through the coil fastened between the two prongs. This causes the style of the fork A to inscribe a straight line on the smoked glass.

If now the fork A is also caused to vibrate, it will tend to make this straight line longer or shorter, according as it moves in the same direction as the fork B, or in an

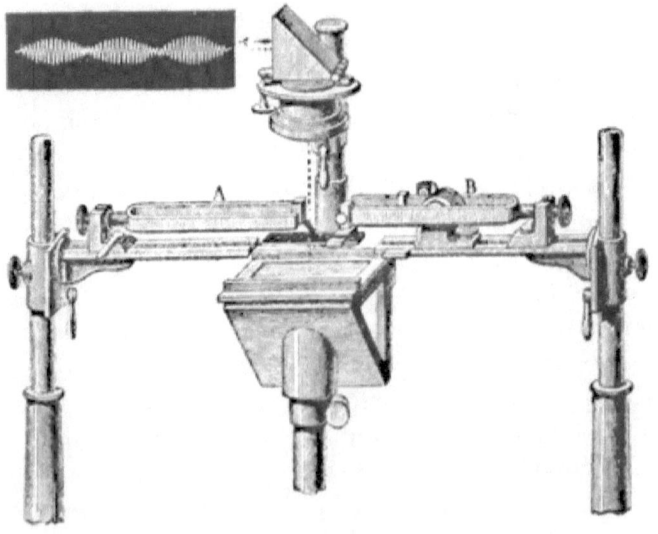

Fig. 142.

opposite direction. When, then, the two forks are in unison, they will reinforce or enfeeble each other according as they are in the same or in opposite phases. This reinforcement or enfeeblement will be indicated by the line traced on the glass, which will be longer or shorter when the two forks are simultaneously acting than when only one is in motion. When the fork A is moved in a line parallel to its axis, the straight line on the glass will change into a beautiful sinuous curve like those shown in the second lecture. The objective and the right-angled prism at the top of the lantern enable me to project on the screen all the figures that the style of one fork may inscribe on the glass of the other.

I disturb the unison of the two forks by moving the sliding weights on the fork B. When both forks are at rest the result of this disturbance of unison is to cause the line inscribed on the glass plate to alternately lengthen and shorten, as we see by the image on the screen. The number of alterations in any given time will depend on the number of beats per second made by the two forks; and the number of beats, as we have seen, depends on the difference of the frequencies of the forks. If there is only one beat per second, the alterations in the length of the line will occur once every second. If there are two or more beats per second, the lengthening and shortening of the line will take place correspondingly often. Under these circumstances, if the fork A is moved slowly and uniformly to the left, — that is, in a direction parallel to its axis and to the length of the plate, — we observe a sinuous line as before, but one whose indentations have a varying amplitude from a maximum to zero. This variation in the amplitude of the curves shown on the screen exhibits to the eye the difference in the rates of vibration of the two forks, while their beats declare the same thing to the ear.

I now adjust the sliding weights again, and while the two forks are in vibration I move A to the left, as before, and you have the result on the screen as a beautiful undulating curve, which tells more clearly than words the nature of the combined motion of the two forks. The forks used are not tuned to give any particular note, nor are they constructed to give a very loud sound; but if you will listen attentively, you will be able to perceive beats succeeding each other at the rate of about two per second. And if you compare the number of beats with the rhythmic action of the image on the screen, you will find that the beats produced synchronize perfectly with the formation of the spindle-shaped segments of the sinuous curve on the screen.

M. Lissajous has taught us how to vary this experiment so as to obtain the same results in an equally striking and pleasing manner. His method is so beautiful, and its applications are so general and of such importance, that every one interested in acoustics should be familiar with it. We are again indebted to M. Mercadier for devising for us a modified form of Lissajous' original apparatus. Mercadier's apparatus is more convenient than the one Lissajous

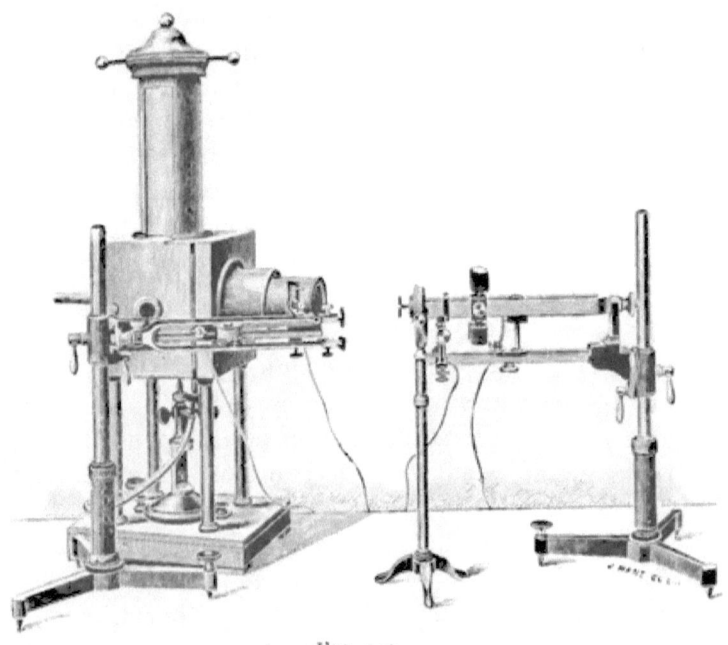

FIG. 143.

used, and enables me to show Lissajous' figures, as they are called, to a large number of persons at the same time.

We use two tuning-forks similar to those used in the preceding experiment. Both are mounted, so as to be kept in vibration at will by an electric current. The only respect in which the forks now used differ from those just employed is that the style and vibrating plate are replaced by polished steel mirrors attached to the ends of the prongs of each fork. One of the forks (Fig. 143) is so

placed that its mirror receives a beam of light coming
from the lantern to the left. The light is then reflected
from this fork to the mirror on the second fork, and thence
reflected to the screen, through a lens, supported on an
appropriate stand. One Grenet cell is connected with

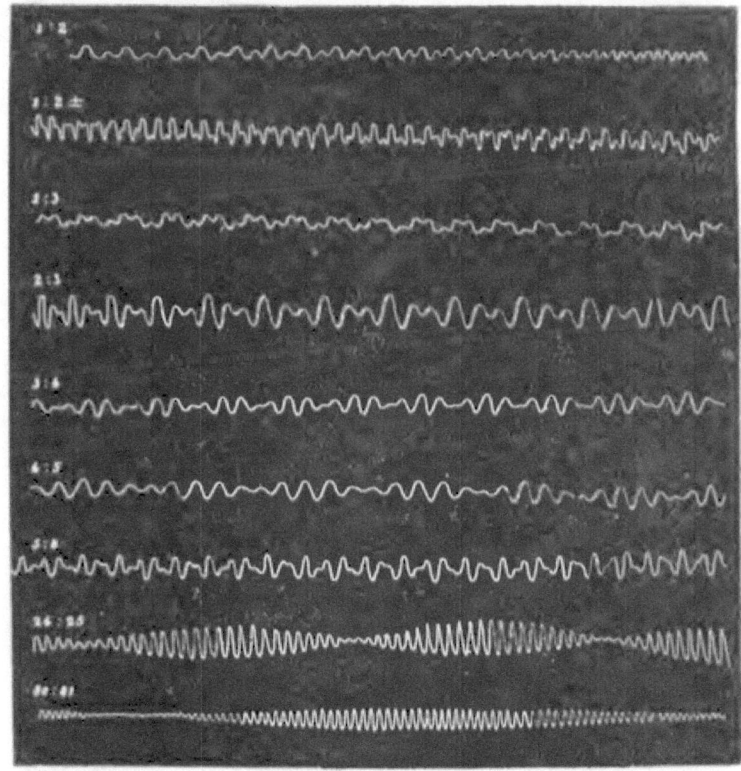

FIG. 144.

each fork, which is thus kept vibrating as long as may be
desired. When the two forks are in unison, they tend
to reinforce or to weaken each other, according as they
are in the same or in opposite phases.

When the forks are so adjusted that they vibrate in the
same plane, the image of light seen on the screen can be
made to go through all the various changes, and in the
same manner, as the inscriptions on the smoked glass in

our last experiment. The forks are now so adjusted that they differ by a semitone, — that is, their rates of vibration are as 24 : 25. The result is the beautiful curve (Fig. 144)

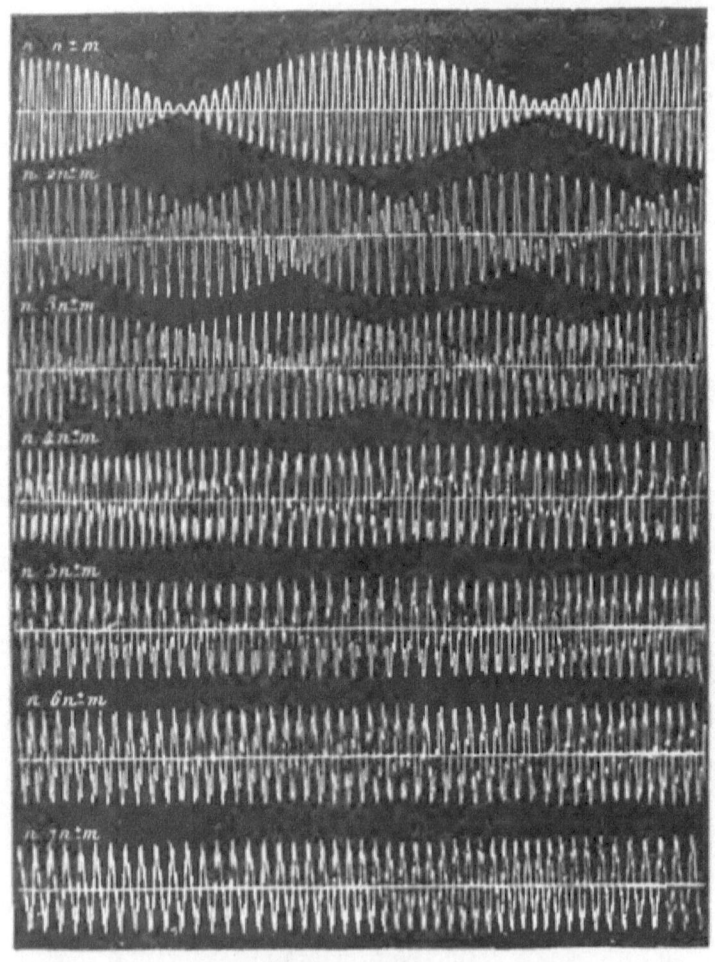

FIG. 145.

now on the screen. If we diminish the interval so that the relative frequencies of the two forks are as 80 : 81, we get a smaller interval, known to musicians as a comma. As seen on the screen, — see adjoining figure, — its image resembles that corresponding to the interval of a semitone, except that the number of sinuosities is greater for the comma, while their amplitude is less. Fig. 144 also shows a number of curves corresponding to simpler intervals. In Fig. 145 are several beautiful and complex curves obtained by Koenig from the altered harmonic intervals indicated at the left-hand side of the figure.

Nothing can give us a better idea of the nature of beats than the figures we have just been studying. The swellings and contractions of the indentations seen on the screen are the exact counterparts of the condition of the atmosphere in this hall. The reinforcements and interferences of sound so beautifully depicted in the different figures we have seen, tell us how the atmosphere that surrounds us is alternately agitated and quiescent, and why it is that we perceive in rhythmic order the varying periods of resonance and silence.

These experiments are made specially to appeal to the eye. I shall now make an experiment that will appeal with equally telling effect to the ear.

Before you (Fig. 146) is a superb instrument designed by Dr. Koenig, by means of which we are enabled to study the phenomena of beats with more satisfaction than with any other instrument we have yet seen. It is a powerful C_2 tuning-fork, actuated by electricity, and fixed before a large adjustable copper resonator. Both branches of the fork are hollow, having been bored by a drill of small diameter. These borings unite with each other in the stem of the fork, where they communicate with a small reservoir of mercury. The mercury can be made to move up and down the branches of the fork by means of a small piston that works in a cylindrical piece of steel, which serves as the reservoir. By raising the mercury, the number of vibrations of the fork is lessened, and its note lowered in proportion. By lowering the mercury, the note is correspondingly raised. We thus have the means of readily changing the frequency of the fork within a comparatively wide limit, and of having a note whose intensity remains unchanged. Dr. Koenig appropriately calls this a fork of variable pitch.

Beside it stands another fork exactly similar, except that it is not provided with the arrangement for changing its frequency. The pitch of this second fork is constant. By properly adjusting the height of the mercury in the fork of variable pitch, we can bring it into unison with the fork of constant pitch. If we now connect each fork with a single Grenet cell, the forks are at once set in vibration.

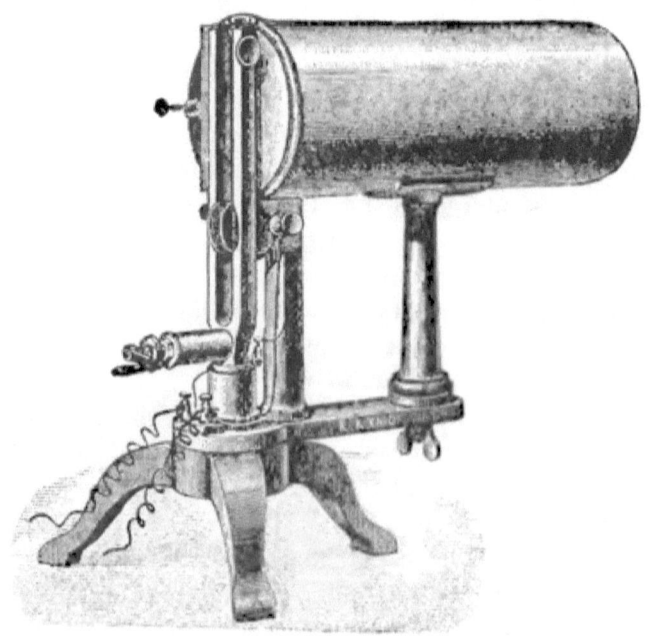

FIG. 146.

You hear little or no sound as yet, because the resonators are closed. One is now opened, and then the other, when you hear notes of exceeding purity and volume. At present the two forks are in unison, and the notes produced seem to proceed from a single source of sound. By raising or lowering the mercury, we can disturb the unison. The slightest movement of the piston is sufficient to change the relative frequencies of the two forks, and to induce beats.

The beats are now very slow, because the piston has

been moved but slightly, and the rate of vibration of the fork has been affected but little. You can, however, perceive a rising and falling of the sound, although each beat persists for several seconds, because of the extraordinary power of the sounds that engender these beats. The notes emitted are as nearly simple tones as may be, for the forks have been so constructed that all the upper partials have been quenched. We have, then, nothing to consider except the primes, and the beats to which, by virtue of their different rates of vibrations, they give rise.

Changing the position of the mercury in the fork still more, we can hear several beats a second. Watch in hand, I count the number now heard in ten seconds. There are thirty; that is, three for each second. I have all along been raising the mercury in the bores of the fork. This has been equivalent to weighting its prongs, and causing them to move more slowly. The number of vibrations has consequently been reduced, and the note correspondingly lowered. The number of beats tells us exactly the extent of this change. C_2 executes 128 vibrations per second, and the fork of variable pitch makes, therefore, three less; namely, 125 per second.

Raising the mercury still higher in the fork, the beats become so rapid that it is difficult, if not impossible, to count them. It is, indeed, difficult to count beats when there are more than four per second; and their enumeration is almost equally difficult when the number falls below one a second. It requires practice to count them with any degree of accuracy when there are two each second. Their enumeration is easiest when there are three or four per second.

The tuning of musical instruments, as now used, is effected solely by counting, or at least by estimating the beats generated by various notes that are successively sounded two by two. Proficiency in tuning requires not only an accurate ear, but also long years of practice during several hours each day. Without the aid of beats, any approximation to correct tuning with the unassisted ear would be impossible. Without beats, it is hardly possible for even the most accurate ear to tune just intervals, not to speak of the more complicated intervals employed in our so-called tempered instruments.

Mr. Ellis, in referring to this matter, says: "But few ears could be trusted to tune a succession of perfect fifths and fourths. Herr G. Appunn"—the brother of Anton Appunn, who made some of the high-pitch forks used in our second lecture—"told me that it cost him an immense labor to tune thirty-six notes, forming perfect fifths and fourths, upon an experimental harmonium, and he had the finest ear for the appreciation of intervals that I ever heard of. The accumulation of almost insensible into intolerable errors besets all attempts to tune by a long series of similar intervals. Even octaves are rarely tuned accurately through the compass of a grand pianoforte."

In the early part of the lecture it was stated that the number of beats engendered when two slightly dissonant notes were sounded, is equal to the difference of the frequencies of the notes. This is true; but it would be misleading to have you left under the impression that beats are produced only when two notes are near unison. But this is just what is taught by most writers on sound and music, and by those especially who follow Helmholtz. Koenig, however, by a most exhaustive series of experiments over almost the entire compass of sound, has demonstrated, by means of the most perfect instruments that mechanical ingenuity could devise, that the generally accepted theory of beats must be materially modified to correspond with the results of his investigations. No one, I think, will question the accuracy of the statements of one who is known to be so careful as Koenig, and who is recognized as an expert of the greatest eminence in all that concerns the science of acoustics.

According to Koenig, beats are produced not only when the intervals are small, but also when the frequencies of the generators of sound are widely separated from each other. In his experiments he was able to distinguish beats made by disturbed harmonic intervals up as far as the eighth and tenth partial. Thus, by taking C_1 of 64 vibrations as the prime, and C_4, making 512 vibrations, and three octaves above C_1, he was able, by slightly altering the frequency of either fork, to obtain beats. And although C_4 is the eighth partial of C_1, the beats were quite distinct, but not so loud as those yielded by two forks nearly in unison. More than this, under favorable circumstances he succeeded in obtaining beats with the intervals $C_1 : D_4 — 64 : 576$, or $1 : 9$,— and $C_1 : E_4 — 64 : 640$, or $1 : 10$.

Helmholtz and others have imagined that these beats were due to the upper partials of the forks used, or to the resultant tones, about which we shall see more presently; but Koenig took care to use forks that gave no upper partials whatever. Throughout his admirable investigation "On the Sounding of Two Tones at the Same Time,"[1] he studiously eschewed the use of forks that gave other than simple tones. Upper partials and resultant tones, therefore, cannot afford any explanation of the facts observed; namely, that two simple tones, of widely separated frequencies, give rise to beats as well as those which are only slightly removed from unison.

But this is not the only discovery made by Koenig concerning the production of beats. He has also demonstrated that two simple tones, called generators, are competent to excite two sets of beats that are quite different from each other. These beats he distinguishes as upper and lower beats. Their frequency for any given interval may be determined from the following law, which in all cases agrees with the results of experiment: —

The frequencies of the beats are equal to the differences between the number of vibrations of the upper generator and the vibration-numbers corresponding to the two multiples of the lower generator, between which the vibration-number of the upper generator is found.

Thus, according to this law, for the interval $2 : 5$, with the

---

[1] Quelques Expériences d'Acoustique, pp. 87 *et seq.*

notes C_2: E_3, giving respectively 128 and 320 vibrations per second, the upper number, 5, of the interval ratio lies between 4 and 6. But these numbers are the second and third multiples of the lower number, 2. The frequencies of the two sets of beats will, therefore, be found by subtracting 4 from 5, = 1, for the lower beat, and 5 from 6, = 1, for the upper beat. The ratio, then, of the frequency of the lower generator to that of the lower beats will be 2 : 1, or, taking the vibration-number, 128, of the generator, the beat-frequency, as compared with it, will be 64. Similarly, the ratio representing the frequency of the upper generator and that of the upper beats will be 5 : 1, or 320 : 64. The frequencies both of the lower and upper beats in this case are equal.

If, however, we take the interval 3 : 8 for the notes C_2 : F_3, with vibrations equal to 128 : 341.3, we shall find that the frequencies of the upper and lower beats are different. Thus, taking the interval ratio, 3 : 8, of the two generators named, we find that the number 8 of the upper generator lies between 6 and 9, the first and second multiples of the number expressing the relative frequency of the lower generator. The relative frequencies, accordingly, of the upper and lower beats will be $8 - 6 = 2$, and $9 - 8 = 1$. That is, the frequency of the lower beats will be to the lower generator as 2 : 3, or, as the number of vibrations of the lower generator is 128, the number of beats will be 85.3. In like manner, the ratio of the relative frequency of the upper generator and the upper beats being 8 : 1, their absolute frequencies will be 341.3 : 42.6. The frequency of the upper beats, in this instance, is just one half that of the lower beats.

But it would be a mistake to infer, from what has been said, that both upper and lower beats are heard in every instance in which beats are produced. Such is not the case. More frequently only one set of beats is audible.

In going from unison, 1 : 1, to the octave, 1 : 2, or from the octave, 1 : 2, to the twelfth, 1 : 3, we shall find that the lower beats extend a little over the lower half of each interval, and the upper beats over a little more than the upper half. Over a short space near the middle of each interval, both sets of beats are heard with varying degrees of distinctness. In higher periods of intervals, as from 1 : 3 to 1 : 4, from 1 : 4 to 1 : 5, etc., the audibility of both upper and lower beats has a more limited range. This is explained by the fact that in each period the upper beats are more feeble than the lower beats. As a consequence, the intensity of both upper and lower beats diminishes from period to period in proportion as we ascend from lower to higher periods.

Illustrations showing the order of occurrence of lower and upper beats, and of their occurrence together, are easily found. Thus the interval, 8 : 9, according to what has been stated, should give only lower beats. Taking the notes $C_1 : D_1$, whose vibration-numbers are 64 : 72, we have only lower beats, whose frequency, 8, is equal to the difference between the frequencies of the two generators. With the interval 8 : 15, we have only upper beats, the relative frequency of which is $1 \cdot 8 \quad 2 = 16. \quad 16 - 15 = 1$. Choosing the interval $C_1 : B_1$, whose vibration-ratio is 64 : 120, we obtain upper beats having a frequency of 8. According to the rule just given, we double the frequency of the lower generator, 64, which gives us 128, and subtract from this the vibration-number, 120, of the upper generator, whereby, as above, we have 8 as a remainder. With $C_2 : F_2$, whose vibration-ratio is 128 : 170.6, giving an interval 3 : 4, and near the middle of the octave, we have both upper and lower beats. $170.6 - 128$ gives us 42.6 as the frequency of the lower beats; and $128 \times 2 = 256$, and $256 - 170.6 = 85.4$, gives us the frequency of the upper beats. But when two generators separated by an interval of a fifth are employed, — that is, when their frequencies are as 2 : 3, — then the frequencies of the upper and lower beats are invariably equal.

The frequency of the beats, as we have seen, increases as the generators depart from unison. At first their frequency is very low, and can easily be counted. Gradually it becomes more and more rapid, the beats changing into a roll, and then into a confused rattle.

The question now arises, "Can beats link themselves together so as to give rise to a continuous sound?" Lagrange and Dr. Thomas Young, the latter of whom gave the subject much attention, thought they could. Helmholtz and his followers say No. Koenig takes up the subject, and by a long series of the most careful observations, with large tuning-forks especially constructed for the purpose, comes to the conclusion that beats can and do change into sounds when their number attains a certain limit. We shall take a hurried review of Koenig's investigations, when, I think, you will be content to accept his views as, in the main, correct.

In 1714 Tartini, the celebrated Italian violinist and musical composer, discovered that when two notes were simultaneously sounded on the violin with sufficient intensity, they gave rise to a third note distinct from both. He called them *terzi suoni*,— third sounds. They are often called, after their inventor, Tartini's tones. They are likewise variously denominated *differential*, *resultant*, and *combinational* tones. Koenig calls them *beat-notes*, or *beat-tones*. Tartini made his discovery the basis of a new system of music,— a system which he developed in his "Trattato di Musica, Secondo la Vera Scienza dell' Armonia," published in 1754, and in a second work on "Dei Principii dell' Armonia Musicale," published in 1767.

Helmholtz distinguishes two kinds of combinational tones,— viz., *differential* and *summational* tones. The former are called differential tones, because their frequencies are equal to the difference of the vibration-numbers of the generating tones. The latter are designated summational tones, because their frequencies are equal to the sum of the vibration-numbers of their generators. For reasons that will appear as we go along, I shall, after Koenig, call both of these tones beat-notes, or beat-tones.

For the ordinary harmonic intervals,— that is, those comprised between unison and a major sixth,— it is quite true that we obtain tones whose frequencies are equal to the difference of their primaries. But it is only these few intervals that afford a basis for the name differential tones, and the various theories with which they have been associated. In the following table are exhibited the beat-tones — the so-called differential tones — of the more common musical intervals: —

Intervals.	Ratio of Frequencies.	Difference.	The Beat-tone is deeper than the Lower Generator by
Octave	1 : 2	1	0
Fifth	2 : 3	1	An octave
Fourth	3 : 4	1	A twelfth
Major third	4 : 5	1	Two octaves
Minor third	5 : 6	1	Two octaves and a major third
Major sixth	3 : 5	2	A fifth
Minor sixth	5 : 8	3	A major sixth

Putting this result in musical notation, showing the generating tones as minims and the beat-tones as crotchets, we have, —

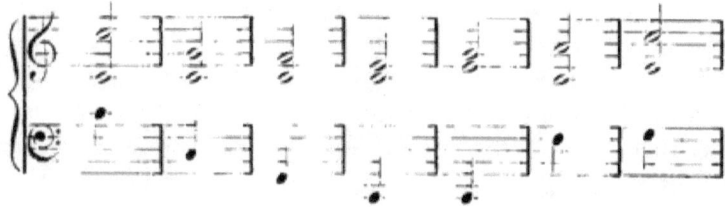

By means of the tuning-forks before you it is easy to render these beat-tones audible. Taking the two forks, C_4 and G_4, whose interval is 2 : 3, and whose frequencies are 512 and 768 respectively, we obtain, on exciting the two forks, a loud and distinct beat-tone, C_3, whose frequency is $768 - 512 = 256$. By sounding simultaneously C_4 and F_4, — interval-ratio 3 : 4, and frequencies 512 : 682.6, — we have a beat-note which, as above indicated, is a twelfth below the lower generator; namely, F_2 of 170.6 vibrations. In like manner, C_4 and E_4, — interval 4 : 5, frequencies 512 : 640 — give us C_2 of 128 vibrations as a beat-note. Proceeding in like manner, it would be easy to render audible the beat-notes due to all the other intervals of the above table.

The rule for determining what are the beat-tones for any two generators is precisely the same as that given for calculating the number of beats produced by two sources of sound. The law governing both beats and beat-tones is identical. This is what might be expected if Koenig's theory, that beats when sufficiently numerous change into beat-tones, is true. Beats are best observed with grave notes, where the difference in frequency is necessarily small. Beat-tones, on the contrary, are best studied with the higher notes, whose vibration-numbers give a correspondingly greater difference of frequency. According to Koenig, beats are best heard with tuning-forks below C_4 of 512 vibrations. Above C_4 all the intervals, except those very near unison, give rise to beat-tones of greater or less intensity.

"But," you will say, "if the law governing beats and beat-tones be the same, we should have upper and lower beat-tones as well as upper and lower beats?" And so we have. And it is precisely these upper beat-tones, whose existence is not explained by Helmholtz's theory, that, with many other stubborn facts, contribute to render his theory untenable. Thus, for the intervals above considered, $C_4 : G_4$; $C_4 : F_4$; $C_4 : E_4$, we have, in addition to the lower beat-notes, C_3, F_2, C_2, also the upper beat-notes, C_5, F_3, and G_3. When the two beat-notes coincide, as the lower and upper beat-notes C_3, they tend to reinforce each other, and generate a proportionally louder sound. When they differ by an octave, as F_2 and F_3, they give rise to a note in which each seems to predominate alternately. The effect of the beat-tones C_2 and G_3 sounding together is the same as would be produced by two weak primaries of the same interval sounding at the same time.

For the intervals given in the table on page 323, the theory of differential tones may apply; but there are many other intervals where the beat-tones are not equal to the difference between the frequencies of their primaries.

The same difficulty obtains with summational tones. We can show experimentally the existence of beat-tones which are entirely different from summational tones, and which Helmholtz's theory is incompetent to explain.

Koenig's law regarding beat-tones is best illustrated with heavy forks emitting acute sounds. On the table is a set of twelve such forks, ranging from C_5 to C_7. With these forks we are able to get beat-tones that are extraordinarily loud and pure. We take two of them and clamp them in a heavy iron support, specially constructed for the purpose (Fig. 147). When sounded, they yield the notes C_6 and B_6,— interval 8 : 15, frequencies 2048 : 3840,— whence we get, as an upper beat-tone, C_3, of 256 vibrations. Taking the frequencies of the notes in question, we have, according to Koenig's law, $2048 \times 2 = 4096$; $4096 - 3840 = 256$. But there is no differential tone here. The differential

FIG. 147.

tone, if one existed, should, in this case, be a note having a frequency of 1792,— a number obtained by subtracting 2048 from 3840,— and would, consequently, have a pitch equal to the seventh partial of the note actually heard, $256 \times 7 = 1792$.

With the forks $C_5 : D_6$,— intervals 4 : 9, frequencies 1024 : 2304,— we have only a lower beat-tone, C_3,— $1024 \times 2 = 2048$; $2304 - 2048 = 256 = C_3$. The differential tone in this case, if such existed, should be $2304 - 1024 = 1280 = E_3$,— a major third above the lower generator ; but no such tone is audible.

The forks C_5 and F_6 — interval 3 : 8, frequencies 1024 : 2730.8 — give both upper and lower beat-tones; but, again, there is no differential tone. The beat-tones in this case are F_2 and F_4; the differential tone, if any existed, should be A_5. Here the upper generator, 8, lies between the second and third multiples of the lower generator, 3; that is, between 6 and 9. By subtraction we have the differences 2 and 1; $8 - 6 = 2$, and $9 - 8 = 1$. The lower beat-note thus forms with the lower generator the interval 2 : 3, and the former is, consequently, a fifth below the latter. The upper beat-note makes, with the upper generator, the interval 1 : 8, which throws the beat-note three octaves below F_6, and makes it, as above, F_3, of 341.3 vibrations, as against 2730.8 vibrations of F_6.

We have seen how two primary tones may give rise to beats and beat-tones. The question may now arise, Can these beat-tones give rise to other beats and beat-tones in the same manner as primary tones do? For the sake of distinction we shall call the beats and beat-tones produced by two given generators *primary beats* and *beat-tones*. Can, then, primary beat-tones, like their generators, give rise to beats and beat-tones also? They can. And the beats and beat-tones thus produced are called *secondary beats* and *beat-tones*. The great merit of Koenig's investigations is that he has been able to establish the law by which such beats and beat-tones are generated. I have not time to illustrate it in detail. It is sufficient to say that it is essentially the same as the law governing primary beats and beat-tones.

A little consideration will make it evident that secondary beats and beat-tones can be heard only when the sounds of the generators are very acute and very intense. I will pass by the secondary beats, and give you two examples of secondary beat-tones. For this purpose I shall employ for the first example two forks having the interval 8 : 11, and executing respectively 2048 and 2816 vibrations per second. The first fork corresponds to C_6, and the second emits a note between F_6 and G_6. The note it gives is, in reality, the eleventh partial of C_2, — the frequency of C_2 multiplied by 11 giving 2816, the frequency of the fork in question.

When, therefore, these two forks are set in vibration, there are produced the primary lower beat-tone, G_4, of 768 vibrations, and the primary upper beat-tone, E_5, of 1280 vibrations. But besides these two beat-tones we may hear clearly a third note, C_4, of 512 vibrations. This is the secondary beat-tone, and is equal to the difference between the frequencies of the two primary beat-tones, G_4 and E_5, — $1280 - 768 = 512$.

I now take two similar forks, whose interval is $8:13$, and whose frequencies are $2048:3328$ vibrations. These forks answer to C_6, as in the preceding instance, and the thirteenth partial of C_2, — $256 \times 13 = 3328$. The lower primary beat-note yielded in this case is E_5. $3328 - 2048 = 1280 = E_5$. The upper primary beat-note is G_4, of 768 vibrations. $2048 \times 2 = 4096$. $4096 - 3328 = 768 = G_4$. The difference between the frequencies of these two beat-tones, as in the case of the first two forks, is 512, — $1280 - 768 = 512 = C_4$. You will observe that the secondary beat-tones for both the intervals assumed, — $8:11$ and $8:13$, — give rise to the same note, C_4. The primary beat-tones for both intervals are likewise the same, namely, G_4 and E_5. They, however, occur in an inverse order for the two intervals. In the interval $8:11$, G_4 is the lower beat-tone, while E_5 is the upper; whereas in the interval $8:13$, E_5 is the lower, and G_4 the upper beat-tone.

But we may go farther. If the primary beat-tones can originate beats and beat-tones, we might expect that the partials of any two prime tones would similarly produce beats and beat-tones. Koenig maintains that the partials of compound tones do produce such beats and beat-tones, and that they have the same frequencies as have Helmholtz's summational tones. For this reason, he concludes that there are no summational tones, as called for by Helmholtz's theory, and, for reasons based on facts adduced in the foregoing experiments in connection with primary and secondary beats, he rejects altogether the theory of differential tones. He sums up in one sentence the results of his admirable investigations on these subjects, by stating that "*so far we have no experimental demonstration of the existence either of differential or summational tones.*"

Beat-tones cannot be explained on Helmholtz's theory, for the reason, as we have seen, that in many cases they have different frequencies from those of differential and summational tones, whereas differential and summational tones can in all cases be accounted for on Koenig's theory of beat-tones, whether produced directly by generators, or by primary beat-tones, or by partials in the case of compound tones. And although as yet Koenig's conclusions are not concurred in by all investigators, I have no doubt that they will be eventually accepted as the only satisfactory solution of the facts to which they refer.

So far we have been using tuning-forks for the production of beats and beat-tones. They have been employed because they are so constructed as to give absolutely simple notes, and because, having their vibration-numbers stamped on them, we can always be sure of the intervals with which we are working. Most, if not all, of the prime tones, beats, and beat-tones, were, I think, audible to all of you, because the forks are made to give remarkably loud sounds. But the forks used, especially those of the higher pitch, give sounds of very short duration, and for this reason it is sometimes difficult to catch at once the beats and beat-tones that one wishes to hear.

Koenig, to whose fertile inventive faculty we owe so many of our best acoustical apparatus, has devised an instrument for giving us beat-tones that can be maintained for any length of time. Such an apparatus is before you. It is composed essentially of a wheel, whose circumference is provided with a cloth band, which is wetted in a small reservoir partly filled with water, and which rubs against two glass tubes (Fig. 148), tuned to the intervals, giving the beat-tones one wishes to observe. The friction of the cloth throws the tubes into longitudinal vibration, and they are thus made to yield loud, pure notes. By means of this instrument, beat-tones can be heard as long as their primaries. The apparatus is provided with twelve glass

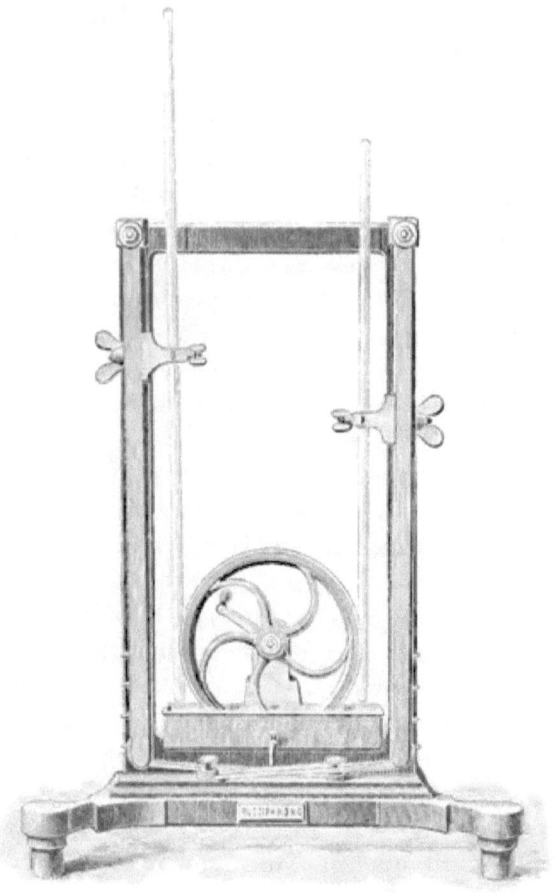

FIG. 148.

tubes attuned to notes extending from C_6 to the twenty-third partial of C_3; that is, to a note having 5888 vibrations per second, — a note, therefore, far above the highest note of the pianoforte.

Taking two tubes, so as to give C_6 and D_6, — interval,

8:9; frequencies, 2048:2304,—we have, on turning the wheel, a distinct lower beat-note, corresponding to C_3, of 256 vibrations. Tubes C_6 and G_6—interval, 2:3; frequencies, 2048:3072—give a C_5 that is remarkably pure and strong. In this case both the upper and the lower beat-notes coincide, as is always the case when the generators are separated from each other by an exact fifth.

We conclude from our experiments with tuning-forks and glass tubes that beats give rise to continuous sounds. Will beats in all cases, however produced, change into a continuous sound, when their number is sufficiently large? Koenig answers this question in the affirmative. It will be interesting here to repeat some of the experiments which he made in connection with the subject, as they will give us a clearer idea of the nature of beats and beat-tones than it would be possible to obtain in any other way.

One of the simplest experiments is with a wooden wheel, about fifteen inches in diameter, an inch and a half thick, and having one hundred and twenty-eight teeth. If a thin, elastic piece of wood be pressed against these teeth, and we then gradually increase the speed of rotation of the wheel, you at first hear a succession of taps, and then a confused rattle, that persists even when the wheel makes an entire revolution per second, and gives, consequently, one hundred and twenty-eight separate taps in that period of time. But along with these taps, provided they are not too noisy, we may hear the note C_2, of one hundred and twenty-eight vibrations. The number of impulses giving rise to the rattle heard and the note C_2 are in this case exactly the same.

If, however, we substitute a small piece of cardboard for the piece of wood, the rattle disappears almost entirely, and the note C_2 becomes much more distinct. When the wheel is given a half of a revolution per second, a rattle is heard, resulting from sixty-four shocks per second; and the sound C, corresponding to sixty-four vibrations, is entirely drowned in the noise that prevails. We learn from this experiment that the same instrument may originate beats and tones at the same time, both of which are perceived by the ear as such. The number of impulses giving rise to these different sensations is, as is evident, the same in both cases. The experiment also proves that we may have as many as one hundred and twenty-eight distinct impulses, or beats, without having a continuous audible sound.

But what, it may be asked, is the lowest sound that can be produced by what are unmistakably beats? Koenig replies to this question by a series of tuning-forks constructed especially for this purpose. Such a set we have here. It is composed of eight powerful forks, between B_6 and C_7, and so tuned that the first seven give, with the eighth, 256, 128, 64, 48, 40, 32, and 26 beats per second, respectively, corresponding, therefore, to the notes C_3, C_2, C_1, G_{-1}, E_{-1}, C_{-1}, and a note making twenty-six vibrations per second.

If we take two forks, one making 3968 vibrations, and the other, C_7, 4096 vibrations, and strike them both vigorously with an ivory hammer, we hear, along with the very acute notes proper to the forks, a deep, grave note, wonderfully pure, corresponding to C_2, of one hundred and twenty-eight vibrations per second. At the same time, however, is heard a peculiar rolling noise, due to beats. Taking forks vibrating 4032 and 4096 times a second, and proceeding as before, we have, as a beat-tone, a note making sixty-four vibrations per second. This is C_1. This beat-tone, like the preceding, is exceedingly pure and distinct. Forks executing 4096 and 4048 vibrations per second yield G_1, having forty-eight vibrations per second. When the frequencies of the forks are 4056 and 4096, the beat-tone resulting therefrom is E_1, whose frequency is 40. We are rapidly approaching the limits of audible sounds; but we can go down still farther. We take two forks whose frequencies are 4064 and 4096, and whose interval is 127 : 128, — an interval which is much less than a comma. The beat-tone in this case is C_{-1}, of thirty-two vibrations, and when the forks are held close to the ear, the note can be recognized without any difficulty. This, as you remember, is the lowest C used in any musical instruments except the very largest organs. We go down a step lower. This time we choose forks whose rates of vibration per second are 4070 and 4096. The number of beats for these forks, whose interval does not exceed half a comma, is twenty-six. They are remarkable in that they do not produce a continuous sensation, but rather a sensation in which one detects the passage from a continuous sound to a series of separate impulses, just such as are heard in pianos and organs yielding notes below C_{-1}.

At the same time that one has this sensation of a grave tone at the lowest limit of perceptibility, there is audible a characteristic rolling due to twenty-six beats per second. Indeed, it has not been possible, in any of the cases just considered, to separate the rolling of the beats from the accompanying beat-tones. We may hear the beats alone by holding the forks some distance from the ear; but we cannot, even with the loudest beat-tones it is possible to obtain, succeed in entirely quenching the beats so as to hear only beat-tones.

These experiments prove that with two primaries of sufficient intensity, thirty-two beats per second are competent to produce a continuous sound; that beats, to the number of about 128 per second, can be distinguished, whatever the intervals employed; and finally, that between these two limits both beats and beat-tones may be heard at the same time.

From what precedes, we learn that beats, as well as primary impulses, may give rise to continuous tones. Intermittent tones also, like beats, may coalesce to produce a continuous sound. This is also contrary to what Helmholtz teaches, for he tells us "beats and intermissions are identical, and that either, when fast enough, produces what is termed a jar, or rattle."

By means of an apparatus specially devised for the purpose, Koenig proves that intermittent sounds may give rise to a continuous sound. The apparatus consists of a large brass disk (Fig. 149), having near its circumference a circle of sixteen large apertures. We rotate this disk, and excite one of the tuning-forks we have just been using, — C_6, for example, — bringing it near the disk, so that its vibrations may pass through the apertures, as these latter move before the fork. On doing this, we find that, in addition to the note of the fork proper, there is also audible a note due to the intermission of its tone by the revolution of the disk. The disk is now making eight revolutions per second, and as there are sixteen apertures,

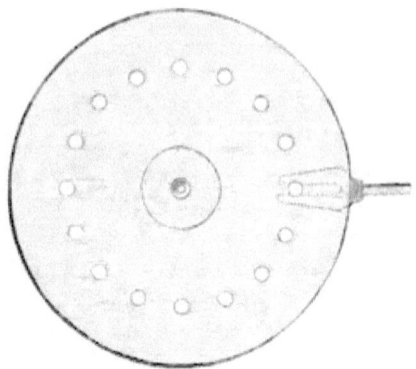

FIG. 149.

the number of intermissions per second amounts to one hundred and twenty-eight. This is equal to the number of vibrations made by the note heard, C_2.

Substituting another fork, C_7, for the C_6 we have been using, and trying it in the same manner, with the velocity of rotation of the disk unchanged, we find that the same note, C_2, is still audible. We might employ other forks of different pitches, and the result would still be the same, as long as there is no change in the speed of rotation of the disk. As soon, however, as we change the velocity of rotation of the disk, the tone due to the intermissions of the note of the fork is changed also. As the speed of the disk is lowered, the note becomes more grave. If we increase the speed of the disk, the pitch of the note is raised in proportion. In all cases the pitch of the resultant tone will, as in the case of beats, depend on the frequency of interruption of the note emitted by the fork.

You will not fail to observe that, in these forks, we have the means of determining the limits of perceptibility of grave sounds. The method is probably the most satisfactory that the acoustician has at his disposal. With all the forks we have used in the experiments just made, the notes, even the lowest of them, are extraordinarily pure and easily heard.

In the experiment just made, a continuous sound was transmitted to the ear intermittently. When the intermis-

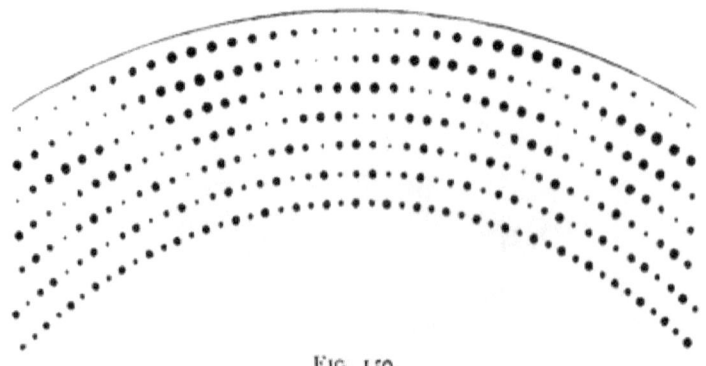

Fig. 150.

sions reached a certain number per second they blended into a continuous tone, the pitch of which was independent of the fork employed. We can observe equally well this passage from intermittent to continuous tones, in sounds that are periodically variable. Koenig proves this experimentally by a disk, a section of which is shown in Fig. 150, having seven circles of holes. Each circle has 192 holes, the diameters of which, for the seven circles, vary periodically 12, 16, 24, 32, 48, 64, and 96 times. In blowing against these circles in succession with a tube in which the diameter equals that of the largest hole, we have, in addition to the sound due to the 192 holes (which is the same for all the circles), the note corresponding to the different periods of variable intensity, — 12, 16, 24, 32, 48,

64, 96. We can assure ourselves of this fact by blowing against seven auxiliary circles, having 12, 16, 24, 32, 48, 64, 96, and 192 holes, all of which have the same diameter, when we shall find that the grave, as well as the acute sounds, really correspond with the different periodic variations indicated by the numbers given.

The foregoing experiments would seem to be conclusive as to the true nature of beats and beat-tones; but Koenig did not stop in his researches on this much-disputed question until he invented the wave-siren. The simplest form consists of a copper disk, whose border is cut in the form of a compound curve, — the resultant of two harmonic curves corresponding to two sounds of any desired interval. The disk we shall first use is bordered by a curve made up of two harmonic curves corresponding to notes giving the interval of a major second, 8 : 9. It is constructed in precisely the same manner as the curve described in the beginning of this lecture (Fig. 140). The intervals, too, in both cases are the same. To make the curves as exact as possible, Koenig first drew them on a very large scale, and then reduced them by photography.

When, now, such a disk is rotated before a tube with a narrow, slit-like aperture fixed parallel to the radius of the disk, the length of the slit being equal to the highest part of the curve, and air is forced through this slit, a motion will be generated in the air corresponding to the law of the curve. The result will be the same as that produced by the sounding together of two perfectly simple tones in which there is no trace whatever of upper partials. With a carefully constructed curve we can always be sure of the interval employed, and consequently of the simplicity of the tones constituting this interval.

When disks for different intervals are rotated slowly, beats are heard; and when the rotation is more rapid, beat-tones are produced corresponding to those produced when tuning-forks for the same intervals are sounded. Thus, for the siren we are now rotating, whose interval is 8 : 9, the resultant beat-note, as with the tuning-forks giving the same interval, is 1; that is, the frequency of the beat-note is 1, as compared with that of the lower of the two notes, whose relative frequency is 8. This means that the lower beat-note is just three octaves below that of the lower note of the major second here given.

By employing a disk (Fig. 151) whose rim is bordered by a curve corresponding to the interval of a major seventh, — 8 : 15, — we should, as with the two tuning-forks of this interval, get an upper beat-note, whose frequency, as compared with its generators, would also be 1. $8 \times 2 = 16$; $16 - 15 = 1$. By taking disks having edges corresponding to curves representing intervals of 8 : 11 and 8 : 13, we get the same results as were obtained with tuning-forks having these same intervals. Like tuning-forks, they give both upper and lower beat-notes, and their frequencies are determined by the same law as that which obtains for the beat-tones of the forks.

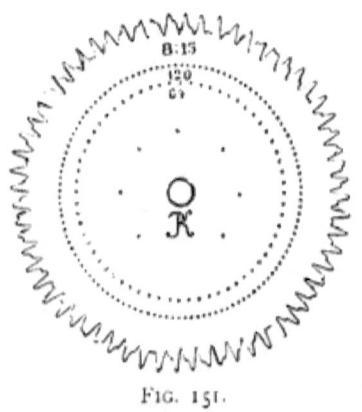

Fig. 151.

Should we wish to study only one interval, we employ a single disk, like the one just used. If, however, we wish to examine a whole series of intervals, and compare the results obtained, we may have recourse to a different form of the apparatus, likewise invented by Koenig. Here, instead of disks, we have four bands of brass fixed on four wheels (Fig. 152), attached to a vertical axis. The edge of each band is so cut as to give, for each edge, the resultant of any two harmonic curves that we may wish to study. These dentated bands, like disks, are caused to revolve before one or more tubes of long narrow apertures, when beat-tones, corresponding to the different intervals, are distinctly heard. An ordinary Seebeck's siren, with several circles of holes corresponding to the primary beat-tones of the curves used, is fastened on the top of the arbor carrying the dentated bands. This serves to assist the ear in determining the notes and intervals due to the different curves. By means of a number of small tubes communicating with a wind-chest, air can be forced through one or more of these circles at the same time. We are thus enabled to compare the tones due to simple primary impulses

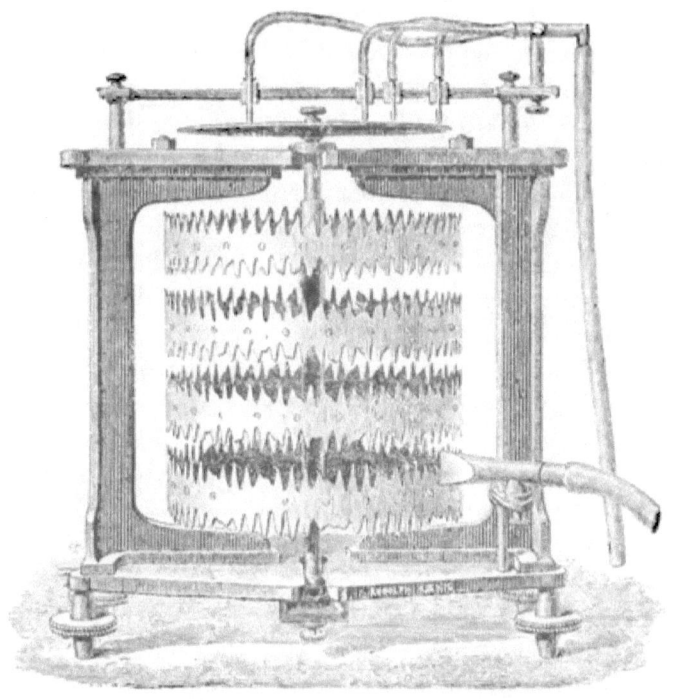

Fig. 152.

with those generated by the crests and troughs of a compound curve passing before a narrow aperture through which air is supplied under greater or less pressure.

The great advantage of the wave-siren is that, as before stated, it gives us perfectly pure tones, free from all admixture of upper partials. The tuning-forks we have been using do this also, but it is difficult to obtain such forks. Moreover, with the wave-siren it is easy to get any interval desired. For this purpose, it is only necessary to combine two harmonic curves, corresponding to the notes whose interval we may wish to investigate. A simple harmonic curve will give a simple note. A curve compounded of two harmonic curves will give simultaneously the notes corresponding to these two simple harmonic curves, and in addition to them, as we have seen, will also yield the beat-tones, upper or lower, or both. Koenig has constructed disks and bands that give the intervals 8 : 9, 8 : 10, 8 : 11, etc., up to 8 : 24. The instrument before you has eight intervals, beginning with 8 . 9, and extending up to 8 · 16; that is, from the major second to the octave.

The evidence, then, that beats may coalesce and blend into a continuous tone, is conclusive. The more the movement of the air, excited by impulses of any kind, differs from a simple pendular motion, the more these impulses will be separately distinguishable, and the less the sound due to their coalescence will be perceptible. On the other hand, the more nearly the periodic motion of the air approaches to a pendular motion, the less distinct will the separate pulses become, and the stronger the resultant tone. Wherefore, with the almost absolutely pendular motion of tuning-forks, the separate impulses beyond 32 or 36 cease to be perceived, and the sound resulting therefrom predominates.

We leave to physiologists to explain why it is that we can perceive simultaneously beats and beat-tones of the same frequency, which are originated in the same sonorous body or bodies. The phenomena observed evidently depend on some as yet unexplained capacity which the organ of hearing possesses of appreciating certain impulses as separate, while at the same time it causes them to coalesce in such a manner as to give rise to the sensation of a continuous tone.

And we leave to physiologists the explanation of another difficulty that must have presented itself to every one who has given any attention to the subject of beats and beat-tones.

Are beats and beat-tones subjective or objective? Are the sensations experienced due to resultant wave-motion arising from two generators of sound, or are they entirely independent of such wave-motion? If the air be disturbed by a vibratory motion occasioned by the resultant action of two sonorous bodies yielding beats or beat-tones, one should be able to recognize such aërial disturbances by means of membranes and resonators. These should vibrate in sympathy with any resultant wave-motion that may be generated, and the sound due to such motion should be perceptibly reinforced by resonators.

But is this the case? Helmholtz and others say that it is. They assert, therefore, that beats and beat-tones[1] have an objective existence, and appeal to various experiments made in support of their opinion. Koenig, Preyer, and Bosanquet, who have given the subject a more careful and more detailed investigation than Helmholtz, maintain, on the other hand, that beats and beat-tones are entirely subjective, — that they are generated independently of any vibratory motion existing externally to the ear. We have, then, according to this view, the sensation of beats and tones which have no corresponding objective reality. This, however, does not imply that such sensations are the product of the imagination, because such is not the case. It means that the beats and beat-tones perceived are excited solely within the ear, — let physiologists explain how, — and that, unlike other similar sensations, they do not correspond to any mode of motion outside of the ear.

Cross has made an experiment — which any one may repeat — that seems to be conclusive in favor of the subjective character of beats and beat-tones. If one listens to two sounds competent to yield a beat-tone, — one sound coming from a generator near by, and the other from a distance over a telephone wire, — the beat-tone will be heard the same as if the sonorous bodies were both near the ear, and acted on the tympanic membrane

---

[1] Called by Helmholtz *differential* and *summational* tones. He does not recognize the existence of beat-tones as explained in the text.

directly. The same result is obtained when both sonorous bodies are at a distance from the ear and from each other, and when the sounds they emit are conveyed to the ear by different conductors, and heard by means of separate telephones. With such an arrangement, the formation of a resultant sound-wave, competent to generate the beat-tone perceived, seems to be impossible.

But it is time to conclude. We have been discussing one of the most difficult and warmly-debated questions connected with the subject of sound. Not only have Koenig and Helmholtz entered the lists against each other, but several other physicists, almost equally distinguished, have made the matter an issue of considerable moment. Among these may especially be mentioned, W. Preyer, G. Appunn, R. H. M. Bosanquet, and Lord Rayleigh. I have endeavored, without entering too much into detail, to give you what may be regarded as experimentally proved regarding this most vexed question of beats and beat-tones. Those of you who may be desirous of knowing more about the subject, I must refer to the researches of the investigators just mentioned. I commend especially to your consideration the account of the very elaborate series of experiments of Dr. Koenig on beats and beat-tones, as given in his admirable " Quelques Expériences d'Acoustique."

CHAPTER IX.

QUALITY OF SOUND.

SOUNDS, as we have learned, differ one from another in three ways, — in loudness, in pitch, and in quality. Loudness, as we saw, depends on the amplitude of vibration of the particles of the sonorous body, and pitch is due to the rapidity of their vibration. What, then, is the cause of quality? The answer to this most interesting, and, I may add, most difficult question, I shall endeavor to give you in to-day's lecture. I shall ask you to give me your closest attention, as we are entering upon a question which, to all except the few who have made it a matter of special investigation, is either entirely misunderstood, or known only by name.

We are all aware, as a matter of experience, that the tone of a violin, even when the pitch is the same, differs from the tone of a flute, a clarinet, a guitar, or a pianoforte. So, too, may the tone of one violin differ from that of another violin, or the tone of one pianoforte differ from that of another pianoforte, and that, too, when the pitch and loudness of the notes sounded are the same. The tone of a Steinway " Grand " is different from that of a Weber or a Chickering " Grand ;" and the tones of a modern violin are vastly different from those emitted by an Amati, or a Guadagnini, or a Stradivarius. Even different players evoke different tones from the same instrument. No beginner can call forth from a pianoforte the purity of tone that responded to the touch of a Liszt, a Chopin, or a Rubinstein, nor can a tyro on the violin draw from the instrument the sweet, smooth, soul-stirring notes that it would yield to a Joachim, a Remeyni, or a

Paganini. The nature of the tones, then, varies with the instrument used, and varies, too, according to the method of manufacture, the materials used, and the way in which they were seasoned or tempered, and according as the performer is a master or a beginner in the art of music. More than this. The nature of the tones elicited from an instrument may depend even on the mood or the condition of health of the performer. Thus, as is obvious, the differences arising from various causes are almost infinitely varied and variable.

It is to these very marked differences of tone, emanating from different causes, and produced by different performers, that we give the general name "quality." The word "character" is also used to express the same thing. The French word *timbre* is likewise employed. The Germans use the very expressive term *klang-farbe*, which, literally translated, means, "clang-color," or "clang-tint." I do not think, however, that we can well improve on the time-honored word "quality,"—a word that is familiar to you all, as designating those differences of tone about which we are now speaking.

Knowing, then, what is meant by quality of tone, we proceed now to investigate its origin. And in order that we may have a better understanding of the subject under consideration, it will be well to take a hasty review of the ground over which we have travelled.

It had long been suspected that the quality of tone depended on the mode of vibration of the sonorous body,—that is, on the form of the wave corresponding to the tone emitted; but nothing certain was known about the matter until Helmholtz took up the subject, about thirty years ago. His profound "Lehre von den Tonempfindungen," published in 1863, cleared up what until that time had been an enigma that had baffled all attempts at its solution.

In this great work he proves that the quality of a tone is due to the number and relative intensity of the partial tones that accompany the fundamental. The way for this grand generalization had been paved by several other investigators, but Helmholtz was the first to give it expression, and experimentally to demonstrate its truth. One of the first to throw light on this mysterious subject was the illustrious Father Mersenne. Speaking of Aristotle, he says, "He seems to have been ignorant of the fact that every string produces five or more different sounds at the same time, the strongest of which is called the natural tone of the string, and alone is accustomed to be taken notice of, for the others are so feeble that they are perceptible only to delicate ears. . . Not only the octave and the fifteenth, but also the twelfth and major seventeenth are always heard, and, over and above these, the major twenty-third (the ninth partial), about the end of the natural sound."[1]

Sauveur, one of the founders of acoustics, made a special study of these sounds accompanying the fundamental. "On plucking a harp-string," he says, "a delicate and practised ear may, in addition to the fundamental, hear other and more acute sounds produced by portions of the string, which, as it were, separate themselves from the string vibrating as a whole, in order to start up vibrations of their own."

Later on Chladni took up the subject, and showed that compound sounds are produced by organ-pipes, wind instruments, and bells, as well as by strings. Rameau, the eminent French composer, made it, in 1722, the basis of his system of musical harmony.

In his admirable article on Sound, written for the "Encyclopædia Metropolitana," Sir John Herschel says, "It was long known to musicians that besides the principal or fundamental note of a string, an experienced ear could detect in its sound other notes, related to this fundamental one by fixed laws of harmony, and which are called, therefore, harmonic sounds. They are the very same, which by the production of distinct nodes may be insulated, and, as it were, cleared from the confusing effect of co-existent

[1] Harm., Lib. IX. Prop. 33.

sounds. They are, however, much more distinct in bells and other sounding bodies than in strings, in which only delicate ears can detect them."

From a communication made to the French Academy in 1875, it appears that Monge, the famous French mathematician, was one of the first to divine the true cause of the quality of sounds. Speaking of the sounds emitted by vibrating strings, Monge asserted it as his belief that their quality was due to the order and number of the vibrations of the aliquot parts of the string in question. And he added, further, that if one could succeed in suppressing the vibrations of these aliquot parts, all strings, of whatever material made, would yield tones of the same quality.

In 1817, Biot, who had been a pupil of Monge about twenty years previous, reproduced in his " Précis Élémentaire de Physique Expérimentale " the theory of his master in a somewhat modified form.

" All sonorous bodies," he says, " yield simultaneously an infinite number of sounds of gradually decreasing intensity. This phenomenon is similar to that which obtains for the harmonics of strings; but the law for the series of harmonics is different for bodies of different forms. May it not be this difference which produces the particular character of sound, called *timbre*, which distinguishes each form of body, and which causes the sound of a string and that of a vase to produce in us different sensations? May it not be owing to the diminution of the intensity of harmonics of each series that we find agreeable certain concords that would be intolerable if produced by sounds equally loud? And may not the quality of each particular substance — of wood or metal, for instance — be due to the superior intensity of one or another harmonic?"

In the first edition of his excellent " Traité de Physique," published in 1855, eight years before the appearance of Helmholtz's great work, M. Daguin has the following paragraph: " In musical instruments *timbre* is due most frequently to feeble sounds which accompany the fundamental. Sometimes these concomitant sounds arise from the vibrating parts themselves, which thus render audible several sounds at the same time. At other times the vibrating body transmits these tremors to other parts of the instrument. . . . *Timbre* may also be due to the manner in which the velocity of the parts in the vibrating body varies during each oscillation. The curves representing sonorous waves may be of variable form, and the wave of rarefaction may be different from that of condensation. It may even be that there are interruptions between the successive waves."

To get a clear idea of the order of sequence of these harmonic sounds, or upper partials, as we have been calling them, let us write out in musical notation the first nine upper partials of C_2:[1]

C_2	C_3	G_3	C_4	E_4	G_4	$A_4\sharp$	C_5	D_5	E_5
1	2	3	4	5	6	7	8	9	10

The seventh note, represented approximately by $A_4\sharp$, — it is, in fact, a little higher than $A_4\sharp$, — although called an harmonic in acoustics, is not considered as such in music. The same is true of D_5, the ninth partial. Either of these sounded simultaneously with the prime with sufficient intensity would cause the most jarring discord.[2]

Having thus refreshed our memories regarding a few points developed in the preceding lectures, we are now prepared to follow Helmholtz in his investigations as to the quality of sound. He tells us, as has already been stated, that the quality of a sound depends on the number of upper partials present, and their relative intensity. Mersenne, Sauveur, Chladni, and others tell us what these partials are, and when they are generated. In order to produce all the different modifications of quality ascribed to them, they should possess considerable intensity as com-

---

[1] Compare the notes here given with those in Chapter IV.
[2] See Chapter X.

pared with their primes. We should, in a word, be able to hear them and distinguish them from the prime note which they accompany, and to which they give their characteristic quality.

In order to hear these upper partials it is not necessary, as might be supposed, to have a particularly acute ear. An ordinary ear, when the attention is properly directed, can perceive them in many instances, and a little practice will enable one to single out one or more of them from any sound that may contain them.

There are, of course, some tones that are practically devoid of upper partials. Such tones are emitted by stopped organ-pipes, and by certain specially constructed tuning-forks. These, as has been stated, are called simple tones, in contradistinction to those having upper partials, and which are denominated compound tones. The flute gives nearly a simple tone, while stringed and reed instruments, open organ-pipes, brass wind instruments, as also the human voice, are particularly rich in upper partials, and are, therefore, good instances of compound tones.

Here, too, we must distinguish between *single* and *composite* tones. A single tone, which may be simple or compound, is a tone emitted by one sounding body. A composite tone is made up of tones — simple or compound — from several sources of sound. Simple tones are characterized by purity and softness, whereas compound tones are distinguished for richness and brilliancy. But simple tones, however pure, are dull, and appear to be more grave than they really are. Compound tones, on the contrary, are bright and crisp, and often partake, in a marked manner, of the acuteness of their upper partials. For this reason even musicians often make a mistake of an octave in estimating the pitch of a given compound sound, taking the pitch of the first upper partial for that of its prime.

Upper partials are most easily heard when they are inharmonic, as in the case of bells. I strike the large Japanese gong on the table, and you at once hear distinctly several tones of quite different pitch. The lowest is deep, mellow, and powerful, and resembles the tone of a cathedral bell. The upper partials are clear and pure, and although not all constituting harmonic intervals with their prime, they still combine in such a way as to produce a pleasing effect. I excite another gong, similar to the first, and while sounding alone the result is similar to that obtained with the first gong; but the bell, being smaller, its prime and upper partials have a higher pitch. When I sound both together you perceive a certain jarring and harshness that disclose, in a most striking manner, the influence of the inharmonic partials. The primes of the two gongs form a comparatively good concord, making very nearly the interval of a fourth; but the upper partials are so far from harmonizing with each other or with their primes that they generate discord. That, however, to which I wish especially to direct your attention is the number of different notes — five or six at least — which can be distinctly separated from the general mass of sound.

The inharmonic upper partials heard so well in bells are also given forth with remarkable intensity by most tuning-forks and metal bars. I give the fork I hold in my hand a vigorous blow with an ivory hammer, and, in addition to the prime note of the fork, you hear distinctly the tinkle of high upper partials. They are, however, quite evanescent, while the prime tone persists for some length of time.

On the table is an instrument called the metallophone. It consists, as you know, of a number of steel bars, which, when struck, vibrate in the same manner as the tuning-fork. When I strike one of these bars, you hear the upper partials as distinctly as in the case of the tuning-fork. If I strike in succession a number of bars separated from each other by harmonic intervals, the primes of these bars will give a pleasing sensation; but the upper partials, not harmonizing with each other, will produce a jingle that is anything but agreeable. But, as in the case of the gongs and tuning-forks just used, the number of separate notes that can be distinguished in the very composite note produced is much greater than the number of sonorous bodies originating the sounds.

There is, then, no difficulty in hearing inharmonic upper partials. But just now we are more interested in detecting the presence of harmonic upper partials. They are, indeed, found in specially constructed bells and tuning-forks along with inharmonic partials; but we shall turn our attention to sounds in which harmonic partials so predominate over those that are inharmonic that the latter are practically imperceptible.

I hold in my hand a long, narrow, open organ-pipe, made of copper. It differs from wider pipes in the fact that it is capable of giving, with differences of pressure, a series of upper partials of remarkable purity and intensity. By forcing air through the pipe, we can, at will, produce any harmonic desired, or the pressure of wind can be so regulated as to cause two partials to sound at the same time. You now hear the fundamental and its octave, and in such a way that you have no difficulty whatever in recognizing the presence of both notes.

We now try a pipe that is exactly similar to the last one, except that it is stopped, instead of open. This pipe, as you know, will also readily yield upper partials. But, unlike the open pipe, whose partials follow in the order both of even and odd numbers, — 1, 2, 3, 4, 5, etc., — the stopped pipe will give only such partials as correspond to the odd numbers 1, 3, 5, etc. As with the open pipe, we can, by varying the pressure of air admitted into the pipe, elicit from it, at pleasure, any of the partials that it is capable of yielding. In like manner we can cause it to emit two notes simultaneously. Just now it is sounding its prime and its twelfth, both of which you can distinguish with ease.

It is scarcely possible to render the upper partials of strings audible to all of you, as they are, in most instances, much less distinct than those to which you have been listening. I shall, however, show you how they may be detected, and leave any of those present who may be sufficiently interested in the matter to make the experiments at their leisure.

In making such experiments, it will be well to look, first, for the upper partials corresponding to odd numbers, as they are most readily heard. Thus, it is easier to hear the third and the fifth partials than to perceive the second and the fourth. Sounding beforehand a note of the pitch of the partial one wishes to observe, will materially aid in hearing such partial when a compound tone containing it is produced.

Both the pianoforte and the harmonium are good instruments on which to study upper partials. Suppose, then, we employ the piano, and wish to hear G_3, which is the third partial of C_2. All that is necessary, in order to hear this note in the compound note C_2, is to strike gently the note G_3, and, after it dies out, to strike strongly C_2, when our ear, already prepared for the note G_3, hears it distinctly in the note C_2. In the same manner we may hear E_4, which is the fifth partial of C_2. A little practice will also enable one to hear the first and second octaves of the prime. On one of the louder stops of a harmonium one may hear, in addition to the preceding, even the seventh and the ninth partials. The two latter are inaudible on the pianoforte, because it is so constructed that they are either totally or partially eliminated.

On the sonometer we should proceed in a different way. If we wish to hear the third partial, for instance, we should gently press a feather on one of the corresponding nodes, and then excite the string by plucking it. In this way we can perceive distinctly the note that is due to the vibration of the third part of the string, as well as that caused by the string vibrating as a whole. In a similar manner, we could render audible several other partials. The third and fifth partials, thus excited, are sufficiently intense to be heard at some distance, with comparative facility. By employing thin strings, which are especially rich in loud upper partials, Helmholtz was able to recognize partials up to the sixteenth.

It is still more difficult to hear the upper partials of the human voice; but even these can be perceived with a little attention and practice. Let a powerful bass voice sing E_2, to the word "awe;" then gently sound on the pianoforte B_3, which is the third partial of E_2, and after the note of the piano dies away, one will still continue to hear, in the voice of the singer, the continuation of the note emitted by the pianoforte. In the same way, if the note be sung to the broad sound of a, as in "father," one may hear G_4, which is the fifth partial of E_2.

Under favorable circumstances, and by giving the matter special attention, one may hear some of the upper partials of the human voice without the assistance of any apparatus whatever. Rameau was thus able to distinguish them with the unaided ear. Seiler, of Leipsic, says that while listening to the voice of the night watchman at a distance, he was able to hear, first the third partial, and then the prime of the note uttered. Garcia relates that in listening to his own voice in the quiet of the night he could detect both the octave and the twelfth of the note he sang. I have heard the same two partials in the voice of a muezzin in Cairo calling the faithful to prayer. But when I heard them, the circumstances were especially favorable. The muezzin had a remarkably powerful, rich voice, the night was unusually still, and the minaret on which stood the servant of the Prophet was only a short distance from the place where I happened to be at the time.

To distinguish more clearly and more readily the upper partials existing in any compound tone, Helmholtz constructed the resonators with which you are already familiar. This is, in reality, only a modification of the resonant case first used by Marloye to strengthen the prime tone of a tuning-fork. Helmholtz's first resonators were made from bottles and from the spherical portions of glass retorts. He also employed conical forms made of pasteboard, tin, or zinc. But by far the best and most useful, as well as the most sensitive resonators, are such as are made by Koenig, and which are especially designed to reinforce strongly one tone only. The conical resonators sometimes used have the disadvantage of strengthening the intensity of all the upper partials at the same time that they augment the prime.

With a series of spherical resonators as made by Koenig, the dimensions of which are accurately calculated to give the maximum of resonance for only one particular note, any one, even though entirely unskilled in the study of musical sounds, is able at once, and without the slightest difficulty, to single out a number of the upper partials found in any compound tone of such instruments as the violin, harmonium, or pianoforte. These resonators enable those who have trained musical ears to detect the presence of partials that are entirely imperceptible to the unaided ear, and to extend their investigations in the study of compound sounds in a manner that would otherwise be quite impossible. By means of resonators as many as sixteen partials of the human voice have been heard, while in reed pipes the number has been swollen to twenty.

Koenig has increased the delicacy and extended the usefulness of the resonator by coupling it with the manometric capsule. In this way the experiment is made to appeal to the eye instead of to the ear. As a consequence, a person who is entirely deaf can analyze a compound tone as well as one who has a most delicate musical ear.

Let us connect this stopped organ-pipe, C_2, with the acoustic bellows. By suitably regulating the pressure of the air we can cause the pipe to speak separately either its prime, C_2, or its twelfth, G_3. Not only this, we can so adjust the pressure of the wind that we can detect without difficulty the presence of both these tones at the same time. By applying to the ear the resonator corresponding to the note G_3, one can readily hear the note, when without the resonator only the note C_2 would be audible.

By connecting the resonators corresponding to the notes

C_2 and G_3, with two manometric capsules, and gently sounding the pipe so that only its prime is audible, we can show that G_3 is really present with C_2, although unheard. The flame-image corresponding to the fundamental note is shown in 1, Fig. 153. 3 is the flame-image of the twelfth, and shows that it executes just three times as many vibrations as its fundamental. Both flames combined give 1:3, which shows the components of the sound under analysis as well as if each partial were examined separately. For a similar reason a sonorous body, yield-

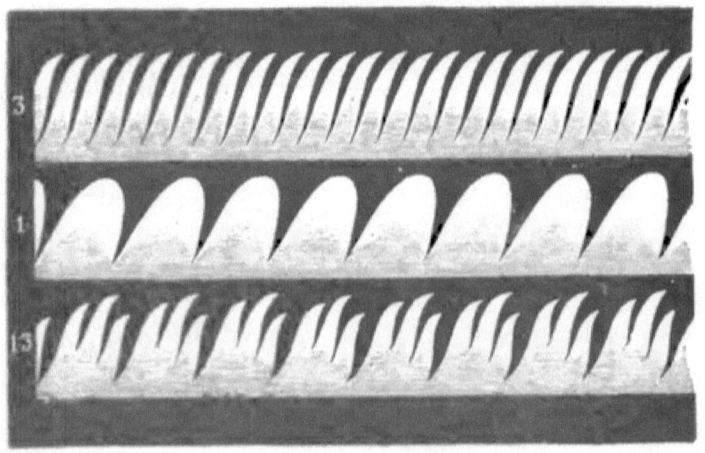

FIG. 153.

ing in succession its prime and its octave, would give respectively the flame-images 1 and 2, Fig. 154. Both partials, sounding simultaneously, would yield a flame-image like 1:2 of the figure.

By employing a larger number of properly tuned resonators, it would be just as easy to show the flame-images corresponding to five or six partials as it is to show those corresponding to two. I may here add, however, that neither resonators alone, nor resonators attached to manometric capsules, can be used for very acute sounds. They are practically useless for all sounds above C_5.

On the screen is a photograph of an instrument having

eight resonators (Fig. 155), exactly like those we have been using, except that they are mounted on a stand. The nipple of each resonator is connected by a rubber tube with a capsule, whose jet is placed before a revolving mirror. The resonators are turned to the notes C_2, C_3, G_3, C_4, E_4, G_4, the seventh partial of C_2, and C_5. If a compound tone whose prime is C_2 is emitted before the opening of the resonators, the flame-images reflected from the mirror will at once disclose the number and the order of the upper partials of the sound. When an open organ-pipe, whose

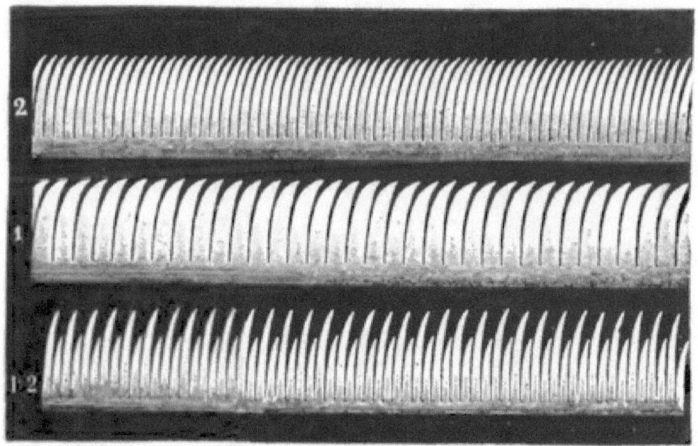

FIG. 154.

prime is C_2, is caused to speak, five or six flame-images declare the presence of as many upper partials in the compound tone. The flame-image corresponding to the third partial is very markedly agitated.

The instrument just referred to, having only a small number of resonators, answers very well for demonstrations, but could not be employed in investigations in which other notes than those to which the resonators are attuned are submitted for examination. In the latter case a series of universal resonators would be required. Such an apparatus — one that was exhibited by Dr. Koenig at the Centennial Exposition at Philadelphia in 1876 — I now show

354 SOUND AND MUSIC.

you, in order that you may have a better idea of its *modus operandi*. The resonators of this splendid apparatus (Fig. 156) are like that described in our seventh lecture (Fig. 125). They are supported in a frame, NCV, and are connected with manometric capsules whose jets are supplied

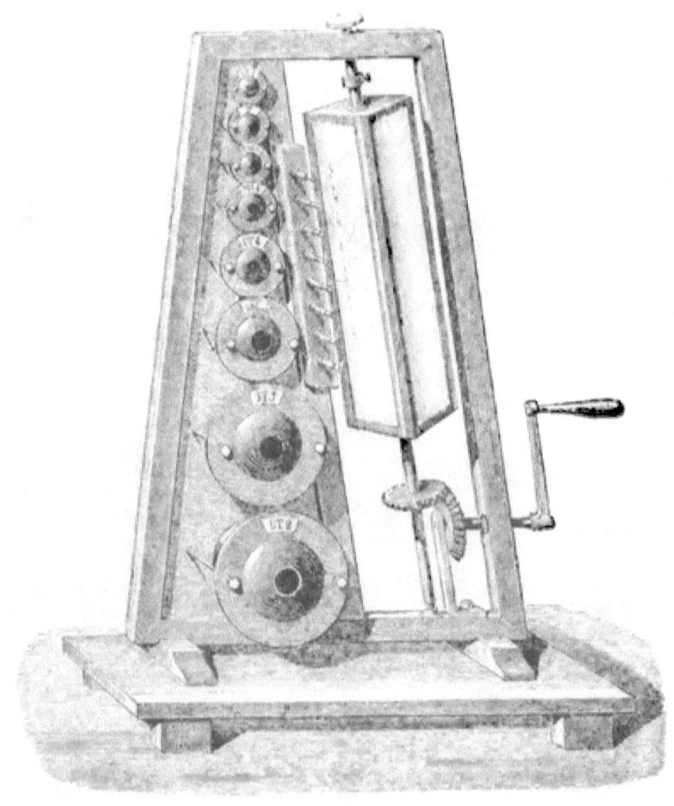

FIG. 155.

with gas, entering through the tube D. The mirror AB is rotated before the jets by the crank M. The resonators can be so adjusted that all the upper partials between C_1 and C_5 can be studied. For the lower notes, the resonators are so arranged that as many as nine partials may be observed. These cylindrical resonators are fully as sensitive as those which are spherical, and, like the latter, they indicate the presence of partials as high as C_5. Such a series of resonant spheres or cylinders has been well likened to a set of chemical reagents. As such reagents enable the chemist to prove the presence of various elements and compounds, so do resonators afford the acous-

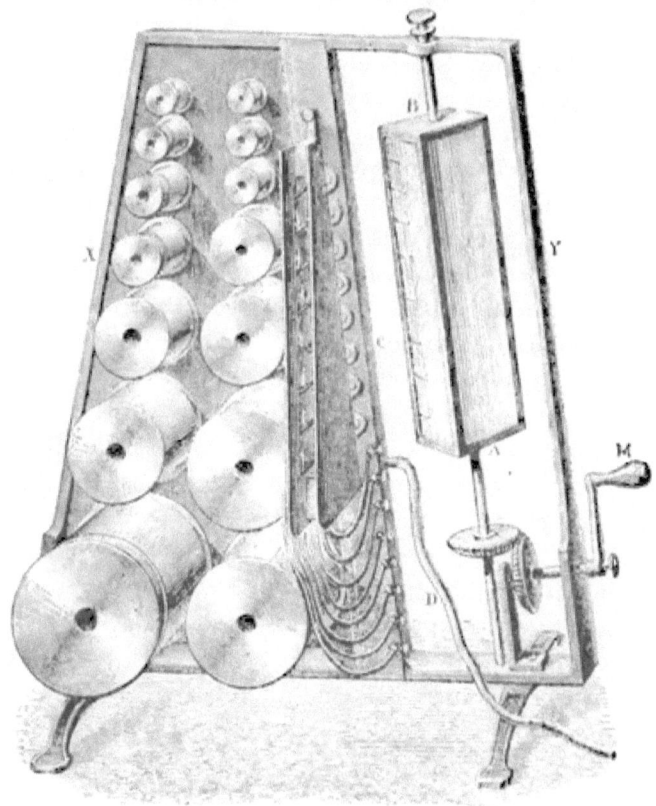

Fig. 156.

tician the means of analyzing any compound note into its constituent partials.

Such an instrument puts us in possession of an admirable means of investigating the nature and composition of vowel-sounds. Why does one vowel-sound differ from another; or why is it that the same pair of vocal cords are capable of sounding more than one vowel at all? The pitch and the loudness of two vowels sung to the same note may be identical. The only way in which the vowels can differ from one another is that in which the sound of the violin, for instance, differs from that of the clarinet. Vowels accordingly differ from one another because their quality is different; because the number and relative intensities of the upper partials accompanying the fundamental are not the same; because the various forms assumed by the oral cavity in the pronunciation of the different vowels are unlike; and because the mouth, acting as an easily adjustable resonator, tends, according to the form assumed, to reinforce one partial more than another when any given vowel is articulated.

Thus when u, like oo, as in "toot," is sung to C_1 before the series of resonators just exhibited, one has, in addition to the prime, evidence of the octave, which is quite intense, and occasionally also of a very feeble twelfth.

When o, as in "no," is sung, the vibrating flames declare the presence of strong third and fourth partials, while the octave is weaker than in u. Even a fifth partial may be observed in o, but it is extremely weak.

The action of the vowel a, as in "ah," extends, as is shown in the vibrating flames, as far as the seventh partial; but it is the fourth, fifth, and sixth that vibrate with the greatest intensity. Singing e, as in "there," the fundamental, as indicated by the flame-images, is accompanied by the octave and the twelfth, — the former feeble, the latter intense. The double octave and its third vibrate with medium intensity. In addition to these, there is also a trace of the seventh partial.

I, as in "machine," sung to C_2, shows that the prime is accompanied only by its first octave.

No more beautiful nor convincing proofs could be desired than those furnished by carefully tuned resonators and manometric flames, that the different vowels, like all musical sounds of different quality, are the result, not of any peculiar action of the vocal cords, but depend solely on the varying admixture of certain partials, of varying intensities, with the fundamental.

But what are the notes that specially distinguish the five vowels just mentioned from each other? Donders first paved the way for an answer to this delicate question by his discovery that the cavity of the mouth for different vowels is attuned to different pitches. Helmholtz, Koenig, and others took up these investigations, and, by means of tuning-forks, determined the pitches of the notes that are most reinforced by the resonance of the oral cavity during the pronunciation of the different vowels. Their experiments have led to the remarkable discovery that resonance is the same for men, women, and children, and that the proper tones of the mouth are nearly independent of age or sex.

From a series of forks prepared for researches on vowel-sounds, I select one which excites the maximum resonance in the mouth when it is shaped for articulating the vowel *u* as pronounced in Italian, viz., as *oo*. Holding the fork before my mouth thus formed, the resonance, as you observe, is very marked. Holding the same fork before a suitably tuned resonator, I obtain a similarly reinforced sound, and one identical in quality.

I try another fork somewhat smaller, and find that this resounds most strongly before the mouth when it assumes the form required for the pronunciation of the vowel *o*. When the form of the mouth is changed, its resonance for this particular fork is much diminished.

Taking another fork, and adjusting the mouth, you hear it distinctly resounding to the fork as in the previous instances; but the sound now heard is that of broad *a*, as in "father."

Similarly, with smaller forks, I excite, by sympathetic resonance, in the air of the oral cavity, sounds corresponding to *e* and *i*. These latter tones, however, are much higher in pitch than those corresponding to the vowels *u*, *o*, and *a*, and their resonance is correspondingly less intense.

According to Koenig's investigations, the notes that are most strongly reinforced by the air in the cavity of the mouth during the articulation of the vowels *u, o, a, e, i*, are $B_2\flat$, $B_3\flat$, $B_4\flat$, $B_5\flat$, $B_6\flat$, respectively. These notes, as is obvious, differ from each other by an octave, and their respective vibration-numbers are 224, 448, 896, 1792, and 3584. In musical notation they would be written as follows: —

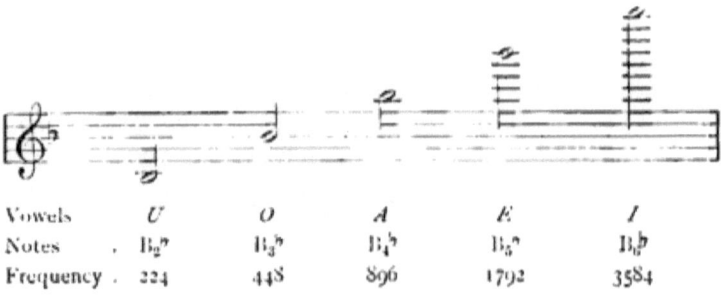

Vowels	*U*	*O*	*A*	*E*	*I*
Notes	$B_2\flat$	$B_3\flat$	$B_4\flat$	$B_5\flat$	$B_6\flat$
Frequency	224	448	896	1792	3584

We have here a simpler form of instrument devised by Koenig for exhibiting the flame-images corresponding to the different qualities of the various vowel-tones sung to the same note, and for showing the transformations that these images undergo when the same vowels are sung to different notes. It is essentially a manometric capsule, like those we have been using, except that it is connected with a funnel-shaped mouthpiece (Fig. 157). *A* of the figure shows a cross-section of the capsule, and *M* is the revolving mirror in which the images of the flame are visible. When one sings into the mouthpiece connected with the manometric capsule, the flame is agitated, and the images seen in the revolving mirror disclose the slightest shades in the quality of the tones emitted; and as the number and intensity of the upper partials of any note vary with the pitch, the flame-images will show a corresponding change in form as the sound produced passes from a grave note to one more acute. For the lower notes, and particularly for the grave vowels, like *u, o, a*, there is an exuberance of partials that is entirely absent in notes of higher pitch, especially in those of the vowel *i*.

QUALITY OF SOUND. 359

When i is sung to C_3, the flame-image produced shows that it is practically a simple tone, and unaccompanied, therefore, by any partials whatever.

The qualities of different vowel-sounds, and their transformations for the various notes from C_1 to C_3, are beautifully depicted in Fig. 158, which gives, in a compendious form, the results of the careful and laborious observations of Dr. Koenig on the subject of vowel-sounds as studied

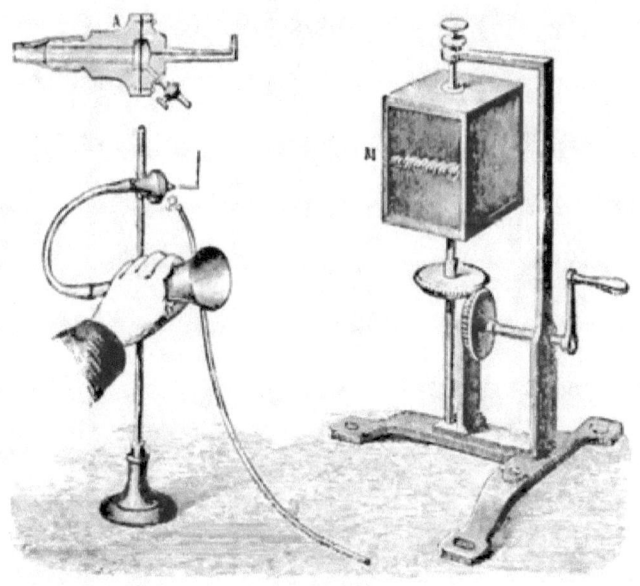

FIG. 157.

with manometric flames. OU, at the head of the first column, is intended to give the Italian sound of u, while the names of ut, re, etc., are given according to the French style, instead of that which we have adopted in these lectures.

Many consonants, as well as the vowels, give characteristic flame-images. The so-called semi-vowels, m and n, give images that are so nearly alike they are practically indistinguishable. Fig. 159 exhibits their images for the notes C_2, E_2, G_2, C_3. In Fig. 160 we have the very remarkable image that characterizes the peculiar sound of the letter *r*.

The dependence of the quality of tone on the number

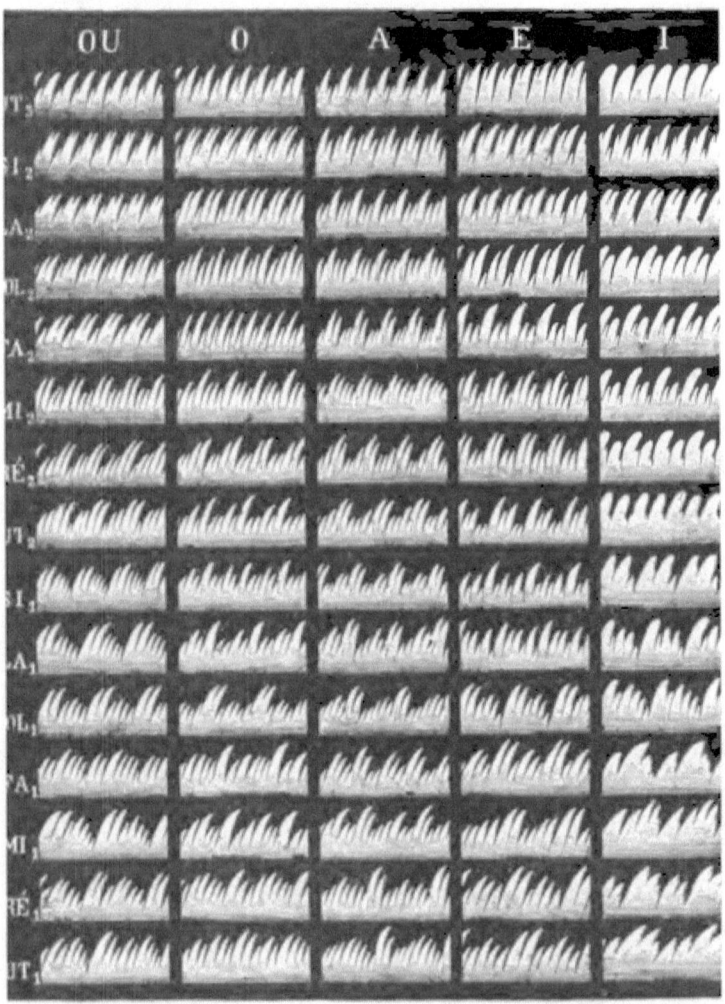

Fig. 158.

and relative intensity of the upper partials that accompany their prime, can be very strikingly shown by a simple experiment that any one can make on the pianoforte.

Raise all the dampers of the instrument, and directing the voice towards the sounding-board, sing loudly the vowel *a*, as in "ah," and you will hear the sound of the same *a* distinctly repeated by the strings that emit notes corresponding to the fundamental and upper partials of the voice. In like manner sing *o*, as in "oh," and the echo will give back with surprising clearness a full, sonorous *o*. *A*, as in "bay," is likewise re-echoed with astonishing exactness. *E*, *i*, and *u* are also heard, but not so loud as *a* or *o*.

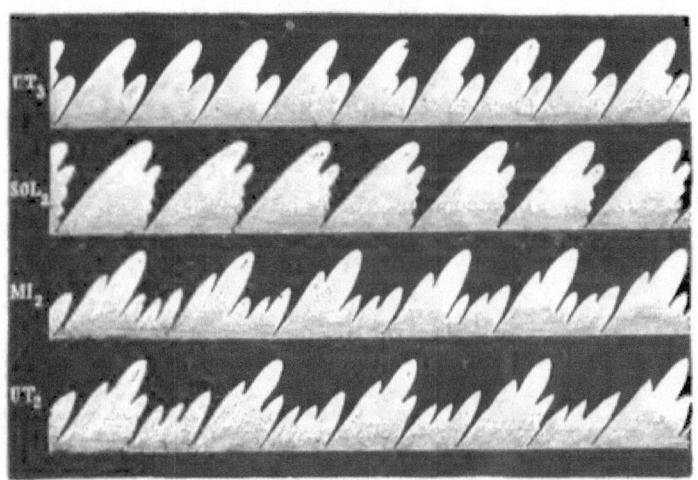

Fig. 159.

Sound a clarinet near the sounding-board, and the quality of the tone of this instrument will be imitated with remarkable fidelity.

All the various sounds mentioned single out and excite to vibration certain strings that, by themselves, would give the elementary constituents of the compound tone in question. These simple experiments prove as conclusively as the more elaborate ones we have made that all compound tones are composed of simple ones, and that quality of tone, as demonstrated in so many ways, is intimately associated with the number and intensity of the partials existing in the tone examined.

Thus far the method we have employed in investigating the quality of sound has been analytical. We have learned the difference between simple and compound tones, and have seen how we can accurately determine the number and relative intensity of the simple tones that coexist in any given compound tone. We have studied particularly the methods of sound-analysis devised by Helmholtz and Koenig, and have found that, with one or two exceptions, all musical sounds are composed of two or more simple tones, and that it is mainly the presence of these partials that enables us to distinguish from each other the sounds proceeding from different sonorous bodies.

FIG. 160.

We are now prepared to make another step in advance, — to study the quality of sound synthetically. After Helmholtz had succeeded in effecting the analysis of sound, by the means just considered, he proceeded to confirm the results thus obtained by synthesis. By analysis he was able to determine the number and the relative intensity of the partials constituting a tone of determinate quality. His next problem was to take these partials, of the number and intensity revealed by his analysis, and put them together in such a manner as to obtain a tone of the same quality as that which had been subjected to analysis. The result was that the two processes — analysis and synthesis — corroborated each other in a most remarkable manner. The problem that had so long baffled musicians and acousticians was at last solved, and we are now able to account for the quality of a tone, as well as for its pitch and its intensity.

In investigating synthetically the quality of a sound, it is essential that we should have simple tones. Stopped organ-pipes, which, as we have learned, give nearly simple tones, might be used, and sometimes are used; but it is found more advantageous to use tuning-forks, whose tones are reinforced by suitable resonators. Tuning-forks thus made give us simple tones, whose vibrations are nearly pendular.

For the artificial production of tones of different qualities, quite a number of forks, of different pitches, are required. As is evident from what has been said regarding the components of compound sounds, we can employ only such tones as those whose frequencies are to each other as the whole numbers 1, 2, 3, 4, etc. Hence, the application of the method is limited to comparatively grave sounds. For should the prime of the compound tone to be studied be very acute, its upper partials would have such a high pitch that it would be impossible to reinforce them with resonators; and unless thus strengthened they would be useless for the purpose under consideration.

On the table is a series of ten tuning-forks placed in front of resonant cases. The larger fork, C_2, gives 128 vibrations, while the other nine forks are tuned to give exactly the nine upper partials of C_2. Starting with C_2 as the prime, these partials would be in the order of succession, C_3, G_3, C_4, E_4, G_4, seventh upper partial, — between $A_4\sharp$ and $B_4\flat$, — C_5, D_5, E_5.

When the prime C_2 is sounded, we have the pure, simple tone that is characteristic of a good tuning-fork. The tone heard in this case is as nearly a perfectly simple tone as it is possible to obtain. In addition to the prime, the octave is now excited, and the two tones blend together so perfectly that they appeal to the ear as only one note. Indeed, it requires considerable effort for the ear to separate one note from the other. But the compound tone heard when the two forks, C_2 and C_3, are sounded together, is quite different from the pure, simple tone emitted by C_2 alone. The second, as all can perceive, is fuller and richer than the first.

The prime C_2 and its first five upper partials, C_3, G_3, C_4, E_4, G_4, are now set in vibration. As with the two forks, the tones of the six forks now so coalesce that the resultant tone seems to proceed from one source of sound. So perfect is the combination that it is exceedingly difficult for the unaided ear to single out the notes that are emitted by the individual forks. With resonators, however, this could be done with the greatest facility, and in a way that would surprise those that have never had any experience with such appliances.

But what I wish specially to direct your attention to is the brilliancy and volume and harmoniousness of the tone you now hear, as compared with that produced by one fork, or by two forks. By exciting simultaneously all the forks in the series, except the seventh and ninth partials, we obtain a tone that is proportionally brighter. Introducing the seventh and ninth partials into the mass of sound now heard, the quality is at once changed. We have introduced elements of discord, although their influence in this case is not so great as they would be in sounding with one of the forks separately, because the volume of tone of the eight other forks is so great that it partially extinguishes the tones of the inharmonic intruders. We could not have a more striking or more beautiful illustration of the dependence of the quality of a tone on the number of partials accompanying a given fundamental, than that afforded by this experiment. The compound sound emitted by the series of forks — omitting the seventh and ninth — here used reminds one of the fulness, mellowness, and softness of the tones of a French horn in the hands of a *maestro*.

But for experiments on the synthesis of sounds, it is necessary to have, not only simple tones, but tones that can be sustained at will. Those afforded by the forks just used diminish rapidly, and for that reason are not well suited for the work of synthesis we now have in hand. And then, again, it is important that we should be able to regulate the intensities of the various simple tones introduced; and to do this accurately a special contrivance is necessary. In other words, if we would do exact work in the synthesis of sounds, a specially devised apparatus is almost indispensable.

Such an apparatus, as made by Koenig, is now before you. It is a modification of the one first devised by Helmholtz, and with which he carried on his celebrated researches on the quality of vowel and other compound sounds. It is one of the most ingenious of acoustic instruments, and enables us to effect, in a most striking manner, the composition of many compound sounds, and to show, what we have demonstrated analytically, how much the quality of a sound depends on the harmonic partials that are associated with the fundamental.

As seen in Fig. 161, this apparatus is composed of ten tuning-forks, giving the series of harmonic partials, starting from C_2, of one hundred and twenty-eight vibrations, as a prime. They are fixed vertically between the poles of electro-magnets which are traversed by an electric current that can be rendered intermittent by a tuning-fork so constructed as to close and break the circuit exactly one hundred and twenty-eight times per second. Each fork is provided with an accurately tuned cylindrical resonator, whose orifice, when the instrument is in use, is brought as near as possible to the vibrating prongs of its associated fork. The orifices of the various resonators can be more or less opened by keys in connection with them. When the resonators are closed, the tuning-forks, although vibrating, are scarcely audible, because the boards on which they rest are insulated from their common support by rubber tubes glued to their lower surface; and this has the effect of almost completely damping the sounds that would otherwise be heard with considerable intensity. As soon, however, as any of the resonators are opened, by pressing on the proper keys, the sounds of the tuning-forks burst forth with exceeding power and volume.

The best tones to select for imitation with the instrument before us are the vowel-sounds, because they are free from the various noises that always accompany other musical sounds. Even aside from this fact, I should now choose vowel-sounds, as a matter of convenience, and to show also

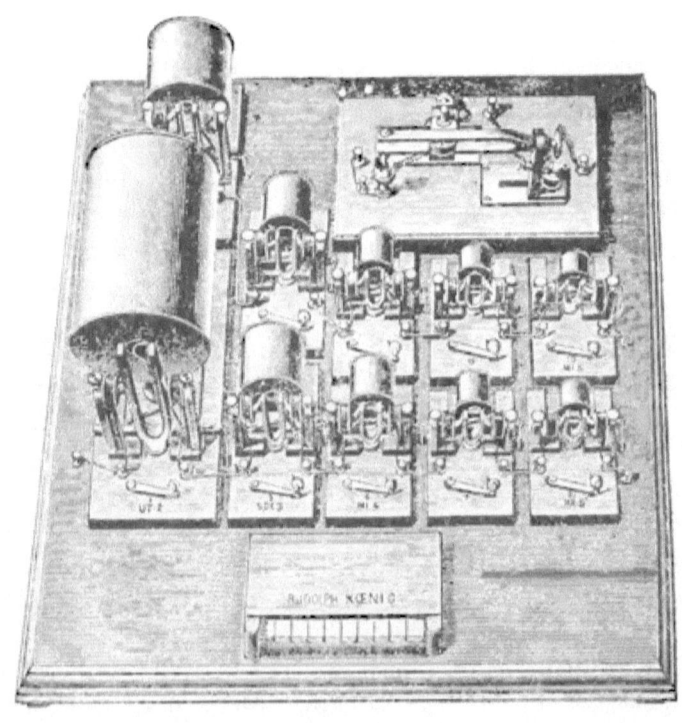

FIG. 161.

how the results we have arrived at analytically are confirmed by the synthetic method. When making the analysis of sounds by means of resonators and manometric flames, we employed vowel-sounds. The results then obtained may now serve as a guide in our synthetic work, and allow us to pick out at a glance the upper partials found in the various vowels, and regulate their intensities according to the flame-images corresponding to the different vowels.

Thus we saw that when u, pronounced as oo, was sung before the resonators, there was, in addition to the fundamental, an indication of a strong second partial, and occasionally, of a very weak third partial. If then the forks C_2 and C_3 are sounded with their corresponding resonators wide open, and G_3 is sounded feebly, we should obtain a compound sound resembling u. The forks are sounded, and at once you hear a tone that certainly approaches the one sought.

O, according to our flame-reactions, is made up of a strong prime and strong third and fourth partials, while its octave is comparatively feeble, and its fifth partial feebler still. The forks required in this instance will be those emitting the prime C_2, and the partials C_3, G_3, C_4, E_4. Opening the resonators of the proper forks according to the indications given by the flame images, we obtain a tone that you must admit bears a striking resemblance to the sound of the vowel o as it is sung.

In the tone of the vowel a, according to its analysis, there are no fewer than seven partials. The prime, fourth, fifth, and the sixth are the strongest. The others are of various degrees of feebleness. The forks required for a are, therefore, C_2, C_3, G_3, C_4, E_4, G_4, and the seventh partial. Sounding these with their corresponding resonators more or less opened, according as they are to reinforce the tones of the forks strongly or feebly, we have as a resultant tone an imitation of the vowel a.

To imitate the sounds of the vowels e and i is less easily accomplished, because of the high pitch of their upper partials, and because of the difficulty in rendering the tones of their upper partials sufficiently intense.

In our flame-analysis of the vowel e we found the prime C_2 accompanied by an octave and a twelfth, the former feeble, the latter very loud. Besides these, there were present the fourth and fifth partials of medium intensity, and a trace of the seventh. Compounding the simple tones of the forks according to these reactions, we obtain a faint reproduction of the tone of the vowel e.

Analytically, *i* is composed of a prime and its octave, both of which are very intense. But the same difficulty that was in our way in the analysis of this vowel, and of sounds of high pitch generally, now confronts us in its reproduction,—the difficulty of getting resonators strongly to reinforce high partials. For this reason it is impossible to imitate the tone of *i* in a way that even approximates the fidelity of the imitations of the graver vowels, especially *u*, *o*, and *a*. But, you will say, in none of these cases is the imitation perfect. The resemblance of the artificial sounds to the natural ones is, at best, more or less fanciful.

I admit that we have not, in the experiments made, been able to reproduce the vowel-sounds with all their characteristic shades of difference. And what is said for vowel-sounds may be said of all other sounds. But even granting the impossibility of effecting such a composition, we have accomplished enough to show that we have discovered the foundation of quality in tone, and this is all that has been attempted.

Moreover, in addition to the effect that upper partials, of varying number and intensity, have in modifying the quality of their prime, and in the case of vowel-sounds, for instance, of impressing on the resultant tone that quality that characterizes it, we must not forget to take into consideration the conformation of the mouth, the condition of the vocal cords, the pressure of the air urged through the glottis, and a score of other conditions that it would be quite impossible exactly to reproduce by any artificial contrivance, however perfect.

And more than this. There is a factor of more or less influence in determining the quality of sound, about which I have yet said nothing, but which is of sufficient importance to merit serious consideration. I refer to difference of phase. Helmholtz, whose conclusions respecting the influence of upper partials in modifying the quality of tone have already been given, denies that quality is in any way affected by difference of phase. Indeed, the complex apparatus that we have just used was partially devised to show that the quality of sound is entirely independent of difference of phase. In summing up the results of his investigations on this subject, he states explicitly that "the quality of the musical portion of a compound tone depends solely on the number and relative strength of its partial simple tones, and in no respect on their difference of phase."

To this conclusion, which Helmholtz lays down as "an important law," Dr. Koenig takes exception, and by a number of cleverly devised apparatus, constructed especially for the purpose, he shows that difference of phase affects the quality of tone to such an extent that its influence cannot be neglected.

To appreciate Koenig's experiments, and understand the apparatus by which they were made, we must recall what was said in our seventh lecture about the combination of waves representing notes of the same and of different periods, and of notes of the same and of different phases. Then, however, only waves corresponding to notes whose periods were equal, or were to each other in the ratio 1 : 2, or 1 : 3, were combined. But it is possible, and even easy, by following the rules there laid down, to combine any number of simple waves, whether of the same or of different phases.

In Fig. 162, drawn by Professor Mayer, we have beautifully illustrated the combination of the six harmonic curves corresponding to the first six partials of a musical note. The elementary curves are shown in the upper part of the figure; the resultant in the lower part. In order to bring out the characteristic flexures of the resultant, the amplitudes of the curves are made to vary as their wave-lengths. But it must not be inferred that the intensities of the partials of a musical note vary according to the amplitudes here given. Neither must it be concluded that the amplitudes, as compared with the wave-lengths, are nearly so great in nature as in the curves in the diagram. As a matter of fact, in sonorous vibrations, the amplitude of vibration of the oscillating particles, as compared with the wave-lengths, must be infinitely small, in order that the law of the "superposition of displacements" may be rigorously true.

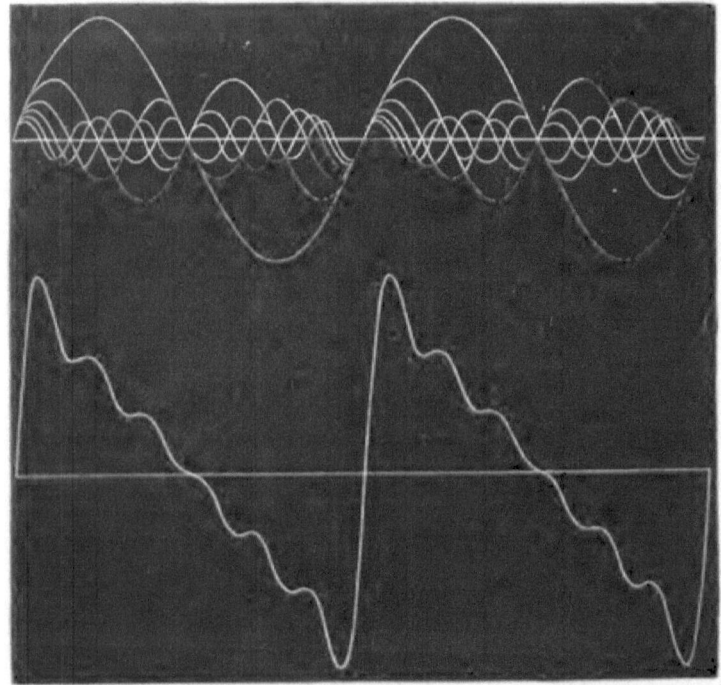

Fig. 162.

The resultant curve given in the foregoing illustration has a special interest from the fact that it closely resembles the vibrational figure executed by a violin-string, as determined by Helmholtz by means of a vibration-microscope. A comparison of the latter curve (Fig. 163) with the former, shows how nearly the two are alike. If the violin had yielded a tone of exactly six partials, and of the same intensities as indicated in Fig. 162, the two resultant curves would be identical in appearance.

Professor Mayer gives us another remarkable illustration of the coincidence of vibrational forms obtained by different

QUALITY OF SOUND. 371

methods. In Fig. 164, *A* shows the indentations made in a sheet of tin when the vowel *a* is sung into the mouth-piece of a phonograph. *B* exhibits a transverse section of these indentations. *C* gives in outline the form of a manometric flame which has been set in vibration by the sing-

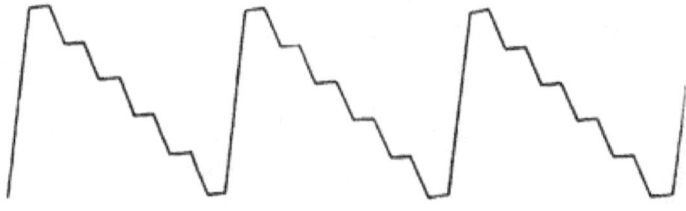

Fig. 163.

ing of the same vowel, *a*. The similarity of forms in the two cases is beyond question.

In Fig. 165, *a*, we have in the upper horizontal line four curves, whose periods are 1:2: 3:4: 5:6: 7:8; and represent sounds whose intensities are equal. The four curves give the resultants of the eight simple curves, when they coincide at their point of departure, indicated by *o*,

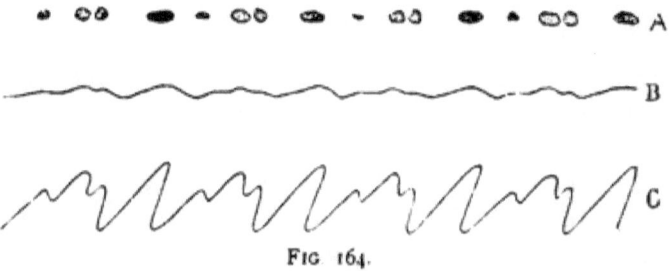

Fig 164.

and when their difference of phase is equal to $\frac{1}{4}$, $\frac{1}{2}$, or $\frac{3}{4}$ of their wave-lengths. In the same figure, *b*, we have four curves, representing likewise curves of equal intensities, and having periods that are to each other as the odd numbers 1 : 3 : 5 : 7. etc. As in *a*, there are differences of phase corresponding to *o*, $\frac{1}{4}$, $\frac{1}{2}$, and $\frac{3}{4}$ of a wave-length.

Sounds in which all the upper partials have the same intensities as their fundamental are probably never produced by any of the natural sonorous bodies with which we are familiar. When required in music, they are produced by bringing out simultaneously a series of sounds bearing to each other the relations of harmonic partials, as in the compound stops of the organ.

But it frequently happens in nature that sonorous bodies possess qualities of tone due to the presence of harmonic partials that decrease in intensity according to a determinate law. Such is the case with reeds not provided with pipes; with strings emitting only one of their proper tones; and with tuning-forks having long, thin branches, and executing vibrations of considerable amplitude.

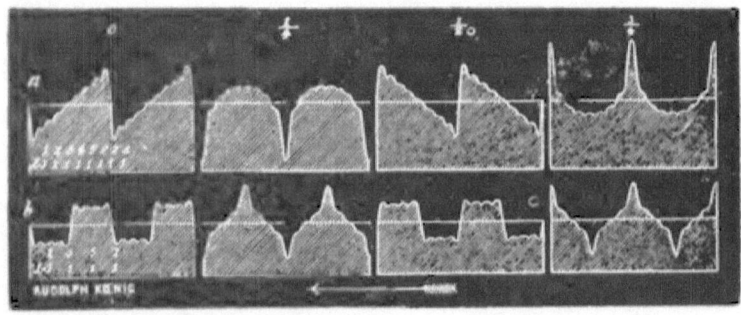

FIG. 165.

In Fig. 166, a, are four curves of four different phases, which are the resultants of ten harmonic curves, whose periods are as $1:2:3:4:5:6:7:8:9:10$, and whose amplitudes vary inversely as the numbers expressing their order. In b, c, and d we have still different curves representing sounds whose partials, with their relative intensities, are indicated by the numbers given.

If, now, these curves are cut in the circumferences of metal disks, or on the margins of metal bands attached to wheels, we have reproduced, in a modified form, the wavesiren which we had occasion to use in studying the nature of beats and beat-tones. The principles employed in constructing a wave-siren for exhibiting beats and beat-tones, and one for showing the quality of tone produced by various harmonic partials, of the same or different phases, are identical.

A siren, as employed for the latter purpose, is now before you. As you observe, it consists essentially of three bands of brass, fastened to three wheels supported on a vertical axis (Fig. 167), which is caused to revolve by a crank. On the margins of the two lower bands are cut four curves, each corresponding to the first twelve partials of a sound, the intensities of which partials are inversely as the order of their sequence. The difference of phase exhibited by these four curves corresponds to the coinci-

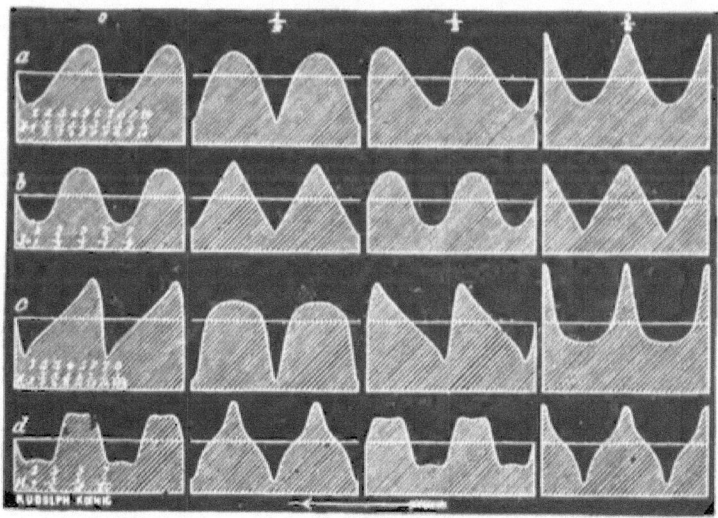

Fig. 166.

dence of origin in the first curve, o, and to differences of $\frac{1}{4}$, $\frac{1}{2}$, and $\frac{3}{4}$ of a wave-length in the three others.

The upper band has cut into its edges two curves, produced by the combination of harmonic curves representing the first six odd partials, whose intensities also decrease inversely as the numbers denoting their order of succession. When revolving on their axes, these curves pass before the narrow openings of six tubes which are connected with a common reservoir, and which, by means of suitable keys, can be opened at will. When air is blown against any of these curves, and they are revolved with a sufficient rapidity, a sound is generated whose quality varies according to the number of the constituent harmonic curves in the resultant compound curve. With this apparatus, then, we are able to compare the results given by two series of different harmonic partials, and to compare also the results afforded by the same series of partials when their phases are different.

If we now direct a stream of air against the four lower serrations in succession while they are made to rotate with

FIG. 167.

a suitable velocity, you immediately perceive that there is a marked difference in the quality of the sounds produced by the different serrated bands. The curve, having a difference of phase of $\frac{1}{2}$, is found to give a tone of greater power and brightness than any of the three others. The minimum of power and brightness is afforded by the curve whose difference of phase is $\frac{3}{4}$, while the two remaining curves, corresponding to differences of phase of o and $\frac{1}{4}$, yield a tone intermediate in quality between those furnished by the curves whose differences of phase are $\frac{1}{2}$ and $\frac{3}{4}$.

Here, then, we have curves corresponding to partials whose number and intensity, in the four cases considered, are precisely the same. The very marked difference observed in the quality of the tones cannot, therefore, depend on the number and intensity of these partials, but must be due to some other factor which is not common to the four curves. This factor is the difference of phase of the curves, and this alone it is that differentiates the quality corresponding to one curve from that given by any of the others.

Trying, in the same manner, the two serrations of the upper band, whose curves correspond to the first six odd partials, we obtain tones that are entirely different from each other, and entirely different from those afforded by the indentations of the two lower bands. We note that there is in this case, also, the same difference of quality of tone for the phases $\frac{1}{4}$ and $\frac{3}{4}$ as was observed in two of the four preceding curves.

But Koenig was not satisfied with the results afforded by these compound curves until he had verified them by other means. He had, indeed, constructed his curves with the greatest care, and on a large scale, reducing them afterwards by photography; and it would seem that the evidence furnished by the experiments made was conclusive. To prove, however, that the difference of quality in the instances just referred to was, without all peradventure, due solely to difference of phase, Koenig devised still another form of wave-siren.

The essential parts of this ingenious piece of mechanism (Fig. 168), — a photograph of which is projected on the screen, — are sixteen copper disks, mounted on a sort of cone-pulley, and connected by suitable tubes with a powerful wind-chest. The disks have cut in their edges sixteen simple harmonic curves, corresponding to the first sixteen partial tones, and they increase in diameter from the first to the last. A movement of rotation causes them to pass before the tubes attached to the wind-chest, and they can be so arranged that each disk will yield a simple tone, corresponding to a simple pendular vibration. With these simple tones, one can form various compound tones of varying qualities, in the same manner as was effected with our tuning-forks and resonators.

But besides being able to reproduce compound tones

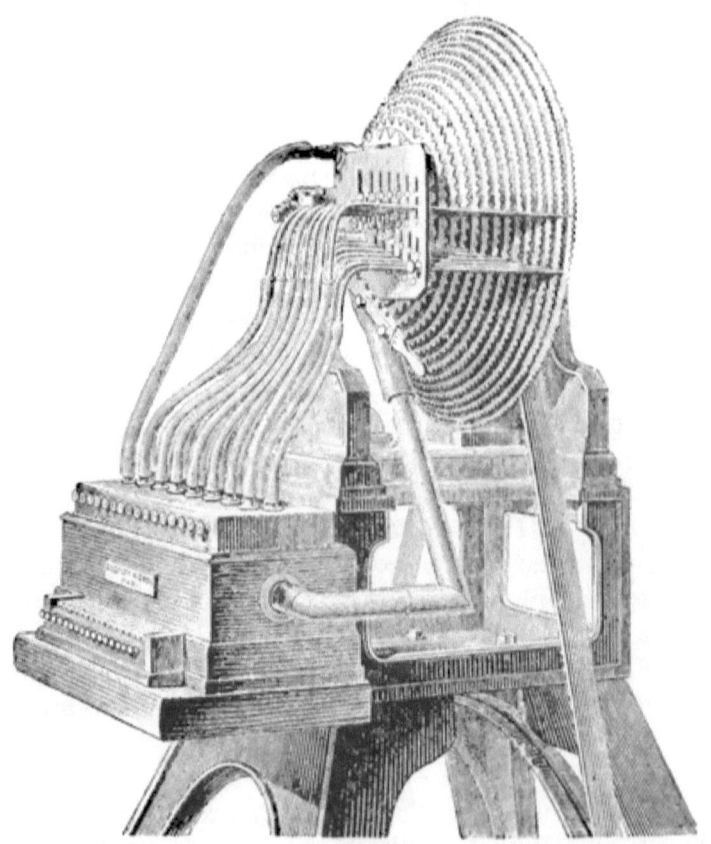

FIG. 168.

differing from each other in the number and intensity of their constituent partials, as was done with the tuning-forks, a special disposition of the apparatus in question enables the experimenter to adjust the air-tubes so that he can have instantly any difference of phase he may desire. Such being the case, he is in a position to show the influence of difference of phase on quality of tone.

And, as was anticipated, the results arrived at with these sixteen disks, giving, at will, either simple or compound tones of the same or of different phases, were entirely in accord with those given by the wave-siren with which we have been experimenting, all of whose curves are compound, and made according to a determinate law.

It is not necessary, however, to have recourse to the elaborate apparatus we have been considering, to show the marked influence of difference of phase on quality of tone. A crucial experiment, also indicated by Koenig, can be made with a much simpler form of instrument.

To the rotator before you is attached a disk (Fig. 169), whose edge is cut in the form of a harmonic curve. Revolving this disk, and directing a current of air against it in such wise that the narrow slit of the tube through which the wind passes is parallel to the radius of the disk, we obtain a feeble, but very sweet note.

FIG. 169.

The note is simple, — just such a note as would be produced by simple pendular vibrations.

If, however, we incline the slit-like opening of the tube either towards the right or the left of the radial line, we at once obtain a stronger and a harsher note. With the proper inclination of the slit, the note emitted assumes the quality due to a free vibrating reed, whose partials are distinctly recognizable. When we incline the slit in the direction of rotation of the wheel, the simple note is changed into a compound note whose prime is accompanied by a series of partials of decreasing intensities having a difference of phase of $\frac{1}{2}$. When it is inclined in the opposite direction, the same partials accompany the prime, but with a difference of phase of o.

We are thus enabled, while using the same partials, to change from one phase to another with the greatest rapidity. The result is very striking indeed. In this way we discover that the notes whose partials have no difference of phase are round and pure, while, on the contrary, those engendered by partials whose difference of phase is equal to half their wave-length, are more harsh and nasal. The difference of quality in the two tones thus generated can well be characterized in comparing them to the vowels *o* and *a*. As the inclination on the slit to the radius of the disk is augmented, this difference becomes more pro-

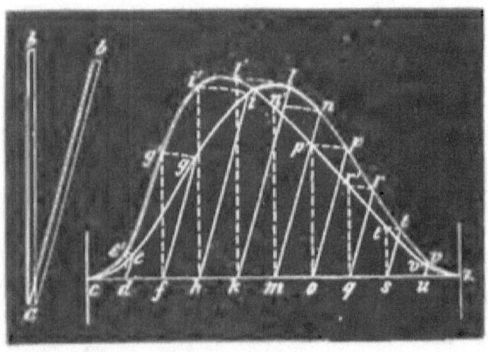

FIG. 170.

nounced, and eventually becomes so great that the qualities of the two notes emitted no more resemble each other than do the two vowels mentioned.

A little consideration will make it evident why a change in the position of the slit before a harmonic curve should give rise to tones of such different qualities. Let $c, e, g, i \ldots z$ (Fig. 170), represent a harmonic curve which is made to pass before the vertical slit $a\,b$. Under such circumstances the perpendiculars of the curve that are successively opposite the slit will vary according to the law of sines, and we shall have a simple tone corresponding to one produced by simple pendular vibrations. If, however, the slit is inclined, the parts of the curve that are successively covered by the slit will vary according to a law which is entirely different.

QUALITY OF SOUND. 379

The result in such a case would be as if the slit were made to move before the curve $c, c', g', i' \ldots z$, which is obtained by cutting the sinusoid by the straight lines $dc, fg, hi, \ldots$ parallel to ab', and erecting at the points $d, f, h, \ldots$ the perpendiculars dc', fg', and hi', equal in length to the lines $dc, fg, hi \ldots$ The change of intensity and quality of tone, due to the inclination of the slit to the right or to the left of the vertical, manifests itself so quickly and with such distinctness that the position requisite for the production of a perfectly simple tone can be determined with the greatest accuracy by the ear alone, without any assistance whatever from the eye.

We can, therefore, no longer entertain any doubt regarding the influence of difference of phase on determining the quality of sound. In the instances just considered, its influence is very marked, and we have no reason for believing that its influence is different in other tones which are characterized by similar differences of phase. Of course the chief factors in determining the quality of any given tone are the number and relative intensity of its partials; but in no case is the effect due to difference of phase in these partials so slight that it can be entirely overlooked. Considering the facts in the case, as disclosed by the experiments made, we can in truth affirm, in the words of Koenig, "that if the changes in the number and relative intensity of partials give rise to such differences of quality as we observe in instruments belonging to different families, or such as distinguish the human voice in the different vowels, the changes in the difference of phase for these same partials are competent to produce differences of quality at least as sensible as those which are remarked in instruments of the same kind, or in the same vowels as sung by different voices."

If now we were asked to give an answer to the question we proposed to ourselves at the beginning of this lecture, regarding the cause of the quality of sound, we should be able to give it without hesitation. The answer would be that given by Helmholtz, with a correction for the difference of phase, and would read as follows: The quality of the musical portion of a compound tone depends on the number and relative intensity of its partial simple tones, and on the differences of phase under which these partial tones enter into composition.

Here I must call your attention to a remarkable mathematical confirmation of the truth of what has been stated regarding the influence possessed by the harmonic partials in modifying the quality of their fundamental. It shows a most intimate connection between two subjects, mechanics and acoustics, that are popularly supposed to be as widely separated from each other as are the antipodes.

The distinguished French mathematician, Fourier, has demonstrated that every periodical vibration, of whatever form, may always be separated into a series of simple pendular vibrations. This means that when we represent the vibrations by curves, there is no periodic form of curve that cannot be compounded out of harmonic curves whose lengths are inversely as the numbers 1, 2, 3, 4, etc. More than this. He has indicated the means for calculating for each compound curve the number, amplitude, and difference of phase of its constituent simple curves.

The law just enunciated, which is generally known as Fourier's theorem, when translated from the language of mechanics into the language of acoustics asserts, what experiment has also shown to be true, that every compound musical tone is composed of a definite number of simple tones, whose relative frequencies follow the same law as that which governs the sequence of harmonic partials.

But, as we have seen, there are comparatively few instances in which a prime tone is accompanied by partials which are perfectly harmonic. In the majority of cases the upper partials are more or less inharmonic. With such tones Fourier's theorem has nothing to do.

While experimenting with his large compound wave-siren (Fig. 167), Koenig discovered that it was impossible, with any combination of partials that he could make, to reproduce the peculiar strident tones of certain reed and wind instruments. Neither could he successfully imitate vowel-sounds. He tried every combination of partials and every variation of intensity and phase, but in vain.

He then devised a modified form of wave-siren that he thought would afford some solution of the difficulty. Instead of having the edge of the disk cut into the form of a curve corresponding to a series of harmonic partials, he made the indentations in some of his sirens correspond to a fundamental, accompanied by certain perturbed harmonics. In others the indentations corresponded to sinusoidal forms, on which are superposed a number of wavelets of various shapes and sizes. I shall show you only two of these sirens, in order that you may have some idea of the nature of the experiments made, and the conclusions to which they lead.

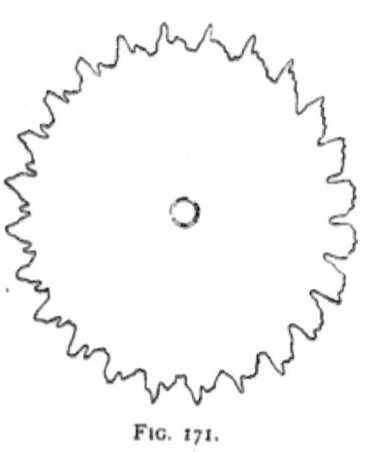

Fig. 171.

The edge of the disk before you (Fig. 171) answers to a curve corresponding to a tone compounded of a prime and four perturbed harmonic partials. The fundamental consists of 24 waves. The first upper partial consists of 49 waves ($2 \times 24 + 1$); the second of 75 ($3 \times 24 + 3$); the third of 101 ($4 \times 24 + 5$); and the fourth of 127 waves ($5 \times 24 + 7$). The resultant curve embraces 24 waves, all different in form, and some of them very irregular in outline. When air is blown through a narrow slit against the teeth of this disk, a very disagreeable and slightly intermittent sound is the result.

In the second disk (Fig. 172), we have twenty-four sinusoidal waves, in the sides of which have been made with a file a number of ripples of various forms and sizes. The crests and troughs, however, remain untouched. For this reason the vibrations made by this siren are of equal amplitude and isochronous. This disk, unlike the one just used, gives a sound which, although somewhat raucous, possesses a definite musical quality.[1]

From these and a number of similar experiments made by Koenig, it is found that we have yet much to learn before we can answer the many questions that still arise regarding the nature of the quality of sound. We know, indeed, in a general way the cause of the quality of sound, and this is a great step forward; but we cannot yet analyze the elements of any particular tone. To be sure, we may be able to determine the number of partials present, and even their relative intensities. This is comparatively easy work. But in addition to this we must know the various differences of phase that characterize the partials of any given tone. And, more than this, we must know how far the partials of a tone are from being truly harmonic, and in what respects the harmonic partials differ from the tones of subdivision, if both sets be present at the same time. The difficulties are many, and apparently insuperable; but judging from what has been done during the past thirty years, we need not despair of being able eventually to give not only a general definition of quality, but also one that will apply in the case of any particular tone.

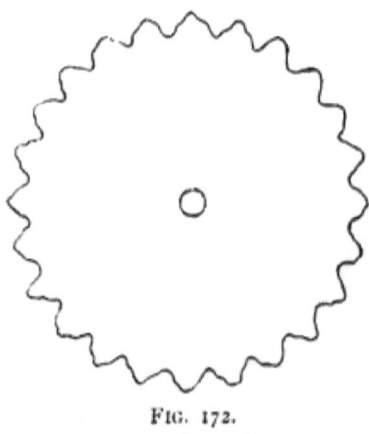

FIG. 172.

We are now prepared to answer a question that must have presented itself to all of you before this, and that is, How is the ear able to hear several tones at the same time?

[1] Ueber Klänge mit ungleichförmigen Wellen. (Annalen der Physik und Chemie. Neue Folge. Band XXXIX. 1890).

It is evident that a given particle of air, or a given point of the drumskin of the ear, can have but one direction of motion at any one instant of time. Hence the motion imparted to any particle of air, or a point of the tympanic membrane, must be that resulting from the compounding of all the simple motions corresponding to all the simple tones existing in the various tones perceived by the ear. Remembering how harmonic curves are combined to form

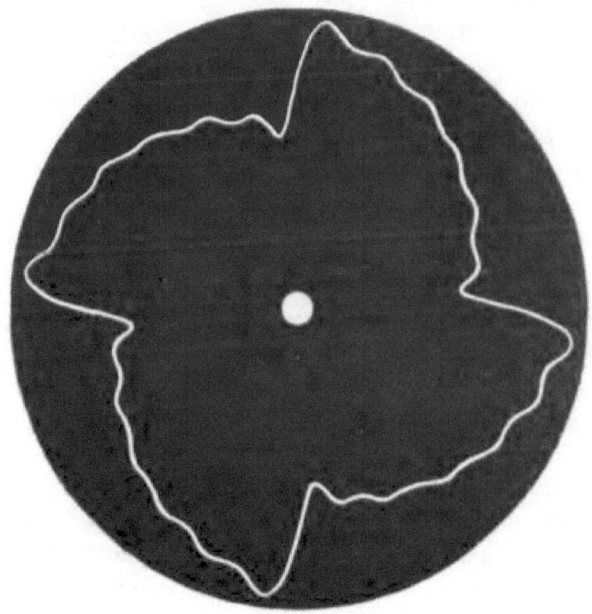

FIG. 173.

compound curves, and having in mind that any given point in such compound curves can have motion in only one direction at any given instant, we can readily understand how the resultant of any number of simple or compound tones impresses on the tympanum of the ear a motion that at any determinate moment is simply either outwards or inwards.

By means of a glass disk devised by Professor Mayer we are able to study in a most satisfactory manner the nature of the motion imparted to any particle of matter under the combined influence of two or more vibratory movements of different periods. On the disk (Fig. 173) is traced a curve that corresponds to four of the resultant curves of Fig. 162. The disk is now placed before the condenser of the lantern and projected on the screen. At present you see the image of the entire curve. If, however, a piece of cardboard with a narrow slit be placed before the disk, with the slit in the direction of one of the radii of the disk, we shall see only a single luminous point, all the rest of the curve being covered by the cardboard. When the disk is slowly rotated, the point of light reproduces exactly the kind of vibratory motion which characterizes a material particle under the joint influence of the first six harmonic motions generating a given musical note composed of six partials. The to-and-fro motion of the luminous point, although perfectly periodic, has a peculiar irregular, halting character. If a single harmonic curve were traced on the disk, instead of the resultant of six such curves, the vibratory movement of the point of light would be quite different. It would then oscillate backward and forward like the pendulum of a clock. In other words, we should have pictured to us the simple harmonic motion corresponding to a simple musical tone.

How the ear resolves this resultant motion into its constituents, and analyzes the mass of composite tone into its simple components, is a question we leave to physiologists to answer. It is a fact that the ear does make the analysis, and unravels with unerring accuracy the most complex sonorous vibrations. Its superiority over the eye in this analytic power is most remarkable. The most intricate mazes of tone are at once traced to their origin, with the greatest facility, by the ear; whereas the eye, in any attempt to separate luminous vibrations of different periods, would surely and utterly fail.

And when we stop to think on the very small size of the external passage of the ear, and its capacity to recognize at one and the same time a multiplicity of tones of the most diverse quality, our wonder increases. It is only then that we begin to realize what a truly marvellous organ is the ear. And if we are to accept as true the theory propounded by Helmholtz, and based on the discoveries of Corti, Hasse, Hensen, and others, our admiration must become even greater. According to this theory, there are in the basilar membrane of the human ear several thousand fibres, each of which is set in sympathetic vibration by a vibratory motion of a certain definite period. These fibres are connected with the constituent filaments of the auditory nerve, and by them the various simple pendular motions which are singled out from the complex vibratory motions, excited by most sonorous bodies, are transmitted to the brain, where they are translated into the sensation we call sound.

If this theory be true, — it is certainly very plausible, — we have afforded us a simple mechanical explanation of the perception of sounds of various pitches and qualities, as far as their vibratory motions are concerned, that compels the mind to recognize the stupendous results which the Creator accomplishes by the simplest means, and to see in the astonishing phenomena of audition evidences of Divine power and wisdom as striking as any disclosed in the whole realm of animated nature.

But sympathetic vibrations excited in the fibres of the basilar membrane, by vibrations of determinate periodicity which are external to the ear, are evidently only a reproduction in the organ of hearing of sympathetic motions which are similar to those excited in all forms of sonorous bodies whose frequencies are identical. This, however, granting it to be true, does not afford any explanation of the sensation of sound. We may offer explanations, based on the principles of mechanics, as to how vibratory motions of various kinds are related to each other, and as to how the motions of one period may give rise to motions of the same or of different periods; but this does not afford a solution of the enigma that confronts us, nor does it shed any light on the nature of the action of the brain. This brings us again to the borderland of mystery. When we can comprehend the nature of the link that binds mind and matter, then, and not till then, may we hope to have some insight into the nature of the phenomena here presented to us, to understand how motion can originate sensation, and how vibrations of different periods can be changed, translated, as it were, into what appeals to our senses, as heat, light, and sound.

CHAPTER X.

MUSICAL INTERVALS AND TEMPERAMENT.

THE sounds with which the acoustician deals range in frequency from sixteen to nearly fifty thousand vibrations per second. Of these, only a comparatively small number are employed in music, and they must always bear to each other certain definite relations of pitch. The ratios of frequencies which characterize such sounds are called *intervals*. Thus, two notes whose frequencies are as $2:1$ constitute the interval of an octave. Two notes whose vibration-numbers are as $3:2$ give the interval of a fifth. These intervals are independent of the position that the notes may occupy on the scale. Provided the ratio of their frequencies remains the same, the interval retains the same name, whether the notes are in one part of the scale or in another.

The *gamut*, or *diatonic scale*, embraces a series of eight notes, the first and last of which have the same names, and are separated from one another by the interval of an octave. The notes of the gamut have been designated by the letters —

$$C, \quad D, \quad E, \quad F, \quad G, \quad A, \quad B, \quad C_2.$$

Considering the frequency of C as unity, the frequencies of the notes of the scale, including the *tonic*, or first note, will be proportional to the numbers —

$$1, \quad \tfrac{9}{8}, \quad \tfrac{5}{4}, \quad \tfrac{4}{3}, \quad \tfrac{3}{2}, \quad \tfrac{5}{3}, \quad \tfrac{15}{8}, \quad 2.$$

Dividing each of these notes by that which precedes it, we obtain the intervals between the successive notes of the scale. The intervals of the major scale are as follows: —

C,	D,	E,	F,	G,	A,	B,	C$_2$.
$\frac{9}{8}$,	$\frac{10}{9}$,	$\frac{16}{15}$,	$\frac{9}{8}$,	$\frac{10}{9}$,	$\frac{9}{8}$,	$\frac{16}{15}$.	

The consecutive intervals from C to C$_2$ are called *a second, a major third, a fourth, a fifth, a major sixth, a major seventh,* and *an octave* respectively. C, from which the intervals are reckoned, is called the *tonic,* or *key-note.* Musicians call the fifth note above the key-note the *dominant,* and the fifth note below, the *sub-dominant.* When the key-note is C, the dominant is G, and the sub-dominant is G in the octave below C.[1]

In the foregoing scale, as will be observed, there are only three different intervals, viz., $\frac{9}{8}$, $\frac{10}{9}$, and $\frac{16}{15}$. The first, $\frac{9}{8}$, is called a *major tone;* the second, $\frac{10}{9}$, is named a *minor tone;* and the last is known as a *major* or *diatonic semitone.* The last interval, although called a semitone, is a little more than the half of a major tone. Adding together two semitones, — which is done by multiplying the frequency-ratio, $\frac{16}{15}$, by itself, — we obtain a number which is slightly greater than $\frac{9}{8}$: — $\frac{16}{15} \times \frac{16}{15} = \frac{256}{225}$; $\frac{256}{225} : \frac{9}{8} :: 2048 : 2025$. Two semitones are therefore greater than a major tone in the ratio of 2048 : 2025. Subtracting a major semitone from a minor tone gives a *minor* or *chromatic semitone,* $\frac{10}{9} \div \frac{16}{15} = \frac{25}{24}$. This interval is the smallest usually employed in music. A less interval, and one of considerable importance in theoretical music, is a *comma.* It is yielded by subtracting a minor from a major tone, $\frac{9}{8} \div \frac{10}{9} = \frac{81}{80}$. Tones, like major and minor tones, that differ from each other by only a comma, are considered in music to have the same value. The same may be said of major and minor semitones. The ratio between these two being less than a comma, — $\frac{16}{15} \div \frac{25}{24} = \frac{128}{125}$, — they are regarded as semitones of equal value.

---

[1] When necessary, the subdominant is transposed into the octave of the tonic.

The various notes of the diatonic scale are, with respect to their frequencies, related to one another as follows: —

Tonic.	Second.	Major Third.	Fourth.	Fifth.	Major Sixth.	Major Seventh.	Octave.
C_3	D	E	F	G	A	B	C_4
256	288	320	341.3	384	426.6	480	512
1	$\tfrac{9}{8}$	$\tfrac{5}{4}$	$\tfrac{4}{3}$	$\tfrac{3}{2}$	$\tfrac{5}{3}$	$\tfrac{15}{8}$	2

Using the smallest whole numbers expressing these ratios, we have —

24 27 30 32 36 40 45 48

All the intervals here given, with the exception of the second and the major seventh, are what are known as *consonant* intervals. The second and the seventh form intervals that are called *dissonant*. The ratios corresponding to the former are expressed by small whole numbers, and the more consonant the interval, the smaller the whole number expressing the ratio. Hence, after unison, the most consonant interval is the octave. After the octave come in succession the fifth, the fourth, the major third, and the major sixth.

Dissonant intervals, on the contrary, are characterized by ratios composed of large numbers, and the amount of dissonance to which any two sounds may give rise may, at least in the middle portion of the musical scale, be determined by the ratio of their vibration-frequencies. Thus the interval of a major tone, $\tfrac{9}{8}$, is, in the lower portions of the musical scale, markedly dissonant. A diatonic or a chromatic semitone, whose vibration ratios are respectively $\tfrac{16}{15}$ and $\tfrac{25}{24}$, are, in similar portions of the scale, far more dissonant. The intervals $\tfrac{2}{1}$, $\tfrac{3}{2}$, $\tfrac{4}{3}$, are called respectively the perfect octave, the perfect fifth, and the perfect fourth, to distinguish them from certain diminished or augmented intervals of the same name. They are said to form *perfect consonances*, in contradistinction to the intervals $\tfrac{5}{4}$, $\tfrac{5}{3}$, and the minor third, $\tfrac{6}{5}$, and the minor sixth, $\tfrac{8}{5}$, which are denominated *imperfect consonances*. The minor third is obtained by subtracting a chromatic semitone from a major third: $\frac{5}{4} \times \frac{24}{25} = \frac{6}{5}$. Similarly, a minor sixth is equal to a major sixth less a chromatic semitone, $\frac{5}{3} \times \frac{24}{25} = \frac{8}{5}$.

From the foregoing we observe that the sum of two intervals is obtained by multiplying, not by adding, their ratios together. Thus a fifth added to a fourth yields an octave, $\frac{3}{2} \times \frac{4}{3} = \frac{12}{6} = 2$. When we wish to subtract one interval from another, we divide the ratio of one by that of the other. Thus, a fifth minus a major third equals a minor third, $\frac{3}{2} \div \frac{5}{4} = \frac{12}{10} = \frac{6}{5}$.

The various intervals thus spoken of are written in musical notation as follows: —

	Perfect unison.	Chromatic semitone.	Diatonic semitone.	Minor tone.	Major tone.	Minor third.	Major third.	Perfect fourth.	Perfect fifth.	Minor sixth.	Major sixth.	Major seventh.	Perfect octave.
Ratio of vibration	1	$\frac{25}{24}$	$\frac{16}{15}$	$\frac{10}{9}$	$\frac{9}{8}$	$\frac{6}{5}$	$\frac{5}{4}$	$\frac{4}{3}$	$\frac{3}{2}$	$\frac{8}{5}$	$\frac{5}{3}$	$\frac{15}{8}$	2
Logarithm of ratio	0	18	28	46	51	79	97	125	176	204	222	273	301

In addition to the intervals given in the above table there are several others used in music, obtained by the inversion of the former; but we have no time to consider them here.

In the preceding diagram, as will be remarked, the intervals are expressed in logarithms[1] as well as by fractions. In point of clearness and intelligibility the logarithmic are much superior to fractional values. By means of logarithms we can tell at a glance the interval between any two sounds whatever, provided we know the numbers of their vibrations. It is immaterial whether they belong to the

---

[1] The logarithms, it will be noticed, are considered as whole numbers, the usual index and decimal point being omitted.

musical scale or not. Expressed in logarithms, the interval of a comma is 5; the interval between C♯ and D♭, called an enharmonic diesis, is 6; while that of a mean semitone, as employed on tempered instruments, is 25.

To find the sum of two intervals, we add together their logarithmic values. The logarithms of the intervals of a fourth and a fifth are, as given above, 125 and 176 respectively. But 125 + 176 = 301, the value of an octave. A major third, 97, added to a minor third, 79, equals a fifth, 176. The difference between two intervals is found by subtracting the logarithm of the lesser interval from that of the greater. A fourth, 125, minus a major third, 97, is equivalent to 28, a diatonic semitone. A major tone, 51, less a minor tone, 46, gives a comma, 5.

From what has been said, we learn that from the very large number of different sounds only a small proportion of them can be used for purposes of music; and those that are so used must form a certain fixed determinate series. We cannot slide, or proceed by a continuous transition, from one sound to another, but must advance by degrees; that is, we must ascend or descend by definite steps.[1] In the octave there are seven such steps, of varying size and position. Between these steps of unequal height, the demands of our modern music sometimes require the interposition of other steps, of lesser magnitude. Such a succession of sounds is called a *scale*, from the Latin word *scala*, "ladder," or "stairway." The French use the word *échelle*, which also means a ladder. The German term for scale is still more expressive. It is *tonleiter*, — that is, a "tone-ladder," or a ladder of musical sounds.

A question now naturally suggests itself. Is the diatonic scale, of which we have been speaking, something conventional and empirical, or is it founded on some law of Nature? The majority of musicians, I am inclined to think, would claim for the scale a natural origin. It so

---

[1] As an ornament, under the name *portamento*, a continuous slide is sometimes permitted in vocal and instrumental music. In instruments with fixed notes, as is obvious, a slide is impossible.

well satisfies our ideas of cadence, modulation, and tonality, it comes so natural to sing it, it is so pleasing to the ear, that there is a wide-spread impression that it must rest on natural laws, and is therefore quite independent of all æsthetical principles.

The late M. Fétis, the eminent musical historian, says in reference to this subject: "It is an opinion generally held that the succession of sounds known in the modern music of European nations, and formulated by their major and minor scales, is the result of some fundamental and immutable law, and that diatonic music — *i. e.*, music in which the sounds succeed one another in tones and semitones — is the music of Nature.

"According to the doctrines of many theorists and historians of the art, the sentiment of the necessity of these diatonic relations of sound ought to have preceded every other conception of tonality, and man would have been incapable of imagining a kind of music inconsistent with these relations.

"I do not hesitate to declare that this opinion is absolutely contrary to what history teaches us by facts of the most unquestionable authority.

"We learn by these facts that diatonic music is not the most ancient; on the contrary, we have proof that none of the nations of antiquity adopted it, and that there exist still peoples to whom it is entirely strange The examples of music of the ancients are sufficient to prove the non-existence of this assumed natural law of diatonic progression It is not difficult to establish among primitive nations systems of sounds differing altogether from it; and it is possible to trace the progressive transformations by which the modern diatonic scale has been developed, at a comparatively late period, from some of the primordial systems differing from it almost entrely."[1]

The first one to adopt a succession of notes that approached our modern diatonic scale was Pythagoras, the

---

[1] Quoted from "Histoire Générale de la Musique." par E. F. Fétis, in "The Philosophy of Music," by Mr. William Pole, F.R.S

founder of theoretical music.[1] The diatonic scale now used was introduced by Zarlino, and the first account of it is found in his "Instituzioni Armoniche," published in 1558. According to numerous and varied experiments made by MM. Cornu and Mercadier, the best performers on stringed instruments still follow the Pythagorean scale when playing a melody, and adopt that of Zarlino only when they play pieces in which two or more notes are sounded simultaneously. Accepting their results as true, — and they seem to be well established, — we must conclude that the scale of Pythagoras is more suitable for melody; while the modern diatonic scale — the scale of Zarlino — is preferable for harmony.

All nations that have had any pretensions to anything approaching a musical system have adopted the division of the scale into cycles of octaves. The Chinese divide the octave theoretically into twelve equal parts, corresponding to our semitones. Practically, however, they use only five notes, whose intervals correspond to the black notes of the pianoforte. The same pentatonic division of the octave is also found to a certain extent in the so-called Scotch music.

The Arabs recognize both the octave and the fifth in their system of music. But their system is even more complex than that of the Chinese. It is divided into sixteen or seventeen unequal intervals, and is entirely different from anything that obtains among Western nations.

The Hindoos theoretically divide the octave into twenty-two parts. Their practical scale, however, consists of only seven degrees. In addition to the octave and the fifth, they also employ the interval of the fourth.

---

[1] The intervals of the Pythagorean scale are as follows: —

C	D	E	F	G	A	B	C_2
$\frac{9}{8}$	$\frac{9}{8}$	$\frac{256}{243}$	$\frac{9}{8}$	$\frac{9}{8}$	$\frac{9}{8}$	$\frac{256}{243}$	

In this scale, as will be observed, there are only two intervals, — the tone and the semitone, or hemitone as it was called by the Greeks. The intervals of the fourth, the fifth, and the octave are the same as in Zarlino's scale. The major third, sixth, and seventh are increased by a comma, while the semitone is diminished by a like amount.

The music of the Persians, like that of the Hindoos, is characterized by the subdivision of the octave into minute intervals. But while the latter had, at least in theory, twenty-two divisions, the former had twenty-four. Each interval, therefore, of a Persian octave would be equivalent to what we call a quarter tone.

The Persian system of music has a special interest for us, because of its influence on Greek music, from which our own was eventually evolved. The Oriental nations of to-day, like the Greeks of ancient times, had a delicate estimation of sounds that to us is quite astonishing. The Greeks frequently used quarter tones, as do the Arabs and Persians of the present time. It is for this reason that an analysis of the music of Oriental nations has always been such a puzzle to musicians and scientific men. Even now, after all the study that has been bestowed upon the musical systems of the Orient, there are still wanting many important data to enable us to form a correct theory regarding even one of the numerous systems that there prevail.

It is sufficient, however, for our present purpose to know that different musical systems have obtained during the course of the world's history; that even now there are various systems in vogue, whose differences are so great that, with the exception of the octave and the fifth, they have scarcely anything in common. From these facts, and from what precedes, it is, then, evident that the diatonic scale has not that basis in Nature that so many people maintain it has. It is, on the contrary, the outgrowth of long centuries of study and experiment, and the product of the æsthetic sense of the untold number of musicians and composers who have given us our present system of music, and made it what it is to-day.

But although the diatonic scale, in its entirety, is not the scale of Nature — that is, a series of notes dictated by certain physical or physiological laws — that it is so often claimed to be, it would be a mistake to contend that it has no foundation whatever in Nature or on Nature's laws.

There are, at least, parts of the scale that have a natural origin, and seem to arise from the very nature of sound itself. But the parts of the scale that can be shown to rest on an undeniable physical basis are a very small proportion of the scale taken as a whole.

The first interval that can be proved to have a natural origin is unquestionably the octave. We have learned that nearly all musical sounds are compound, and that it is possible, even by the unaided ear, to recognize some of the constituents of a given compound note. Among those most readily detected in stringed instruments, such as were used by the Greeks, would be the second and third harmonic partials. But these constitute the octave and the twelfth of the fundamental, and, as has been stated, can be recognized even in the human voice. And for people like the Greeks, who had such acute ears for small intervals of tone, it would be unreasonable to suppose that they were incapable of hearing the partials that can be perceived by even an untrained musical ear.

Again, the octave is, from its very nature, only a replicate — a kind of repetition — of the fundamental. So much is this the case that even practised musicians sometimes mistake the second for the first partial. And then, furthermore, we must not forget the natural tendency, with which every one is cognizant, that there is to sing in octaves. Thus, a boy or a woman, in accompanying a melody sung by a bass voice, or played on a bass or barytone instrument, will naturally sing an octave higher. And provided they have an average musical ear, they can do this without any musical education whatever. "When, then, a higher voice," says Helmholtz, "executes a melody an octave higher than a grave voice, we hear again a part of what we heard before; namely, the evenly numbered partial tones of the grave voice, and at the same time we hear nothing that we had not previously heard."

The third partial, or the twelfth above the prime, is, as you know, just a fifth above the second partial. In many instances it can be more readily detected in a compound tone than the octave itself. And so perfectly does the interval of the fifth answer the requirements of the ear that even unpractised singers find it quite natural to take a fifth to a chorus that does not quite suit the pitch of their voice.

What has been said of the octave and the fifth may, in a limited manner, be predicated also of the fourth. But I do not think that we can claim a natural origin for any of the other intervals of the diatonic scale.

The fact that the intervals of the octave, the fifth, and the fourth have a physical basis in the partials of compound tones accounts most probably for the manner of tuning the earliest forms of the Greek lyre. The lyre, as we are informed by Boethius, was, to the time of Orpheus, an instrument of four strings, whose intervals would be represented by the notes $C: F: G: C_2$. Only the order of succession of the notes is indicated by the letters given, as their pitch is unknown.

The remaining intervals of the diatonic scale are more or less arbitrary and the results of numberless experiments to secure such notes as would best answer the purposes of melody and harmony. No one who has examined the subject would for a moment maintain that there is anything in Nature to suggest the intervals of a tone or a semitone. We readily sing the diatonic scale, with its different tones and semitones, as a matter of education; but it is quite certain that no one uninstructed in music would ever naturally sing this scale, however accurate and delicate his ear.

But another question now presents itself. Why was not the octave divided into equal instead of unequal parts? The answer generally given to this question is that it would be difficult for the ear to appreciate uniform divisions, and because, too, of the difficulty, if not impossibility, of the unaided voice to divide the octave into any given number of equal parts. Hence the unequal divisions, some of which were suggested by the harmonic partials that now characterize our major scale.

A succession of single tones, in an order pleasing to the ear, constitutes what is called *melody*. An air or tune sung by a single voice or played on an instrument of any kind, one note at a time, is a melody. As to its structure, music was first developed in the form of melody. Indeed, according to Helmholtz, melody is the essential basis of music. It has been cultivated from the earliest times, and in the musical systems of most of the Oriental nations it is the only form of music yet known.

The simultaneous sounding of two or more tones whose intervals are concordant produces *harmony*, and the combination of two or more notes that are thus harmonious constitutes *a chord*.[1] Two notes constitute a *dyad*, three form a *triad*, and four a *tetrad*. In order that a chord may be consonant, all the intervals composing it must be concords. Three notes, whose rates of vibrations are as $1 : \frac{5}{4} : \frac{3}{2}$, or as $4 : 5 : 6$, — that is, a triad made up of a tonic, a major third, and a fifth, give us the *perfect major chord*. To this chord it is usual to add the octave of the tonic, which gives us four notes that are separated from each other by the intervals $\frac{5}{4}, \frac{6}{5}, \frac{4}{3}$. By changing the order of these intervals so that they read $\frac{6}{5}, \frac{5}{4}, \frac{4}{3}$, we obtain the *perfect minor chord*. As you will observe, the only difference between the major and the minor chords is in the order in which the intervals $\frac{5}{4}$ and $\frac{6}{5}$, the major and minor thirds, succeed each other. In the former chord the major third comes first; in the latter it is the minor third that takes precedence. These two chords are at the basis of our modern system of music; and although the difference in ratios of their constituent intervals is very slight, their effect on the ear and the mind is so great that they are

---

[1] Hauptmann, the great authority on musical theory, draws a very precise distinction between melody and harmony. The former, according to him, conveys the idea of motion, the latter the idea of rest. Melody must go on, otherwise it ceases to be melody. In harmony, however, even though it stand still, the musical idea is complete. There are, indeed, progressions in harmony, but these constitute a succession of distinct ideas, each more or less complete in itself. In melody, on the contrary, it is succession only that forms one idea as a whole.

employed to express entirely different ideas and passions. In musical notation the perfect major and minor chords are written: —

These chords may be inverted in various ways, and caused to go through quite a cycle of changes; but we have not the time to consider them here.

The essential distinction, then, between melody and harmony is seen to be that in the former there is a succession of simple notes, while in the latter we have a chord or a succession of chords. And this, in truth, is the great difference between the music of the ancient nations, who knew little or nothing of harmony, and our modern music; between the systems of music that still prevail in the semi-civilized nations of Asia and that which obtains amongst the more cultured peoples of Europe and America.

We have seen that concords follow each other in the order of smoothness, — from the interval of the octave to that of the minor sixth. But the smoothest intervals are by no means the most gratifying to the ear. This is shown in the frequent use of thirds and sixths in two-part music as compared with the employment of the concords. Thirds and sixths, at least in our modern music, are considered to have a charm and richness that the fifth, the fourth, and the octave possess in only a comparatively inferior degree. Certain æsthetic reasons have been assigned for this preference, but it seems to result rather from habit and education. Time was when both thirds and sixths were used very sparingly by musicians, and when they were considered at best as only imperfectly consonant. Both these intervals were unknown to the Greeks and the Romans, and were introduced into our present system of music in comparatively recent times.

An interval of special interest to acousticians and to theoretical musicians is the harmonic, or sub-minor seventh, the vibration-frequencies of whose notes are 4:7. But this interval, although in some instances more harmonious than the minor sixth, 5:8, is not used in practical music. No satisfactory explanation seems to have been yet offered why it has not been adopted. The most that can be said against it is that it is strange, and that it has an effect on the ear that is quite different from that of any of the intervals with which we are familiar. It cannot be urged, as is sometimes done, that the interval is dissonant, because, as just stated, it is often less so than an interval that is frequently employed, — the minor sixth. Indeed, the sub-minor seventh is, in some instances at least, quite pleasing and harmonious, and it may in certain cases contribute very materially to the richness and brilliance of certain chords played on instruments that are tuned in pure intonation.

Having spoken at some length of scales, intervals, and chords, we are now prepared for their experimental examination. For this purpose we shall use tuning-forks and sirens, as they are better adapted to our purpose than anything else.

Before you is a set of tuning-forks on resonant cases, giving the diatonic scale. They embrace the octave extending from C_3 to C_4. When they are sounded in succession the musicians present will find that the intervals, although mathematically exact, are slightly different from those to which they are accustomed. Some of the notes appear too flat, others too sharp. The reason for this will be manifest when we come to consider the tempered scale which is now universally used in music.

When the notes constituting the consonant intervals of which we have been speaking are sounded simultaneously, the result is entirely different from that yielded when the same notes are sounded on any of our keyed instruments like the organ or pianoforte. I sound in succession the fifth, the fourth, the major and the minor thirds, and the sixth, and they all give consonances that are marvellously pure and harmonious. And not only do we hear the notes that are emitted by the forks that are agitated by the bow, but also their corresponding beat-tones. They come forth at times so loud and clear that it is difficult to believe that they are not produced by corresponding forks. I now sound C_4 and the seventh harmonic partial of C_2. The frequencies of the notes of these forks are as 4:7. We have, therefore, the tabooed harmonic, or the sub-minor seventh. The result, I think all will confess, is almost as gratifying to the ear as some of the consonant intervals to which you have just been listening. I can even fancy that some of the musicians present would be glad to have this interval introduced into our musical system forthwith. The effect is new, I admit, but I think that not even the most pronounced partisans of our present system of music would declare it to be unpleasant. In the music of the future it may be reckoned as a consonance. Who knows? The major thirds and sixths, and still more the minor thirds and sixths, had to struggle a long time for recognition. But it came at last, and they are now among the most popular intervals in music. And so may it be in a measure with the sub-minor seventh. It has many friends even now, and their number is daily increasing. Music is pre-eminently a progressive art, and it is difficult to foresee what modifications it will admit in the not distant future.

A siren devised by Oppelt enables us to push our investigations still farther. This instrument — an elaborate form of the instrument invented by Seebeck — consists of a large disk of copper (Fig. 174), pierced with 24 concentric circles of holes. Fifteen of the circles yield simple notes, 5 give different intervals of the diatonic scale, and the remaining ones furnish 4 of the more common chords.

The siren is now mounted on a rotator and caused to revolve. When a stream of air is directed by means of a suitable tube against any of the circles of holes, you hear notes exactly like those produced by Seebeck's siren. Blowing against the circle having 12 holes, and then against that having 24 holes, we produce, as you hear, two notes that are separated from each other by the interval of an octave. There are other circles having 36, 72, 96, 144, and 192 holes. 36 and 72, 72 and 144, 96 and 192, taken in pairs, have the same ratio, viz., 1 : 2, and hence give the same interval as the circles having 12 and 24 holes. The circles that have respectively 12 and 18 apertures — ratio 2 : 3 — yield the interval of a fifth. Similarly, the circles having 12 and 15 holes — ratio 4 : 5 — give the major third. In like manner, we might by suitable combi-

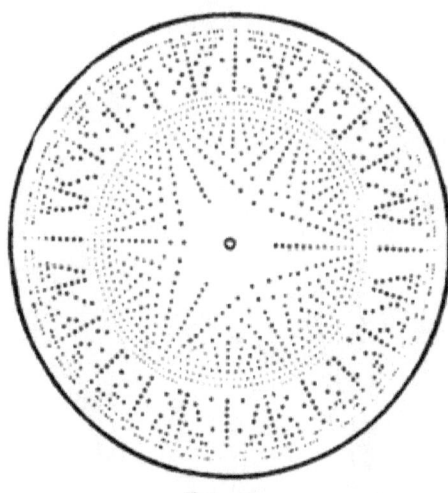

FIG. 174.

nations obtain all the other intervals of which we have been speaking.

But the important fact in this experiment, and the one to which I wish especially to direct your attention, is that these intervals are entirely independent of the pitch of the notes composing them. Whether the disk be rotated rapidly or slowly, the frequency-ratio of any two notes remains the same. Provided, then, that the relative pitch of any two notes remains constant, the interval remains unchanged, whatever the position of the interval in the scale.

From the intervals we have been considering, it is but a step to chords of three or more notes. We shall try here only the perfect major chord, — C, E, G, — the relative frequencies of whose notes is 4 : 5 : 6 When a current of air is directed against the holes composing this chord, and the disk is caused to revolve, the harmony at once bursts forth pure and clear. Whether the disk move slowly or rapidly, whether the pitch of the notes be high or low,

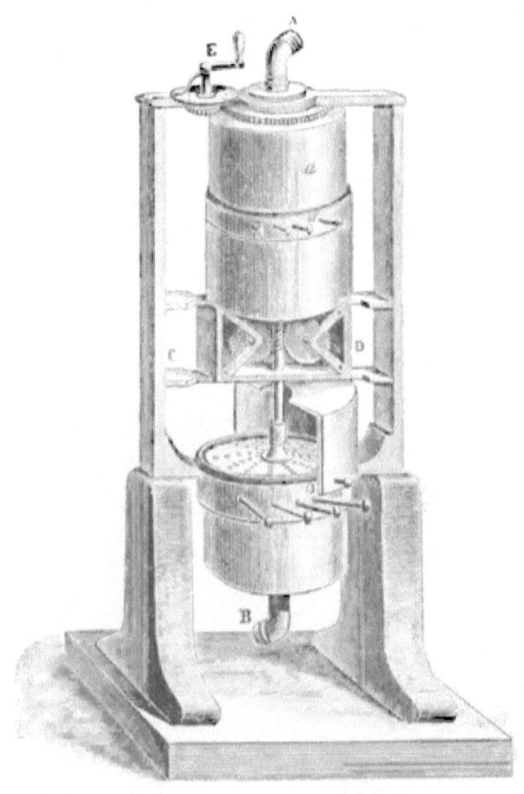

FIG. 175.

the character of the chord, as you perceive, remains unchanged.

But let me make you acquainted with a more elaborate and a more available instrument than the siren of Oppelt. Before you (Fig. 175) is a double siren devised by Helmholtz. It is composed of two of Dove's polyphonic sirens, connected by a common axis. Dove's siren differs from the siren of Cagniard de la Tour in having two or more circles of holes, — that of Cagniard de la Tour having, as you remember, only one. The Dove sirens used in the instruments before you have each four series of holes, disposed in concentric circles. The lower disk presents four series, of 8, 10, 12, and 18 holes; the upper disk has four others, of 9, 12, 15, and 16 apertures. If, therefore, the circle having 8 holes yields the note C_1, the siren, at the same velocity of rotation, will give the notes C_1, E_1, G_1, D_2 for the lower disk, and the notes D_1, G_1, B_1, and C_2 for the upper. The instrument, consequently, is competent to produce all the more important intervals and chords we have been considering, and serves admirably to bring out all the characteristics of the diatonic scale.

The orifices A and B are connected with an acoustic bellows by means of an India-rubber tube. When air is urged into A, the upper siren alone sounds. When air is admitted into the lower siren, it only becomes vocal. If, however, air be admitted into both orifices simultaneously, both sirens become sonorous. The number of revolutions made by the sirens is recorded by the clock-work CD. The keys at a and b correspond each to a series of orifices in the parts of the air-chambers opposite the openings A and B. By means of a toothed wheel and pinion at E, not only the disk of the upper siren, but also the air-chamber above the disk, can be made to rotate both forwards and backwards. Both the upper and lower sirens are surrounded by brass boxes, divided into halves so as readily to be attached to or removed from the instrument. One half the box is removed from the lower siren, while both halves are seen enclosing the one above. These boxes act as resonators, and their office is to augment the volume of the prime, while the upper partials of the compound tone of the siren are correspondingly damped. The moment the tone of the siren is in unison with that of the box, the note emitted bursts forth with extraordinary purity and power.

When air is simultaneously urged into both wind-chests, with the two circles of twelve apertures open, we have perfect unison. If, now, a series of 8 holes in the lower, and 16 in the upper siren be opened, we obtain the interval of an octave. Opening the series of 9 in the upper and 18 holes in the lower siren, the same interval is given, although the absolute rates of vibration have been increased. But the ratio of the two rates remains the same, being in both cases as $1:2$. Opening a series of 10 apertures in the lower, and 15 in the upper siren, or of 12 holes in the upper and 18 in the lower, we have, in both instances, the interval of the fifth, because in both cases the ratio of the rates of vibration is as $2:3$. By opening the series of 9 and 12, or of 12 and 16, — in both of which cases the ratio is $3:4$, — we obtain the interval of a fourth. Similarly the two series of 8 and 10, and 12 and 15, yield the interval of a major third, expressed by the ratio $4:5$. In like manner the series 10 and 12, or 15 and 18, give the interval of a minor third, whose frequency-ratio is $5:6$. When we open the series having 8 and 9 apertures, we obtain the interval of a major tone. The series 9 and 10, for a like reason, give the interval of a minor tone. The series whose orifices number 15 and 16 respectively yield, when sounded at the same time, the interval of a major semitone.

The last three intervals, when the siren is moving at an ordinary velocity, are remarkably dissonant. The reason of this is because of the beats, which are very loud and distinct. We can, however, so increase the velocity of the siren as to cause the beats corresponding to the intervals $8:9$ and $9:10$ to coalesce and give rise to pure, clear beat-tones. The harshness of the interval is now far less than it was before. This experiment succeeds particularly well with the interval corresponding to a major tone, $8:9$. The beat-tone in this case is three octaves below the lowest constituent of the interval, but it is sufficiently loud to be heard throughout the hall.

Helmholtz's siren affords us a simple means of illustrating the phenomena of beats and interference. If we open the two series of twelve orifices each, and urge air through the sirens, we have, as just seen, perfect unison. The sound from one siren reinforces that from the other, and the result is a much greater volume of tone than either one, singly, is competent to produce. This, however, holds true only when the apertures in the sirens have the same motion with reference to the orifices in the wind-chests. But, as we have seen, we are able, by means of the wheel and pinion, E, to turn the upper cylinder either in the same direction in which the siren moves, or in the direction opposite. When the cylinder is rotated so that its orifices meet those of the siren, the apertures pass each other more rapidly than when the cylinder is motionless. The pitch of the note of the upper siren is thus rendered higher than the pitch of the note from the lower one, and the result, as declared by the powerful beats, is interference. For every complete revolution of E there are produced four beats, for the prime tone of the instrument. If the motion is reversed, the orifices of siren and cylinder pass each other less frequently, and the result is that the pitch of the note emitted by the upper siren is lower than the pitch of the note from the lower siren. Again, we have interference, and beats are heard as before. If one revolution of E towards the right give rise to four beats, and heightens the pitch of the upper siren by four vibrations, a single revolution to the left will lower the pitch by the same amount, and the tone of the upper siren will have four vibrations less than the tone of the lower one. It is obvious that we have here another illustration of Doppler's principle, which was discussed *in extenso* in our third lecture.

So far, we have been studying musical intervals acoustically. But we can also study them mechanically and optically. Indeed, paradoxical as it may appear, the most delicate and most accurate means at our disposal for examining musical intervals is the optical method. We shall consider this presently. As an introduction to it, we shall investigate the nature of the vibrations of the compound pendulum devised by Professor Blackburn, of Glasgow, in 1844.

A modified form of such an instrument (Fig 176) is before you. The bob is a thick disk of lead, into which is fitted a glass funnel filled with fine sand. Instead of a single string, as is used in an ordinary pendulum, we have here an arrangement calculated to give a much more complicated motion. When the pendulum, as shown in the figure, oscillates in a direction at right angles to the cross-piece from which it is suspended, its length is equal to the distance from the lower part of the cross-piece to the centre of the disk. If, however, the pendulum move in a direction parallel to the line joining the two upright pieces, its length will then be measured from the point r — a small ring of metal — to the centre of the disk. If moved in either direction, as stated, the motion will be in a straight line, — the direction in one case being perpendicular to what it is in the other. But if the pendulum is started from the point D, which is in a line making an angle of forty-five degrees with the line joining the two uprights, we get quite a different result. In this case, the sand from the funnel will trace a curve instead of a straight line, the nature of the curve depending on the relative lengths of the two pendulums. I say *two* pendulums, for that in reality is what we have. The

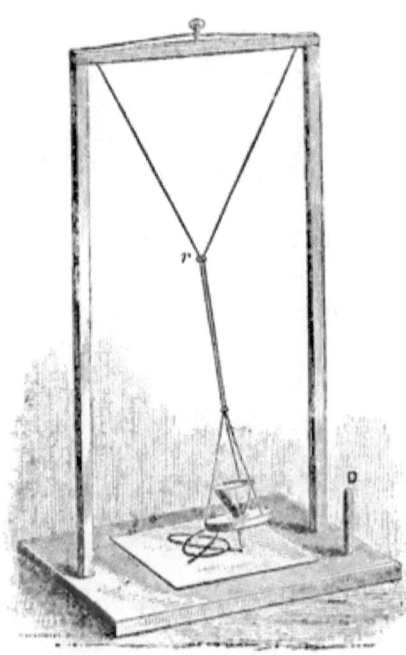

FIG. 176.

point of support for the shorter pendulum is the metal ring r, and the point of support of the longer one is the lower part of the cross-bar.

If the shorter curve is one fourth the length of the longer one, the former will execute twice the number of vibrations that the latter will in the same period of time. This is in accordance with the law that the times of the vibrations of any two pendulums vary inversely as the square roots of their lengths. But the bob cannot move in two directions

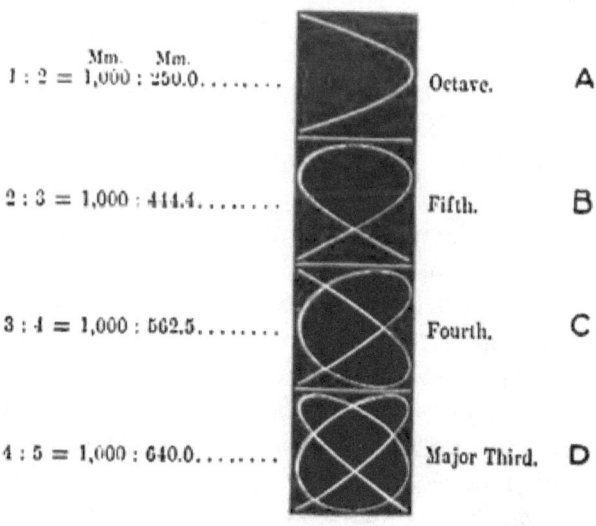

Fig. 177.

at the same time. It will, consequently, move along a path intermediate between the two straight lines just spoken of, and the resultant due to the combination of the two vibrations is a parabola, — A (Fig. 177). The rates of vibrations of the two pendulums in the case just considered are as 1 : 2. But this ratio also expresses the interval of the octave. The figure A therefore is the curve that corresponds to this interval.

If we change the position of the ring r so as to alter the relative lengths of the two pendulums, and start the bob from D, as before, we shall obtain an entirely different figure from the one just exhibited. Making the lengths of the two pendulums as $4:9$, the sand from the funnel will describe figure B. But the square roots of 4 and 9 are 2 and 3 respectively. While, therefore, the longer pendulum makes two vibrations, the shorter one executes three. But the ratio $2:3$ expresses the interval of the fifth, and hence figure B may be considered as the visible expression of this interval.

Making the relative lengths of the two pendulums 9 and 16, — the square roots of which are 3 and 4, — we obtain figure C, corresponding to the interval of the fourth. Similarly, if we make the lengths of the pendulums as $16:25$, we shall obtain figure D. The square roots of 16 and 25 are respectively 4 and 5. But these ratios express the vibration ratio of the major third. Figure D, consequently, corresponds to this interval. In the same manner, by changing the relative lengths of the pendulums, we could obtain figures corresponding to all the intervals in music. We should find that the figures expressing the intervals become more complex as the numbers representing the intervals become larger.

The figures just given are produced only when the bob starts from the point D, or from some point similarly situated with reference to the straight line between the two uprights and the one intersecting it at right angles. If the bob be made to start from points other than those mentioned, entirely different figures will be produced.

Mr. Tisley has invented a compound pendulum, which, for the variety, beauty, and delicacy of the figures it is competent to produce, is in every way superior to the one we have been using. Such a one, connected with a vertical lantern, is now before you. It consists of two pendulums, $P P'$, balanced on knife-edges at $A A'$. From the points $c' c$ project two brass arms cp and $c'p$, which, when the pendulums are at rest, are at right angles to each other. These arms are given perfect freedom of motion in every direction by being connected with the pendulums by ball-and-socket joints at c and c'. By means of the threads t

and t', connected with delicate adjustable springs attached to the arms cp and $c'p$, the tracing point at p may be readily lowered and raised without in any way affecting the vibrations of the pendulums. Sliding brass plates are attached to the pendulum rods, and are intended to receive the weights, which serve the purpose of bobs. The sum of the weights ordinarily varies from five to twelve pounds. The relative lengths of the two pendulums are altered at will by placing the weights at different heights. W is a smaller weight sliding along the pendulum rod, and is counterpoised by the weight T. These small weights enable one to adjust the pendulums very accurately, and to change, if need be, their rates of vibration even while in motion.

On the condenser of the vertical lantern rests a plate of glass blackened by camphor-smoke. The pendulums are so adjusted that one of them

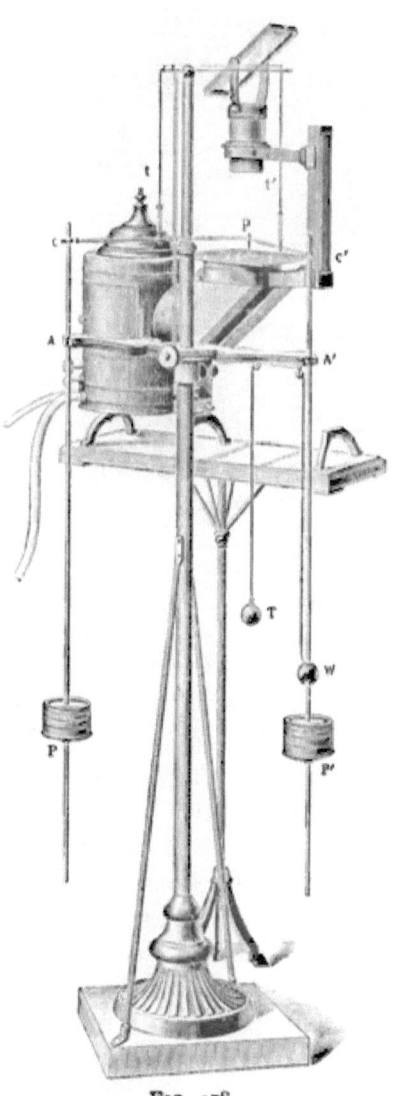

FIG. 178.

vibrates twice while the other executes three vibrations. If, then, they be both made to oscillate simultaneously, they should cause the tracing-point, p, to describe a curve corresponding to the musical interval of a fifth. The pendulums are started, and instantly there flashes out on the screen, where all was darkness before, a beautiful bright curve, which becomes more and more complicated. Finally, the tracing-point has returned to its starting-point, and the curve delineating the interval of a fifth is complete. But as the pendulums continue to vibrate there is inscribed on the plate a second figure within the first. Both are identical in all respects except size. The reason of this is due to the gradually decreasing amplitude of oscillation of the pendulums. Thus, by allowing the pendulums to vibrate for some moments, a number of figures, equally beautiful and equally symmetrical, are inscribed on the glass plate, one within the other. We have now on the screen a visible expression (Fig. 179) of the sonorous vibrations composing the interval of a perfect fifth. By sliding the weight, W, up or down the rod, we should disturb the perfection of the interval, and introduce corresponding changes in the figure.

FIG. 179.

FIG. 180.

Only a moment is required to adjust the pendulums for the interval of a fourth. Substituting a new glass plate for the one now on the lantern, and setting the pendulums going as before, we have designed for us a figure that is even more beautiful and more complex than that corresponding to a fifth. As before, we have a series of curves within curves (Fig. 180), as elegant in form as they are marvellous in regularity. By suitably adjusting the relative lengths of the pendulums, it is manifest that we could secure an infinite number of tracings, corresponding not only to all the intervals used in music, but also answering to all possible rates of vibration.

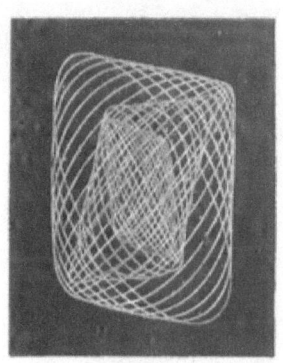

Fig. 181.

In Fig. 181 we have a tracing that is quite different from anything that we have yet seen. A slight change in the relative lengths of the pendulums is all that is required to transform some of the simpler figures we have been studying into others of bewildering intricacy. And yet, notwithstanding the maze-like complexity of these tracings, they are, one and all, as faultlessly symmetrical as they are novel and exquisite.

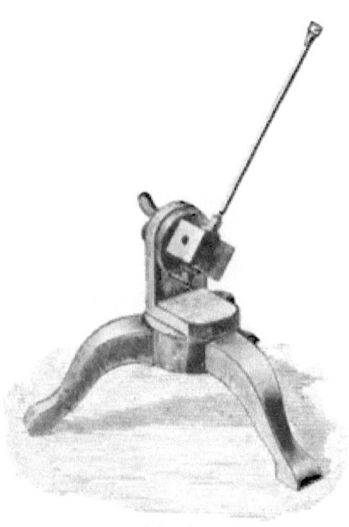

Fig. 182.

In 1827 Wheatstone devised a simple little contrivance for showing the figures corresponding to the various musical intervals, that reproduces admirably all the various curves afforded by the pendulum. To this little piece of apparatus he gave the name of "caleidophone." It is nothing more than an elastic rod of steel (Fig. 182) attached to a firm support. If the rod be cylindrical, and its flexural rigidity for all transverse directions be the same, it will, when set in vibration, move in one plane, like a simple pendulum. But if the flexural rigidity be unequal, either through lack of homogeneity of the material of the rod, or on account of its form, there will be a composition of two rectangular vibrations that are, as in the compound pendulum, mutually perpendicular. Thus, if Oba

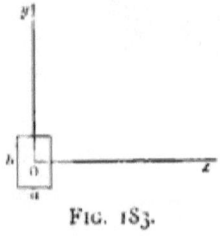

Fig. 183.

(Fig. 183) be the cross-section of a prismatic rod, the rod will tend to vibrate more rapidly in the direction Oy than in the direction Ox. If, however, the rod be flexed to some point intermediate between the lines Oy and Ox, and then set free, it will no longer vibrate in a single plane, but will execute a curve varying as the ratio of the sides a and b. If $a:b$ as $1:2$, the curve due to the compounding of the two rectilinear vibrations will be that corresponding to the interval of the octave. The rod before us is made to give the figure of the octave.

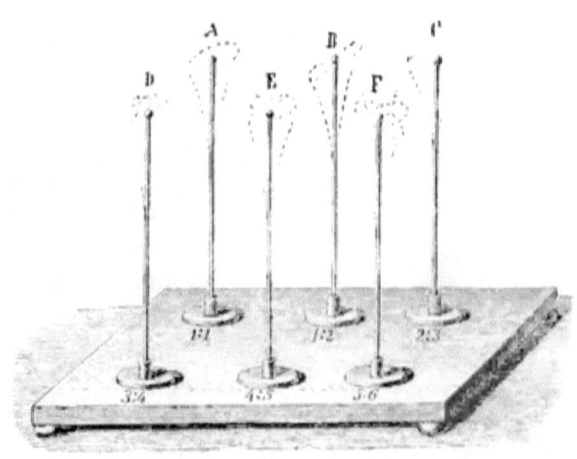

Fig. 184.

At its upper extremity is a small, highly polished mirror, which reflects a beam of light coming from our lantern. On the ceiling is depicted the curve of the figure 8, answering to the curve of the octave.

If, in place of the rod just used, we were to take others,

in which $a : b = 2 : 3,\ 3 : 4,\ 4 : 5$, or $5 : 6$, we should obtain curves corresponding to the fifth, the fourth, the major, and the minor thirds respectively. On the table is a small stand in which are fixed six rods (Fig. 184) so constructed that they give all the common intervals from unison to the minor third.

The rods, so far employed, are competent to describe curves corresponding only to a single interval each. But Lippich has devised a universal caleidophone (Fig. 185), with which we are able to obtain figures answering to any interval whatever. It consists of a long strip of steel fastened at its lower end to a solid support. To the upper end of the strip is attached a similar strip of steel, the direction of the greater cross section of the latter being perpendicular to that of the former. The two pieces of metal are so connected that the upper one is capable of being adjusted so that its length may bear any desired ratio to that of the lower strip. The bright bead at the upper extremity of the adjustable strip reflects light in the same manner as the similar apparatus that we have just used. It is manifest, from what has been said, that this form of caleidophone, simple as it appears, is capable of yielding as great a variety of curves as the compound pendulum. The results of the one beautifully corroborate those of the other, and both fully respond to all the requirements of theory regarding the composition of the rectangular vibrations of pendulums and elastic rods.

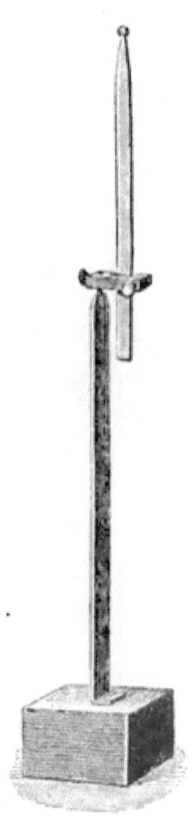

Fig. 185.

But, you may ask, where is the connection between the figures we have been studying and the musical intervals to which they are said to correspond? Neither the pendulums nor the rods emit any sound whatever. The latter may, indeed, in some cases, yield notes, but they are at best very faint. It is important, therefore, to establish a connection that cannot be gainsaid between the various curves given, and the musical intervals that they are said to represent. The optical method of M. Lissajous, discovered in 1857, shows the connection in a most remarkable manner, and at the same time affords the most delicate method of tuning sonorous bodies that is known to science.

We have already had occasion to see something of Lissajous' method, but not precisely in its bearing on

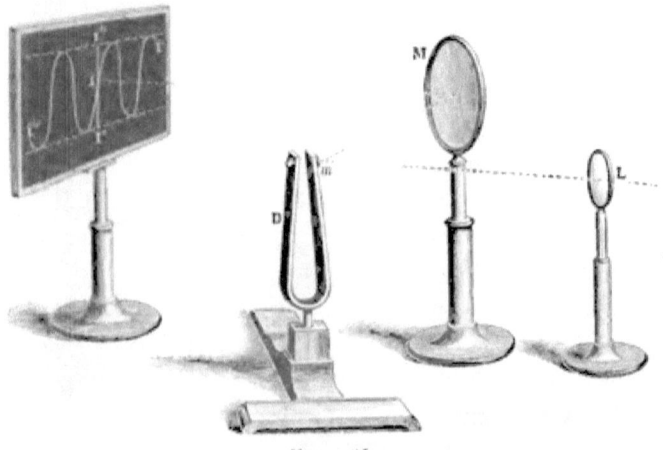

FIG. 186.

musical intervals. This method, which is now so celebrated, and which is now always employed when it is desired to have intervals of tuning-forks, or other instruments, absolutely exact, is, in principle, only a modification of Wheatstone's discovery. In place of rods, Lissajous used tuning-forks, to one of the branches of which are attached small mirrors.

For the sake of illustration, I shall use the simplest form of apparatus. A beam of light from our lantern passes through the lens L (Fig. 186), and impinges on the mirror m of the upright fork D. The light is reflected from the mirror, m, of the fork D to the mirror M, and thence to the screen. While the fork is quiescent, only a bright spot of light is seen on the canvas. As soon, however, as the fork is set in motion, the spot of light, *l*, becomes a vertical line, *l l*, parallel to the branches of the fork. If, now, the mirror, *M*, be rotated about its vertical axis, the straight line is transformed into a beautiful sinuous curve, *i" i"*. This change of a luminous point into a straight line, and then into an undulating curve of light, is, as you know, due to the persistence of impressions made on the retina.

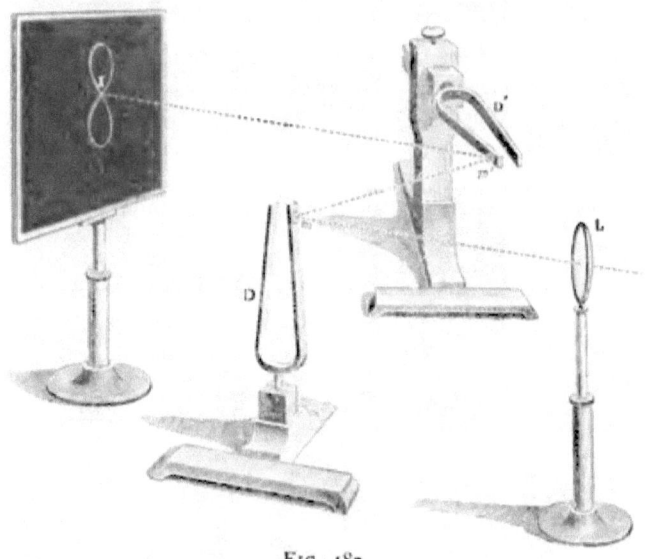

FIG. 187.

Let us now substitute for the mirror *M* a second fork, *D'*, whose plane of vibration is perpendicular to that of the fork *D*. If the fork *D* remain in quiescence, and *D'* be caused to oscillate, the point of light on the screen will describe a horizontal line which is parallel to the branches of the fork. This line is perpendicular, therefore, to that made by the fork *D*. Both forks are excited, and we have now on the screen a curve (Fig. 187), which, we have said, corresponds to the interval of an octave. But how do we know this? Because, aside from the fact that the frequencies of the forks are stamped on their stems, we can, on listening to them, hear that one yields a note exactly an octave higher than that emitted by the other.

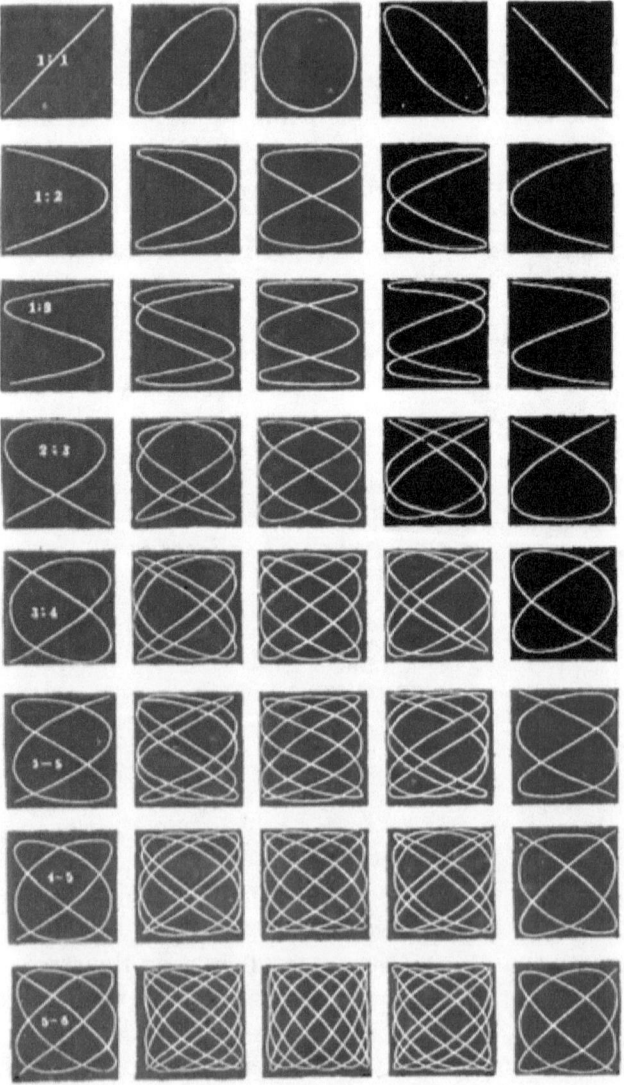

Fig. 188.

By taking forks whose frequencies are as 1 : 1, 1 : 2, 1 : 3, 2 : 3, 3 : 4, 3 : 5, 4 : 5, and 5 : 6, we may obtain all the curves exhibited in Fig. 188. There can be no doubt about the figures corresponding to the intervals named, because, when the forks are sounded, the ear tells us at once what the intervals are, and these, we find, always correspond to certain characteristic curves. In Fig. 188 there are five curves — for unison, the curves may become straight lines — for each interval corresponding to the different phases in which the forks may happen to vibrate. As a matter of fact, if the intervals are not absolutely exact, there is an indefinite number of forms for the curve distinguishing each interval, and there is a constant change, while the forks are vibrating, of one form into the other. Thus, when two forks are in perfect unison, their characteristic curve is a circle. It may also be an

Fig. 189.

ellipse, or a straight line, depending on the phases of vibrations of the forks. But if the unison be disturbed, even never so slightly, we immediately observe a change, more or less rapid, from a circle into an ellipse, from an ellipse into a straight line, and from a straight line back into a circle. At one time the ellipse, as also the straight line, is inclined to the right; at another, to the left. Each cycle of changes shows all possible forms intermediate between a straight line and a circle. What has been said of the transformation undergone by forks whose unison is disturbed may be iterated regarding the changes that may characterize any of the intervals whose curves are given in the adjoining figure.

In Fig. 189 we have two phases of a more complicated curve, — that corresponding to the interval of a major second, — whose vibration-frequencies, as you remember, are 8 : 9.

By using Mercadier's electric forks, which we have had occasion to employ more than once heretofore, we can, by means of the movable weights on the branches, have the intervals so accurately adjusted that the curves will suffer no variation whatever. The figure yielded, whatever it may be, or whatever phase it may present, will then remain fixed and invariable as long as the forks are in vibration.

This fact, as is evident, can be used to advantage in what has been aptly termed optical tuning. All that is necessary is to have a standard tuning-fork, executing any given number of vibrations per second. To simplify the work as much as possible, Lissajous invented what is known as an optical comparator, or vibration microscope. An improved form of this instrument was subsequently devised by Helmholtz. It differs from that of Lissajous in being provided with an electro-magnet, so that it can be kept in vibration as long as may be desired. Such a comparator (Fig. 190) is before you. It is composed of an electric fork, attached to a solid support, and a microscope. The objective of the microscope is borne by one of the prongs of the fork, which makes a right angle with the tube. When the fork is set in motion the objects visible in the field of the microscope seem to move in the same direction as does the fork. If now a second tuning-fork, whose prongs are perpendicular to those of the first, be caused to oscillate, a point on the second fork will appear to describe a curve, whose form will depend on the vibration-frequencies of the two forks used. If the intervals of the fork be perfect, some of the forms seen in Fig. 188 will appear, and the form first seen will persist as long as the interval remains undisturbed. If, however, the interval be

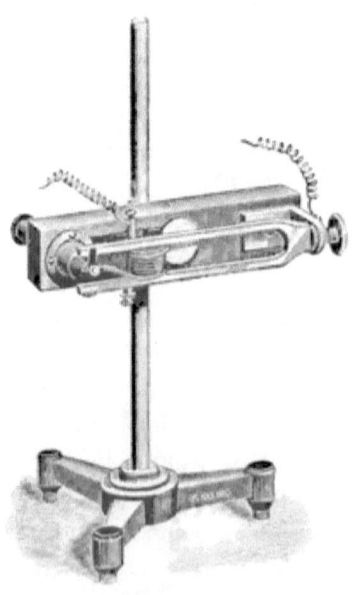

FIG. 190.

perturbed in any way whatever, by a change in the temperature of the forks, for instance, the figure seen is no longer constant. It immediately begins to pass through a cycle of changes, producing some of the various curves in Fig. 188. The longer the time required for effecting a complete cycle of changes, the nearer the intervals of the forks are perfect. The vibration-microscope before us is made to execute exactly 128 vibrations per second. If, now, the figure yielded by this fork, and a second one supposed to be in unison with it, go through a cycle of changes in ten minutes, it means that our comparator executes $10 \times 60 \times 128 = 76800$ vibrations, while the other fork, during the same period, makes one vibration more or one vibration less than this number. The percentage of error in this instance is very slight indeed.

This method of tuning may be applied to any sonorous bodies whatever, and is incomparably superior to any other method we have yet seen. It affords us a means of determining, without any assistance whatever from the ear, any musical interval with a precision that is virtually absolute. By this means a deaf person can tune with almost infinitely greater exactitude than would be possible for the most delicate and most practised musical ear.

Koenig's clock-fork, or tonometer (Fig. 191), is a more elaborate form of comparator than Lissajous' vibration microscope. As an instrument of precision, it is wellnigh perfect. It consists of a large tuning-fork, making sixty-four vibrations per second, which, like Lissajous' comparator, is connected with a microscope. Each prong is provided with a micrometer screw having a heavy head, by means of which the rate of the fork can be adjusted with the utmost precision. Between the prongs is a delicate thermometer for indicating the temperature. The escapement of the clock, with which the fork is connected, is so regulated that the tuning-fork performs the same functions as does the pendulum or balance-wheel in an ordinary clock. The vibratory motion of the fork is rendered continuous by the impulse it receives from the escapement-wheel at each vibration. It was by means of this marvellous piece of mechanism that Koenig determined the frequency of the *Diapason Normal* of the French Conservatory, and proved that its pitch was slightly different from what it was supposed to be. It is this instrument also that he used in determining the frequencies of many

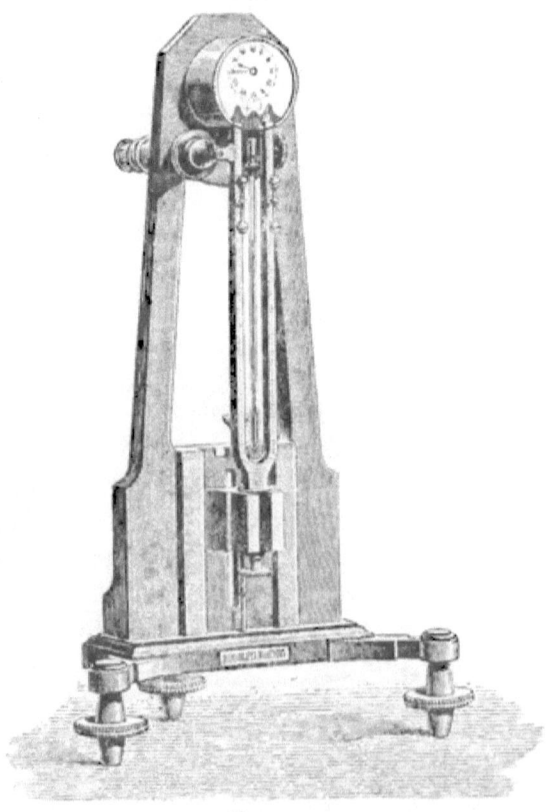

FIG. 191.

of the forks that we have been using in the course of these lectures. Hence their unfailing accuracy, — an accuracy that it would be impossible to secure by any other known means.

M. Lissajous, in connection with M. Desains, has furnished us with another method of obtaining acoustic figures corresponding to any given musical interval. It is known as the graphical method, and may be viewed as supplementary to the optical method which we have just examined. We have already had occasion, especially in the eighth lecture, to employ the graphical method, so that the principle involved is quite familiar to you. We shall now have recourse to a more delicate piece of apparatus than any we have yet employed when using this method. The instrument before you (Fig. 192) consists of two large tuning-forks fastened to a heavy cast-iron base. A prong of one of the forks carries a piece of smoked glass, while a prong of the other bears a light style. The forks, which

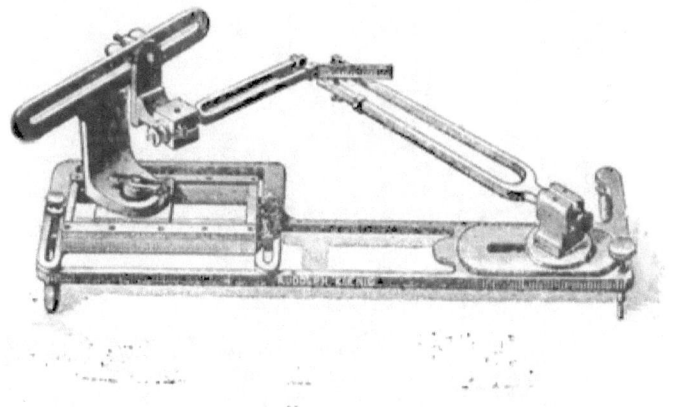

FIG. 192

are in perfect unison, are now placed at right angles to each other and set in vibration. On moving the fork, to which the style is attached, along a groove, a beautiful trace, corresponding to the interval 1 : 1, — unison, — is given on the smoked glass. Here, as in the optical method, we have the composition of two rectilinear motions, and the result is a curve, Fig. 193, which is characteristic for the interval named. Employing forks whose vibration-frequencies are as 1 : 2, 1 : 2 ±, 5 : 6, and 15 : 16, we obtain the elegant tracings exhibited in the adjoining figure.

All the various methods we have used for elucidating the nature of musical sounds admirably supplement each other, and unequivocally substantiate all the deductions of theory. In observing the intimate connection between simple mathematical ratios and musical consonances, we cannot help calling to mind the saying of Pythagoras, "All is harmony and number." The relations between simple numbers and musical harmony is indeed so marked as to arrest the attention of even the most casual observer. There is something of truth, therefore, in Leibnitz's definition of music, when he says it is "an occult exercise of the mind unconsciously performing arithmetical calculations." [1]

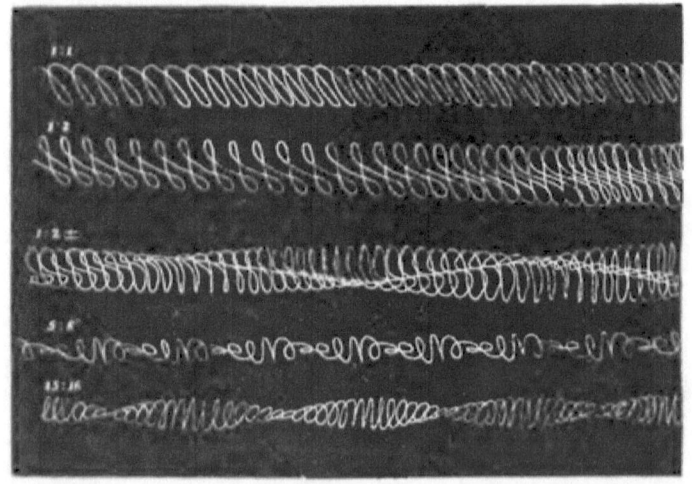

FIG. 193.

We have frequently, in the course of our lectures, used the words *consonance* and *dissonance*, and spoken of intervals as being *consonant* or *dissonant*. It is now time that we should understand the full signification of these terms, and inquire into the causes of consonance and dissonance, and learn why some intervals produce dissonant, and some consonant sensations.

Every one knows, whether he have an ear for music or not, that two or more sounds simultaneously produced

[1] "Musica est exercitium arithmeticæ occultum nescientis se numerare animi."

may in certain instances have a harsh, jarring effect, while in other cases the result of the combination of several notes is pleasing and harmonious. This, however, is only saying that there is such a thing as dissonance as contradistinguished from consonance, that certain musical intervals are rough and grating, while others are smooth and flowing, but it does not offer any explanation of the phenomena observed.

According to the great geometer, Euclid, "Consonance is the blending of a higher with a lower tone. Dissonance is incapacity to mix, when two tones cannot blend, but appear rough to the ear." The illustrious Euler, as the result of profound mathematical investigations, concludes that the mind is pleasurably or unpleasurably affected according as the musical intervals heard are simple or complex. As stated by Helmholtz, "Consonance is a continuous, dissonance an intermittent, sensation of tone."[1] These definitions, however, are little more than statements of a fact. Even the definition of Helmholtz, often as it has been quoted, does not give us the desired information. Indeed, before the investigations of Koenig on the nature of beats, and the researches of Mayer on residual sonorous sensations, a philosophical distinction between consonance and dissonance was an impossibility.[2] But strange as it may seem, the profound and painstaking researches of these two distinguished physicists seem to be entirely

[1] "Consonanz ist eine continuirliche, Dissonanz eine intermittirende Tonempfindung."

[2] As early as the beginning of the last century, Sauveur had outlined the true theory of consonance and dissonance, but it was allowed to fall into oblivion. "Beats," he tells us, "do not please the ear because of the inequality of the sound, and it is quite likely that it is the absence of beats which renders octaves so agreeable. Following out this idea, it is found that the chords in which beats are not heard are precisely the ones which musicians treat as consonances, and that those in which beats are heard are dissonances. When a chord is dissonant in one octave and consonant in another, it is because there are beats in one, and none in the other. Such a chord is deemed an imperfect consonance" ("Histoire de l'Académie Française" for the year 1700, page 143). Most of the acoustical discoveries of Sauveur are to be found in the Memoirs of the French Academy of Sciences.

ignored. They were the first to give us quantitative determinations of the relations between different tones, all previous determinations being only qualitative, — and the first to put us in possession of the facts necessary to draw the line of demarcation between intervals that are consonant and those that are dissonant. In their works we find the key to the solution of the most vexed questions of musical harmony. And yet, with the exception of a published lecture by Prof. S. P. Thompson,[1] and a few brief notices by Mr. A. J. Ellis,[2] their admirable investigations and the important laws which they disclose are, by English readers at least, virtually unknown.

Koenig's researches, as we have seen, revealed the fact that beats, when sufficiently numerous, may coalesce so as to produce a musical note. Hence the beat-tones, which are commonly known as grave harmonics, differential notes, resultant notes, etc. Professor Mayer finds, by a long series of most arduous observations,[3] extending over the entire musical scale, that the time during which the sensation of sound persists in the ear after the vibrations of air near the tympanic membrane have ceased, varies with the pitch of the note observed. The results of Professor Mayer's experiments are given in the following table: —

N.	V	B.	D
C_1	64	16	$\frac{1}{16} = .0625$ sec.
C_2	128	26	$\frac{1}{26} = .0384$ "
C_3	256	47	$\frac{1}{47} = .0212$ "
G_3	384	60	$\frac{1}{60} = .0166$ "
C_4	512	78	$\frac{1}{78} = .0128$ "
E_4	640	90	$\frac{1}{90} = .0111$ "
G_4	768	109	$\frac{1}{109} = .0091$ "
C_5	1024	135	$\frac{1}{135} = .0074$ "

[1] The Physical Foundation of Music; being an Exposition of the Acoustical Researches of Dr. Rudolph Koenig of Paris, delivered in the Royal Institution of Great Britain, June 13, 1890.
[2] See Ellis's Helmholtz.
[3] See The American Journal of Science and Arts, October, 1874.

In Column N are given the names of the notes, and in Column V their corresponding frequencies. Column B exhibits the smallest number of beats per second which the note must make with another note in order that the two may constitute the nearest consonant interval. The duration of the beats in fractions of a second are given in Column D. Thus the lowest number of beats that C_1 can give with another note in order that the sensation may be continuous, is 16. The duration of the residual sensation for C_1 is consequently the $\frac{1}{16}$ of a second. But $64:64+16=C_1:E_1$, the interval of a major third. For the next higher octave, we have, according to the table, $128:128\times 26 = C_2:E_2$. In this instance a minor third is the nearest consonant interval. For the notes C_3 and C_4 the nearest consonant intervals are respectively about $\frac{1}{4}$ and $\frac{1}{2}$ of a semitone less than a minor third. C_5 forms a consonance with a note that is but a single tone higher, while C_6 makes a consonance with a note that is separated from it by an interval which is less than a semitone.

This is certainly contrary to all the generally received opinions of musicians, who consider the intervals of whole tones and semitones as invariably dissonant. They admit, it is true, especially when their attention is called to the fact, that the dissonance of these intervals is less in the higher than in the lower parts of the scale. But they will persist in calling the intervals of whole tones and semitones dissonant, in whatever part of the scale these intervals may happen to be found. Facts, however, are stubborn things, and Professor Mayer has demonstrated that intervals universally regarded by musicians as dissonant are, at least in the higher parts of the scale, quite perfect consonances. Similarly, intervals in the lower parts of the scale that musicians always treat as consonances, Professor Mayer shows are, in reality, dissonances. Thus, the nearest consonant interval for C_1, according to the above table, is a major third. But both in this part of the scale and in that below, musicians make use of a minor third which is demonstrably dissonant.

The conclusions arrived at by Koenig and Mayer establish the fact that whenever two notes, whatever their position in the scale, are separated by an interval sufficiently large to allow the beats to blend into a continuous tone, the result is consonance. When the beats do not blend, there is dissonance. The cause of dissonance, therefore, is beats, which, like a flickering light, give rise to a discontinuous sensation. When the sensation is made continuous by the coalescing of the beats, the result is consonance. These statements may be regarded as two laws, but laws that admit of exceptions. We saw in Lecture Eighth that the same generator may produce, at one and the same time, both beats and beat-tones of the same number of vibrations. We learned also that the same phenomenon is exhibited, especially well, by means of heavy tuning-forks of high pitch.

I sound the two forks C_5 and D_5, which form a major second, and at once, in addition to the notes corresponding to these two forks, we hear a deep beat-tone identical with the note produced by a fork, having a frequency of C_2. I do not think that any of the musicians present would pronounce the effect dissonant; and yet, according to musical theory, the interval of C_5 and D_5 always produces dissonance. In a similar manner are sounded the forks D_5 and E_5, separated from each other by a minor tone. The beat-tone is the same as before, — C_2. In both instances the effect is strange, if you will, but certainly not dissonant, in the sense in which the term is ordinarily understood.

We now take the forks E_6 and F_6, separated from each other by a semitone. When both are sounded together, we hear, in addition to the proper notes of the forks, the deep beat-tone F_2, which breaks forth with astonishing clearness. Again, if we employ the forks B_6 and C_7 — likewise separated by the interval of a semitone — we have produced, when they are sounded simultaneously, a beat-tone, C_3, of singular volume and power. Even in these cases, where the interval between two generators is only a semitone, the result is smooth and continuous. The sounds of the forks are acute, it is true; but the effect of the combination is neither harsh nor grating on the ear. No appreciable beats are heard in either case, and the interval of a semitone in this region of the scale must be pronounced a consonance, musical theory to the contrary notwithstanding.[1]

Mr. Ellis obtained similar results from two flageolets.[2] When one instrument yielded $F\sharp_6$, and the other G_6, the beat-tone produced would have been G_2, had the interval been pure; but as it was, the beat-tone approximated F_2 more closely than G_2. What is remarkable in this case is that no beats whatever are perceptible, and the beat-tone generated is far below any note that the instrument itself is capable of producing.

All the interesting phenomena which we have just been examining can be beautifully shown by means of a species of harmonium now before you.[3] It was specially designed by Mr. Ellis as an instrument for demonstrating the facts on which musical theory depends. It is tuned by means of a set of forks so as to give intervals that are perfectly pure. It is essentially an experimental instrument, and its range is too limited for the purposes of practical music.

By sounding simultaneously the two notes constituting any of the ordinary musical intervals, we at once hear the corresponding beat-tone burst forth with surprising clearness and strength. Testing some of the notes in the upper part of the scale, which are separated by a tone or a semitone, we obtain a result that is essentially the same as those yielded by tuning-forks and flageolets. Both kinds of intervals yield smooth and distinct beat-tones, and frequently without any perceptible traces of beats. This, then, is an additional illustration of the fact that the inter-

---

[1] I have repeated the foregoing experiments for the distinguished violinist. Remenyi, and he fully concurs in the views herein expressed regarding the nature of consonance and dissonance.

[2] Ellis's Helmholtz, pp 153 and 173.

[3] The violin and violoncello also serve the same purpose admirably.

vals of a tone and a semitone, far from being dissonant, may, in the higher regions of the musical scale, be quite consonant.

It must, however, be observed that compound tones, such as those given by reeds, do not always give such pleasing effects as do the simple tones of tuning-forks. The reason of this is that although the primes of compound tones may be consonant, the upper partials may, and often do, beat with their primaries and with each other, and thus give rise to a roughness of tone that is never observed in the case of the same intervals when simple tones are tried.

It is obvious that what has been said of consonance and dissonance, as considered in any of the musical intervals, applies with equal truth to chords composed of three or more notes. Chords are consonant when unaccompanied by beats; they are dissonant when beats are present. Occasionally the beats, especially those resulting from the upper partials of compound tones, are so feeble that they are quenched almost, if not entirely, by the louder continuous tones of the chords. When the beats are so feeble as not to be recognized in the mass of the tone, or so weak as not to produce any disagreeable effect on the ear, they are viewed as being virtually absent, and the chords are regarded as consonant. It is also important to bear in mind that chords, like intervals, may be dissonant in one part of the scale, and consonant in another. It is a mistake, then, for the reasons adduced, to attempt to draw a line of demarcation between consonance and dissonance either in the case of intervals or of chords. Nature has indicated no such boundary lines, and it is futile for musicians — as many of them often do — to pin their faith to theories that can be disproved by the simplest experiments.

In order to exhibit at a glance the comparative dissonance and consonance of the different intervals of the scale from C_2 to C_3, Helmholtz constructed a diagram, of which Fig. 194 is a slightly modified reproduction. The intervals are indicated by distances measured off on the horizontal line C_3, C_5. Their relative dissonances and consonances are denoted by the perpendiculars from the curve to the horizontal base-line. As will be observed, the curve from C_3 to C_4 is somewhat different from that extending from C_4 to C_5. The curve for octaves above C_5, or below C_3, would show corresponding differences, — the consonances being more numerous in the upper, and less numerous in the lower regions of the musical scale. This curve was calculated for the compound note of a violin. The curves corresponding to the notes yielded by other instruments would, of course, exhibit different outlines, and be modified according to the relative number and intensity of the partials present. Mr. Sedley Taylor, in referring to this curve, picturesquely says: "If we regarded the outline as that of a mountain chain, the discords would

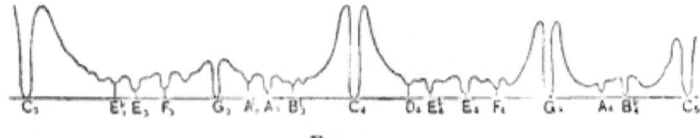

FIG. 194.

be represented by peaks, and the concords by passes. The lowness and narrowness of a particular pass would measure the smoothness and definition of the corresponding musical interval."

So far we have been considering only exact intervals, and only one scale, the natural, or diatonic, scale of C major. But musicians, in order to secure all the variety and effects that characterize our modern music, must employ a large number of scales in both the major and the minor modes. Hence the necessity for additional notes, and hence, also, the origin of the so-called chromatic scale. This scale contains 12 instead of 7 — or, counting the octave, 13 instead of 8 — notes within the interval of the octave. By the addition of 5 additional semitones, the whole notes are sharpened or flatted by a chromatic semitone; and the octave is thus divided into 13 semitones. These 13 semitones are all that are usually employed within the octave of such keyed instruments as the organ, harmonium, and pianoforte.

But if pure intervals are to be preserved, the number of intervals to the octave should be much greater. The reason of this is, that the sharp of one note is not, as is so often supposed, the same as the flat of the note following. Thus, if C_3 have a frequency of 256 vibrations, the vibration-numbers of $C\sharp_3$ and $D\flat_3$ will be respectively 266.66 and 276.48. Between these two notes, usually considered as the same, there is, as will be observed, a difference of nearly ten vibrations. Again, $E\sharp_3$ and $F\flat_3$ give, respectively, 333.33 and 327.68 vibrations, the former being higher than the latter. The vibration-numbers of $B\sharp_3$ and $C\flat_4$ are 500 and 491.52, in the order named, the sharp of the lower note having a higher pitch than the flat of the upper one. In the octaves above C_3 the differences in the number of vibrations between the sharps and flats of two adjoining notes is proportionately greater.

If, in like manner, we should flat and sharp all the eight notes of the octave, we should obtain twenty-four notes to each octave; and this for one key simply. Similar differences would be observed between the sharps and flats of the notes of the remaining twenty-three major and minor scales.

From what has been said it is obvious that the thirteen tones of the chromatic scale are entirely inadequate to the purposes of music, if pure intervals are to be preserved, and if the performer is to have the power to modulate from one key into another. Mr. Ellis has calculated that theory requires no less than seventy-two keys to the octave, in order that the musician may have complete command over all the keys employed in modern music.

The mechanical difficulties in the way of constructing instruments with such a large number of keys to the octave, not to speak of the difficulties that such an arrangement would entail on the composer and the performer, have given rise to various kinds of compromises, known as systems of *tempering*, or *temperament*.

Temperament is "*the division of the octave into a number of intervals such that the notes which separate them may be suitable in number and arrangement for the purposes of practical harmony.*"

The first system of temperament — known as *unequal*, or *mean tone*, temperament — was introduced by Zarlino and Salinas in the sixteenth century. The object of this form of temperament was to render the more common scales fairly accurate, while the others are ignored. Such a system of tuning limited the player to a part only of the keys now in use. It had, however, the advantage of giving smoother consonances than when all the scales are used, and retained its ground in parts of Europe and Great Britain until only a few years ago. Even now there are organists who prefer it to the systems now in use.

The system of temperament which now prevails almost universally is known as that of *equal temperament*. Its introduction is generally ascribed to Johann Sebastian Bach, in the early part of the last century. There seems, however, to be no doubt that it was known long anteriorly to that period. In his "Harmonie Universelle," Mersenne gives the correct numbers of the ratios for equal temperament, and says of it that "it is the most used and the most convenient, and that all practical musicians admit that the division of the octave into twelve semitones is easier for the player."[1] In his "Harmonicorum," published in 1648, he makes substantially the same statement.[2]

But whoever may have been the inventor of equal temperament, it prevails now, to the almost entire exclusion of other systems. It has the advantage of simplifying the construction of keyed instruments, and of rendering less

---

[1] His words in reference to equal temperament are, that it is "le plus usité et le plus commode, et que tous les practiciens avouent que la division de l'octave en 12 demitons leur est plus facile pour toucher les instruments" (Livre III. prop. 12).

[2] Speaking of the division of the octave into twelve equal semitones, — thirteen counting the octave of the tonic, — he says, "Quod temperamentum omnium facillimum esse fatebuntur organarii, cum illud ad praxim redegerint" (Liber IX. prop. 19).

difficult the work of composer and performer; but it sacrifices much of the beauty and harmony of effect that would result from just intonation.

In equally tempered instruments, the only interval accurately tuned is the octave. All the other intervals are more or less out of tune. The fifth is somewhat flatted, whereas the thirds and sixths are much sharped. When the notes of the tempered scale are sounded in succession, no deviation from pure intonation is observable, except by trained musical ears. When, however, two or more notes are sounded simultaneously, especially on instruments which, like the organ or the harmonium, give sustained tones, the departure from pure intonation is at once remarked, even by those who have no ear whatever for music. Beats, more or less numerous, are found to accompany all intervals except the octave. Fortunately, however, for the pianoforte, these beats are evanescent, and hence the effect is not so jarring as with the harmonium or the organ. It was indeed its adaptability to the pianoforte that gave the system of equal temperament the long lease of life that it has enjoyed. And it was the simplicity of the system, more than anything else, that tended to develop the pianoforte and make it what it is to-day, — the "voice of the composer," and the most popular of instruments.

But notwithstanding all the advantages claimed for it, equal temperament deprives us of one of the greatest charms of music, — that of the vivid contrast afforded us by the close juxtaposition of consonant and dissonant chords. This is at once seen by comparing the effect of a piece of music played on an instrument tuned in just intonation, with that of the same piece played on an instrument tuned in equal temperament. A still more striking way of showing the marked difference between music as executed according to pure intonation and according to equal temperament, is to have a quartet of accurate voices sing first according to the former system, unaccompanied, and then according to the latter, accompanied by the pianoforte. The contrast between the purity and brilliancy of the concords of pure intonation, and the harshness and dulness of those of equal temperament, is so decisive as to appeal to any one who has even an ordinary ear for music. Hence it would be much better if singers were taught by accompanying them with the violin or 'cello instead of the piano.

It is pure intonation that renders the music played on slide trombones and string quartets of a character so superior to that executed on ordinary keyed instruments. The instruments of the trombone and violin family are not, like the pianoforte and organ, limited to a few notes, but, like the human voice, are competent to produce an indefinite number of tones and intervals that are absolutely pure.

It is because music sung and played in pure intonation is of such excellence that it should receive more attention than is ordinarily given it. There are, it is true, those who think that the duodecimal division of the octave is quite sufficient for all purposes of melody and harmony, and that nothing better can be had, and who accordingly regard all who favor a change as unreasonable innovators. But it must be admitted by all who have examined the subject that our present musical system is far from perfect. No one, I take it, will refuse to encourage pure intonation, where, as in vocal and stringed harmony, it can be secured as readily as intonation that is confessedly faulty and unnatural.[1]

There is no insuperable obstacle to the introduction of pure intonation into all forms of orchestral music. It would of course necessitate some changes in the forms of instruments as now made, but the changes demanded would not by any means be so great or so numerous as is usually imagined. The labors and experiments of Helmholtz, Bosanquet, Ellis, Poole, White, and Colin Brown have demonstrated that pure intonation is possible, even with keyed instruments like the organ and the harmonium.

[1] See Appendix II

It may therefore be accepted as a fact that we are yet in a state of transition as regards the system of intonation to be employed in music, and that the not far distant future will witness the introduction of many modifications of the tempered system now in vogue.

Mr. Ellis states the case well when he says that "Equal temperament, or what tuners give us for it, — a very different thing generally, — has indeed become a temporary necessity. . . . But the discoveries of Helmholtz have sounded the knell of equal temperament, which must henceforth be regarded as a theoretical mistake and a practical makeshift, — a good servant, dismissed for becoming a bad master, and now merely retaining office until a successor is installed. . . At any rate, just intonation, even upon a large scale, is immediately possible. And if I long for the time of its adoption in the interests of the listener, still more do I long for it in the interests of the composer. What he has done of late years, with the rough and ready tool of equal temperament, is a glorious presage of what he will do in the future with the delicate instruments which acoustical science puts into his hands. The temporary necessity for equal temperament is passing away. Its defects have been proved to be ineradicable. An intonation possessing none of these defects has been scientifically demonstrated. It is feasible now on the three noblest sources of musical sound, — the quartet of voices, the quartet of bowed instruments, and the quartet of trombones. The issue is in the hands of the composer. Can any one doubt the result?"[1]

I have now only a few brief observations to make, and my task is finished. In what I have said I have confined myself solely to the elucidation of the subject of physical acoustics, and of its simpler relations to the physical basis of musical harmony. The subject of physiological acoustics, which Johann Müller, Helmholtz, Gavarret Preyer, and others have treated so ably, I have touched upon but

[1] "Illustrations of Just and Tempered Intonation," extracted from the Proceedings of the Musical Association of London, 1874-75.

incidentally, and only when it was found necessary to throw light on the physical aspect of the questions under discussion. Only the merest reference has been made to the subject of musical æsthetics. This was foreign to the scope of our work. Although physics and mathematics are intimately connected with music as a science, they have little or nothing to do with it as an art. The æsthetics of music, therefore, is something that must be considered apart from any of the physical and mathematical relations that have been investigated at such length. To show you how important it is not to lose sight of this observation, I shall quote for you a few paragraphs from one of the greatest authorities on musical æsthetics, Dr. Eduard Hanslick, of Vienna. He says,—

"Finally, let it be observed that musical beauty has nothing to do with mathematics. The idea entertained by certain writers, even those who should know better, regarding the part played by mathematics in musical composition, is singularly vague. Not satisfied with the facts that the vibrations of tones, the differences of intervals, consonance and dissonance, may be traced to mathematical relations, they are convinced that the beauty of a piece of music is also grounded on numbers. The study of harmony and counterpoint is for them a kind of *cabala* which teaches composition by calculation. . . .

"Although mathematics furnishes an indispensable key for the investigation of the physical basis of the tonal art, its importance in musical composition must not be overrated. In a tone-poem, be it beautiful or not beautiful, nothing is calculated mathematically. Creations of the fancy are not arithmetical problems. All monochord experiments, sound-figures, proportions of intervals, etc., are out of place here. The department of æsthetics begins where these elementary relations cease. Mathematics prepares only the simple material for intellectual treatment, and remains concealed in the simplest relations; but musical conceptions come to light without its assistance. . . . What converts music into a tone-poem, and raises it out of the category of physical experiments, is something free and spiritual, and, therefore, something incalculable. Mathematical calculation has as much participation in the art work of music as it has in the productions of the other arts, but no more."[1]

In music we have a beautiful illustration of how science and art go together hand in hand, how one aids the other, how science explains art, and how art often forestalls the conclusions of science. The two working together, with a common end in view, have made music what it is to-day, — the solace and the delight of our race. And we have every reason to hope that the music of the future will be even a closer approximation to those " pure strains ethereal" of which the poet sings, and which we are ever wont to associate with that blessed Fatherland, which is filled

> " With acclamation and the sound
> Symphonious of ten thousand harps that tune
> Angelic harmonies."

[1] Vom Musikalich-Schönen, von Dr Eduard Hanslick, Professor in the University of Vienna.

APPENDIX.

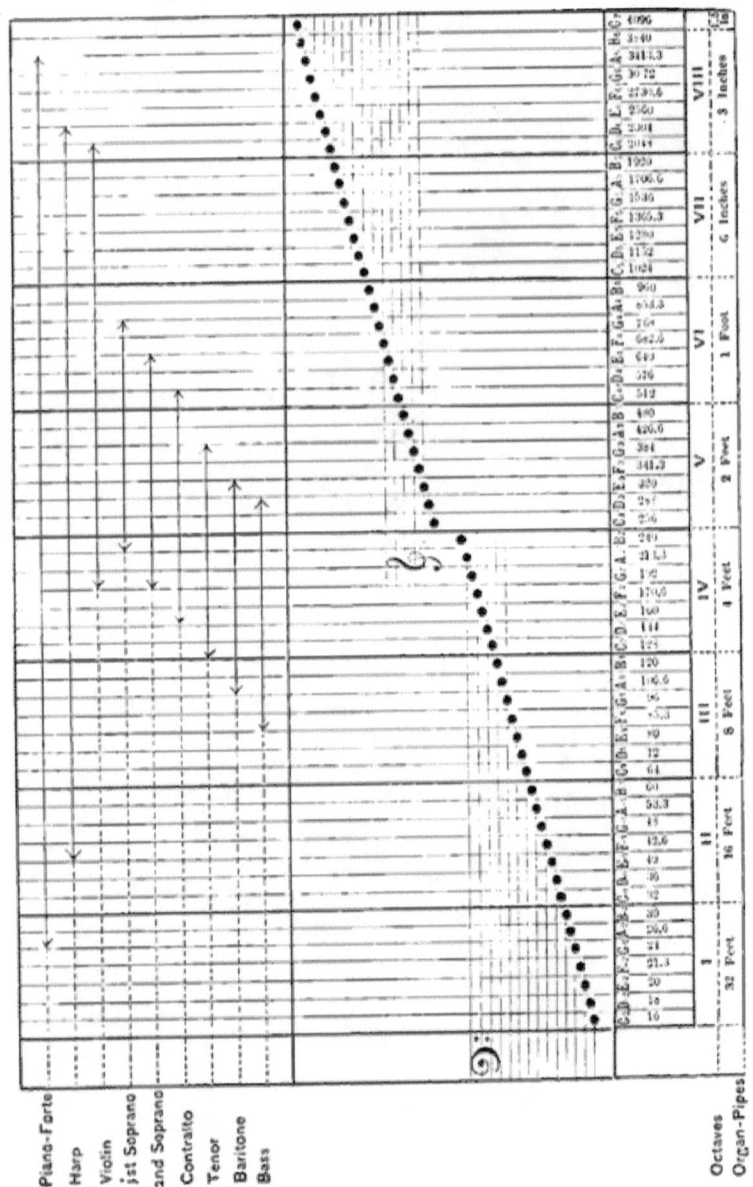

TABLE OF THE COMPASSES OF VOICES AND INSTRUMENTS.

APPENDIX.

I.

FREQUENCIES OF NOTES OF THE MUSICAL SCALE, AND COMPASSES OF THE HUMAN VOICE, AND OF SOME OF THE MORE COMMON MUSICAL INSTRUMENTS.

FOR purposes of reference and comparison there are exhibited in the diagram on page 438 the notes of the musical scale, and the frequencies of these notes according to the standard — physicists' pitch — used throughout this volume. Knowing the frequency-ratios of the different intervals, as detailed in Chapter X., it is an easy matter to calculate the vibration-number of any determinate note according to French or international pitch.

There are also given the various compasses of the human voice, and of a few of the musical instruments in most general use. The compass of the ordinary organ is only seven octaves; but in the larger instruments it is, as indicated in the diagram, fully eight octaves. In some exceptional cases the range may extend half an octave higher.

Inasmuch as the positions of notes are frequently referred to the corresponding organ-pipes, the lengths of pipes for the lowest notes — the C's — of the different octaves are here specified. Thus the lowest octave of the organ is often called the 32-foot octave; the next higher is known as the 16-foot octave; while the other octaves above this are in like manner designated from the lengths of the pipes yielding the lowest notes.

Sometimes, however, special names are given to some of the octaves. Thus the octave of C_{-2} is denominated the sub-contra, and that of C_{-1} the contra octave. The octave of C_1 is called the great, while that of C_2 is known as the tenor, or little octave. The octaves C_3 and C_4 are termed the middle and treble octaves respectively, and the two following — those of C_4 and C_5 — are, in the order named, spoken of as the octaves in alto and in altissimo. The octave of C_3 is likewise styled the one-stroked octave, while the octaves C_4, C_5, and C_6 are named respectively the two-stroked, three-stroked, and four-stroked octaves.

The pianoforte is classed as a seven-octave instrument, although its compass is sometimes less and sometimes greater. Similarly only the *average* compasses are given for the violin, harp, and the human voice. A reference to Chapter II. will show that the pitch, both for male and female voices, may in certain instances vary within a considerable range.

In connection with the foregoing I would call attention to the desirability of having some uniform system of indicating the notes of the different octaves of the musical scale. We saw in Chapter II. that there are several systems in vogue, those in Germany and England being quite different from the one that obtains in France. This lack of uniformity is often a source of much embarrassment, and even of grave error.

Now that an international standard of pitch has been adopted, it would be a great boon both to students and general readers if some uniform method of naming the notes could be established. A very slight modification of the French system would, it seems to me, answer admirably all practical purposes. Thus, if instead of calling the lowest C, corresponding to sixteen vibrations, C_{-2}, C'', $\underline{C}$, or Ut_{-2}, as is now the custom, it were called C_1, and the C's following were designated C_2, C_3, C_4, etc., it would greatly simplify matters both for acousticians and musicians. It would then be an easy matter to locate any note, from that of the 32-foot organ-pipe to that of the most acute note perceptible by the human ear. The C of the sub-contra octave of the organ being C_1, the highest G of Appunn's forks — eleven and a half octaves above C_1 — would be known as G_{12}.

II.

PLAYING IN PURE INTONATION.

THAT good violinists and violoncellists, when unaccompanied by equally tempered instruments, execute pieces of music written for harmony, in pure intonation, is well known. This accounts for the remarkable purity and fulness of tone that characterize the playing of such artists as Remenyi, Joachim, Popper, Wilhelmj, and Ole Bull. In listening to such performers, one can always hear distinctly the *Tartini*, or beat-tones, that add such richness and volume to violin music. Virtuosi like those named give their theoretical value not only to octaves, fifths, and fourths, but also to thirds and sixths. Indeed, we may well doubt whether such artists could, when unaccompanied, play a major third out of tune, as required by the system of equal temperament. Remenyi tells me that when he is not accompanied by a keyed instrument, he instinctively plays in pure intonation, and that he *feels* the difference between notes like D♯ and E♭, or G♯ and A♭, for instance, of which equal temperament can take no account.

Even in playing melodies, the best violinists play according to the just, and not according to the tempered, scale. This has been proved conclusively by the experiments of Delezenne and others. It is true that the experiments of Cornu and Mercadier seem to point to the Pythagorean scale as the scale of melody; but even granting this to be the case, it may be accepted as a demonstrated fact that whether violinists play according to the Pythagorean or the modern diatonic scale, they do *not* play according to the scale of equal temperament.

An interesting crucial experiment, showing that good violinists play in pure intonation, and not according to equal temperament, was made by Helmholtz, with the aid of Herr Joachim. For this purpose a specially constructed harmonium, giving pure intervals, was employed. It was thus discovered that the intervals played by the distinguished violinist were exactly the same as those given

PYTHAGOREAN SCALE	THE MODERN DIATONIC AND CHROMATIC SCALES		MODERN SCALE OF EQUAL TEMPERAMENT	
C₄ — 512 Vibs.		C₄ — 512 Vibs.		C₄ — 512 Vibs.
HEMITONE 28		SEMITONE 28		
B₃ — 484		B₃ — 480		B₃ — 483.2
TONE 51	A₃♯ — 414.4	MAJOR TONE 54	B₃♭ — 461	B₃♭ — 456.1 / A₃♯
A₃ — 432		A₃ — 426.7		A₃ — 430.5
TONE 51	G₃♯ — 400	MINOR TONE 46	A₃♭ — 409.6	A₃♭ — 406.4 / G₃♯
G₃ — 384		G₃ — 384		G₃ — 383.6
TONE 61	F₃♯ — 355.5	MAJOR TONE 54	G₃♭ — 364.6	G₃♭ — 362 / F₃♯
F₃ — 341.3		F₃ — 341.3		F₃ — 341.7
HEMITONE 23		SEMITONE 28		
E₃ — 324		E₃ — 320		E₃ — 322.5
TONE 51	D₃♯ — 300	MINOR TONE 46	E₃♭ — 307	E₃♭ — 304.4 / D₃♯
D₃ — 288		D₃ — 288		D₃ — 287.3
TONE 51	C₃♯ — 266.7	MAJOR TONE 54	D₃♭ — 276	D₃♭ — 271.2 / C₃♯
				MEAN SEMITONE 25
C₃ — 256		C₃ — 256		C₃ — 256

by the harmonium. The intervals specially selected were thirds and sixths, and Helmholtz found that these intervals as played by Joachim were always perfect, and never equally tempered, thirds and sixths.

I have made a similar experiment with the eminent artist Remenyi, — he using the violin, and I an harmonium tuned in just intonation. The results arrived at were identical with those obtained by Delezenne and Helmholtz.

In order that the reader may see at a glance the principal scales spoken of in this work, and have a graphical representation of the differences between pure and equally tempered intervals, between sharps and flats, I append the accompanying diagram,[1] calculated for the octave extending from C_3 to C_4. The frequency of C_3, 𝄞 , is 256 vibrations per second, — the same as used throughout the book. By inspection of the diagram it will be noticed that the semitones have not the same value in any of the scales. Again, in the Pythagorean scale there are only two different intervals, the whole tone and the semitone, or hemitone; whereas in the modern diatonic scale there are, as we have learned, three different intervals, the major and minor tones, and the semitone. A very marked difference is likewise observed between the sharps and flats; the latter, contrary to what musicians teach, being higher in pitch than the former. The only interval that is common to the three scales is the octave. The intervals of the equally tempered scale are, as indicated, all of exactly the same magnitude, the deviations from pure intonation being evenly distributed among the different intervals of the octave. The relative values of the intervals of the three scales are given in logarithms. They may also, as is obvious, be obtained from the vibration-numbers of the various notes as given in the diagram.

[1] A combination of some diagrams, slightly modified, given in Pole's "Philosophy and Music."

INDEX.

INDEX.

ACADEMY of Sciences, French, determines velocity of sound, 96, 97
Acoustics, 16, 141.
  father of, 57
  recent progress of, 16, 17.
Air columns, subdivision of, in organ-pipes, 221-224.
  condition of, under influence of vibratory motion, 221-224.
Air-pump, used to show necessity of medium for transmission of sound, 39.
Analysis of vowel-sounds, 355-357.
Apparatus, Helmholtz's, for synthesis of sounds, 366.
Appunn, 82-84, 88, 171, 340.
Arago, 97, 98, 299.
Aristotle, 343.
  on production of sound, 19.
  on propagation of sound, 42.
  on time required for transmission of sound, 94.
Audiphone, 211.
Audition, Helmholtz's theory of, 385.
  range of, for different persons, 91.

BACH, 431
Bacon, Lord, on the nature of sound, 19.
Barry, 251, 253.
Basilar membrane, 385.
Bassoon, 242.
Beats, 6.
  law governing, 319.
  lower and upper, 319.
  primary and secondary, 326.
  yielded by singing-flames, 305.
Beat-apparatus, Koenig's, 315.
  notes and beat-tones, 322.
    primary and secondary, 326.
  tone apparatus, Koenig's, 329.
  tones, heavy tuning-forks for, 325.
  and beats, subjective, 339.
Bell, best form of, 205.
  founding, laws governing, 205.
  partials of, 205.
  Savart's, 270.
  vibrating segments of, 204.
Bernouilli, D., 103, 141, 169, 219.
  on laws governing nodes of organ-pipes, 218.

Bernouilli, J., 137.
Biot, 82, 102, 187, 344.
Blackburn's pendulum, 406.
Bosanquet, 339, 340, 433
Bosscha's method of measuring the velocity of sound, 107, 108.
Boyle's law, 98.
Bourget's researches on the vibrations of membranes, 208.
Bureau de Longitudes determines the velocity of sound, 97, 98.
Byron, Lord, on Nature's music, 37.

CAGNIARD DE LA TOUR'S mill-siren, 30.
  siren, 62-66, 403.
Caleidophone, Wheatstone's, 411-413.
Carlyle, on music of Nature, 37
Cauchy, 169, 191.
Cavaillé-Coll, 217.
  his formula for making organ-pipes, 237.
Character of sound, 342
Chladni, 58, 79, 82, 83, 107, 128, 141, 167, 173, 178, 187, 189, 191, 193, 195, 197, 198, 211, 248, 256, 258, 345
Chladni's figures, explanation of, 193-195.
  on plate vibrating *in vacuo*, 199.
  rotating, 201.
  great work, 169.
  view of the tuning-fork, 174.
  laws of vibrating plates, 202.
  method of determining pitch, 60.
  observations on upper partials, 343.
  tonometer, 171
Chords, perfect major and minor, 397.
Chromatic scale, 429, 430, 441.
  semitone, 388.
Claque-bois, 178, 179.
Clarinet, 242.
Clock-fork, Koenig's, 74, 419, 420.
Colladon and Sturm measure velocity of sound in water, 104, 105.
Comma, 388.
Comparator, optical, 418.
Compasses of the human voice and of various musical instruments, 43, 90, 100, 437.
Composite tones, 346.

Compound tones, 143, 346.
Consonance, 260.
Consonance and dissonance, diagram illustrating, 429.
　　difference between, 422–429.
Consonances, imperfect and perfect, 390.
Consonant intervals, 389.
Consonants, flame-images of, 359–362.
Cornet-a-piston, 245
Cornu, 393, 443.
Corti's discoveries, 385
Cottrell's experiment, 116.
Crest of wave, 67.
Curve of sines, or harmonic curve, 67.
Curves corresponding to various intervals, 313, 314.
　　described by vibrating piano-wires, 165.
　　illustrating beats, 302.

DAGUIN, 276, 277.
　　on timbre, 344
D'Alambert, 137.
Delezenne, 443.
Desain's and Lissajous' graphical method, 420, 421
Despretz, 82, 83.
Diapason Normal, 63, 74, 76.
Diatonic scale, 79, 387, 391–393.
　　conventional, 391–395, 443, 444.
　　semitone, 388.
Diffraction of sound, 126, 127
Dissonance and consonance, difference between, 422–429.
Dissonant intervals, 389.
Distance travelled by sonorous vibrations, 127–129.
Dominant, 388.
Donders' researches on vowel-sounds, 357.
Doppler's principle, 110, 112, 405.
Duboscq, 309.
Duhamel's vibroscope, 65
Dulong, 256.
　　measures the velocity of sound in gases, 103.

EAR, accuracy of, 92.
　　rapidity of its appreciation, 92.
　　external, auditory passage of, 278, 279.
　　sensitiveness of, for different notes, 91.
　　training of, 93.
Echo, simple, multiple, polysyllabic, 119.
Echoes, remarkable, 120, 121.
Electrographic method of determining pitch, 70.
Ellis, 82, 85, 148, 242, 244, 318, 424, 427, 430, 433, 434.
Embouchure, 216.
　　de cor, 243.
Equal temperament, 431
　　scale of, 441.
Euclid, on consonance and dissonance, 423.
Euler, 137, 169, 208, 423.
Evolution in science, 42.
Exner, 93.

FARADAY, 198, 248.
Fétis, M., 392.
Fifth, a, 388.
Figures, Lissajous', 417.
Films, vibrating, 271.
Flageolet, 238.
Flame-images of vowels and consonants, 359–362.
Flame, manometric, 229–231.
Flames, sensitive, 251–254.
　　singing, 247–251
Flute, 238.
　　Bernouilli's, 229.
　　or flue pipes, 217.
Fog-signals, 125.
Fourier's theorem, 380.
Fourth, a, 388.
French horn, 244
　　pitch, adoption of, 76, 77.
Frequencies of notes of the musical scale, 439, 440.
Frequency, 69.
Fresnel's experimentum crucis, 300.
Fundamental note, 140

GALILEO's experiment on pitch, 57.
Galton's whistle, 87
Gamut, 79–81, 387.
Gases, velocity of sound in, 103.
Gavarret, 434.
Gay-Lussac, 97.
Germain, Mlle. Sophie, 191.
Geyer, 251, 253.
Govi, 251.
Graphical method of obtaining acoustic figures, 420, 421
　　determining pitch, 69.
Grimaldi, 299.
Guericke's, Otto von, experiment showing that sound cannot travel in vacuo, 30.
Guy of Arezzo, 79

HANDEL, 77.
Hanslick on musical esthetics, 435, 436
Harmonic curves, Mayer's combination of, 370.
　　motions, 52, 67.
Harmonics, 140, 148, 153.
　　in music, 151–153.
Harmonicons, glass and rock, 35.
Harmonium tuned in pure intonation, 427.
Harmony, 397.
Harp, Marloye's, 184.
Hasse, 385.
Hauptmann, on melody and harmony, 397.
Hawksbee's experiment on the transmission of sound, 40.
Hearing, range of, for different persons, 91.
Helmholtz, 58, 82, 83, 88, 134, 144, 175, 274, 304, 318, 319, 322, 340, 345, 350, 362, 365, 368, 369, 370, 379, 385, 395, 418, 423, 428, 433, 434, 443, 444.

Helmholtz, his apparatus for the synthesis of sounds, 366.
   his distinction between a musical sound and a noise, 35.
   his double siren, 402-405.
   on influence of difference of phase on quality of sound, 309.
   on melody, 397.
   on quality of sound, 342, 343.
   his researches on vowel-sounds, 357.
   his theory of audition, 385.
   his work on sound, 17.
Hemony, 205.
Henry, Joseph, 125.
Hensen's discoveries, 385.
Herschel, Sir John, 203, 296, 343.
Hertz's experiments, 299, 300.
Hipkins, 148.
Houghton's illustration of noises giving rise to musical sounds, 37.
Hüber, 141.
Humboldt, 97, 118, 119, 128.
Huygens, 262, 266.
Hydrogen singing-flame, 31.

INTERFERENCE, partial and total, 287.
   apparatus, Koenig's, 296.
   of vibrations of tuning-fork, 288, 289.
   shown by means of manometric pipes, 292, 293.
Intervals, consonant and dissonant, 389.
   logarithmic value of, 390, 391.
   musical, 323, 387, 390.
Intermittent sounds which give rise to continuous sounds, 332-334.
Intonation, just, 432-434.
   playing in, 443, 444.
Isochronism, some effects of, 263.
Isochronous, meaning of word, 23.

JEWS-HARP, 172.
Joule's thermal unit, 172.

KASTNER's pyrophone, 251.
Key-note, 388.
King, a form of Chinese musical instrument, 35.
Kircher, Father, 120.
Kirchhoff, 191, 208.
Koenig, Dr. R., 58, 83, 84, 86, 112, 149, 151, 179, 190, 218, 234, 235, 265, 276, 280, 281, 318, 319, 322, 324, 327, 328, 330, 334, 349, 351, 353, 362, 365, 369, 375, 377, 379, 380, 382, 423, 426.
   his acoustic apparatus, 18.
   his clock-fork, 74, 419, 420.
   on the influence of the difference of phase on the quality of sound, 378.
   his researches, 17.
   his researches on vowel-sounds, with tuning-forks, 357, 358.
Kohlrausch, 93.
Kundt's method of determining the velocity of sound, 107, 256.
   sound-figures, 256, 257.

LAGRANGE, 137, 191.
Lampman on the music of Nature, 37.
Laplace, 103, 105.
   his correction of Newton's formula, 100.
Larynx, model of, 246.
Le Conte's discovery of sensitive flames, 251.
Leibnitz's definition of music, 422.
Le Roux's determination of the velocity of sound, 101.
Light and sound vibrations compared, 88.
Liquids, velocity of sound in, 105.
Lissajous, 63, 74, 169, 309, 312, 418, 419.
   his graphical method, 420, 421.
   his experiment showing interference, 291.
   his optical figures, 417.
   optical method of studying musical intervals, 414-420.
Locke, on the nature of sound, 20.
Locomotive whistle, action of, 218.
Logarithmic value of intervals, 390, 391.
Loudness of sound, law governing, 55.
Lucretius on propagation of sound, 101.
   on origin of wind instruments, 213.
Lyre, Greek, 396.

MACH, 112.
   his apparatus for illustrating the propagation of sound-waves, 51.
Major scale, 392.
   chord, 397.
   semitone and major tone, 388.
Manometric flame, Koenig's, 229-231.
Mariotte's law, 68, 69.
   apparatus for illustrating transmission of sound, 48.
Marloye, 24, 83, 132, 133, 350.
   his harp, 184.
Mayer, Prof. A. M., 92, 107, 187, 370, 383, 425, 426.
   his mechanical equivalent of a sonorous vibration, 56, 57.
   his electrographic method of determining pitch, 70.
   his sound-mill, 281.
   his tracings, 72.
Melde's experiments with vibrating strings, 157-162.
Melody, 397.
   Helmholtz on, 397.
Mean-tone temperament, 431.
Melodiaphone, 277.
Membrane, basilar, 385.
Membranes, vibrating, 207-210.
Mercadier, 303, 417, 443.
   his electro-magnetic forks, 160, 309, 312.
   his radiophone, 33.
Mersenne, Father, 23, 55, 69, 77, 99, 140, 141, 218, 219, 237, 280, 345.
   his acoustic researches, 57-59.
   his determination of the velocity of sound, 95, 96.
   his determination of pitch, 58, 59.
   on equal temperament, 431.

Mersenne, Father, on laws of vibrating strings, 135-137.
　on quality of sound, 343.
　on quality of sound, tubes and drums, 203, 236.
Metallophone, 35, 179.
Meteors, explosion of, 128.
Microscope, vibration, 418.
Mill-siren of Cagniard de la Tour, 30.
Minor scale, 392.
　chord, 397.
　semitone and minor tone, 388.
Mirror, revolving, 231.
Monge, on quality of sound, 344.
Monochord, 132.
Motion, harmonic or pendular, 52, 67.
　effect of, on pitch of sound, 110-113.
Mouth instruments, 216.
　piece of horns, 243.
　pipes, 217.
Mozart, 79, 90.
Müller, Johann, 246, 434.
Music, Arabian, Chinese, Greek, Hindoo, Persian, Scotch, 393, 394.
　boxes, 172.
　Leibnitz's definition of, 422.
Musical intervals, 323, 387, 390.

NAIL-FIDDLE, 172.
Napoleon Bonaparte's interest in Chladni's experiments, 191.
Newton, 99, 103, 105.
　on the nature of sound, 47.
　on the velocity of sound, 98-101.
Noble and Pigott, 145.
Nodes, 146.
　not motionless, 156.
　and ventres of organ-pipes, 226-234.
Noise, as distinguished from a musical sound, 34.
Norremberg's apparatus for showing interference, 293.
Notes of the scale, various methods of indicating, 80, 81.
Notes, beat-, 322.

OBOE, 242.
Octave, an, 388.
　pentatomic division of, 393.
Ohm, G. S., 150.
Ophicleide, 245.
Oppelt's siren, 400.
Optical comparator, 418.
　expression of beats, 309-315.
　method of studying musical intervals, Lissajous', 414-420.
Oral cavity, resonance of, 357, 358.
Organ, acoustic, 218.
　pipe, description of, 216.
　　large manometric, 233.
　　open, law of, 220.
　　stopped, law of, 220, 221.
　　subdivision of air-column in, 221-224.
　　nodes and ventres of, 226-234.

Organ-pipe, theory and experiment regarding, 235-237.
Orpheus and Amphion, legends of, 282.
Oscillation, meaning of term, 22.

PAPUS, experiment on the transmission of sound, 40.
Partial tones, order of succession, 140.
Partials, harmonic and inharmonic, 149, 153.
　upper, resonance of, 280.
Pendular motion, 52, 67.
Pendulum, Blackburn's, 406.
　Tisley's compound, 408, 409.
Period, and periodic, meaning of terms, 23
Periodically variable tones, 334.
Periods, vibrations of same, and of different, 283-286.
Phase, meaning of, 45.
　identity of and difference of, 283-285, 290, 291.
　difference of, influence of, on quality of sound, 368-379.
Phonautograph, 70.
Pipes, flute, or flue, and mouth-pipes, 217.
　organ, 216.
Pitch, 60.
　as affected by motion, 110-113.
　determined by the siren, 64.
　French, adoption of, 76, 77.
　Mersenne's determination of, 59.
　standard, 75-77.
Plateau, 141.
Plates, vibrations of, 191-202.
　vibrating, laws of, 202.
Playing in pure intonation, 443, 444.
Poisson, 160, 191, 208.
Polarized light, applied to the study of a vibrating body, 187-189.
Popocatepetl, silence on summit of, 41.
Portamento, 391.
Preyer, 82, 83, 84, 339, 340, 434.
Pyrophone, 251
Pythagoras, 132-134, 392.
Pythagorean scale, 393, 441, 443, 444.

QUALITY of sound, 342.
Quincke's apparatus for showing interference, 294.

RADIOPHONE described, 33.
Rameau, 41, 343, 350.
Ramsey's theory of smell, 21.
Range of hearing for different persons, 91.
Ray of sound, 114.
Rayleigh, Lord, 111, 130, 206, 263, 340.
　on Laplace's correction of Newton's formula, 100.
Reed, description of, 240.
　double and single, 239.
　free and striking, 240.
　instruments, 216.
　pipe, 239.
　vibrating, 172.
Reflection of sound, 114-123.
Refraction of sound, 123-125.

Regnault, 103.
   his determination of the velocity of sound, 101.
Remenyi, 341, 427, 441.
Resonance, 266.
   of oral cavity, 357, 358.
   of upper partials, 280.
Resonator, adjustable, Daguin's, 276.
   Helmholtz's, 274-276, 350, 351.
Revolving mirror, Wheatstone's, 231.
Riccati, 141, 160.
Rucker, Trevelyan's, 29.
Rods, free at one end, 173, 174.
   free at both ends, 177, 178.
   longitudinal vibrations of, 179-186.
   transverse vibrations of, 170-179.

SALINAS, 431.
Sauveur, 70, 82, 83, 141, 142, 146, 148, 151, 210, 345, 423.
   his determination of pitch, 59.
   on upper partials, 343.
Savart, Félix, 28, 82, 83, 138, 181, 190, 191, 200, 201, 207, 211, 218, 235, 236, 254.
   his bell, 270.
   his law of vibrating tubes, 203.
   his method of determining nodes of sonorous pipes, 225.
   his tube, 28.
   his wheel, 29, 60, 61.
Savart, Nicolas, 138.
Scale, 301.
   chromatic, 429, 430, 441.
   diatonic, 387, 391-393, 441, 443, 444.
   conventional, 391-395.
   of equal temperament, 441, 443, 444.
   musical, frequencies of notes of, 439, 440.
   uniform system of indicating notes of, desirable, 440.
   Pythagorean, 393, 441-444.
Schaffgotsch, 251.
Scheibler's tonometer, 74, 309.
Schneebeli's theory of aerial vibration in pipes, 217.
Schwedoff's apparatus for illustrating the laws of vibrating strings, 162-165.
Scott and Koenig's phonautograph, 70.
Second, a, 388.
Seebeck, 169.
   his siren, 30, 61.
Seiler, Madame, 279.
Semitone, chromatic, diatonic, major, minor, 388.
Seneca on the origin of sound, 19, 38.
Sensitive flames, 251-254.
Seventh, a, 388.
   harmonic or sub-minor, 400.
Shells, spherical, 46.
Shore, John, inventor of the tuning-fork, 24.
Simple tones, 346.
Sines, curve of, 67.
Singing-flames, 247-251.
   hydrogen, 31.
   yielding beats, 305.

Single tones, 346.
Sinusoid, 67.
Siren of Cagniard de la Tour, 62-65.
   Helmholtz's double, 402-404.
   Koenig's, 18.
   Oppelt's, 400, 402.
   wave, 335-338.
Sixth, a major, 388
Sling, musical, 31.
Smith's air-reed, 217.
Smoke-jet, sensitive, 251.
Solids, velocity of sound in, 106.
Son rauque, 190.
Sondhaus, 124.
Sonometer, 133, 155, 166.
Sound, character of, 342.
   definition of, 19-22.
   figures, in vibrating tubes, Kundt's, 256, 257.
   how produced, 21, 22.
   mill, 281.
   pitch of, 60.
   propagation of, 42-53
   quality of, 342.
   shadow, 126.
   timbre of, 342.
   diffraction of, 126, 127.
   reflection of, 114-123.
   refraction of, 123-125.
   and light vibrations compared, 88.
   of subdivision, 149.
Sounds, acute, limits of audibility of, 83.
   grave, limits of audibility of, 82.
Stancari's experiment, 59.
Standard pitch, 75-79.
Stone, 92.
Straw-fiddle, 178.
Strehlke, 169.
String, as understood in acoustics, 131, 138.
Sub-dominant, 388.
Superposition of vibrations, 154, 155.
Sympathetic sounds and vibrations, 266.
Synchronous motion, instances of, 263.
Synthesis of sounds, 365-368.

TARTINI, 322.
Taylor, Brook, 137.
   Sedley, 271, 429.
Temperament, equal, and mean-tone, 431.
   scale of equal, 431, 435, 443, 444.
Tensile strength of pianoforte-wires, 137.
Terquem, 190.
Tetrad, 397.
Theorem, Fourier's, 380.
Thermal unit, Joule's, 57.
Third, a major and a minor, 388.
Thompson, S. P., 424.
Timbre, 342.
Tisley's compound pendulum, 408, 409.
Tones, beat, combinational, differential, resultant, summational, 322.
   composite, compound, simple, single, 346.
   major and minor, 388.
   shell, Wordsworth on, 278.
   periodically variable, 334.

Tonic, 387, 388.
Tonometers, 74-76, 171, 300, 419, 420.
Torsional vibrations, 167, 189, 190.
Trevelyan's rocker, 29.
Triad, 307.
Trombone, 244.
Trough of wave, 67.
Trumpet, 245.
Trumpets, ear and speaking, 122, 123.
Tubes, sonorous, laws of, 218.
Tuning by means of beats, 308, 309.
    of musical instruments, 317, 318.
Tuning-forks, inventor of, 24.
    mode of vibration of, 289.
    heavy for beat-tones, 322.
    Koenig's, 18.
    of variable pitch, 315, 316.
Tyndall, 119, 125, 251.

UNDULATION, meaning of term, 67.

VAN DEN GHEYN, 205.
Velocity of sound in air, 94-104.
    of sound in gases, 103.
    of sound in liquids, 105.
    of sound in solids, 106.
    of sound, Mersenne's measurement of, 95.
Ventral segments, 146.
Ventres, 146.
    and nodes of organ-pipes, 226-234.
Vibration microscope, 418.
    number, 69.
Vibrations, complete or double, semi or single, 22.
    amplitude of, 23.
    of aerial columns of sonorous tubes, mode of, 216, 217.
    longitudinal, 160, 165, 179, 186.
    torsional, 167, 189, 190.
    transverse, 160, 165, 170, 179.
    superposition of, 154, 155.

Vibratory movements, 23.
Vibroscope, Duhamel's, 65.
Violin string, vibrational figure of, 371.
Violon de fer, 172.
Vitruvius on propagation of sound, 43.
Voice, compass of, 90.
Vowels, flame-images of, 359, 360.
Vowel-sounds, analysis of, 353-357.
    researches on by Donders, Helmholtz, and Koenig, 357, 358.

WALLIS, 145.
Walloston, 83.
Wave-siren, 335-338.
    compound, 376.
Wave-systems of various kinds, 284, 285.
Weber's observations, 289.
Wertheim, 32, 218, 234, 235, 256.
    his method of measuring the velocity of sound in liquids, 105, 106.
Wheatstone, 100, 193, 231, 248.
    his caleidophone, 411-413.
Wheel, Savart's, 29, 60, 61.
Whewell on a passage from Aristotle, 42.
Whistle, Galton's, 87.
Wind-instruments, 216.
    origin of, 213.
Wordsworth, on shell-tones, 278.

XYLOPHONE, 35.

YOUNG, DR. THOMAS, 69, 147, 148, 165, 299, 322.

ZAMMINER, on the French-horn, 244.
Zarlino, diatonic scale, introduced by, 393.
    and Salinas on unequal or mean-tone temperament, 431.

www.ingramcontent.com/pod-product-compliance
Lightning Source LLC
Chambersburg PA
CBHW022139300426
44115CB00006B/253